Penguin Business

Management and Motivation

Victor H. Vroom is John G. Searle Professor of Organization and Management at Yale University. Considered an international expert on leadership and decision making, he came to Yale in 1972 as Chairman of the Department of Administrative Sciences and Associate Director of the Institution for Social and Policy Studies. When the School of Management was founded in 1976, Professor Vroom was named to its original board of permanent officers. As a teacher and researcher, he has focused on the psychological analysis of behavior in organizations. He is the author of several books and over fifty articles. His 1964 book, *Work and Motivation*, is regarded as a landmark in that field and his 1973 volume, *Leadership and Decision Making* is widely cited as a breakthrough in the study of leadership in formal organizations. his latest book is *The New Leadership* published in 1988.

A native of Canada, Professor Vroom received his B.S. and M.A. degrees in psychology from McGill University in 1953 and 1955. After receiving his Ph.D in psychology from the University of Michigan in 1958, he was named Study Director in Michigan's Institute for Social Research and lecturer in psychology. He later served as Assistant Professor of Psychology at the University of Pennsylvania and Associate Professor of Psychology at the Carnegie Institute of Technology. In 1966, he was named Professor of Psychology and Industrial Administration at Carnegie-Mellon's Graduate School of Administration. Professor Vroom has been elected president of the Society of Industrial and Organization Psychology and is a Fellow of the American Psychological Association. He is a consultant to several major corporations, including General Electric, Bell Labs, GTE and American Express and currently serves on the Board of Trustees of the Connecticut Savings Bank.

Edward L. Deci is professor of Psychology and Director of the Human Motivation Program at the University of Rochester, New York. He holds a Ph.D in psychology from the Carnegie-Mellon University and has also studied at the University of Pennsylvania, University of London, Hamilton College, and at Stanford University, where he was an interdisciplinary post-doctoral fellow.

Professor Deci has done research on many aspects of human motivation and is author of the following books; *Intrinsic Motivation* (1975), *The Psychology of Self-Determination* (1980) and *Intrinsic Motivation and Self-Determination in Human Behaviour* (1985). He is a fellow of the American Psychological Association and a member of many other professional associations, and has lectured and consulted for universities, public school systems, corporations and mental health agencies throughout the world. He also has a private practice in psychotherapy.

Management and Motivation

Selected Readings

Edited by Victor H. Vroom and Edward L. Deci

Penguin Books

PENGUIN BOOKS

Published by the Penguin Group
27 Wrights Lane, London W8 5TZ, England
Viking Penguin Inc., 40 West 23rd Street, New York, New York 10010, USA
Penguin Books Australia Ltd, Ringwood, Victoria, Australia
Penguin Books Canada Ltd, 2801 John Street, Markham, Ontario, Canada L3R 1B4
Penguin Books (NZ) Ltd, 182–190 Wairau Road, Auckland 10, New Zealand

Penguin Books Ltd, Registered Offices: Harmondsworth, Middlesex, England

First published in Penguin Education 1970
Reprinted in Penguin Books 1989
10 9 8 7 6 5 4 3 2 1

Printed and bound in Great Britain by
Cox & Wyman Ltd, Reading
Set in Monotype Times

Copyright acknowledgement for items reproduced in this volume
will be found on page 381

Contents

Introduction:
An Overview of Work Motivation [1]

If you look at a group of persons who are performing the same job, you will note that some do it better than others. This is true whether the group consists of secretaries, clerks, assemblers, salesmen or managers. Furthermore, if you have some quantitative measure of their contribution to the organization, you will probably find that the best person in each group is contributing two, five or perhaps ten times what the poorest is contributing. These observations raise a question of psychological interest – what are the causes of these differences in performance? One answer that has been given is that these differences reflect varying abilities or skills on the part of individual workers. People have had different amounts and kinds of experiences and vary in the degree to which they possess the necessary intellectual and other endowments to learn from this experience. This assumption has led to a number of different strategies on the part of organizations for improving worker performance. It has led for example to an attempt to select workers for a particular job who have the abilities or skills which are necessary for its performance. It has also led to an emphasis on training – systematic attempts on the part of the organization to develop the necessary abilities or skills on the part of workers. Finally, it has led to changes in the content of jobs to make them consistent with the existing abilities or skills in the labour force.

There is, however, another assumption which can be made about the origin of differences in performance among people doing the same kind of work, and this assumption leads to somewhat different organizational strategies for improving job performance. The assumption of which we now speak is that differences in performance among people doing the same kind of work reflect differences in their motivation. At any given point in time people vary in the extent to which they are willing to direct their energies towards the attainment of organizational objectives.

1. We wish to thank Miss Danielle Marton for assistance with the clerical aspects of preparing this volume.

Introduction

It is now fairly clear that both of these statements are true. In other words, the performance of a person on a job is considered as a function of two different kinds of variables. One of these refers to the ability or skill of the individual to perform the job and the second refers to his motivation to use this ability or skill in the actual performance of the job. It is also fairly clear that performance is not equal to the sum of an individual's ability and motivation, but rather to the product of these two variables. Increasing the motivation of persons high in ability will lead to a greater increase in performance than increasing the motivation of persons low in ability. Similarly, there is more to be gained from increasing the ability of individuals who are high in motivation than of individuals who are low in motivation. In short, the effects of each of these variables (ability and motivation) on performance is dependent upon the existing amount of the other.

It is the second of these two variables – motivation – that is the basic concern of this book. The problem of motivating employees is as old as organized activity itself, but it has only been within the last half century that the scientific method has been brought to bear on its solution. This relatively short period of time has seen the beginnings of attempts to apply the conceptual and methodological tools of the behavioural sciences, particularly psychology, to the relationship between man's motivation and his work as well as to the managerial issues involved in that relationship.

In this book we will not be dealing in any systematic or intensive way with motivation as a basic psychological process. The reader interested in such an orientation is referred to Atkinson (1964); Bindra and Stewart (1966); or Cofer and Appley (1964). Our concern is with the intersection between the study of human motivation and the practice of management. Since the now famous Hawthorne studies (Roethlisberger and Dickson, 1939) and the work of Lewin and his associates on democratic leadership (Coch and French, 1948; Lewin, Lippitt and White, 1939) a great deal of research has been conducted on human motivation in the work place. This research has relevance for such managerial problems as job design, leadership style, the design of compensation or promotional systems and a number of others. In this volume we will attempt to portray some of this research along with its managerial implications.

The question of what motivates workers to perform effectively is not an easy one to answer. Many aspects are as yet unexplored and there are many other alternative ways of characterizing and organizing what is known about the relationship between motivation and management. One way of conceptualizing different approaches is in terms of the assumptions which they make about human motivation and the implications of these assumptions for managerial practice. Looking at the problem in this way, there appear to us to be three major approaches underlying the work discussed in this volume. Let us think of these approaches as managerial or organizational strategies for stimulating motivation.

The first of these approaches might, for lack of a better term, be described as paternalistic in nature. It assumes that people will be motivated to perform their jobs effectively to the extent to which they are satisfied with these jobs. The more one rewards workers the harder they will work. The greater the extent to which an employee's needs are satisfied in his job, the greater the extent to which he will respond, presumably with gratitude or loyalty, by producing effectively on that job.

The essence of this approach is to make the organization a source of important rewards – rewards for which the only qualification is membership in the organization. In other words, the rewards which are utilized in this approach might be termed unconditional rewards in the sense that the amount of rewards that any individual receives is not dependent in any clear-cut way on how he behaves within the organization, but rather on the fact that he is a member of that organization.

Let us look at some of the practices which are used in organizations and are consistent with this approach. The first things which come to mind and meet the conditions that we have described above are various fringe benefits. Examples are pension plans, group insurance, subsidized education, recreation programmes, comfortable working conditions and the like. Also qualifying as instruments of the paternalistic approach are high wage levels, across the board wage increases, job security and predictable promotion patterns.

This approach also has some implications for the relationship between the manager and his subordinates. If the manager were to apply this approach to its fullest extent he would seek to arrange the conditions of work so that people would feel comfortable, happy and secure. His primary goal would be to see to it that his subordinates were able to get the things that they wanted, and he would assume that as a consequence of this support the subordinate would display enthusiasm and loyalty.

Some of the assumptions underlying this approach and the empirical evidence for these assumptions are contained in Part Two of this volume. In that section you will find studies bearing on the determinants of employee satisfaction and the relationship between satisfaction and various indices of employee performance including turnover and the effectiveness with which an employee performs his role. The evidence indicates that these unconditional rewards have undoubtedly been effective in helping companies to attract and to hold people. It is, however, exceedingly doubtful whether the rewards did much by way of motivating these people while they were in the organizations.

There is little evidence that any of the policies that we have described have had any direct effect on worker productivity or performance. The distinction which is necessary here is the distinction between a person's satisfaction with the job and his motivation to perform effectively in that job. It was once assumed that these two things went hand in hand, that a person who was satisfied with his job would necessarily be an effective performer. During the last twenty years there have been a large number of research studies conducted in order to test the correctness of this assumption, and the results, reviewed in the article by Brayfield and Crockett (Reading 5), show no consistent or meaningful relationship between them. Effective performers were as likely to be dissatisfied with their jobs as they were to be satisfied with them and ineffective performers were as likely to be satisfied as they were to be dissatisfied. It should be added, however, that a fairly consistent negative relationship has been observed between job satisfaction and turnover. In other words, people who are satisfied with their jobs are less likely to leave the organization than people who are dissatisfied.

It might be concluded from this that the paternalistic approach was not a very effective strategy for dealing with the problem of motivating workers to perform effectively in their jobs. It operated primarily on job satisfaction and indirectly on people's decisions about whether or not to stay in the organization, but it had relatively little effect on people's decisions about how much they would produce while in the organization.

The second approach or strategy for motivating people within organizations has its roots in the scientific management methods of Taylor (Reading 20). It is based on the assumption that a person will be motivated to work if rewards and penalties are tied directly to his performance, thus the rewards are conditional rather than unconditional. In short, they are attached to and made contingent upon effective performance.

The clearest example of the use of rewards as a means of motivating performance may be found in individual wage incentives. It is also manifest in such practices as promoting individuals on the basis of their merit and in recognizing and rewarding people for special accomplishments. In addition, penalties are typically made contingent upon falling below some minimal standard of performance. Examples of this would include warnings, reprimands or even dismissals for violating rules and procedures. The assumptions underlying this strategy are what McGregor (Reading 22) calls the Theory X approach to management. The methodology of this approach constitutes an external control system. It is necessary to define the standards to be used in the allocation of the rewards and penalties in as objective or measurable a fashion as possible. These standards may be formulated in terms of the methods used by the individual when carrying out his job or in the results which he achieves. It is also necessary to monitor the behaviour of the individual to observe the extent to which these standards are attained or adhered to. The final ingredient of the system is the consistent allocation of the rewards and penalties based on the observations of performance.

This approach to motivation rests on a rather substantial foundation of psychological research and theory. The foundation is what psychologists have termed the Law of Effect or the principle of reinforcement. Succinctly it states that if a person undertakes an action and this action is followed by a reward, the probability that the action will be repeated is increased. On the other hand, if the person undertakes an action which is ignored or followed by a punishment, that behaviour is less likely to be repeated.

Introduction

Research has provided support for these propositions in a large number of different situations. It is also consistent with many of the findings reported in Opsahl and Dunnette (Reading 10) concerning the role of financial compensation in industrial motivation as well as the evidence reported in Reading 17 by Georgopoulos, Mahoney and Jones which suggests that effective performers are more likely than ineffective performers to view performance on their present jobs as a means to the attainment of wage increases and promotion to higher level positions.

On the other hand, there appear to be significant limitations on an approach to motivation which is based exclusively on external control. These limitations are more apparent in some situations than in others, but they seriously weaken the universal applicability of an approach to motivation based solely on externally mediated rewards and penalties.

One of the limitations stems from the kinds of rewards and penalties which can be utilized by such an approach. In Reading 2, Maslow portrays a conception of the range of human needs. It is clear from this analysis that there are an exceedingly large number of outcomes which are potentially gratifying or aversive to human beings and only a small number of these outcomes are under direct managerial control. It is particularly difficult for the external control system to encompass the higher order needs for esteem and self-actualization. In addition it is evident from the findings cited in Tannenbaum (Reading 15) that certain rewards and penalties relevant to social needs are under the control of the informal organization, and these sanctions may work in opposition to the formal control system.

A second limitation to the external control system stems from its reliance on some reasonably objective method of measuring or assessing performance. This is clearly possible in many rank-and-file positions in production or in sales, but it becomes increasingly difficult as one moves to positions of a staff or managerial nature. As Katz notes in Reading 19, the interdependence of positions frequently makes it difficult or impossible to trace results to the efforts of one individual. In addition, events in the environment of the organization, such as adverse market conditions or labour disputes, weaken the relationship between the behaviour of the incumbent and the measurable results of his performance. Organizationally mediated rewards and penalties have most clear-cut motivational effects where the outcomes on the basis of which the rewards and penalties are allocated are under the control of the individual. Where such control is weakened, the motivational advantages tend to break down.

Within the last twenty to twenty-five years, a third approach to motivation has become discernable in the writings of people such as McGregor (Reading 22), Likert (Reading 23) and Maier and Hayes (Reading 24). It has frequently been termed participative management. Whereas paternalistic management assumed that man can be induced to work out of a feeling of gratitude to the system, and the external control system associated with scientific management assumed that man can be induced to work by the expectation of gain for doing or the expectation of loss for not doing, participative management assumes that individuals can derive satisfaction from doing an effective job *per se*. They can become ego-involved with their jobs, emotionally committed to doing them well and take pride from evidence that they are effective in furthering the objectives of the company. The assumptions underlying a participative approach to management are more completely documented by McGregor in Reading 22 when he talks about Theory Y.

One of the basic elements of the different theories of participative management is the integration of the planning and the doing. The term 'management by objectives' expresses a similar idea. In essence, the discretionary component of jobs is enlarged and the programmed component is reduced. The person is given broad goals or objectives and is enabled to determine for himself how they are to be achieved. The basic assumption is that if a person has freedom in determining how he will do his job, then he will regard his job as more of a challenge than if he is told exactly what to do and when to do it.

A second common element is the reduction in the use of authority as a means of control. Leavitt (Reading 27) deals with this in his concept of power equalization. In essence, the supervisor or manager plays a helping role rather than an authoritative one. He is there as a resource for his subordinates to use, but he resists imposing his ideas on his subordinates concerning how their jobs should be done. To quote from

15

McGregor, 'The manager is a teacher, a consultant, a colleague, but very rarely a boss.'

Finally, in the participative management approach there is much more reliance on the utilization of work groups as problem-solving and decision-making units. On matters affecting the entire unit, the supervisor does not make decisions autocratically and issue orders to subordinates, but rather he meets with his sub-ordinates as a group and shares problems with them and encour-ages them to participate with him in finding solutions to these problems. This opportunity to participate in the decision-making process is assumed, with considerable justification, to create involvement or commitment on the part of subordinates and enhance identification with corporate goals and objectives.

The reader should note that in discussions of participative management little mention is made of either compensation or promotion. Incentives for effective performance are in the task or job itself or in the individual's relationship with members of his working team, not in the organizationally mediated consequences of task performance. The emphasis is on creating conditions under which effective performance can be a goal rather than a means to the attainment of some other goal, and the philosophy is one of self-control or self-regulation rather than organizational control.

There are some indications that participative management may be more applicable to some organizational conditions than to others. It seems to have been less influential at lower levels in organizations where the nature of the technology frequently permits little discretion in how a job is done, and where the situa-tional demands are fairly constant and predictable and simply require repetition of well codified or defined routines. It has been more influential at higher organizational levels and in research and development functions where problems are complex and roles are continually changing in response to altered situational demands. Leavitt has discussed this problem in detail in Reading 25.

Since the emphasis on internal control and self-regulation in participative management assumes a particular set of needs or motives to be characteristic of man – most notably those at the higher end of Maslow's hierarchy – it is possible that the effectiveness of participative management may also be dependent on the strength of these motives among the people to be managed. A few studies (French, Israel and As, 1960; Marrow, 1964; Vroom, 1959) have suggested significant personality or cultural differences in response to participative management. Maslow (1965) has speculated that the principles of participative management are most useful in managing persons with strong needs for self-actualization and are primarily applicable in the more highly developed countries.

So far we have been discussing these three approaches to motivation as if they were incompatible with one another. We have been treating paternalistic, scientific and participative managements as though an organization must select from among them, or as though an organization which moved towards one approach necessarily moved away from the others. It is now appropriate to examine that issue more closely. Paternalistic and scientific managements do represent opposite poles on one continuum. The former employs uniformity in reward levels among occupants of the same role while the latter, which is based on reward levels tailored to the performance of the occupant, employs inequality or variance in rewards and penalties among such occupants. Certain aspects of scientific and participative managements are, however, much less incompatible. It is possible to set up conditions such that individuals are rewarded through wage increases and promotions for effective performance and at the same time to establish conditions conducive to their maximum involvement in their jobs and in the organization. In such a system people would be both challenged by their jobs and rewarded by the organization for doing them well. They would be given maximum freedom or discretion in planning their jobs with the knowledge that they would be evaluated on the basis of the objective results they achieved and not on the basis of their adherence to arbitrary rules or supervisory whims and fancies.

Inconsistencies between these two approaches to motivation occur if rewards and penalties are based on the way in which the job is done rather than the results achieved. This effectively reduces the discretion permitted an individual in how he does his job, which causes – according to the advocates of participative management – a decrease in motivation.

Introduction

The term scientific management typically carries with it connotations other than that of merely allocating rewards and penalties based on performance. As conceived by Taylor, it also means maximum separation of the planning from the doing. The worker is effectively 'programmed' from the outside eliminating any need for thinking or judgement on his part about how the job should be done. It is in this sense – the separation rather than integration of the planning and doing – that scientific and participative managements are incompatible with one another.

In this volume we have drawn together a collection of papers and articles which we feel presents a comprehensive picture of the work being done in the field of motivation and management. We have included three kinds of papers. First, there are summary or review articles, which review the results of research related to some significant aspect of the problem in order to provide the reader with an integration and an overview of that area. Secondly, we have included reports of specific empirical investigations to give the reader some flavour of the nature of the research methodology and the kinds of investigations that are cited in the review articles. Finally, we have included articles of a theoretical nature which attempt to develop models or theories to account for a wide range of empirical findings.

We hope that those readers with a background in psychology will be able to see the connexion between psychological theories on the one hand, and research and applications to the management of large-scale organizations on the other. We also hope that the students of management can acquire both an acquaintance with one of the disciplines on which the practice of management depends and some concrete ideas concerning its relevance to their chosen profession.

References
ATKINSON, J. W. (1964), *An Introduction to Motivation*, Van Nostrand.
BINDRA, D., and STEWART, J. (eds.) (1966), *Motivation*, Penguin Books.
COCH, L., and FRENCH, J. R. P. (1948), 'Overcoming resistance to change', *Hum. Rel.*, vol. 1, pp. 512–33.
COFER, C. N., and APPLEY, M. H. (1964), *Motivation: Theory and Research*, Wiley.
FRENCH, J. R. P., ISRAEL, J., and As, D. (1960), 'An experiment on participation in a Norwegian factory', *Hum. Rel.*, vol. 13, pp. 3–19.

LEWIN, K., LIPPITT, R., and WHITE, R. K. (1939), 'Patterns of aggressive behavior in experimentally created social climates', *J. soc. Psychol.*, vol. 10, pp. 271–99.

MARROW, A. J. (1964), 'Risks and uncertainties in action research', *J. soc. Iss.*, vol. 20, pp. 5–20.

MASLOW, A. H. (1965), *Eupsychian Management: A Journal*, Dorsey-Irwin.

ROETHLISBERGER, F. J., and DICKSON, W. J. (1939), *Management and the Worker*, Harvard U.P.

VROOM, V. H. (1959), 'Some personality determinants of the effects of participation', *J. abnorm. soc. Psychol.*, vol. 59, pp. 322–7.

Part One Why Men Work

Most conceptions of the process of motivation begin with the assumption that behaviour is, at least in part, directed towards the attainment of goals or towards the satisfaction of needs or motives. Accordingly, it is appropriate to begin our consideration of motivation in the work place by examining the motives for working. Simon (Reading 1) points out that an organization is able to secure the participation of a person by offering him inducements which contribute in some way to at least one of his goals. The kinds of inducements offered by an organization are varied, and if they are effective in maintaining participation they must necessarily be based on the needs of the individuals.

Maslow (Reading 2) examines in detail what these needs are. He points out not only that there are many needs ranging from basic physiological drives such as hunger to a more abstract desire for self-actualization, but also that they are arranged in a hierarchy whereby the lower-order needs must to a large degree be satisfied before the higher-order ones come into play.

One of the most obvious ways in which work organizations attract and retain members is through the realization that economic factors are not the only inducement for working as indicated by Morse and Weiss (Reading 3). In line with the social, esteem and self-actualization needs discussed by Maslow, factors such as associations with others, self-respect gained through the work, and a high interest value of the work can serve effectively to induce people to work.

1 Herbert A. Simon

Administrative Behaviour

Excerpts from chapters 1 and 6 of Herbert A. Simon, *Administrative Behavior*, Macmillan, New York, 2nd edn, 1957, pp. 4, 110–11, 115–17. (First published in 1947.)

Value and Fact in Decision

A great deal of behavior, and particularly the behavior of individuals within administrative organizations, is purposive – oriented towards goals or objectives. This purposiveness brings about an integration in the pattern of behavior, in the absence of which administration would be meaningless; for, if administration consists in 'getting things done' by groups of people, purpose provides a principal criterion in determining what things are to be done. [. . .]

Inducements

Individuals are willing to accept organization membership when their activity in the organization contributes, directly or indirectly, to their own personal goals. The contribution is direct if the goals set for the organization have direct personal value for the individual – church membership is a typical example of this. The contribution is indirect if the organization offers personal rewards – monetary or other – to the individual in return for his willingness to contribute his activity to the organization. Employment in a business concern is a typical example of this. Sometimes these personal rewards are directly related to the size and growth of the organization – as in the case of the stockholders of a business; sometimes, not very directly – as in the case of most wage earners. The characteristics of these three bases for participation are sufficiently distinct to make it worthwhile to consider them separately; personal rewards deriving directly from the accomplishment of the organization objective; personal inducements offered by the organization and closely related to its size and growth; and personal rewards derived from inducements offered by the organization but unrelated to the organization size and growth. Organizations are ordinarily made up of three groups of individuals, in each of which one of these types of motivation prevails; and it is the presence of these three groups that gives administration its specific character.

The phrase 'personal goals' which is used here should be understood in a broad sense. It is by no means restricted to egoistic goals, much less to economic goals. 'World peace' or 'aid to the starving Chinese' may be just as much a personal goal for a particular individual as another dollar in his pay envelope. The fact that economic incentives frequently predominate in business and governmental organizations should not obscure the importance of other types of inducements. Nor should intangible egoistic values, such as status, prestige, or enjoyment of organization associations, be forgotten.

In business organizations the 'customers' are a group that has, predominantly, the first type of motivation – direct interest in organization objectives; employees, the third type; and the entrepreneur the second type. This is true, of course, only to a very rough approximation.

The members of an organization, then, contribute to the organization in return for inducements that the organization offers them. The contributions of one group are the source of the inducements that the organization offers others. If the sum of the contributions is sufficient, in quantity and kind, to supply the necessary quantity and kinds of inducements, the organization survives and grows; otherwise it shrinks and ultimately disappears unless an equilibrium is reached.[1] [. . .]

Incentives for Employee Participation

To an employee of a non-volunteer organization the most obvious personal incentive that the organization offers is a salary or wage. It is a peculiar and important characteristic of his relation with the organization that, in return for this inducement, he offers the

1. This idea of an equilibrium is due to C. I. Barnard. See Barnard (1938), pp. 56–9 and chs. xi and xvi.

organization not a specific service but his undifferentiated time and effort. He places this time and effort at the disposal of those directing the organization, to be used as they see fit. Thus, both the customer relation (in the commercial organization) and the employee relation originate in contract, but in contracts of very different sorts. The employment contract results in the creation of a continuing authority relation between the organization and the employee.

How can this be? Why does the employee sign a blank check, so to speak, in entering upon his employment? First, from the viewpoint of the organization, nothing would be gained by offering an inducement to the employee unless the latter's behavior could be brought into the system of organization behavior through his acceptance of its authority. Second, from the viewpoint of the employee, the precise activities with which his time of employment is occupied may, within certain limits, be a matter of relative indifference to him. If the orders transmitted to him by the organization remain within these limits of acceptance, he will permit his behavior to be guided by them.

What determines the breadth of the area of acceptance within which the employee will accept the authority of the organization? It certainly depends on the nature and magnitude of the incentives the organization offers. In addition to the salary he receives, he may value the status and prestige that his position in the organization gives him, and he may value his relations with the working group of which he is a part. In setting his task, the organization must take into consideration the effect that its orders may have upon the employee's realization of these values. If the employee values white-collar status, for example, he may be completely unwilling to accept assignments that deprive him of that status even when the work he is asked to perform is not inherently unpleasant or difficult.

There is great variation among individuals in the extent to which opportunities for promotion act as incentives for participation. Promotion is, of course, both an economic and a prestige incentive. Burleigh Gardner has pointed out the importance for administrative theory of the presence in organizations of certain highly 'mobile' individuals, i.e. individuals who have a strong desire for advancement. It would be a mistake (which Gardner carefully avoids) to assume that these desires provide a strong incentive in all individuals.[2]

We find, then, that those participants in organization who are called its employees are offered a variety of material and non-material incentives, generally not directly related to the attainment of the organization objective nor to the size and growth of the organization, in return for their willingness to accept organization decisions as the basis for their behavior during the time of their employment. The area within which organization authority will be accepted is not unlimited, and the boundaries will depend on the incentives that the organization is able to provide. In so far as these incentives are not directly dependent upon the organization objective, modification of that objective will not affect the willingness of employees to participate, and hence the latter group will exert little influence in the determination of the objectives.

References
BARNARD, C. I. (1938), *The Functions of the Executive*, Harvard U. P.
GARDNER, B. B. (1945), *Human Relations in Industry*, Irwin.

2. On this and other aspects of the problem of incentives see Gardner (1945), chs. i and viii.

2 A. H. Maslow

A Theory of Human Motivation

Abridged from A. H. Maslow, 'A theory of human motivation',
Psychological Review, vol. 50, 1943, pp. 370–96.

The Basic Needs

The physiological needs

The needs that are usually taken as the starting-point for motivation theory are the so-called physiological drives. Two recent lines of research make it necessary to revise our customary notions about these needs: first, the development of the concept of homeostasis, and, second, the finding that appetites (preferential choices among foods) are a fairly efficient indication of actual needs or lacks in the body.

Homeostasis refers to the body's automatic efforts to maintain a constant, normal state of the blood stream. Cannon (1932) has described this process for the water content of the blood, salt content, sugar content, protein content, fat content, calcium content, oxygen content, constant hydrogen-ion level (acid-base balance) and constant temperature of the blood. Obviously this list can be extended to include other minerals, the hormones, vitamins, etc.

We cannot identify all physiological needs as homeostatic. That sexual desire, sleepiness, sheer activity and maternal behavior in animals are homeostatic, has not yet been demonstrated. Furthermore, this list would not include the various sensory pleasures (tastes, smells, tickling, stroking) which are probably physiological and which may become the goals of motivated behavior.

In a previous paper (Maslow, 1943) it has been pointed out that these physiological drives or needs are to be considered unusual rather than typical because they are isolable and because they are localizable somatically. That is to say, they are relatively independent of each other, of other motivations and of the organism as a whole, and, in many cases, it is possible to demonstrate a localized, underlying somatic base for the drive. This is true less generally than has been thought (exceptions are fatigue, sleepiness, maternal responses), but it is still true in the classic instances of hunger, sex and thirst.

It should be pointed out again that any of the physiological needs and the consummatory behavior involved with them serve as channels for all sorts of other needs as well. The person who thinks he is hungry may actually be seeking more for comfort or dependence than for vitamins or proteins. Conversely, it is possible to satisfy the hunger need in part by other activities such as drinking water or smoking cigarettes. In other words, these physiological needs are only relatively isolable.

Undoubtedly these physiological needs are the most prepotent of all needs. What this means specifically is that, in the human being who is missing everything in life in an extreme fashion, it is most likely that the major motivation would be the physiological needs rather than any others. A person who is lacking food, safety, love and esteem would most probably hunger for food more strongly than for anything else.

If all the needs are unsatisfied, and the organism is then dominated by the physiological needs, all other needs may become simply non-existent or be pushed into the background.

It is quite true that man lives by bread alone – when there is no bread. But what happens to man's desires when there *is* plenty of bread and when his belly is chronically filled?

At once other (and 'higher') needs emerge and these, rather than physiological hungers, dominate the organism. And when these in turn are satisfied, again new (and still 'higher') needs emerge and so on. This is what we mean by saying that the basic human needs are organized into a hierarchy of relative prepotency.

One main implication of this phrasing is that gratification becomes as important a concept as deprivation in motivation theory, for it releases the organism from the domination of a relatively more physiological need, permitting thereby the emergence of other more social goals. The physiological needs, along with their partial goals, when chronically gratified cease to exist as active determinants or organizers of behavior. They now exist only in a potential fashion in the sense that they may emerge again to dominate the organism if they are thwarted. But a want that is satisfied is no longer a want. The organism is dominated and its behavior organized only by unsatisfied needs. If hunger is satisfied, it becomes unimportant in the current dynamics of the individual.

This statement is somewhat qualified by a hypothesis to be discussed more fully later, namely, that it is precisely those individuals in whom a certain need has always been satisfied who are best equipped to tolerate deprivation of that need in the future; furthermore, those who have been deprived in the past will react to current satisfactions differently from the one who has never been deprived.

The safety needs

If the physiological needs are relatively well gratified, there then emerges a new set of needs, which we may categorize roughly as the safety needs. All that has been said of the physiological needs is equally true, although in lesser degree, of these desires. The organism may equally well be wholly dominated by them. They may serve as the almost exclusive organizers of behavior, recruiting all the capacities of the organism in their service, and we may then fairly describe the whole organism as a safety-seeking mechanism.

Although in this paper we are interested primarily in the needs of the adult, we can approach an understanding of his safety needs perhaps more efficiently by observation of infants and children, in whom these needs are much more simple and obvious. One reason for the clearer appearance of the threat or danger reaction in infants is that they do not inhibit this reaction at all, whereas adults in our society have been taught to inhibit it at all costs. Thus even when adults do feel their safety to be threatened, we may not be able to see this on the surface.

The average child in our society usually prefers a safe, orderly, predictable, organized world which he can count on and in which unexpected, unmanageable, or other dangerous things do not happen and in which, in any case, he has all-powerful parents who protect and shield him from harm.

The healthy, normal, fortunate adult in our culture is largely satisfied in his safety needs. The peaceful, smoothly running, 'good' society ordinarily makes its members feel safe enough from wild animals, extremes of temperature, criminals, assault and murder, tyranny, etc. Therefore, in a very real sense, they no longer have any safety needs as active motivators. Just as a sated man no longer feels hungry, a safe man no longer feels endangered.

Other broader aspects of the attempt to seek safety and stability in the world are seen in the very common preference for familiar rather than unfamiliar things, or for the known rather than the unknown. The tendency to have some religion or world-philosophy that organizes the universe and the men in it into some sort of satisfactorily coherent, meaningful whole is also in part motivated by safety-seeking. Here too we may list science and philosophy in general as partially motivated by the safety needs (we shall see later that there are also other motivations to scientific, philosophical or religious endeavour).

Otherwise the need for safety is seen as an active and dominant mobilizer of the organism's resources only in emergencies, e.g. war, disease, natural catastrophes, crime waves, societal disorganization, neurosis, brain injury, chronically bad situations.

Some neurotic adults in our society are, in many ways, like the unsafe child in their desire for safety, although in the former it takes on a somewhat special appearance. Their reaction is often to unknown, psychological dangers in a world that is perceived to be hostile, overwhelming and threatening.

The neurosis in which the search for safety takes its clearest form is in the compulsive-obsessive neurosis. Compulsive-obsessives try frantically to order and stabilize the world so that no unmanageable, unexpected or unfamiliar dangers will ever appear (see Maslow and Mittlemann, 1941). They hedge themselves about with all sorts of ceremonials, rules, and formulae so that every possible contingency may be provided for and so that no new contingencies may appear. They are much like the brain-injured cases, described by Goldstein (1939) who manage to maintain their equilibrium by avoiding everything unfamiliar and strange and by ordering their restricted world in such a neat, disciplined, orderly fashion that everything in the world can be counted upon. They try to arrange the world so that anything unexpected (dangers) cannot possibly occur. If, through no fault of their own, something unexpected does occur, they go into a

A. H. Maslow

panic reaction as if this unexpected occurrence constituted a grave danger. What we can see only as a none-too strong preference in the healthy person, e.g. preference for the familiar, becomes a life-and-death necessity in abnormal cases.

The love needs

If both the physiological and the safety needs are fairly well grati-fied, then there will emerge the love and affection and belonging-ness needs, and the whole cycle already described will repeat itself with this new center. Now the person will feel keenly, as never before, the absence of friends or a sweetheart or a wife or children. He will hunger for affectionate relations with people in general, namely, for a place in his group, and he will strive with great intensity to achieve this goal. He will want to attain such a place more than anything else in the world and may even forget that once, when he was hungry, he sneered at love.

In our society the thwarting of these needs is the most com-monly found core in cases of maladjustment and more severe psychopathology. Love and affection, as well as their possible expression in sexuality, are generally looked upon with ambiva-lence and are customarily hedged about with many restrictions and inhibitions. Practically all theorists of psychopathology have stressed thwarting of the love needs as basic in the picture of maladjustment. Many clinical studies have therefore been made of this need and we know more about it perhaps than any of the other needs except the physiological ones (see Maslow and Mittelmann, 1941).

One thing that must be stressed at this point is that love is not synonymous with sex. Sex may be studied as a purely physio-logical need. Ordinarily sexual behavior is multi-determined, that is to say, determined not only by sexual but also by other needs, chief among which are the love and affection needs. Also not to be overlooked is the fact that the love needs involve both giving *and* receiving love (see Maslow, 1942; and Plant, 1937, ch. v).

The esteem needs

All people in our society (with a few pathological exceptions) have a need or desire for a stable, firmly based, (usually) high evalua-tion of themselves, for self-respect, or self-esteem, and for the

31

esteem of others. By firmly based self-esteem, we mean that which is soundly based upon real capacity, achievement and respect from others. These needs may be classified into two subsidiary sets. These are, first, the desire for strength, for achievement, for adequacy, for confidence in the face of the world, and for independence and freedom.[1] Second, we have what we may call the desire for reputation or prestige (defining it as respect or esteem from other people), recognition, attention, importance or appreciation.[2] These needs have been relatively stressed by Alfred Adler and his followers and have been relatively neglected by Freud and the psychoanalysts. More and more today, however, there is appearing widespread appreciation of their central importance.

Satisfaction of the self-esteem need leads to feelings of self-confidence, worth, strength, capability, and adequacy of being useful and necessary in the world. But thwarting of these needs produces feelings of inferiority, of weakness, and of helplessness. These feelings in turn give rise to either basic discouragement or else compensatory or neurotic trends. An appreciation of the necessity of basic self-confidence and an understanding of how helpless people are without it, can be easily gained from a study of severe traumatic neurosis.[3]

The need for self-actualization

Even if all these needs are satisfied, we may still often (if not always) expect that a new discontent and restlessness will soon develop, unless the individual is doing what he is fitted for. A

1. Whether or not this particular desire is universal we do not know. The crucial question, especially important today, is, 'Will men who are enslaved and dominated inevitably feel dissatisfied and rebellious?' We may assume on the basis of commonly known clinical data that a man who has known true freedom (not paid for by giving up safety and security but rather built on the basis of adequate safety and security) will not willingly or easily allow his freedom to be taken away from him. But we do not know that this is true for the person born into slavery. The events of the next decade should give us our answer. See discussion of this problem in Fromm (1941), ch. v.

2. Perhaps the desire for prestige and respect from others is subsidiary to the desire for self-esteem or confidence in one's self. Observation of children seems to indicate that this is so, but clinical data give no clear support of such a conclusion.

3. See Kardiner (1941). For more extensive discussion of normal self-esteem, as well as for reports of various researches, see Maslow (1939).

musician must make music, an artist must paint, a poet must write, if he is to be ultimately happy. What a man *can* be, he *must* be. This need we may call self-actualization.

This term, first coined by Kurt Goldstein, is being used in this paper in a much more specific and limited fashion. It refers to the desire for self-fulfilment, namely, to the tendency for one to become actualized in what one is potentially. This tendency might be phrased as the desire to become more and more what one is, to become everything that one is capable of becoming.

The specific form that these needs take will of course vary greatly from person to person. In one individual it may be expressed maternally, as the desire to be an ideal mother, in another athletically, in still another aesthetically, in the painting of pictures, and in another inventively in the creation of new contrivances. It is not necessarily a creative urge although in people who have any capabilities for creation it will take this form.

The clear emergence of these needs rests upon prior satisfaction of the physiological, safety, love and esteem needs. We shall call people who are satisfied in these needs, basically satisfied people, and it is from these that we may expect the fullest (and healthiest) creativeness.[4] Since, in our society, basically satisfied people are the exception, we do not know much about self-actualization, either experimentally or clinically. It remains a challenging problem for research.

The preconditions for the basic need satisfactions

There are certain conditions which are immediate prerequisites for the basic need satisfactions. Danger to these is reacted to almost as if it were a direct danger to the basic needs themselves. Such conditions as freedom to speak, freedom to do what one

4. Clearly creative behavior, like painting, is like any other behavior in having multiple determinants. It may be seen in 'innately creative' people whether they are satisfied or not, happy or unhappy, hungry or sated. Also, it is clear that creative activity may be compensatory, ameliorative, or purely economic. It is my impression (as yet unconfirmed) that it is possible to distinguish the artistic and intellectual products of basically satisfied people from those of basically unsatisfied people by inspection alone. In any case, here too we must distinguish, in a dynamic fashion, the overt behavior itself from its various motivations or purposes.

wishes so long as no harm is done to others, freedom to express oneself, freedom to investigate and seek for information, freedom to defend oneself, justice, fairness, honesty, orderliness in the group are examples of such preconditions for basic need satisfactions. Thwarting in these freedoms will be reacted to with a threat or emergency response. These conditions are not ends in themselves but they are *almost* so, since they are so closely related to the basic needs, which are apparently the only ends in themselves. These conditions are defended because without them the basic satisfactions are quite impossible, or at least, very severely endangered.

If we remember that the cognitive capacities (perceptual, intellectual, learning) are a set of adjustive tools, which have, among other functions, that of satisfaction of our basic needs, then it is clear that any danger to them, any deprivation or blocking of their free use, must also be indirectly threatening to the basic needs themselves. Such a statement is a partial solution of the general problems of curiosity, the search for knowledge, truth and wisdom, and the ever persistent urge to solve the cosmic mysteries.

An act is psychologically important if it contributes directly to the satisfaction of basic needs. The less directly it so contributes, or the weaker this contribution is, the less important this act must be conceived to be from the point of view of dynamic psychology.

The desires to know and to understand

So far, we have mentioned the cognitive needs only in passing. Acquiring knowledge and systematizing the universe have been considered as, in part, techniques for the achievement of basic safety in the world or, for the intelligent man, expressions of self-actualization. Also freedom of inquiry and expression have been discussed as preconditions of satisfactions of the basic needs. True though these formulations may be, they do not constitute definitive answers to the question as to the motivation role of curiosity, learning, philosophizing, experimenting, etc. They are, at best, no more than partial answers.

This question is especially difficult because we know so little about the facts. Curiosity, exploration, desire for the facts, desire to know may certainly be observed easily enough. The fact that they often are pursued even at great cost to the individual's safety is an indication of the partial character of our previous discussion. In addition, the writer must admit that, though he has sufficient clinical evidence to postulate the desire to know as a very strong drive in intelligent people, no data are available for unintelligent people. It may then be largely a function of relatively high intelligence. Rather tentatively, then, and largely in the hope of stimulating discussion and research, we shall postulate a basic desire to know, to be aware of reality, to get the facts, to satisfy curiosity or, as Wertheimer phrases it, to see rather than to be blind.

This postulation, however, is not enough. Even after we know, we are impelled to know more and more minutely and microscopically, on the one hand, and, on the other, more and more extensively in the direction of a world philosophy, religion, etc. The facts that we acquire, if they are isolated or atomistic, inevitably get theorized about, and either analysed or organized or both. This process has been phrased by some as the search for 'meaning'. We shall then postulate a desire to understand, to systematize, to organize, to analyse, to look for relations and meanings.

Once these desires are accepted for discussion, we see that they too form themselves into a small hierarchy in which the desire to know is prepotent over the desire to understand. All the characteristics of a hierarchy of prepotency that we have described above, seem to hold for this one as well.

We must guard ourselves against the too easy tendency to separate these desires from the basic needs we have discussed above, i.e. to make a sharp dichotomy between 'cognitive' and 'conative' needs. The desire to know and to understand are themselves conative, i.e. have a striving character, and are as much personality needs as the 'basic needs' we have already discussed.

Further Characteristics of the Basic Needs

The degree of fixity of the hierarchy of basic needs

We have spoken so far as if this hierarchy were a fixed order but actually it is not nearly as rigid as we may have implied. It is true that most of the people with whom we have worked have seemed to have these basic needs in about the order that has been indicated. However, there have been a number of exceptions.

1. There are some people in whom, for instance, self-esteem seems to be more important than love. This most common reversal in the hierarchy is usually due to the development of the notion that the person who is most likely to be loved is a strong or powerful person, one who inspires respect or fear and who is self-confident or aggressive. Therefore, such people who lack love and seek it, may try hard to put on a front of aggressive, confident behavior. But essentially they seek high self-esteem and its behavior expressions more as a means to an end than for its own sake; they seek self-assertion for the sake of love rather than for self-esteem itself.

2. There are other, apparently innately creative people in whom the drive to creativeness seems to be more important than any other counterdeterminant. Their creativeness might appear as self-actualization released not by basic satisfaction but in spite of lack of basic satisfaction.

3. In certain people the level of aspiration may be permanently deadened or lowered. That is to say, the less prepotent goals may simply be lost and may disappear forever, so that the person who has experienced life at a very low level, i.e. chronic unemployment, may continue to be satisfied for the rest of his life if only he can get enough food.

4. The so-called 'psychopathic personality' is another example of permanent loss of the love needs. These are people who, according to the best data available (Levy, 1937), have been starved for love in the earliest months of their lives and have simply lost forever the desire and the ability to give and to receive affection (as animals lose sucking or pecking reflexes that are not exercised soon enough after birth).

5. Another cause of reversal of the hierarchy is that when a need has been satisfied for a long time, this need may be underevaluated. People who have never experienced chronic hunger are apt to underestimate its effects and to look upon food as a rather unimportant thing. If they are dominated by a higher need, this higher need will seem to be the most important of all. It then becomes possible, and indeed does actually happen, that they may, for the sake of this higher need, put themselves into the position of being deprived in a more basic need. We may expect that after a long-time deprivation of the more basic need there

will be a tendency to re-evaluate both needs so that the more prepotent need will actually become consciously prepotent for the individual who may have given it up very lightly. Thus, a man who has given up his job rather than lose his self-respect, and who then starves for six months or so, may be willing to take his job back even at the price of losing his self-respect.

6. Another partial explanation of *apparent* reversals is seen in the fact that we have been talking about the hierarchy of prepotency in terms of consciously felt wants or desires rather than of behavior. Looking at behavior itself may give us the wrong impression. What we have claimed is that the person will *want* the more basic of two needs when deprived in both. There is no necessary implication here that he will act upon his desires. Let us say again that there are many determinants of behavior other than needs and desires.

7. Perhaps more important than all these exceptions are the ones that involve ideals, high social standards, high values, and the like. With such values people become martyrs; they will give up everything for the sake of a particular ideal, or value. These people may be understood, at least in part, by reference to one basic concept (or hypothesis) which may be called 'increased frustration tolerance through early gratification'. People who have been satisfied in their basic needs throughout their lives, particularly in their earlier years, seem to develop exceptional power to withstand present or future thwarting of these needs simply because they have strong, healthy character structure as a result of basic satisfaction. They are the 'strong' people who can easily weather disagreement or opposition, who can swim against the stream of public opinion, and who can stand up for the truth at great personal cost.

I say all this in spite of the fact that there is a certain amount of sheer habituation which is also involved in any full discussion of frustration tolerance. For instance, it is likely that those persons who have been accustomed to relative starvation for a long time are partially enabled thereby to withstand food deprivation. What sort of balance must be made between these two tendencies, of habituation on the one hand, and of past satisfaction breeding present frustration tolerance on the other hand, remains to be worked out by further research.

Degrees of relative satisfaction

So far, our theoretical discussion may have given the impression that these five sets of needs are somehow in a stepwise, all-or-none relationship to one another. We have spoken in such terms as the following: 'If one need is satisfied, then another emerges'. This statement might give the false impression that a need must be satisfied 100 per cent before the next need emerges. In actual fact, most members of our society who are normal are partially satisfied in all their basic needs and partially unsatisfied in all their basic needs at the same time. A more realistic description of the hierarchy would be in terms of decreasing percentages of satisfaction as we go up the hierarchy of prepotency.

As for the concept of emergence of a new need after satisfaction of the prepotent need, this emergence is not a sudden, saltatory phenomenon but rather a gradual emergence by slow degrees from nothingness.

Unconscious character of needs

These needs are neither necessarily conscious nor unconscious. On the whole, however, in the average person, they are more often unconscious. It is not necessary at this point to overhaul the tremendous mass of evidence which indicates the crucial importance of unconscious motivation. It would by now be expected, on *a priori* grounds alone, that unconscious motivations would on the whole be rather more important than the conscious motivations. What we have called the basic needs are very often largely unconscious although they may, with suitable techniques and in sophisticated people, become conscious.

The role of gratified needs

It has been pointed out above several times that our higher needs usually emerge only when more prepotent needs have been gratified. Thus gratification has an important role in motivation theory. Apart from this, however, needs cease to play an active determining or organizing role as soon as they are gratified.

What this means, for example, is that a basically satisfied person no longer has the needs for esteem, love, safety, etc. The only sense in which he might be said to have them is in the almost metaphysical sense that a sated man has hunger or a filled bottle has emptiness. If we are interested in what *actually* motivates us and not in what has, will, or might motivate us, then a satisfied need is not a motivator. It must be considered for all practical purposes simply not to exist, to have disappeared. This point should be emphasized because it has been either overlooked or contradicted in every theory of motivation I know.[5] The perfectly healthy, normal, fortunate man has no sex needs or hunger needs, or needs for safety or for love or for prestige or for self-esteem, except in stray moments of quickly passing threat. If we were to say otherwise, we should also have to aver that every man had all the pathological reflexes, e.g. Babinski, etc., because if his nervous system were damaged, these would appear.

It is such considerations as these that suggest the bold postulation that a man who is thwarted in any of his basic needs may fairly be envisaged simply as a sick man. This is a fair parallel to our designation as 'sick' of the man who lacks vitamins or minerals. Who is to say that a lack of love is less important than a lack of vitamins? Since we know the pathogenic effects of love starvation, who is to say that we are invoking value questions in an unscientific or illegitimate way, any more than the physician does who diagnoses and treats pellagra or scurvy? If I were permitted this usage, I should then say simply that a healthy man is primarily motivated by his needs to develop and actualize his fullest potentialities and capacities. If a man has any other basic needs in any active, chronic sense, then he is simply an unhealthy man. He is as surely sick as if he had suddenly developed a strong salt hunger or calcium hunger.[6]

If this statement seems unusual or paradoxical the reader may be assured that this is only one among many such paradoxes that will appear as we revise our ways of looking at man's deeper

5. Note that acceptance of this theory necessitates basic revision of the Freudian theory.

6. If we were to use 'sick' in this way, we should then also have to face squarely the relations of man to his society. One clear implication of our definition would be that (a) since a man is to be called sick who is basically thwarted, and (b) since such basic thwarting is made possible ultimately only by forces outside the individual, then (c) sickness in the individual must come ultimately from a sickness in the society. The 'good' or healthy society would then be defined as one that permitted man's highest purposes to emerge by satisfying all his prepotent basic needs.

motivations. When we ask what man wants of life, we deal with his very essence.

Summary

1. There are at least five sets of goals which we may call basic needs. These are, briefly, physiological, safety, love, esteem and self-actualization. In addition, we are motivated by the desire to achieve or maintain the various conditions upon which these basic satisfactions rest and by certain more intellectual desires.

2. These basic goals are related to one another, being arranged in a hierarchy of prepotency. This means that the most prepotent goal will monopolize consciousness and will tend of itself to organize the recruitment of the various capacities of the organism. The less prepotent needs are minimized, even forgotten or denied. But when a need is fairly well satisfied, the next prepotent ('higher') need emerges, to dominate in turn the conscious life and to serve as the center of organization of behavior, since gratified needs are not active motivators.

Thus man is a perpetually wanting animal. Ordinarily the satisfaction of these wants is not altogether mutually exclusive but only tends to be. The average member of our society is most often partially satisfied and partially unsatisfied in all of his wants. The hierarchy principle is usually empirically observed in terms of increasing percentages of non-satisfaction as we go up the hierarchy. Reversals of the average order of the hierarchy are sometimes observed. Also it has been observed that an individual may permanently lose the higher wants in the hierarchy under special conditions. There are not only ordinarily multiple motivations for usual behavior but, in addition, many determinants other than motives.

3. Any thwarting or possibility of thwarting of these basic human goals, or danger to the defenses which protect them or to the conditions upon which they rest, is considered to be a psychological threat. With a few exceptions, all psychopathology may be partially traced to such threats. A basically thwarted man may actually be defined as a 'sick' man.

4. It is such basic threats which bring about the general emergency reactions.

5. Certain other basic problems have not been dealt with

40

because of limitations of space. Among these are (a) the problem of values in any definitive motivation theory; (b) the relation between appetites, desires, needs and what is 'good' for the organism; (c) the etiology of the basic needs and their possible derivation in early childhood; (d) redefinition of motivational concepts, i.e. drive, desire, wish, need, goal; (e) implication of our theory for hedonistic theory; (f) the nature of the uncompleted act, of success and failure and of aspiration level; (g) the role of association, habit and conditioning; (h) relation to the theory of interpersonal relations; (i) implications for psychotherapy; (j) implication for theory of society; (k) the theory of selfishness; (l) the relation between needs and cultural patterns; (m) the relation between this theory and Allport's theory of functional autonomy. These as well as certain other less important questions must be considered as motivation theory attempts to become definitive.

References

CANNON, W. B. (1932), *The Wisdom of the Body*, Norton.

FROMM, E. (1941), *Escape from Freedom*, Farrar & Rinehart.

GOLDSTEIN, K. (1939), *The Organism*, American Book Co.

KARDINER, A. (1941), *The Traumatic Neuroses of War*, Hoeber.

LEVY, D. M. (1937), 'Primary affect hunger', *Amer. J. Psychol.*, vol. 94, pp. 643–52.

MASLOW, A. H. (1939), 'Dominance, personality, and social behavior in women', *J. soc. Psychol.*, vol. 10, pp. 3–39.

MASLOW, A. H. (1942), 'The dynamics of psychological security–insecurity', *Char. Pers.*, vol. 10, pp. 331–44.

MASLOW, A. H. (1943), 'A preface to motivation theory', *Psychosomat. Med.*, vol. 5, pp. 85–92.

MASLOW, A. H., and MITTELMANN, B. (1941), *Principles of Abnormal Psychology*, Harper.

PLANT, J. (1937), *Personality and the Culture Pattern*, Commonwealth Fund.

3 Nancy C. Morse and Robert S. Weiss

The Function and Meaning of Work and the Job

Nancy C. Morse and Robert S. Weiss, 'The function and meaning of work and the job', *American Sociological Review*, vol. 20, 1955, pp. 191–8.

With the increasing complexity and industrialization of society, work for many people has become more and more simply a means towards the end of earning a living. However, we are in danger of over-generalizing this trend and pushing it to its logical conclusion, expecting that working serves *only* a means function.[1] The present study of the meaning of work among a national sample of employed men indicates that, for most men, having a job serves other functions than the one of earning a living. In fact, even if they had enough money to support themselves, they would still want to work. Working gives them a feeling of being tied into the larger society, of having something to do, of having a purpose in life. These other functions which working serves are evidently not seen as available in non-work activities.

This finding that work has other meanings is consistent with observations of the effect of retirement and the effect of unemployment on men. If men work only for money, there is no way of explaining the degree of dislocation and deprivation which retirement, even on an adequate salary, appears to bring to the formerly employed. The particularly interesting results of this national sample study on the meaning of working are: (a) that working is more than a means to an end for the vast majority of employed men; (b) that a man does not have to be at the age of retirement or be immediately threatened by unemployment to be able to imagine what not working would mean to him; and (c) that working serves other functions than an economic one for men in both middle-class and working-class occupations, but that

1. The same type of over-generalization of a trend was found until recently in the writing on the family. Since the family was changing (and in some ways reducing) its functions, there was some tendency to go to the extreme and predict the dying out of the family altogether.

the non-monetary functions served by working are somewhat different in these two broad classifications of occupations.

The method used to explore the function and meaning of work for employed men was a short 'fixed question–free answer' interview of a random sample of employed men in the United States.[2] We shall report some of the results of the analysis of these interviews with the 401 men studied in the sample.[3]

General Results

The conclusion that working is more than a means for economic support comes primarily from a question in the interview which was designed to remove hypothetically the economic function of working. The question asked the respondents was: 'If by some chance you inherited enough money to live comfortably without working, do you think that you would work anyway or not?'

The interviewer then followed this question with the probe: 'Why do you feel that you would work (not work)?'

Table 1 indicates that 80 per cent of the employed men answered that they would want to keep on working. It might have been expected that such a question would be considered quite unreal to the respondents. The quality of the responses, however, suggested that, while the question was not one for which they had a ready answer, it was one which they took seriously and could consider personally. Furthermore, the vividness and emotionality of their responses to this question indicated that we were tapping an area which was real and meaningful to them. It was almost as if they had never consciously thought about what working meant to them but now that they were presented with the imaginary removal of it, they could see for themselves and verbalize to another person the feelings which had really been there implicitly all the time.

When those who have stated that they would work anyway are

2. This exploratory study was made possible through cooperation with the Economic Behavior Program of the Survey Research Center. The short interview followed a longer interview for that program on consumers' expectations and plans and recent buying experience. The interviewing was done in September 1953.

3. A description of the Survey Research Center sampling method will be found in Kish (1953), especially pp. 230–35. The general interviewing method used is described in Cannell and Kahn (1953).

Table 1

Percentage of Individuals for Whom Working Serves a Non-Monetary Function

Question: 'If by some chance you inherited enough money to live comfortably without working, do you think you would work anyway or not?'

	N	Per cent
Would keep working	314	80
Would not keep working	79	20
Total responding	393	100
Not ascertained	8	
Total sample	401	

asked for their reasons for feeling this way, they give quite a wide variety of answers. Approximately two-thirds of them give what we called positive reasons, that is, they talked of something positive about working (Table 2). The most common types of positive reasons were: working keeps one occupied, gives one an interest; working keeps an individual healthy, is good for a person; and the kind of work is enjoyable. A little more than a third of those who felt that they would want to continue working gave only what we called negative reasons, that is, they talked of some negative consequences of not working. Frequent negative reasons for continuing working were: 'would feel lost if didn't work, would go crazy' and 'wouldn't know what to do with my time, can't be idle'. The fact that 36 per cent of the men who want to continue working give only negative reasons for working (Table 2) indicates that for many men working serves as a means of warding off the dangers of loneliness and isolation. The finding that as many as 14 per cent of the total sample express fears of being lost or going crazy if they did not work lends support to the consideration of work as an important positive element in the emotional economy of many individuals because it serves to anchor the individual into the society.

We should, however, be cautious about inferring too much from the answers to this one question and probe. It does not mean that people cannot readjust to not working; rather it means that not working requires considerable readjustment. The typical employed man does not *at present* have alternative ways of directing his energy and internal resources and does not *at present* have alternative ways of gaining a sense of relationship to his society which are sufficiently important to take the place of working.

The relationship of age to desire to keep working suggests that

Table 2
Reasons for Continuing Working

Question: 'Why do you feel that you would work?'

	N	Per cent
Positive reasons		
Enjoy the kind of work	27	9
To be associated with people	4	1
To keep occupied (interested)	93	32
Justifies my existence	14	5
Gives feeling of self-respect	13	5
Keeps individual healthy, good for person	30	10
Other	4	1
Total positive reasons	185	63
Negative reasons		
Without work, would:		
Feel lost, go crazy	42	14
Feel useless	5	2
Feel bored	11	4
Not know what to do with my time, can't be idle	29	10
Habit, inertia	17	6
To keep out of trouble	3	1
Other	2	0
Total negative reasons	109	37
Total responding	294	100
Not ascertained	20	
Total would work	314	
Total would not work	79	
Not ascertained	8	
Total sample	401	

the nearer the individual is to retirement age (65), the more likely that he will say that he would not work if he did not need to for economic reasons. However, as we can see from Table 3, even in the age group of fifty-five years through sixty-four years almost

Table 3
The Relationship Between Desire to Keep Working and Age

Age category	N	Percentage who would want to work	Percentage who would not want to work	Total percentage
21–34	106	90	10	100
35–44	123	83	17	100
45–54	79	72	28	100
55–64	46	61	39	100
65 or over	38	82	18	100
Total responding	392			
Not ascertained	9			
Total sample	401			

two thirds of the men would want to keep working.[4] The change in feelings about working with age indicates that some of the older men are becoming adjusted to the idea of not working. The high per centage of men over 65 who say they would continue to work even if they did not have to should be discounted. Individuals over 65 frequently have an option, regarding whether they continue to work, and our sample is one of employed men, only. It does not include those who stop work.

The kind of job which the individual now has does not influence strongly his feeling that he would want to keep working at *some* job even if he inherited enough money to live comfortably without working. While the men in the working-class occupations are slightly less likely to want to keep working, over three-quarters of those who are foremen, in the crafts and trades, or who are

4. Friedmann and Havighurst (1954, p. 183), studying five occupational groups of men fifty-five or over, found one-third to two-thirds of the men in their occupational sample wanted to continue working past sixty-five. The approach and findings of this book parallel at many points those reported in this paper, although the present authors were not aware of the Friedmann-Havighurst research until after this study was completed.

Nancy C. Morse and Robert S. Weiss

factory operatives and semi-skilled, would keep on working. The only occupational group which deviates from this over-all pattern is the unskilled. Only slightly over 50 per cent of them would want to continue working.

The degree to which working becomes woven into the pattern of life of the employed man is also attested to by the results on job satisfaction. When asked the question: 'Taking into consideration all the things about your job (work), how satisfied or dissatisfied are you with it?', 80 per cent of the employed men said they were either very satisfied or satisfied with their jobs. This finding suggests that most individuals accommodate themselves to their chances and possibilities in life and in general do not maintain, as conscious aspirations, chances and opportunities not within their scope to realize. However, for many individuals, commitment to working is much deeper than commitment to their particular job. This is attested to by the high frequency with which people answer that they would change jobs, if they inherited enough money to live comfortably without working. Many individuals, including those who say they are satisfied with their jobs, would switch to another job if they could, but few would stop working.

Further evidence that working is serving non-economic functions is found in the kinds of answers the men who want to keep working give to the question: 'Suppose you didn't work, what would you miss most?' Over two-fifths respond with a general feeling that they would lose something important to their well-being if they did not work. Almost a third point directly to the social aspects of working (Table 4).

Occupational Difference

The data presented so far indicate that working serves non-economic functions for the vast majority of employed men. Does it serve different functions, however, for people in different occupations? A sample of 401 men is not large enough to specify in detail the particular functions of work for men in all the various specific occupations. We can, however, examine the meaning of working and the type of satisfactions gained from the job for certain broad classifications of occupations. The basic

47

Table 4
Things Missed If Did Not Work by Those Who Would Want to
Keep Working

Question: 'Suppose you didn't work, what would you miss most?'		
	N	*Per cent*
General feeling		
Feeling of living, belonging, being part of something	6	3
Feeling of doing something important, worthwhile, feeling of self-respect	23	9
Feeling of interest, being interested	12	5
Feeling of doing something, would be restless	62	25
Total expressing general feeling	103	42
Specific things missed		
The kind of work I do	29	12
The people I know through or at work, the friends, contacts	77	31
Regular routine	16	6
Money	5	2
Other	2	1
Total mentioning specific things missed	129	52
Nothing missed	15	6
Total responding	247	100
Not ascertained	67	
Total would work	314	
Total would not work	79	
Not ascertained	8	
Total sample	401	

classification which we have used separates the occupations into
two major categories and one 'offset' category. The two major
divisions which we shall use are middle-class occupations and
working-class occupations. We have separated farming into a

third category because of its unique features such as the fusion of work and non-work, the high degree of self-employment, the rural setting, and the like.

The middle-class occupations differ from the working-class ones on a variety of dimensions. There are substantial differences not only in terms of the characteristics of the people recruited to the jobs, but in terms of the content of the jobs themselves. The middle-class occupations more frequently emphasize verbal and conceptual skills, while the working-class occupations more frequently emphasize skilled use of the body. In addition, there are differences in object-relations. Thus a large segment of the middle-class jobs involve dealing with people, while many of the working-class jobs involve working with tools and machines. Thus while the primary classification of middle-class and working-class occupations may seem to stress differences in prestige and social status between the two sets of jobs, there is actually a whole pattern of differences, a complex of factors, which separates these two groups of occupations.

The types of occupations which we have considered middle class are: professional, managers employed by others and sales. For professional and sales we have followed the census classification,[5] but we have excluded self-employed managers and proprietors from our managerial classification, despite their inclusion in the census system.[6] We have labeled the following occupations as working class: foremen, crafts and trades; machine-operators and semi-skilled; unskilled; and service. The occupations which we have not included in this analysis, in addition to the self-employed managers, are clerical and government service. These

5. The general occupational groupings used by the census and the specific occupations listed under the various census designations are to be found in the Bureau of the Census (1950).

6. While the managers employed by others clearly fall into the middle-class occupational grouping, self-employed managers are a mixed group. The initial coding had been in terms of the census classification and it would have been necessary to go back and recode the occupations. Thus while an owner of a realty company would be in a middle-class occupation, the operator of a gasoline station or a restaurant worker who owns part of the business would be more appropriately classified in the working-class occupations. The self-employed managers were therefore excluded, as were the other groups which would have required recoding, the clerical and government service workers.

occupations appear to include some jobs which would be classified as working class and some which would be classified as middle class. Along with the farmers these two major classifications of middle class and working class with their sub-headings will form the basis of the occupational analysis.

The findings on the relationship between occupation and certain demographic characteristics for our sample are consistent with those reported by the census. The men in middle-class occupations are better educated are more often white and Protestant and earn more money than those in the working-class occupations. The largest contrasts occur between the 'top' of the middle-class occupations, the professions, and the 'bottom' of the working-class occupations, the services.

Almost the entire group of farmers are self-employed, while nearly all of the other occupational groups are employed by others. The farmers are similar to those in working-class jobs in terms of education and income yet are even more likely to be Protestant than those in middle-class jobs.[7]

These results confirm the idea that by grouping the occupations into middle class, working class, and farming, we have also grouped on a number of other variables. The broad occupational differences cannot, therefore, be interpreted as due to any single factor, but rather as due to a pattern of factors, pertaining to the type of people, type of work, and type of situation or environment in which they live and work.

Function of Working and Occupational Class

The occupational groupings differ much more on the type of function that working plays for them, than they do on the degree to which it serves other functions than the economic one. Many individuals in middle-class occupations emphasize the interest to be found in their jobs and the sense of accomplishment which comes from work well done. On the other hand, the typical individual in a working-class occupation emphasizes the necessity for some directed activity which will occupy his time, his mind and

7. The religious affiliation findings are probably the result of the pattern of immigration into this country. The non-Protestants (primarily Catholics) were in general later immigrants, when farm land was no longer so cheap nor as easily available.

his hands. These conclusions are based on answers given to the question, 'Why would you continue working?' asked of those who said they would continue to work even if they inherited money (Table 5).

For many of those in the middle-class occupations working means having something interesting to do, having a chance to accomplish things and to contribute. Those in working-class

Table 5

Reasons for Continuing to Work by Occupation

Number of Individuals Who Give as Reasons for Working:			
	Interest or accomplishment	To keep occupied	Other	Total
Middle class				
Professional	13	8	3	24
Managerial	6	5	4	15
Sales	6	8	4	18
Total middle class	25	21	11	57
Per cent	(44)	(37)	(19)	(100)
Working class				
Trades	6	44	15	65
Operatives	6	42	9	57
Unskilled	1	9	3	13
Service	1	7	1	9
Total working class	14	102	28	144
Per cent	(10)	(71)	(19)	(100)
Total farmers	6	22	6	34
Per cent	(18)	(64)	(18)	(100)
Total responding				235
Not ascertained				18
Total would work				253
Total would not work and not ascertained				73
Total sample				326*

* Clerical workers, self-employed managers and government workers do not appear in this table.

Chi-square between classes $= 31.77$, significant at the 0.001 level. Chi-squares within middle and working classes are not significant.

occupations view working as virtually synonymous with activity, the alternative to which is to lie around and be bored or restless. For the farmers working is also activity, but the demarcation between work and other areas of life is less sharp than it is for the working-class respondents. As a result many farmers, particularly older farmers, are almost unable to consider a way of life which does not include work.

These differences between the occupational groupings correspond to differences in the content of the middle-class and working-class jobs. The content of the professional, managerial and sales jobs concerns symbols and meanings. Furthermore, the middle-class job imposes a responsibility for an outcome, for successful sales, successful operation of a department or successful handling of a legal case. Thus a life without working to a man in a middle-class occupation would be less purposeful, stimulating and challenging. The content of working-class jobs, on the other hand, concerns *activity*. Working-class occupations emphasize work with tools, operation of machines, lifting, carrying, and the individual is probably oriented to the effort rather than the end. Therefore life without working becomes life without anything to do.

Of course the meaning which work has for the individual is not only affected by the general type of work which he does, but is also determined by the type of person he is. To some extent, at least, there may be selection into occupations so that the person going into a middle-class job has a different social background from one going into a working-class job. The different functions of work may to some extent be attributed to different early learning and socialization of those entering different occupations. Perhaps both the nature of the job and the nature of the jobholders operate together to produce a similarity of orientation towards the place of work in life among people in the same general type of job.

Occupational Differences in Job Attitudes

The major reason for working *at a particular job* may be monetary even though the reasons for wanting to continue to work are not. The extent to which the job is important to the individual for other than monetary reasons is probably best indicated by his response to the question of whether he would continue in the same job if he no longer had to work to earn a living. If the employed man answered that he would want to keep working even if he inherited money, he was then asked: 'Would you still keep on doing the same type of work you are doing now?' The answers to this question, presented in Table 6, indicate very clearly that the farming job and the middle-class occupations, particularly the professional jobs, are much more important to their occupants than are the working-class jobs to their occupants. More than two-thirds of the farmers and more than three-fifths of the men in the middle-class occupations would want to continue in their present type of work even if they inherited enough money so that it was no longer necessary for them to work for a living.

From these results it seems clear that while men almost regardless of job are adjusted to the type of work they are doing, those who have the less interesting, less prestigeful and less autonomous jobs would most like to change their jobs if the opportunity were provided. The most common type of job suggested as a replacement for their present work is going into business for themselves. Many of the men in the working-class occupations said that they would like to go into business for themselves, although they often were not able to say what type of business they would want to go into. These answers seemed to indicate a desire for a more prestigeful, freer job than the one they now had; one which would not, however, require additional formal education and training. The way the man in the working-class occupation thought about going into business for himself was consistent with his view of working as keeping occupied. There was no mention of obtaining a feeling of purpose or accomplishment from this imagined work. He carried over his already developed view of the meaning of work to this new imagined occupation.

We already mentioned that most people are satisfied with their present job. Table 7 shows that the men in the middle-class occupations are more polarized in their answers to the question: 'Taking into consideration all the things about your job (work), how satisfied or dissatisfied are you with it?' Those in the middle-class occupations, particularly the managers, are more likely to give extreme answers. The explanation for this difference between

Table 6

Per Cent of Respondents Who Would Continue to Work and Per Cent Who Would Continue on Same Job

	N	Per cent who would work	Per cent who would continue in same type of work
Middle class			
Professional	28	86	68
Managerial	22	82	55
Sales	22	91	59
Total middle class	72	86	61
Working class			
Trades	86	79	40
Operatives	80	78	32
Unskilled	27	58	16
Service	18	71	33
Total working class	211	76	34
Total farmers	43	86	69
Total would work	253		
Total would not work, not ascertained	73		
Total sample	326*		
Chi-squares between classes		6·87	29·22
p less than		0·05	0·001
Chi-squares within middle class		0·76	0·79
		not significant	not significant
Chi-squares within working class		8·74	6·30
p less than		0·05	0·10

* Clerical workers, self-employed managers and government workers do not appear in this table.

Nancy C. Morse and Robert S. Weiss

the occupational groupings may lie partially in the greater importance of the content of the job to those in the middle-class occupations and partially in the greater opportunity for personal satisfactions in the middle-class jobs. Those in the middle-class

Table 7

Per Cent Satisfied and Dissatisfied with Their Jobs by Occupation

		Percentages			
	N	Very satisfied	Satisfied	Dissatisfied	Total
Middle class					
Professional	28	54	36	10	100
Managerial	22	23	41	36	100
Sales	22	46	36	18	100
Total middle class	72	42	37	21	100
Working class					
Trades	84	32	57	11	100
Operatives	80	25	60	15	100
Unskilled	24	25	54	21	100
Service	16	19	50	31	100
Total working class	204	27	57	16	100
Total farmers	41	29	56	15	100
Total responding	317				
Not ascertained	9				
Total sample	326*				

* Clerical workers, self-employed managers and government workers do not appear in this table.

Middle class is significantly more 'polarized' than the other groups. Chi-square = $9 \cdot 87$, p less than $0 \cdot 05$.

jobs, as a result, react more strongly either in a positive or negative way to the particular job. The man in a working-class job, on the other hand, gets used to his job, adjusts himself to it, perhaps even resigns himself to it.

Perhaps the most interesting findings in this area of job satisfaction are those which indicate the degree to which people do adjust to the job conditions and opportunities which are available to them. People in different occupations do not vary as greatly in whether or not they are satisfied with their jobs as they do in their reasons for their satisfaction. The managers mention salary much more frequently than do the professional and sales people who stress the content of the job itself. The crafts and trades group respond positively to the kind of work they do, while the unskilled mention money, and those in service occupations tend to give as reasons for satisfaction the fact that it is the only type of job they could get and that they like the people they work with and meet. Each of the occupations shows quite a different pattern of satisfaction sources. The general conclusion from these results combined with those on present level of satisfaction would seem to be that most people adjust to the jobs which they have, and base that adjustment on the particular attributes of the job and the job situation. There appears to be a tendency for the individual to react positively to his work situation and to emphasize the favorable aspects of it.

Summary and Conclusions

Using interviews with a national sample of employed men, we have studied the extent to which working serves non-economic functions for the total population and the differential meanings of work and the job for those in different occupations.

The results indicate that for most men working does not simply function as a means of earning a livelihood. Even if there were no economic necessity for them to work, most men would work. It is through the producing role that most men tie into society and, for this reason and others, most men find the producing role important for maintaining their sense of well-being.

To the typical man in a middle-class occupation, working means having a purpose, gaining a sense of accomplishment, expressing himself. He feels that not working would leave him aimless and without opportunities to contribute. To the typical man in a working-class occupation working means having something to do. He feels that not working would leave him no adequate outlet for physical activity; he would just be sitting or lying around. To the typical farmer, just as to the typical individual in a working-class occupation, working means keeping busy, keeping occupied. But work has a much more pervasive importance for the farmer. The boundaries between work and home life are not as sharp for him, and life without work is apt to be difficult to consider. These results confirm what other studies, using other methods, have shown.

We are now going through a period of readjustment of our institutions to the shortening of the work day and week and to the early retirement of individuals from their jobs. The development of means by which individuals can gain the same feelings which they now obtain from work through substitute activities is one possible long-range solution. Another, perhaps, is the development of methods by which individuals might remain productive in their later years. In either case it would seem necessary that the occupation give the individual meaningful (in his own terms) and socially integrating activity.

References

BUREAU OF THE CENSUS (1950), *Alphabetical Index of Occupations and Industries*, 1950 Census of Population, U.S. Dept of Commerce.

CANNELL, C., and KAHN, R. (1953), 'The collection of data by interviewing', in L. Festinger and D. Katz (eds.), *Research Methods in the Behavioral Sciences*, Dryden Press, ch. 8.

FRIEDMANN, E. A., and HAVIGHURST, R. J. (1954), *The Meaning of Work and Retirement*, University of Chicago Press.

KISH, L. (1953), 'Selection of the sample', in L. Festinger and D. Katz (eds.), *Research Methods in the Behavioral Sciences*, Dryden Press, ch. 5.

Part Two Satisfaction: Its Determinants and Effects

Jobs and the environments in which they are performed have seldom been designed to satisfy the needs or motives of those who are to work in them. The principal consideration has been the effectiveness with which the work is carried out and the degree to which the goals of the larger organization are attained. None the less, the fact of the market place – the requirement that persons be found who will be willing to perform them – has resulted in at least minimal attention to the congruence between the nature of jobs and human motives. In addition, the organization of workers into trade unions has augmented their individual bargaining power over wages, hours and the physical conditions of work, and governments have frequently regulated the minimum standards of work.

Within these limits it is evident that there are marked differences in the degree to which individuals derive need satisfaction from their work. Since Hoppock's classic monograph in 1935, a substantial amount of research has been conducted in an attempt to shed light on both the determinants and consequences of these differences.

In this part, we examine some of this research and the conclusions which follow from it. The first three Readings are concerned with the consequences of job satisfaction. Ross and Zander (Reading 4) present one of several empirical studies indicating a relationship between job satisfaction and turnover. The more a person's needs are satisfied in his job, the lower the probability that he will subsequently leave the organization. In Reading 5, Brayfield and Crockett review the evidence concerning the relationship between job satisfaction and job performance. It sheds doubt on the widespread belief that satisfied workers will necessarily be productive workers and that successful efforts to increase work satisfaction will inevitably result in higher productivity. Finally, Kornhauser (Reading 6) presents data indicating a positive relationship between job satisfaction and measures of mental health.

The remainder of the section is concerned with the determinants of job satisfaction. Herzberg (Reading 7) proposes that satisfaction and dissatisfaction be regarded as different dimensions rather than different ends of the same dimension. He argues that satisfaction results primarily from the content of the job whereas dissatisfaction results from the job context. Vroom (Reading 8) reviews the evidence concerning the determinants of peoples' attitudes towards their jobs, a concept which is both conceptually and operationally equivalent to job satisfaction. He concludes with a summary of four classes of variables which should be incorporated into any theory of job satisfaction.

Finally, March and Simon (Reading 9) examine both the factors influencing job satisfaction and those which will effect the probability that the individual will leave the organization.

Reference
HOPPOCK, R. (1935), *Job Satisfaction*, Harper.

4 Ian C. Ross and Alvin Zander

Need Satisfactions and Employee Turnover

Ian C. Ross and Alvin Zander, 'Need satisfactions and employee turnover',
Personnel Psychology, vol. 10, 1957, pp. 327–38.

In this study we establish the fact that the degree of satisfaction
of certain personal needs supplied by a person's place of employment has a significant direct relationship to his continuing to
work for that company. These personal needs are for recognition,
for autonomy, for a feeling of doing work that is important and
for evaluation by fair standards. In addition, knowing important
people in the organization is related to continued employment.
There are some indications that anxiety develops in those employees who state that their needs for autonomy and fair evaluation are not satisfied.

In addition to the degree of need satisfaction provided by the
job, we examined the degree to which the employment situation
limits satisfactions which the worker can receive from his family
and from his community. We found that the extent to which the
job interferes with family and community satisfactions is related
to turnover as strongly as the failure to receive need satisfactions
on the job. But interference with off-the-job sources of satisfaction is not related to experiencing dissatisfaction on the job. We
interpret these results to mean that there are two essentially
different kinds of reasons for leaving the employing organization.
Some people resign for reasons of both kinds: the job itself does
not satisfy needs and it also keeps them from receiving satisfactions from other sources. Most of the people in this study who
resigned, however, felt only one or the other of these two forms
of dissatisfaction. (The interference with off-the-job satisfactions
is probably higher among the people studied than in the population at large since shift work is prevalent in the industry in
which this study was conducted.)

Theoretical Orientation

This study was undertaken in order to determine whether the satisfaction of certain psychological needs by an employment situation has a demonstrable relationship to labour turnover. We were primarily interested in needs which could be satisfied by the social dimensions of the work situation. Of course, all organizations satisfy some of the needs of their members otherwise the membership could not exist because persons would not belong to it. Even the few organizations with involuntary memberships, such as prisons, meet some needs, if only the physical requirements of inmate members. We found it helpful to distinguish between two kinds of need satisfactions that organizations give their members. One kind of need satisfaction is provided by means of money payments. These payments permit the member to obtain need satisfaction by purchasing goods and services that will meet at least some of his needs. The other kind of need satisfaction an organization provides its members results from the intrinsic process of participating in the social system of the organization. For purposes of this study we have distinguished five personal needs that can be gratified on the job. These needs are for affiliation, achievement, autonomy, recognition and fair evaluation. We undertook to find out whether the satisfaction of these needs is important to the members. Our measure of importance was whether the people who are more dissatisfied with regard to these needs are more likely to leave. We used a limited number of needs which we expected to be important and which might be useful in an operational attempt to increase the intrinsic satisfaction of the job situation.

Our objective was to determine to what degree satisfaction of the five personal needs affects the cohesiveness of the industrial organization with which we are concerned. Cohesiveness is the resultant of all the forces acting on all members in the direction of their remaining in the organization. Our major hypothesis was developed by assuming that if satisfaction of these needs is important, those members who are not satisfied will relinquish their membership, which in this industrial case means resigning from their jobs. Thus, we can state our principal operational hypothesis: people who resign will be less satisfied than those who stay with regard to the five needs of affiliation, achievement, autonomy, recognition and fair evaluation.

Design

The design of this study was determined in part by the necessity to handle carefully two important methodological problems while meeting the objectives just described. First, it was necessary to keep the effects of personal satisfactions on the job independent of the effects of earnings and of the needs which can be met by money. To some extent people may be expected to put up with a lack of satisfaction of personal needs in order to obtain money. Also, people who are more financially independent may be willing to experience very little deprivation of personal needs.

The second problem to which our study design was oriented is that of causality in time. In order for our hypothesis to be tested in a meaningful way, it was necessary to obtain measures of dissatisfaction that preceded the act of resignation in time. Measurements taken after the decision to resign has been made are likely to be complicated by the necessity to justify the resignation, by the resigned worker's attempting to be sure that he will be able to re-enter the organization at some time in the future and by the release of tension which the announcement of intention to resign probably brings.

The design of the study will be described in six steps. As each step is discussed, its relevance to the major design problems is made explicit.

The first step was the administration of a questionnaire to 2680 female skilled workers in forty-eight sections of a large company. These sections were located in a number of cities. Since we wanted to measure needs and satisfaction before resignations took place (and thus before the people resigning were identified), a large number of questionnaires was necessary in order that the small percentage resigning within a reasonable period after measurement would constitute a statistically useful number of cases.

The second step consisted in gathering personal data on these employees from supervisors' reports.

The third step was to place each employee in one of six categories depending upon certain personal characteristics. These categories, in general, describe types of domestic situations which influence the likelihood that a woman will need to have a job. These categories are used to help separate the effects of money from on-the-job satisfactions in a manner to be described shortly. We shall refer to the categories as types of employees.

The fourth step was the identification of those employees who resigned during the four-month period following administration of the questionnaires. There were 169 resignations among the 2680 people who completed questionnaires.

As the fifth step, two control cases who did not resign were selected to match each resigned employee. The controls were selected by picking the person of the same type, in the same section, who had next higher seniority with the company and the person with next lower seniority. This method of control provided us with people of comparable experience having the same work, supervision and employee benefits in addition to similar financial circumstances.

The sixth and final step of the design was the comparison of the extent to which the need satisfaction of the control persons was equal to or different from that of those who resigned. According to our general hypothesis, those who resigned should have felt greater dissatisfaction of their personal needs and should have experienced more interference with satisfactions derived from off-the-job sources. Comparisons were made between each resigned employee and the matched control persons. The major hypothesis states that the mean difference is not zero but indicates that greater dissatisfaction is evidenced by the resigned people.

The classifications of types of employee were intended to hold constant for purposes of control, personal characteristics which are economically important and which have a bearing upon the continued employment of women workers. The six types are: single tentatives, married tentatives, objectives, mothers, careerists and permanents. In general, both single and married *tentatives* have events ahead of them which will raise questions about their continued employment. These events are, of course, marriage and motherhood. The *objectives* are people whose terminations are expected when foreseen events take place. A common event is the return of husbands from military service. *Mothers* are a separate class because they have returned to work after an event which often terminates a woman's participation in the labor force. The return of these mothers may indicate responsibilities which are a reason for them to continue working. *Careerists* are those whom the supervisors consider especially motivated to succeed in the industry with which we are concerned. *Permanents* are those who have been employed for a relatively long time and who, for many reasons, are likely to remain employed until they reach retirement age.

These types were so defined that they are not all mutually exclusive. For example, a person may be a mother as well as a careerist. We, therefore, had to decide on an order of priority by which individuals would be placed in only one type. The basic principle used was that a person would be placed in that type which is deemed a stronger predictor of length of service with the organization.

Operational criteria for each type were set up in terms of the personal data given by supervisors. The careerists were selected first. Thus, anyone who might meet the criteria for careerist, permanent and mother was classified as a careerist. From those who were not careerists, we next selected the permanents. Then we selected the objectives, mothers and tentatives in that order. The two classes of tentatives are mutually exclusive so that no ordering decision had to be made between them.

The measurement of satisfaction for the needs of recognition, achievement, and autonomy required a pair of questions for each need. One question measured the strength of the need, and the other the extent to which the need was met by the employment situation. Respondents were asked to indicate their feelings about each question by marking a point on a graphic rating scale. For example, the following pair of items was used to measure the need for recognition and the degree of recognition obtained: 'How important is it to you that you know how well you are doing?' 'How fully are you informed about the quality of your work?' The first question is directed to the strength of the need and the second to the extent that the need was met. For scoring purposes the marks on the accompanying scale were counted as having the values 0 through 9.

The amount of dissatisfaction was computed by subtracting the degree of satisfaction from the strength of the indicated need.

65

This procedure was based on the assumption that it is not how much need satisfaction one receives that is important, but rather the extent to which needs are met or not met. For example, let us compare two workers, A and B, who indicate that their need for recognition is 5 and 8, respectively. Let us assume that they report satisfaction in this area of 4 and 6. In spite of the fact that worker B is receiving greater satisfaction, we consider him less satisfied. His dissatisfaction is 2, i.e. 8 minus 6. Since worker A has only one unit of dissatisfaction (5 minus 4), his needs are met to a greater extent, and by our hypothesis worker A is more likely to remain with the organization.

The method of using the difference gives some protection against differing interpretations among respondents in regard to the scaled values. To the extent that the same relationship is perceived between the two scales (strength of need and satisfaction) by various subjects, the differences in the level of need or satisfaction implied by the words have no effect.

The need for affiliation was measured by a series of paired questions of a similar type. We asked how important it was for the person to know and to be known by the management and the extent to which they were known. We also asked questions about co-workers. The need to be evaluated by fair standards was handled with a single question about fairness of the company's expectations.

The questionnaire also included items on the degree to which the job prevented gratification of needs in family life and social life, as well as questions about anxiety, quality of supervision received and the necessity of having a job.

Results

The results were evaluated by computing, for each resigned employee and each person selected as a control, the extent to which her needs were not met. These scores were computed by subtraction of the degree of each satisfaction received from the amount of the corresponding need expressed. Then from the dissatisfaction scores of the resigned employee were subtracted the mean dissatisfaction scores of the two persons with whom the resigned worker had been matched. These differences between the dissatisfactions of the resigned person and the matched people who remained were the main statistics with which we worked. The standard errors of these differences were computed and evaluated for the 169 sets of resigned workers and comparable employees who remained. Since the hypothesis is that the needs of resigned workers will be satisfied to a lesser degree, the differences are confirmatory of the hypothesis only in one direction of divergence from zero. In the significance tests applied, the probability values quoted are for the one-tailed test.

It is in the area of *recognition* that we find the largest and most significant difference in degree of dissatisfaction between the 169 persons who resigned and their controls. This is evident in the accompanying table. Most of this difference is associated with responses to a question about the extent to which a respondent is informed about the quality of her work. If we take the entire scale of response as having ten units, those who resigned were on the average 0·64 of a unit more dissatisfied than were the comparable persons who stayed. This difference is significantly different from zero in the predicted direction well beyond the 1 per cent level of significance.

In this study the need for *achievement* was interpreted as feeling that one is doing something important when one is working. The resigned employees had 0·23 of a unit greater dissatisfaction in this respect and the difference is significant at the 5 per cent level.

Autonomy was understood to be the extent to which a person is on his own when he works. There was substantially no difference between the resigned workers and the matching continuing workers in regard to the strength of the need for autonomy. There was a substantial difference in the autonomy which they indicated they experienced. Those who resigned reported 0·53 of a unit greater dissatisfaction in the autonomy area at the 2·5 per cent level.

The results for these three needs are summarized in Table 1.

It is worth noting that the strength of the needs for recognition, achievement and autonomy were essentially the same for those who resigned and the matched continuing workers. Both groups also rated their ability to do the work equally. These findings suggest that the resigned and matched continuing workers are approximately the same kind of people but that they receive differentially satisfying experiences in the course of their employment.

In our questions on the *affiliation* need we found that those who stayed wanted to know management better and also reported a greater acquaintance with management. Consequently, their dissatisfaction in the affiliation area was essentially equal to that of the resigned group. Surprisingly, we found that there was no difference in the compared groups' evaluation of the suitability of co-workers for friends.

Table 1

Differences in Satisfactions between Resigned Workers and Matched Continuing Workers

Measurement	Mean difference between* resigned workers and matched continuing workers	p
Strength of need for recognition	0·08	ns
Degree of recognition received	−0·56	0·0025
Dissatisfaction with recognition	0·64	0·0025
Strength of need for achievement	0·15	ns
Degree of achievement received	−0·08	ns
Dissatisfaction with achievement	0·23	0·05
Strength of need for autonomy	0·09	ns
Degree of autonomy received	−0·44	0·025
Dissatisfaction with autonomy	0·53	0·025
N = 169		

* The negative difference (−) means that the scores of the resigned workers were lower.

One question was asked about the standards used in the *evaluation* of workers. The resigned workers rated the fairness of the expectations held by the company as 0·32 of a unit lower than did the controls. This difference is significant at the 5 per cent level. In another section of the questionnaire we asked the respondents to rate their own performance and the company's expectations with regard to five specific items of skill. There was no difference whatsoever in the ratings of own best performance of the two matched groups. However, the resigned workers rated the company's expectations 0·20 of a unit higher, and on three out of the five items, the resigned workers reported significantly higher expectations for their performance. Taken together, these responses seem to indicate that those who resigned thought that more was expected of them. We cannot say whether they considered these expectations unreasonable, but they did not accept them to the same extent as did the workers who remained. Also, the workers who remained did not consider the expectations as difficult as did the ones who resigned.

Anxiety

In addition to our main interest in the effects of need satisfaction on turnover, we had a secondary interest in anxiety as a possible result of dissatisfaction that would increase the likelihood of resigning. Anxiety, in the sense we used it, is typified by feelings of uneasiness which lead to rejection of the perceived sources of the anxiety. It was our desire to find out whether deprivations of the on-the-job satisfactions studied here were associated with anxiety. We also wished to find out if anxiety increased the likelihood that a person would resign.

Only a small part of the questionnaire could be devoted to evaluation of anxiety; thus measurement depends on the responses to eight questions. Two of these questions inquired about the value and representativeness of the quality control checks used by management to measure performance of the respondents. The other six inquired about the frequency of feeling uneasy in specified social situations that occur on the job. Two of these eight anxiety items are significantly related to resigning. Those who left felt that work observations are inferior measures of ability, and they reported more frequent uneasiness when their supervisors stand close behind them. These two items have low but significant correlations with dissatisfaction, with the need for autonomy and for fair evaluation. However, the anxiety differences are fully accounted for in a statistical sense by the correlation of these two items with lack of need satisfaction. When expected anxiety was computed for those who resigned from the relationship of the dissatisfactions to anxiety, it was found to be almost identical with the reported anxiety. We conclude that those who resigned are more anxious than those who remain but that little if any additional dynamic effect on turnover is induced by the anxiety itself.

Job Interference with Other Satisfaction Sources

Three questions about the interference of employment with sources of satisfaction in home or community showed significant differences between the responses of the resigned workers and those of matched people who remained. These questions indicated that those who resigned felt that they were kept from doing things at home, that their jobs were interfering with their social life, and were preventing participation in clubs and similar activities. These differences are all about one-half of a unit on a ten-unit scale and are significantly different from zero at the 3 per cent level, or better.

Since the resigned employees reported greater dissatisfaction on the job and more intereference with family and social life, the possibility was suggested that the dissatisfaction on the job might be due to the outside difficulties. However, when correlations were computed between the various interference responses and the on-the-job lack of need satisfaction, most of the correlation coefficients turned out to be quite small. The largest of these coefficients was $r = 0.22$. While this correlation is significantly greater than zero at the 5 per cent level, it hardly leads us to believe that workers will say very often that they are dissatisfied on grounds of personal needs when actually the job interferes with home life, or vice versa. We have concluded, therefore, that on-the-job deprivations and off-the-job interferences are independent social forces upon workers towards resigning.

Other Items

The responses of the resigned workers on several other questions were not different from those made by persons who stayed with the company. These concerned the quality of supervision, the adequacy of on-the-job training, and the necessity for having a job. The discriminating ability of this last question was to some

Ian C. Ross and Alvin Zander

extent reduced by the control on personal characteristics. The people whose responses were compared are in the same life circumstances because they were matched in respect to their job motivation and thus have essentially similar needs for continued employment. It is also interesting to note that those who resigned did not rate their ability to do the job significantly lower than those who stayed.

We also asked workers whether they feel that the community has respect for workers in this industry and how well the employees' families and friends understand their work. None of these items was found to be significantly related to leaving.

Conclusion

We conclude that workers whose personal needs are satisfied on the job are more likely to remain in the organization. While we are unable to evaluate the comparative importance of earnings as a substitute for direct need satisfaction, the satisfaction of needs has values which are worth developing for the establishment of stable work groups.

71

5 Arthur H. Brayfield and Walter H. Crockett

Employee Attitudes and Employee Performance

Excerpt from Arthur H. Brayfield and Walter H. Crockett, 'Employee attitudes and employee performance', *Psychological Bulletin*, vol. 52, 1955, pp. 396–424.

Morale as an Explanatory Concept in Industrial Psychology

One principal generalization suffices to set up an expectation that morale should be related to absenteeism and turnover, namely, that organisms tend to avoid those situations which are punishing and to seek out situations that are rewarding. To the extent that worker dissatisfaction indicates that the individual is in a punishing situation, we should expect dissatisfied workers to be absent more often and to quit the job at a higher rate than individuals who are satisfied with their work. Since the general proposition about the effects of reward has received a great amount of verification in psychology, it is not strange that it has been carried to the analysis of absenteeism and turnover.

A plausible connexion between satisfaction and performance on the job is less obvious. Let us consider specifically the possible relationship between satisfaction and productivity. Under conditions of marked dissatisfaction it is likely that low productivity may serve as a form of aggression which reflects worker hostility towards management. But the hypothesis that production should increase monotonically with increases in satisfaction apparently rests on the assumption that the worker will demonstrate his gratitude by increased output, or that the increased satisfaction frees certain creative energies in the worker, or that the satisfied employee accepts management's goals, which include high production.

In any event, it is commonly hypothesized that, whatever the causes, increased satisfaction makes workers more motivated to produce. Given this condition, it should follow that increased productivity can be attained by increasing worker satisfaction. We are going to advance the proposition that the motivational structure of industrial workers is not as simple as is implied in this formula. We feel that research workers have erred by overlooking individual differences in motivations and perceptions because of their concern with discovering important and applicable generalizations. Most of what follows is an effort to point out areas in which differences between workmen may make a difference in their adjustment to the situation.

At the outset let us make it clear that we expect the relation between satisfaction and job performance to be one of concomitant variation rather than cause and effect. It makes sense to us to assume that individuals are motivated to achieve certain environmental goals and that the achievement of these goals results in satisfaction. Productivity is seldom a goal in itself but is more commonly a means to goal attainment. Therefore, as has been suggested,[1] we might expect high satisfaction and high productivity to occur together when productivity is perceived as a path to certain important goals and when these goals are achieved. Under other conditions, satisfaction and productivity might be unrelated or even negatively related. In the light of this consideration, we shall center our discussion on an analysis of industrial motivation as it relates specifically to employee satisfaction and to productivity.

For the sake of convenience we may distinguish between threats and rewards as incentives to productivity. Goode and Fowler (1949) have described a factory in which morale and productivity were negatively related but productivity was kept high by the continuance of threats to workers. Here the essential workers – people with considerable skill – were marginal to the labor force because of their sex or because of physical handicaps. Since the plant was not unionized, it was possible for management to demand high productivity from these workers on threat of discharge. This meant that the workers, although most dissatisfied with their jobs, produced at a very high rate because of the difficulty they would face in finding another position should they be discharged.

There is little doubt that threat was widely used as a motivating device in our own society in the past and is presently used in more

1. For some later confirmation of this hypothesis, see Georgopoulos, Mahoney and Jones (1957).

authoritarian societies. However, it is doubtful if any great amount of at least explicit threat is currently used by industries in this country in efforts to increase productivity or reduce absenteeism. First of all, considerable change has occurred in management philosophy over the past fifty years, and such tactics are repugnant to many industrial concerns. Secondly, the growth of unions has virtually outlawed such tendencies except in small, semi-marginal industries which are not unionized.

Threats of discharge, then, probably do not operate as incentives unless the worker falls considerably below the mean in quantity and/or quality of output. For a number of reasons management has settled upon rewards for motivating workers to produce, including such tangible incentives as increased pay and promotion, as well as verbal and other symbolic recognition. Let us examine whether this system of rewards actually provides motivation for increased productivity by the worker.

It is a commonplace observation that motivation is not a simple concept. It is a problem which may be attacked at a number of different levels and from many theoretical points of view. Whatever their theoretical predilection, however, psychologists generally are agreed that human motivation is seldom directed only towards goals of physical well-being. Once a certain minimum level of living has been achieved, human behavior is directed largely towards some social goal or goals. Thus, in our own society, goals such as achievement, acceptance by others, dominance over others, and so on, probably are of as great concern to the average workman as the goals of finding sufficient food and shelter to keep body and psyche together.

We assume that social motives are of considerable importance in industry. We assume, further, that the goals an individual pursues will vary depending upon the social systems within which he is behaving from time to time. Most industrial workers probably operate in a number of social systems. Katz and Kahn (1952) suggest four such systems: first, the system of relations outside the plant, and – within the plant – the systems of relationship with fellow workers on the job, with members of the union and with others in the company structure. We may ask whether job performance, and particularly productivity, is a path to goal achievement within these various sets of social relations.

Arthur H. Brayfield and Walter H. Crockett

Outside the plant

It is often argued that any worker who is motivated to increase his status in the outside community should be motivated towards higher productivity within the plant. Productivity frequently leads directly to more money on the job, or involves movement to jobs with higher prestige or with authority over others. If productivity does result in such in-plant mobility, increased output may enable the individual to achieve a higher level of living, to increase his general status in the community, and to attempt such social mobility as he may desire. In this way productivity may serve as a path to the achievement of goals outside the plant.

The operation of this chain of relationships, however, depends not only upon the rewards given the higher producer, but also upon the original motivation of the workman to increase his status position in the outside community. The amount of status motivation among production-line employees is open to question. Certainly the findings of Warner (Warner and Lunt, 1941), Davis and Gardner (Davis, Gardner and Gardner, 1941) and others (Centers, 1941; Davis, 1948; Ericson, 1947) indicate that there are systematic differences in the goals which are pursued in the different segments of our society. It is not impossible that a very large proportion of America's work force is only minimally motivated towards individual social achievement. The assumption that such a motivation does exist may reflect in considerable part a projection of certain middle-class aspirations on to working-class employees.

Furthermore, it is not unlikely that the reference group against which an individual workman evaluates his success may be only a segment of the community, rather than the community as a whole. An individual whose accomplishments are modest at best when compared with the range of possible accomplishments in the community may have a feeling of great accomplishment when he compares his achievements with those of others in his environment. If this is true, and if he desires to continue to operate within this segment of society, any further increase in rewards within the plant might lead to his exclusion from personally important groups outside the plant rather than to increased prestige in such groups.

Finally, there are many goals outside the industrial plant which may be socially rewarding to the individual and which require only minimal financial and occupational rewards inside the plant. Active participation in veterans' organizations, in churches, in recreational programs and similar activities may be and frequently are carried out by individuals at all positions in the industrial hierarchy. As a matter of fact, to the extent that the individual receives extensive social rewards from such activities he may have only slight interest in his work on the job, and he may continue to remain in industry only to maintain some minimum economic position while carrying out his outside functions. For such an individual, high productivity may lead to *no* important goals.

Relations with other workers in the plant

The studies by Elton Mayo and his associates introduced the work group into the analysis of industry, and a wealth of subsequent investigations have confirmed the importance of on-the-job groups. Throughout these studies has run the observation that members of the work group develop group standards of productivity and attempt to force these standards upon those workmen who deviate. Thus, in the bank wiring room it was the socially maladjusted individual, the deviant from the work group, who maintained a level of production above that of the group even though his native ability was considerably below that of many of the others.

Mathewson's classic (1931) study of restriction of output among unorganized workers was an early demonstration of the operation of group norms.

Schachter *et al.* (1951) have conducted an experiment which indicates that in cohesive groups an individual's productivity may be either raised or lowered, depending upon the kind of communications directed toward him by congenial co-workers. In an actual factory setting, Coch and French (1948) presented existent groups with evidence that a change in job methods and in productivity was necessary if the factory was to remain in a favorable position relative to other, competing factories. These groups, through group discussion, arrived at a decision as to the proper job set up, and modified the group judgement of 'fair' output markedly upward.

There is evidence, then, that the level of performance on the job frequently depends upon a group norm, and that performance level may be changed by changing the group norm in a direction desired by management. This change in the norm probably results from a conviction among the workers that higher production is in their own interest as well as in management's, i.e. that their interest and management's interests coincide. This raises the perplexing question of whether, with regard to productivity, the interests of mangement and labor do, in fact, coincide.

Management, presumably, is interested in higher production as a way of reducing the ratio of cost to output, and thereby bettering management's financial and competitive position. In an expanding market, the argument goes, this makes possible the expansion of the company, increased wages, a larger labor force and general prosperity not only for the corporation but for the employees as well.

The case may not be so attractive to the workers, especially when the market is not expanding and demand for the product is constant, nearly constant or declining. In this event, higher productivity per worker means that fewer people are required for the same level of output, or that fewer hours are worked by the same number of workers. In either case, many workers may lose, rather than gain, by the increase in productivity. It may be argued that in normal times such individuals usually find fairly rapid employment in some other segment of the economy. However true this may be, from the viewpoint of the individual workman this involves a considerable disruption in working habits and in his social life in general, and is to be avoided wherever possible. Viewed in this light the interests of management and labor are inimical.

As psychologists we steer clear of such arguments. But we should be sensitive to the fact that the question is a debatable one, that a final decision will probably rest upon values rather than data, that each side is capable of convincing arguments, and that the perception of a certain inevitable conflict of interests between the two groups is honestly and intelligently held by many people. We should also recognize that any reduction in work force after a joint labor–management effort to increase productivity will likely be interpreted as resulting from the increased productivity,

77

and may lead to a future avoidance not only of high productivity levels but also of labor–management cooperation.

At any rate, we often find that individual workers interpret higher productivity as counter to the interests of the employees. To the extent that this perception constitutes a group norm, such motives as are rewarded through the individual's social relationships with other workmen may be blocked by increased productivity. In such cases, productivity may serve as a path to certain goals, but as a block to social acceptance.

The union structure

One system of relationships of considerable importance in many industrial concerns is the union. In many companies much of what was said in the preceding section may be extended to refer also to the relations of the worker in the system of social relations within the union.

In some plants high productivity is not a deterrent to active union participation. Nevertheless, it probably is true that productivity is seldom a prerequisite for advancement within the union hierarchy. If the individual is oriented towards the union structure, it is unlikely that high productivity will serve as a path to such goals, whatever its effect on other goals he may pursue.

The company structure

We have indicated above that many of the worker's social motives outside the plant, as well as his desires for in-plant associations with fellow workmen and within the union, may be only slightly affected by increase in productivity and sometimes may be blocked by increased productivity. The apparent range of goals that a worker may have is so wide that productivity may be a path to only a few of them.

However, workers are often motivated towards goals within the plant such as turning out a quality product, higher wages and promotion. Let us examine the relationship between satisfaction and productivity for workers who are motivated towards these in-plant goals.

At the start it is evident that productivity and quality are sometimes mutually exclusive. If the individual must concentrate on maintaining high quality work, speed of production probably plays a secondary role. Conversely, if he must emphasize speed, quality often must be reduced to some degree. The speed–quality dilemma is sometimes resolved by making the individual work units so routine and concerned with such minute changes in the material that increased speed will not affect the quality of the product. However, if a worker is more highly motivated when he is performing some meaningful job, the above procedure may be resolving one dilemma by raising another. At any rate, the artisan motivated towards the goal of quality, may be highly satisfied with his job while turning out a very limited number of finished pieces per unit of time. If he is forced to increase productivity and lower in some measure the quality, we might expect his satisfaction to decrease. For such a person satisfaction and productivity would be negatively related.

Consider now the individual who is motivated towards higher wages and promotion. While these rewards may not be exclusively dependent upon job performance, at the same time productivity and other aspects of performance often are weighted heavily at promotion time in most companies. In other words, productivity and other aspects of job performance constitute a path to the goal of promotion and wage increases.

Now it is likely that people with aspirations to change position in the company structure will often be quite dissatisfied with their present position in the company. Aspiration to move within a system implies not only a desire for some different position in the future, but some degree of dissatisfaction with the position one is presently occupying. The amount of dissatisfaction probably depends upon the length of time the individual has occupied this position. Thus, although productivity may be a path to the goal, failure to achieve the goal to date may result in dissatisfaction and the high producer may be less satisfied than the low producer.

Evidence sustaining this point of view is to be found in the Katz, Maccoby and Morse (1950) report of a large insurance company in which the best, most productive workers were also considerably more critical of company policy than were less productive workers. S. Lieberman reports (personal communication) a similar finding in a large appliance factory. A year after all workers in the factory had filled out a questionnaire, Lieberman compared the earlier responses of those who had been

79

promoted to foreman with a matched group of workers who were not promoted. Those promoted had been significantly less satisfied with company practices at the earlier time than had the control group.

Once again the question arises as to what is meant by satisfaction. It may be that extremely high satisfaction is indicative of a certain amount of complacency, a satisfaction with the job as it is, which may be only slightly related to job performance, if it is related at all. On the other hand, individuals who are highly motivated may perceive productivity as a path to their goals, but may also be more realistically critical of whatever deficiencies exist within the organization. They may feel, in addition, that their output is not being rewarded as rapidly as it deserves.

Implications for Future Research

We have arrived at two conclusions: first, that satisfaction with one's position in a network of relationships need not imply strong motivation to outstanding performance within that system and, second, that productivity may be only peripherally related to many of the goals towards which the industrial worker is striving. We do not mean to imply that researchers should have known all along that their results would be positive only infrequently and in particular circumstances. We have been operating on the basis of hindsight and have attempted to spell out some of the factors which may have accounted for the failure of industrial investigators to find positive relationships in their data.

However, certain implications seem logical from the foregoing sections of this report. Foremost among these implications is the conclusion that it is time to question the strategic and ethical merits of selling to industrial concerns an assumed relationship between employee attitudes and employee performance. In the absence of more convincing evidence than is now at hand with regard to the beneficial effects on job performance of high morale, we are led to the conclusion that we might better forego publicizing these alleged effects.

The emphasis on predicting job performance, and particularly productivity, rests upon the acceptance of certain values. That is, the many studies that have used productivity as the criterion to be predicted have been performed because productivity has direct economic value to industry and, presumably, to society at large. But the fact that it has economic value does not mean that job performance is the only, or even the most important, aspect of organizational behavior. From the viewpoint of studying, analysing, and understanding the industrial setting and individual reactions thereto, productivity and other aspects of job performance may be only one of several important factors. It would seem worthwhile to study the causes, correlates and consequences of satisfaction, *per se*. It seems possible, for example, that conditions conducive to job satisfaction will have an effect on the quality of the workman drawn into the industry, the quality of job performance, and the harmony of labor–management relations. Such potential correlates, among others, merit exploration.

Another potentially fruitful approach involves studying the differential effect of particular kinds of mangement practices upon the attitudes and performances of workers with different motives, aspirations and expectations. The appropriate questions may concern how, for particular workers, productivity comes to be perceived as instrumental to the achievement of some goals but not others, while for other workers a different perception develops.

The experimental approach has largely been neglected in this area of industrial research, yet the control of variables that it provides seems essential to the development and refinement of our knowledge in the area. Certainly, where experimentation has been used, as by Schachter and associates (1951) and by Coch and French (1948), the results have been both enlightening for the understanding of present problems and encouraging for its future application. As our concepts become increasingly precise, we may expect an increased use of experimentation both within the industrial setting and in the laboratory.

Perhaps the most significant conclusion to be drawn from this survey is that the industrial situation is a complex one. We have suggested that an analysis of the situation involves analysis not only of the individual's relation to the social system of the factory, the work group and the union, but the community at large as well. It is important to know what motives exist among industrial workers, how they are reflected in the behavior of the workers and how the motives develop and are modified within the framework of patterned social relationships in the plant and in the larger community.

We seem to have arrived at the position where the social scientist in the industrial setting must concern himself with a full-scale analysis of that situation. Pursuit of this goal should provide us with considerable intrinsic job satisfaction.

References

CENTERS, R. (1941), *The Psychology of Social Classes*, Princeton U.P.

COCH, L., and FRENCH, J. R., Jr (1948), 'Overcoming resistance to change', *Hum. Rel.*, vol. 1, pp. 512–32.

DAVIS, A. (1948), *Social Class Influences upon Learning*, Harvard U.P.

DAVIS, A., GARDNER, B. B., and GARDNER, M. R. (1941), *Deep South: A Social and Anthropological Study of Caste and Class*, University of Chicago Press.

ERICSON, M. C. (1947), 'Social status and child rearing practices', in T. M. Newcomb and E. L. Hartley (eds.), *Readings in Social Psychology*, Holt, pp. 494–501.

GEORGOPOULOS, B. S., MAHONEY, G. M., and JONES, N. W. (1957), 'A path–goal approach to productivity', *J. appl. Psychol.*, vol. 41, pp. 345–53. [Reading 17.]

GOODE, W. J., and FOWLER, I. (1949), 'Incentive factors in a low morale plant', *Amer. soc. Rev.*, vol. 14, pp. 618–24.

KATZ, D., and KAHN, R. L. (1952), 'Some recent findings in human relations research in industry', in G. E. Swanson, T. M. Newcomb and E. L. Hartley (eds.), *Readings in Social Psychology*, Holt, pp. 650–65.

KATZ, D., MACCOBY, N., and MORSE, N. (1950), *Productivity, Supervision, and Morale in an Office Situation*, Survey Research Center, University of Michigan.

MATHEWSON, S. B. (1931), *Restriction of Output among Organized Workers*, Viking Press.

SCHACHTER, S., ELLERSTON, N., MCBRIDE, D., and GREGORY, D. (1951), 'An experimental study of cohesiveness and productivity', *Hum. Rel.*, vol. 4, pp. 229–3.

WARNER, W. L., and LUNT, P. S. (1941), *The Social Life of a Modern Community*, Yale U.P.

6 Arthur Kornhauser

Job Satisfaction in Relation to Mental Health

Excerpts from chapter 5 of Arthur Kornhauser, *Mental Health of the Industrial Worker: A Detroit Study*, Wiley, 1965.

Evidence indicates that there are substantial occupational differences of mental health as defined and measured by our indexes[1]. Men in routine production jobs on the average have less satisfactory mental health; those in more skilled and varied types of work have better mental health. Moreover, the findings indicate that the differences of mental health result in large degree from the jobs themselves and their associated conditions quite apart from differences due to the kind of men employed in the different occupations.

This conclusion at once presents the challenging question of what aspects of occupations are important. Which of the myriad characteristics and higher- and lower-level jobs and associated life conditions are the salient determinants of better or poorer mental health? *Why* do we find poorer mental health in low-level occupations?

One can readily offer a long list of plausible explanatory factors – from lower pay, economic insecurity, and disagreeable working conditions to the more intangible influences of status, promotion opportunities, type of supervision and work-group relations,

1. Six component indexes were combined to provide a general measure of mental health. The six parts are the following:
1. An index of manifest anxiety and emotional tension.
2. An index of self-esteem, favorable versus negative self-feelings.
3. An index of hostility – versus trust in and acceptance of people.
4. An index of sociability and friendship versus withdrawal.
5. An index of over-all satisfaction with life.
6. An index of personal morale – versus anomie, social alienation, despair.

These indexes were chosen as ones possessing 'face validity' in reference to mental health. Each is considered a partial indicator. Taken together, they represent an operational definition of mental health for purposes of the study.

simplicity and repetitiveness of job operations and lack of personal control over them, non-use of abilities with consequent feelings of futility, and many more such possible influences on and off the job. Some of these obviously may be more significant than others. In the following chapter [not included in this excerpt] we attempt to estimate the saliency of a number of these variables. In the present chapter we deal with the prior, more basic question whether job-level conditions *as a whole* produce differences of satisfaction and dissatisfaction which are associated with corresponding differences of mental health.

It would surely be a mistake to think in terms of this *or* that causal factor as important. Mental health is a product of complex combinations of influences, varied and shifting, dependent on the values currently emphasized and the expectations aroused as well as on the existing conditions of gratification and deprivation. The attitudes, feelings and behaviors that indicate better or poorer mental health are reactions of a person to his entire life situation; his relationship to the world permits him to maintain a realistic, positive, satisfying belief in himself and his purposeful activities or it does not. The key question for our inquiry is whether lower-level factory jobs do, in fact, offer generally less favorable circumstances than do better jobs for the development and maintenance of good mental health.

The occupations we are comparing clearly present markedly dissimilar opportunities for satisfying self-actualizing lives. It is not simply the objective conditions, however, but the subjective meaning of these that is crucial for mental health. To what extent are the advantages and deprivations perceived and felt as such? We shall focus on the *experienced* gratifications and frustrations of working life in the quest for explanations of occupational differences in mental health. Our central conception is that *job feelings* are crucial intervening processes between the type of work men do and their level of mental health. We expect satisfaction with the job to be associated with better mental health, dissatisfaction with poorer mental health. [. . .]

A vast body of unsystematic observation and literary reporting has called attention to the unsatisfying and allegedly dehumanizing effects of specialized production work. The frustrations, the oppressive goalless boredom and stultification of the assembly line have been repetitiously commented on, deplored and denounced. The conjunction of these prevalent complaints with the pronouncedly poorer mental health at lower occupational levels can scarcely be fortuitous. Rather, it would seem, the expressions of job dissatisfaction mark the scars of unfulfilled desires and expectations that are particularly common at lower skill levels. [. . .]

Summary

Analysis from our research on the issue of mental health can be summarized as follows. Jobs in which workers are better satisfied are conducive to better mental health; jobs in which larger numbers are dissatisfied are correspondingly conducive to poorer average mental health. Moreover, in each occupational category the better-satisfied individuals enjoy better mental health than those less satisfied. Finally, the satisfied in lowest-level jobs have mental-health scores similar to those of workers in higher jobs, and the dissatisfied among skilled and high semi-skilled workers tends to resemble the lower-skill groups (this last for middle-aged only). The evidence as a whole accords with the hypothesis that gratifications and deprivations experienced in work and manifested in expressions of job satisfaction and dissatisfaction constitute an important determinant of workers' mental health. Our interpretation is that job conditions impinge on working people's wants and expectations to produce satisfactions and frustrations which in turn give rise to favorable or unfavorable perceptions of self-worth, opportunities for self-development and prospective gratification of needs. These effects are reflected in the occupational mental-health differences revealed in our assessments.

7 Frederick Herzberg

The Motivation–Hygiene Theory

Excerpt from chapter 6 of Frederick Herzberg, *Work and the Nature of Man*, World Publishing Company, 1966.

With the duality of man's nature in mind, it is well to return to the significance of these essays to industry by reviewing the motivation–hygiene concept of job attitudes as it was reported in *The Motivation to Work*.[1] This study was designed to test the concept that man has two sets of needs: his need as an animal to avoid pain and his need as a human to grow psychologically.

For those who have not read *The Motivation to Work*, I will summarize the highlights of that study. Two hundred engineers and accountants, who represented a cross-section of Pittsburgh industry, were interviewed. They were asked about events they had experienced at work which either had resulted in a marked improvement in their job satisfaction or had led to a marked reduction in job satisfaction.

The interviewers began by asking the engineers and accountants to recall a time when they had felt exceptionally good about their jobs. Keeping in mind the time that had brought about the good feelings, the interviewers proceeded to probe for the reasons why the engineers and accountants felt as they did. The workers were asked also if the feelings of satisfaction in regard to their work had affected their performance, their personal relationships and their well-being.

Finally, the nature of the sequence of events that served to return the workers' attitudes to 'normal' was elicited. Following the narration of a sequence of events, the interview was repeated, but this time the subjects were asked to describe a sequence of events that resulted in negative feelings about their jobs. As many sequences as the respondents were able to give were recorded

1. F. Herzberg, B. Mausner and B. Snyderman, *The Motivation to Work*, Wiley, 2nd edn, 1959.

within the criteria of an acceptable sequence. These were the criteria:

First, the sequence must revolve around an event or series of events; that is, there must be some objective happening. The report cannot be concerned entirely with the respondent's psychological reactions or feelings.

Second, the sequence of events must be bound by time; it should have a beginning that can be identified, a middle and, unless the events are still in process, some sort of identifiable ending (although the cessation of events does not have to be dramatic or abrupt).

Third, the sequence of events must have taken place during a period in which feelings about the job were either exceptionally good or exceptionally bad.

Fourth, the story must be centered on a period in the respondent's life when he held a position that fell within the limits of our sample. However, there were a few exceptions. Stories involving aspirations to professional work or transitions from sub-professional to professional levels were included.

Fifth, the story must be about a situation in which the respondent's feelings about his job were directly affected, not about a sequence of events unrelated to the job that caused high or low spirits.

Figure 1, from *The Motivation to Work*, shows the major findings of this study. The factors listed are a kind of shorthand for summarizing the 'objective' events that each respondent described. The length of each box represents the frequency with which the factor appeared in the events presented. The width of the box indicates the period in which the good or bad job attitude lasted, in terms of a classification of short duration and long duration. A short duration of attitude change did not last longer than two weeks, while a long duration of attitude change may have lasted for years.

Five factors stand out as strong determiners of job satisfaction – *achievement, recognition, work itself, responsibility* and *advancement* – the last three being of greater importance for a lasting change of attitudes. These five factors appeared very infrequently when the respondents described events that paralleled job dissatisfaction feelings. A further word on *recognition*: when it

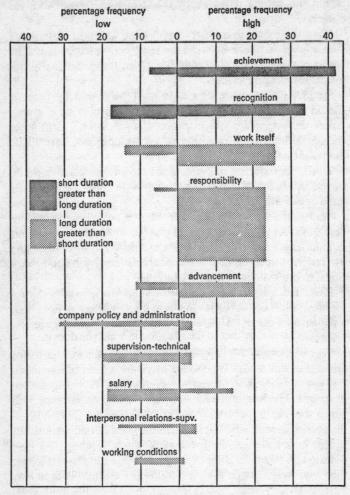

Figure 1 Comparison of satisfiers and dissatisfiers

appeared in a 'high' sequence of events, it referred to recognition for achievement rather than to recognition as a human-relations tool divorced from any accomplishment. The latter type of recognition does not serve as a 'satisfier'.

When the factors involved in the job dissatisfaction events

were coded, an entirely different set of factors evolved. These factors were similar to the satisfiers in their unidimensional effect. This time, however, they served only to bring about job dissatisfaction and were rarely involved in events that led to positive job attitudes. Also, unlike the 'satisfiers', the 'dissatifiers' consistently produced short-term changes in job attitudes. The major dissatisfiers were *company policy and administration, supervision, salary, interpersonal relations* and *working conditions.*

What is the explanation of such results? Do the two sets of factors have two separate themes? It appears so, for the factors on the right of Figure 1 all seem to describe man's relationship to what he does: his job content, achievement on a task, recognition for task achievement, the nature of the task, responsibility for a task and professional advancement or growth in task capability.

What is the central theme for the dissatisfiers? Restating the factors as the kind of administration and supervision received in doing the job, the nature of interpersonal relationships and working conditions that surround the job and the effect of salary suggest the distinction from the 'satisfiers' factors. Rather than describe man's relationship to what he does, the 'dissatisfier' factors describe his relationship to the context or environment in which he does his job. One cluster of factors relates to what the person does and the other to the situation in which he does it.

Since the dissatisfier factors essentially describe the environment and serve primarily to prevent job dissatisfaction, while having little effect on positive job attitudes, they have been named the *hygiene* factors. This is an analogy to the medical use of the term meaning 'preventive and environmental'. Another term for these factors in current use is *maintenance* factors. I am indebted to Dr Robert Ford of the American Telephone and Telegraph Company for this excellent synonym. The 'satisfier' factors were named the *motivators*, since the other findings of the study suggest that they are effective in motivating the individual to superior performance and effort.

So far, I have described that part of the interview that was restricted to determining the actual objective events as reported by the respondents (first level of analysis). They were also asked to interpret the events, to tell why the particular event led to a change in their feelings about their jobs (second level of analysis).

The principal result of the analysis of this data was to suggest that the hygiene or maintenance events led to job dissatisfaction because of a need to *avoid* unpleasantness; the motivator events led to job satisfaction because of a need for growth or self-actualization. At the psychological level, the two dimensions of job attitudes reflected a two-dimensional need structure: one need system for the avoidance of unpleasantness and a parallel need system for personal growth.

The discussion so far has paved the way for the explanation of the duality of job-attitude results. Why do the hygiene factors serve as dissatisfiers? They represent the environment to which man the animal is constantly trying to adjust, for the environment is the source of Adam's suffering. The hygiene factors listed are the major environmental aspects of work.

Why do the motivators affect motivation in the positive direction? An analogy drawn from a familiar example of psychological growth in children may be useful. When a child learns to ride a bicycle, he is becoming more competent, increasing the repertory of his behavior, expanding his skills – psychologically growing. In the process of the child's learning to master a bicycle, the parents can love him with all the zeal and compassion of the most devoted mother and father. They can safeguard the child from injury by providing the safest and most hygienic area in which to practice; they can offer all kinds of incentives and rewards, and they can provide the most expert instructions. But the child will never, never learn to ride the bicycle – unless he is given a bicycle! The hygiene factors are not a valid contributor to psychological growth. The substance of a task is required to achieve growth goals. Similarly, you cannot love an engineer into creativity, although by this approach you can avoid his dissatisfactions with the way you treat him. Creativity will require a potentially creative task to do.

8 Victor H. Vroom

Industrial Social Psychology

Excerpt from Victor H. Vroom, 'Industrial social psychology',
in G. Lindzey and E. Aronson (eds.), *The Handbook of Social Psychology*,
vol. 5, Addison–Wesley, 2nd edn, 1969, pp. 200–208.

Barnard (1938) and Simon (1947) have provided a language for the identification and analysis of conditions under which an organization can induce persons to participate in its activities. Called the inducements-contributions theory, it views each member or participant in the organization as receiving inducements for his participation (which in the case of employees may include pay, recognition, prestige, etc.) and as making payments or contributions to the organization (including the 'cost' to him of his effort and of lost opportunities stemming from his participation in the organization). The individual's decision to participate in the system is determined by the relative magnitude of inducements and contributions when both are measured in terms of the participant's values or motives.

While the language is different the basic idea is seemingly indistinguishable from statements by social psychologists regarding the conditions affecting a person's attraction to a group (Bass, 1960; Cartwright and Zander, 1960; Thibaut and Kelley, 1959). The common ingredient is the notion that the attractiveness of a social system to a person and the probability that he will voluntarily withdraw from participation in it, are related to the consequences of organizational membership, specifically the rewards and punishments, or satisfactions and deprivations incurred as a result of organizational membership.

While such a proposition may appear to be a tautology, it can be made testable by the addition of assumptions about motives which are common to all or at least a majority of persons. Thus, if an economic motive is assumed, namely, that more money is preferred to less money, then the finding that attitudes towards roles in organizations are positively correlated with the pay of the occupant can be explained (Barnett *et al.*, 1952; Miller, 1941; Thompson, 1939). Similarly, other rather plausible assumptions about motives could account for the observed positive relationships between attitudinal measures and (a) amount of acceptance by co-workers (van Zelst, 1951; Zaleznik, Christensen and Roethlisberger, 1958), (b) amount of consideration shown by their superiors (Fleishman, Harris and Burtt, 1955; Halpin and Winer, 1957; Likert, 1961; Seeman, 1957), (c) number of different operations performed in jobs (Walker and Guest, 1952; Wyatt, Fraser and Stock, 1929), (d) amount of influence in decision making (Baumgartel, 1956; Jacobsen, 1951; Vroom, 1960), and (e) level in the organization (Centers, 1948; Gurin, Veroff and Feld, 1960; Hoppock, 1935; Kornhauser, 1965; Morse, 1953; Patterson and Stone, 1942; Porter, 1962; Super, 1939; Uhrbrock, 1934).

There is considerable evidence that these same work role variables are negatively related to objective indicators of the decision not to participate in the organization, such as absences and turnover. Ross and Zander (1957) and Wickert (1951) found that people who reported that they had little influence on decision making had a higher probability of resigning from the organization than those who reported greater influence; Kerr, Koppelmeir and Sullivan (1951) found the highest turnover among persons with the least opportunity for informal interaction; Baldamus (1951) found a positive correlation between the repetitiveness of jobs and the rate of turnover among their occupants; Fleishman, Harris and Burtt (1955) found a negative relationship between supervisory consideration and absenteeism; and Fleishman and Harris (1962) found a negative relationship between consideration and turnover.

While these investigations are all correlational in nature and do not demonstrate that the designated properties of work roles 'cause' the attitudes of their occupants, there is some evidence from field experiments that attitudes do change in the expected direction following changes in these work role variables. Thus Elliot (1953), Guest (1957) and Walker (1950) reported increased job satisfaction following job enlargement; Morse and Reimer (1956) reported more favorable worker attitudes following an increase in their influence in decision making and less favorable attitudes following increased hierarchical control; and Meyer, Kay and French (1965) reported more favorable attitudes towards management and towards the appraisal system on the part of employees, as a consequence of the introduction of a work planning and review system which provided a greater opportunity for subordinates to participate in problem solving and in the setting of performance goals.

While each of the aforementioned variables (pay, acceptance, variety, influence, status) may be safely regarded as dimensions on which larger amounts are preferred to smaller amounts by most persons, it is not unreasonable to assume that individuals may differ in their preferences among them. Individual differences in preferences or motives have proven extremely useful in accounting for differences in people's choices among work roles (Vroom, 1964), and similar reasoning would suggest that they are influential in determining people's affective responses to the work role which they have chosen. While measurements of individual differences in motives have not yet played a major role in research on the determinants of attitudes towards organizations, the few studies which have been conducted have yielded quite promising results.

A field study by Turner and Lawrence (1965) illustrated the importance of including both work role variables and individual difference measures in the same investigation. These researchers set out to determine through correlational methods the consequences of task attributes, such as amount of autonomy, responsibility and variety, on the job satisfaction and absenteeism of rank-and-file workers. A rating scale was developed to measure these task attributes and was used by the researchers in rating forty-seven jobs in eleven companies. The existence of strong positive intercorrelations among the ratings on the dimensions used made it necessary to combine the separate scores into an index score which Turner and Lawrence called the Requisite Task Attribute (RTA) index. Low RTA jobs were simple and undemanding, while high RTA jobs were more complex and required greater knowledge and skill. Contrary to expectation no relationship was found between the RTA scores of jobs and the job satisfaction of their occupants, and only a weak negative relationship was found between the RTA index and absenteeism.

93

Subsequent analyses indicated that these over-all relationships masked two contrasting patterns of response to task variables. The sample of 470 workers studied included two major sub-groups: those living and working in rural or small town settings, who were predominantly Protestant; and those living and working in urban settings, who were predominantly Roman Catholic. When the results for these two groups were analysed separately, the predicted results were obtained for the rural Protestant population and the reverse was obtained for the urban Catholic population. The urban workers tended to express more satisfaction with and exhibit less absenteeism on low RTA jobs while the rural workers tended to be more satisfied with and be absent less frequently from high RTA jobs.

One of the explanations offered by Turner and Lawrence for the unanticipated findings for urban workers utilizes the concept of anomie, originally introduced by Durkheim. Conceivably the urban workers could be characterized by a state of normlessness brought about by industrialization. Sociologists have frequently pointed to the state of normlessness which accompanies lower-class, urban, industrialized social systems. Perhaps highly industrialized and unpleasant conditions of urban life foster alienation from the traditional norms of society, most particularly a lack of concern with upward mobility and self-actualization in work, attributes commonly associated with the American middle class.

Further evidence for this explanation came from a study by Blood and Hulin (1967). The subjects were male blue-collar workers in twenty-one different plants located in different communities throughout the eastern United States. From census data, several indices were found which appeared likely to represent the degree of alienation prevalent in each community. These indices included degree of urbanization, population density and evidence of slum conditions. The results indicate substantial variation in the responses of workers in different communities to apparently similar job situations – variation which is, at least in part, predictable from measures of the alienation in the community. In general the pattern of results is consistent with that obtained by Turner and Lawrence. Workers in communities low in alienation appear to place a high value on demanding, involving jobs while those in communities high in alienation tend to be more satisfied with jobs which are less personally involving and demand less responsibility.

The Turner–Lawrence and Blood–Hulin studies illustrate the difficulty of explaining a person's attitude towards his role solely in terms of the objective properties of that role, and suggest that measures of individual or community differences *and* work role variables can account for a larger proportion of variance in attitude than can either of these sets of variables considered alone. They do not, however, shed much light on the psychological processes underlying the contrasting patterns of response. One wants to know the nature of the psychological dispositions which are associated with the subcultural groupings in these investigations, and how these dispositions are acquired and can be measured.

Other investigators have had considerable success using self-report measures of relevant motives in predicting or explaining the effects of work role variables on the attitudes of role occupants. In conjunction with a large-scale field experiment designed to determine the effects on attitudes and productivity of increased and decreased influence in decision making by rank-and-file workers, Tannenbaum and Allport (1956) used a self-report measure of motivation in an attempt to predict the attitudes of organizational members towards each of two experimentally induced programs of change. Persons were classified as suited or unsuited to each experimental program on the basis of their response to twenty-six questions about what they were 'characteristically trying to do'. This measure was found to be significantly related to the attitudes of individuals towards each experimental program as measured one year later. Individuals classified as suited to a program tended to express greater satisfaction with the program and a stronger desire for it to continue.

Additional evidence of an interaction between a situational variable and a self-report, motivational measure was obtained by Vroom (1960). The size of the correlation between supervisors' judgements of the amount of influence they could exercise over their superiors, and their attitudes towards their jobs was found to vary systematically with the strength of their need for independence as measured by a sixteen-item questionnaire. The correlations between these two variables were 0·55, 0·31 and 0·13, respectively, for supervisors high, moderate and low in need for independence. A similar interaction was found between influence in decision making and the *F*-scale score of the supervisor. No relationship between influence and attitude towards the job was found for supervisors high in authoritarianism; a moderate positive relationship was found for supervisors intermediate in authoritarianism; and a marked positive relationship was found for supervisors low in authoritarianism.

The results of these studies indicate quite clearly that persons' attitudes towards their work roles and the probability that they will choose to continue to occupy them are dependent on both situational and personality variables. The situational variables correspond to the amounts of different kinds of outcomes (e.g. pay, influence, variety) provided by the work roles, and the personality variables correspond to individual differences in the strength of their desire or aversion for these outcomes.

Social Comparison Processes

Thus far we have been viewing the attitudes of the organization member as determined solely by the nature of his individual transactions with the organization. The value he places on organizational membership, as expressed in his statements of the extent to which he is satisfied with his job and the organization, is determined solely by the rewards he derives and the costs he incurs from that membership. There is some evidence that indicates a limitation to this point of view.

Stouffer *et al.* (1949) found numerous instances in which the attitudes of soldiers towards their roles were not predictable from the objective situation which they were facing. For example, there was greater dissatisfaction with promotional opportunities in the army air corps than in the military police, despite the fact that probability of promotion was much higher in the former branch of the service. Furthermore, high school graduates, who typically were assigned to better jobs and had significantly greater chances for advancement than those with less education, expressed greater dissatisfaction with their status and jobs.

Such findings were interpreted, in *ad hoc* fashion, as support for the fact that individuals develop conceptions of proper or equitable levels of reward at least partly from information about the rewards received by others. Dissatisfaction occurs when one's level of reward falls below the proper or equitable level. Translation of such ideas from the realm of a system for accounting for discrepancies between empirical findings and predictions from simpler theories has undoubtedly been aided by the recent development of more precise models of the process (Adams, 1963; Homans, 1961; Patchen, 1961). Problems remain, however, in the coordination of the abstract concepts contained in these models to measurable or manipulable events.

One of the issues that needs to be resolved before predictions can be made and tested concerns the process by which other persons are selected for comparison. It is intuitively obvious that a person does not compare the level of rewards which he receives with all other persons. Information about the reward levels of others is necessary to permit the comparison to occur. It is also likely that further selection takes place within the subset of others about whom information is available. But what are the variables which determine the selection process? This problem has been discussed by others (e.g. Festinger, 1954; Merton and Kitt, 1952) and there has been some research relevant to the industrial scene. Patchen (1961) studied the wage comparisons made by hourly workers in an oil refinery, and Andrews and Henry (1963) studied those of lower- and middle-level managers. In both studies it was found that persons compare their wages not only with the wages of others in the same organization but also with the wages of those who are not organization members. In the latter study, 'outside' comparisons were most typical of highly educated managers.

The specific people used in wage comparisons can be assessed by direct questions or, indirectly, by determining the relative predictability of attitudes from various difference measures. Lawler and Porter (1963) found that the difference between the amount of pay received by a manager and that received by others at his level was a better predictor of the manager's satisfaction with his pay than was the absolute amount of pay that he received. First-line supervisors making more than $12,000 were more satisfied than were company presidents making less than $49,000. In their study of managers in five firms, Andrews and Henry

(1963) found that over-all satisfaction with pay was more highly related to the difference between their wages and the average amount received by others at their level in all five companies than to the difference between their wages and the average received by others at the same level in their own company.

Given that a person has compared the level of reward which he is receiving with that received by another, what determines the affective consequences of the comparison? The more recent theories put forth by Adams, Patchen and Homans assume that the amount of satisfaction or dissatisfaction is not solely a function of differences in reward levels between the two persons, but is also influenced by differences in such variables as merit, seniority, ethnic background, etc., which are considered by the individual to be 'proper' bases for reward allocation. A common theoretical solution has been to treat feelings of inequity or injustice as a response to perceived discrepancies between the ratios of rewards to such 'inputs' or 'investments' on the part of individuals. Thus, in a simple system consisting of only two persons, each of whom has perfect information about the reward levels and other attributes of the other, the proper or equitable level of reward for each is predicted to be dependent on four sets of variables: (a) the level of reward received by the other, (b) the extent to which the other possesses attributes which are potential inputs or investments, (c) the extent to which the individual himself possesses the same attributes, and (d) the rules used by the individual for translating differences in attributes possessed (b and c above) into a proper reward differential. The degree of inequity experienced by the person and his attitude towards the reward system are, in turn, predicted to be a function of each of these variables and of his own reward level.

Needless to say, difficulties in identifying and scaling the relevant variables make it presently impossible to subject the mathematical properties of this model to a definitive test. A crucial problem is found in the measurement of the fourth set of variables listed above. In order to test the theory, it is necessary to know the attributes which are believed by all persons to be proper bases for reward allocation or, alternatively (and perhaps more realistically), to have a method by which differences among persons can be assessed. An unsuccessful attempt by Zaleznik, Christensen and Roethlisberger (1958) to predict the satisfaction scores of forty-seven workers from a reward-investment index obtained by subtracting from the wage level a number of worker attributes assumed to represent 'investments' in their jobs (e.g. age, seniority, education), seems more likely to be attributable to their scaling methods than to deficiencies in the theory which they sought to test.

Adams (1965b) has conducted some research on salaried employees in General Electric which constitutes an attempt to determine empirically the relative weight which people believe should be assigned to various attributes in salary decisions. Manager-subordinate pairs were asked to consider the last time the manager changed the salary of the subordinate and to rate the importance given to each of forty-five factors and the importance which should have been given to each of these factors. The results indicate some differences between managers and subordinates in 'proper' bases for salary decisions, as well as some differences between persons in high and low level positions and among those working in different functional areas.

Adams (1963) and Homans (1961) postulated that perceived discrepancies in ratios of rewards to investments produce feelings of inequity, and consequently negative affect, *regardless of the direction of the discrepancy*. In other words, tension is produced by relative gratification as well as a relative deprivation. Discrepancies produced by 'over-reward' are associated with feelings of guilt, while those produced by 'under-reward' are associated with feelings of anger or unfairness. Most of the empirical evidence concerns the latter situation. In fact, using differences between reports of levels of reward that one should and one is receiving from one's job as a criterion, Lawler (1964) and Porter (1962) found considerable evidence of under-reward but no evidence of over-reward on the part of managers in American firms, a finding which may reflect defensiveness on the part of the respondents or the fact that the over-reward situations are exceedingly short-lived. In a series of experiments Adams (1963, 1965b) has induced the belief on the part of subjects that they were being over-compensated, but these experiments are concerned with effects on performance, not on attitudes. Jaques (1961) reported that a state of disequilibrium is created by

99

discrepancies between actual and equitable levels of pay which vary in intensity with the size of the discrepancy but are independent of its sign. While such a conclusion is consistent with the proposition under discussion, its significance must be tempered by the absence of any indication in the report of the measures used or of the number of subjects on whom observations were made.

The idea that statements of liking for or satisfaction with a role are influenced by relative rather than absolute reward levels can hardly be disputed when stated in its most general form. The problems remaining concern the specific nature of this comparison process. A complete explanation of the role of social comparisons in determining individuals' attitudes towards their roles must specify how specific others are selected for comparison, how information about self and others is combined to yield judgements of the equity or fairness of any reward differential, and by what mechanisms inequity or unfairness will be reduced or eliminated. The last of these questions is explored at some length in a paper by Adams (1965a) which discusses six alternative modes of inequity reduction and presents some assumptions which can provide a basis for initial predictions concerning the choices that will be made among them.

Expected Level of Reward

In the previous section we were concerned with the affective consequences of discrepancies between the level of reward that a person believes he should receive and that which he does receive. From the time of William James, psychological theorists have assumed that individuals compare the level of reward which they receive with that which they expected to receive. Positive discrepancies, in which the attained level of reward exceeds what was expected, have been predicted to produce satisfaction, whereas negative discrepancies, in which the attained level of reward is less than what was expected, have been predicted to produce dissatisfaction. Applying this proposition to the problem under consideration, we would not expect the attitudes of a single member towards his role in the organization to be a linear function of the level of reward which he receives. The relationship between these two variables should be represented by a monotonically increasing piecewise, linear function with the slope being steepest around the expected level.

The basic idea is similar in one respect to that discussed in the previous section. Affective responses to a given level of reward are assumed to be highly variable, and it is assumed that this variation can be accounted for by reference to a standard with which the attained or received level is compared and evaluated. The differences between these two formulations concern the nature of the standard of comparison, its predicted determinants and the predicted consequences of discrepancies between the standard and attained level.

To test the proposition that a person's affective response to a given level of reward varies with the level that he expected, it is necessary to make some additional assumptions about the way in which expectations are formed and are altered by experience. Thus, if we assume that a person's expected level of reward in a given situation is determined solely by the reward levels which he has previously attained in that situation, we can expect that the affective consequences of a given reward level will vary predictably with prior reward levels. Substantial support for this prediction has been obtained from laboratory experiments on contrast effects (Crespi, 1942; Zeaman, 1949) and on extensions of Helson's concept of sensory adaptation levels to the problem of reinforcement (Bevan and Adamson, 1960; Black, Adamson and Bevan, 1961; Collier and Marx, 1959; Helson, 1964). Also consistent with the prediction is evidence that experiences of success and failure are not dependent on the absolute amount of achievement but on the relationship between achievement and level of aspiration where the latter variable is, in large part, determined by previous achievement (Lewin *et al.*, 1944).

While the level of aspiration concept has played an important role in theories about behavior in organizations (Cyert and March, 1963; March and Simon, 1958), there has been little systematic empirical investigation of the way in which attitudes towards or satisfaction with outcomes of organizational membership are affected by previously obtained outcomes or other cues regarding the outcomes which will be obtained. A laboratory experiment conducted by Spector (1956) is suggestive of the kind of results that might be obtained if more explicit attention were given to this variable in research on behavior in organizations. He assigned subjects to four-person groups to work on a simulated military intelligence problem. They were instructed to operate as a team with each man decoding a different part of a series of messages given to the team. The level of reward expected by subjects was manipulated not by controlling rewards received on earlier trials but by verbal communications from the experimenter. Some groups were told that three of the four men would be promoted after completion of the first message, while others were told that only one of every four men would be promoted. Subsequent to completion of the first message, all the members of half of the groups were promoted. This manipulation was independent of the manipulation of the probability of promotion, yielding four experimental conditions corresponding to the various combinations of high and low subjective probability of promotion, and attainment or nonattainment of promotion. The dependent variable was a six-item morale measure which was similar to those used in industrial studies. Morale was found to be highest among subjects who received but did not expect a promotion, and lowest among subjects who expected but did not receive a promotion. There was no interaction between the two independent variables, and mean morale scores were a function of the amount and sign of the discrepancy between attainment and expectation.

Summary

To recapitulate, we have identified four classes of variables which, on the basis of existing evidence, appear to determine the attitude of a person towards his role in an organization and the probability that he will leave it, permanently or temporarily. These four variables are:

1. The amounts of particular classes of outcomes such as pay, status, acceptance and influence, attained by the person as a consequence of his occupancy of that role.

2. The strength of the person's desire or aversion for outcomes in these classes.

3. The amounts of these outcomes believed by the person to be received by comparable others.

4. The amounts of these outcomes which the person expected to receive or has received at earlier points in time.

The nature of the functional relationship between attitudes and these four variables can only be estimated from existing data. Given an outcome or outcome class which is desired by the person, the evidence reviewed suggests that the strength of his attraction towards his role and the probability of his remaining in it increase as the amount of the outcome received increases; decrease as the amount of the outcome received by comparable others exceeds the amount he receives; and increase as the difference between the amount of the outcome received and the amount which he expected and/or has been accustomed to receiving becomes more positive or less negative. On the other hand, if the person is indifferent to the outcome or outcome class, these relationships may be expected to disappear, and if the person has an aversion to the outcome, the signs of the relationships may be expected to reverse.

References

ADAMS, J. S. (1963), 'Toward an understanding of inequity', *J. abnorm. soc. Psychol.*, vol. 67, pp. 422–36.
ADAMS, J. S. (1965a), 'Injustice in social exchange', in L. Berkowitz (ed.), *Advances in Experimental Social Psychology*, vol. 2, Academic Press.
ADAMS, J. S. (1965b), *A Study of the Exempt Salary Program*, General Electric Company, Behavioral Research Services.
ANDREWS, I. R., and HENRY, M. M. L. (1963), 'Management attitudes toward pay', *Indus. Relat.*, vol. 3, pp. 29–39.
BALDAMUS, W. (1951), 'Type of work and motivation', *Brit. J. Sociol.*, vol. 2, pp. 44–58.
BARNARD, C. I. (1938), *The Functions of the Executive*, Harvard U.P.
BARNETT, G. J., HANDELSMAN, I., STEWART, L. H., and SUPER, D. E. (1952), 'The occupational level scale as a measure of drive', *Psychol. Monogr.*, vol. 66, no. 10 (whole no. 342).
BASS, B. M. (1960), *Leadership, Psychology, and Organizational Behavior*, Harper.
BAUMGARTEL, H. (1956), 'Leadership, motivations and attitudes in research laboratories', *J. soc. Iss.*, vol. 12, pp. 24–31.
BEVAN, W., and ADAMSON, R. (1960), 'Reinforcers and reinforcement: their relation to maze performance', *J. exp. Psychol.*, vol. 59, pp. 226–32.
BLACK, R., ADAMSON, R., and BEVAN, W. (1961), 'Runway behavior as a function of apparent intensity of shock', *J. comp. physiol. Psychol.*, vol. 54, pp. 270–4.
BLOOD, M., and HULIN, C. (1967), 'Alienation, environmental characteristics and worker response', *J. appl. Psychol.*, vol. 51, pp. 284–90.
CARTWRIGHT, D., and ZANDER, A. (1960), *Group Dynamics*, Row, Peterson, 2nd edn.

CENTERS, R. (1948), 'Motivational aspects of occupational stratification', *J. soc. Psychol.*, vol. 28, pp. 187–217.

COLLIER, G., and MARX, M. H. (1959), 'Changes in performance as a function of shifts in magnitude of reinforcement', *J. exp. Psychol.*, vol. 57, pp. 305–9.

CRESPI, L. P. (1942), 'Quantitative variation of incentive and performance in the white rat', *Amer. J. Psychol.*, vol. 55, pp. 467–517.

CYERT, R., and MARCH, J. G. (1963), *A Behavioral Theory of the Firm*, Prentice-Hall.

ELLIOTT, J. D. (1953), Increasing office productivity through job enlargement. The human side of the office manager's job, *American Management Association Office Management Series*, no. 134, pp. 3–15.

FESTINGER, L. (1954), 'Motivations leading to social behavior', in M. R. Jones (ed.), *Nebraska Symposium on Motivation*, University of Nebraska Press, pp. 191–218.

FLEISHMAN, E. A., and HARRIS, E. F. (1962), 'Patterns of leadership behavior related to employee grievances and turnover', *Personn. Psychol.*, vol. 15, pp. 43–56.

FLEISHMAN, E. A., HARRIS, E. F., and BURTT, H. E. (1955), *Leadership and Supervision in Industry*, Bureau of Educational Research, Ohio State University.

GUEST, R. H. (1957), 'Job enlargement: a revolution in job design', *Personn. Admin.*, vol. 20, pp. 9–16.

GURIN, G., VEROFF, J., and FELD, S. (1960), *Americans View their Mental Health*, Basic Books.

HALPIN, A. W., and WINER, B. J. (1957), 'A factorial study of the leader behavior descriptions', in R. M. Stogdill and A. E. Coons (eds.), *Leader Behavior: Its Description and Measurement*, Ohio State University, pp. 39–51.

HELSON, H. (1964), *Adaption-Level Theory*, Harper & Row.

HOMANS, G. C. (1961), *Social Behavior: Its Elementary Forms*, Harcourt, Brace.

HOPPOCK, R. (1935), *Job Satisfaction*, Harper.

JACOBSEN, E. (1951), Foreman–steward participation practices and worker attitudes in a unionized factory, *Unpublished Doctoral Dissertation, University of Michigan*.

JAQUES, E. (1961), *Equitable Payment*, Wiley.

KERR, W. A., KOPPELMEIR, G., and SULLIVAN, J. J. (1951), 'Absenteeism, turnover and the morale in a metals fabrication factory', *Occup. Psychol.*, vol. 25, pp. 50–55.

KORNHAUSER, A. W. (1965), *Mental Health of the Industrial Worker: A Detroit Study*, Wiley. [See Reading 6.]

LAWLER, E. E. (1964), Managers' job performance and their attitudes toward their pay, *Unpublished Ph.D Dissertation, University of California*.

LAWLER, E. E., and PORTER, L. W. (1963), 'Perceptions regarding management compensation', *Industr. Relat.*, vol. 3, pp. 41–9.

LEWIN, K., DEMBO, T., FESTINGER, L., and SEARS, P. S. (1944), 'Level of aspiration', in J. McV. Hunt (ed.), *Personality and the Behavior Disorders*, vol. 1, Ronald Press, pp. 333–78.

LIKERT, R. (1961), *New Patterns of Management*, McGraw-Hill. [See Readings 14 and 23.]

MARCH, J. G., and SIMON, H. A. (1958), *Organizations*, Wiley. [See Reading 9.]

MERTON, R. K., and KITT, A. (1952), 'Contributions to the theory of reference behavior', in G. Swanson, T. Newcomb and E. Hartley (eds.), *Readings in Social Psychology*, Holt, 2nd edn, pp. 430–44.

MEYER, H., KAY, E., and FRENCH, J. R. P. (1965), 'Split roles in performance appraisal', *Harv. bus. Rev.*, vol. 43, pp. 123–9.

MILLER, D. C. (1941), 'Economic factors in the morale of college-trained adults', *Amer. J. Sociol.*, vol. 47, pp. 139–56.

MORSE, N. (1953), *Satisfactions in the White-Collar Job*, University of Michigan, Survey Research Center.

MORSE, N., and REIMER, E. (1956), 'The experimental change of a major organizational variable', *J. abnorm. soc. Psychol.*, vol. 52, pp. 120–29.

PATCHEN, M. (1961), *The Choice of Wage Comparisons*, Prentice-Hall.

PATTERSON, D. G., and STONE, C. H. (1942), 'Dissatisfactions with life work among adult workers', *Occupations*, vol. 21, pp. 219–21.

PORTER, L. W. (1962), 'Job attitudes in management: I, perceived deficiencies in need fulfillment as a function of job level', *J. appl. Psychol.*, vol. 46, pp. 375–84.

ROSS, I. C., and ZANDER, A. (1957), 'Need satisfactions and employee turnover', *Personn. Psychol.*, vol. 10, pp. 327–38. [Reading 4.]

SEEMAN, M. (1957), 'A comparison of general and specific leader behavior descriptions', in R. M. Stogdill and A. E. Coons (eds.), *Leader Behavior: Its Description and Measurement*, Ohio State University, pp. 86–102.

SIMON, H. A. (1947), *Administrative Behavior*, Macmillan, New York. [See Reading 1.]

SPECTOR, A. J. (1956), 'Fulfillment and morale', *J. abnorm. soc. Psychol.*, vol. 52, pp. 51–6.

STOUFFER, S. A., SUCHMANN, E. A., DEVINNEY, L. C., STAR, S. A., and WILLIAMS, R. M. (1949), *The American Soldier: Adjustment during Army Life*, vol. 1, Princeton U.P.

SUPER, D. E. (1939), 'Occupational level and job satisfaction', *J. appl. Psychol.*, vol. 23, pp. 547–64.

TANNENBAUM, A. S., and ALLPORT, F. H. (1956), 'Personality structure and group structure: an interpretive study of their relationship through an event-structure: hypothesis', *J. abnorm. soc. Psychol.*, vol. 53, pp. 272–80.

THIBAUT, J. W., and KELLEY, H. H. (1959), *The Social Psychology of Groups*, Wiley.

THOMPSON, W. A. (1939), 'Eleven years after graduation', *Occupations*, vol. 17, pp. 709–14.

Satisfaction: Its Determinants and Effects

TURNER, A. N., and LAWRENCE, P. R. (1965), *Industrial Jobs and the Worker: An Investigation of Response to Task Attributes*, Harvard University, Graduate School of Business Administration, Division of Research.

UHRBROCK, R. S. (1934), 'Attitudes of 4430 employees', *J. soc. Psychol.*, vol. 5, pp. 365–77.

VAN ZELST, R. H. (1951), 'Worker popularity and job satisfaction', *Personn. Psychol.*, vol. 4, pp. 405–12.

VROOM, V. H. (1960), *Some Personality Determinants of the Effects of Participation*, Prentice-Hall.

VROOM, V. H. (1964), *Work and Motivation*, Wiley. [See Reading 16.]

WALKER, C. R. (1950), 'The problem of the repetitive job', *Harv. bus. Rev.*, vol. 28, pp. 54–8.

WALKER, C. R., and GUEST, R. H. (1952), *The Man on the Assembly Line*, Harvard U.P.

WICKERT, F. R. (1951), 'Turnover and employees' feelings of ego-involvement in the day-to-day operations of a company', *Personn. Psychol.*, vol. 4, pp. 185–97.

WYATT, S., FRASER, J. A., and STOCK, F. G. L. (1929), 'The effects of monotony in work', *Industrial Fatigue Research Board Report*, no. 56, H.M.S.O.

ZALEZNIK, A., CHRISTENSEN, C. R., and ROETHLISBERGER, F. J. (1958), *The Motivation, Productivity and Satisfaction of Workers: A Prediction Study*, Harvard University, Graduate School of Business Administration.

ZEAMAN, D. (1949), 'Response latency as a function of the amount of reinforcement', *J. exp. Psychol.*, vol. 39, pp. 466–83.

9 James G. March and Herbert A. Simon

Motivational Constraints: The Decision to Participate

Abridged from chapter 4 of James G. March and Herbert A. Simon, *Organizations*, Wiley, 1958.

Employee Participation: The Participation Criterion

In joining the organization an employee accepts an authority relation, i.e. he agrees that within some limits (defined both explicitly and implicitly by the terms of the employment contract) he will accept as the premises of his behavior orders and instructions supplied to him by the organization. Associated with this acceptance are commonly understood procedures for 'legitimating' communications and clothing them with authority for employees. Acceptance of authority by the employee gives the organization a powerful means for influencing him – more powerful than persuasion, and comparable to the evoking processes that call forth a whole program of behavior in response to a stimulus.

On the assumption that employees act in a subjectively rational manner, we can make some predictions about the scope of the authority relation from our knowledge of the inducements and contributions of the employees and other organization members (Simon, 1952–3).[1] An employee will be willing to enter into an employment contract only if it does not matter to him 'very much' what activities (within the area of acceptance agreed on in the contract) the organization will instruct him to perform, or if he is compensated in some way for the possibility that the organization will impose unpleasant activities on him. It will be advantageous for the organization to establish an authority relation when the employee activities that are optimal for the

1. See Reading 1 for a discussion of inducements and contributions – *Editor*.

organization (i.e. maximize the inducement utility to other participants of the employee's activity) cannot be predicted accurately in advance.

These propositions can be restated in a form that permits them to be tested by looking at terms of the employment contract. A particular aspect of an employee's behavior can be (a) specified in the employment contract (e.g. as the wage rate usually is), (b) left to the employee's discretion (e.g. sometimes, but not always, whether he smokes on the job), or (c) brought within the authority of the employer (e.g. the specific tasks he performs within the range fixed by the job specification).

To construct a series of hypotheses relating employee participation to external variables, we must first establish a criterion for 'participation'. Three methods of measuring participation yield substantially different results. First, we can measure the quantity of production by the individual worker. Second, we can use an absence criterion. Permanent physical absence associated with leaving the company payroll represents the extreme value on the low side. Differences in on-the-job productivity are not captured by the absence criterion but employees are distinguished by their absence rates as well as their turnover rates. Third, we can use a turnover criterion: we can identify participation with the all-or-none phenomenon of being on or off the organization payroll.

Although it may appear at first blush that these measures simply reflect different degrees of disassociation from the organization and, therefore, are simply different points on a continuum, the available empirical evidence indicates no consistent relation among measures of production, absences, and voluntary turnover (Acton Society Trust, 1953; Brayfield and Crockett, 1955; Morse, 1953).[2]

We propose here to use a turnover criterion. At the same time, however, we will attempt to point out how an absence criterion would support similar or different propositions.

Employee Participation: The General Model

We make the general postulate that increases in the *balance of*

2. See Readings 4 and 5 for evidence on this question – *Editor*.

inducement utilities over contribution utilities (4.1)[3] decrease the *propensity of the individual participant to leave* (4.2) the organization, whereas decreases in that balance have an opposite effect [4.2:4.1].

The inducements-contributions balance is a function of two major components: the *perceived desirability of leaving the organization* (4.3) and the *perceived ease of movement from the organization* (4.4) (i.e. the utility of alternatives foregone, [4.1 : 4.3, 4.4]). Although these are not completely independent factors, most of the propositions below are statements about variations in either one or the other of them. The satisfaction (or motivation to withdraw) factor is a general one that holds for both absences and voluntary turnover. Differences between absences and turnover stem not from differences in the factors inducing the initial impulse but primarily from differences in the consequences of the alternative forms of withdrawal. The perceived ease of withdrawal from the organization, on the other hand, frequently is quite different for permanent withdrawal than for absenteeism or sick leave.

Factors Affecting the Perceived Desirability of Movement from the Organization

Some of the factors listed here affect the perceived desirability of movement and others the perceived ease of movement. However, in most cases the intervening variables are not made explicit in the available research and hence at least some of the structure of the theory is not tested directly. Nevertheless, there is sufficient information available to support the existence of two distinct mechanisms. One of the advantages of retaining the intervening variables is that it permits us to use data on absenteeism as possibly relevant to questions of turnover even though (as has been previously indicated) we have theoretical reasons and empirical evidence for believing that absenteeism and turnover are not in all respects well correlated. The reader who wishes to question

3. The numbering of variables and propositions is as follows. If a proposition states that the value of dependent variable 3.7 varies with the value of independent variable 3.3, we will number the proposition '3.7 : 3.3'. The distinctions between dependent and independent variables are not arbitrary, but are assertions about the direction of the causal arrow. Utility is a term (from utility theory) which represents the subjective worth to a person of something, in this case it is of inducements and contributions.

this assumption will, of course, also wish to question the propositions cited here that depend significantly on data gathered from studies of absences.

The literature on the factors associated with employee motivation to leave an organization suggests that the primary factor influencing this motivation is employee satisfaction with the job as defined by him. The greater the individual's *satisfaction with the job* (4.5), the less the perceived desirability of movement [4.3: 4.5]. A fairly wide range of job characteristics is relevant, since individual discontent with employment may reflect any of a number of relatively distinct aspects of the job.

The most reasonable hypotheses about an individual's motivation to withdraw from employment are closely related to the conflict phenomena. We can state three major propositions. First, the greater the *conformity of the job characteristics to the self-characterization held by the individual* (4.6), the higher the level of satisfaction [4.5 : 4.6]. Dissatisfaction arises from a disparity between reality and the ego-ideal held by the individual. The greater the disparity, the more pronounced the desire to escape from the situation.

Second, the greater the *predictability of instrumental relationships on the job* (4.7), the higher the level of satisfaction [4.5 : 4.7]. Ability to predict the cost of attaining a specified volume of production would be an example of such predictability in the job of factory manager. One form of decision-making conflict stems from incomplete predictability. In general and up to a fairly extreme point, increased predictability yields increased satisfaction for most people – particularly in activities that are primarily instrumental.

Third, the greater the *compatibility of work requirements with the requirements of other roles* (4.8), the higher the level of satisfaction [4.5 : 4.8]. As Curle (1949) has pointed out, one of the major reasons for interpersonal differences in work satisfaction is that groups in a society do not always make mutually compatible demands on the individual worker. One would predict that an organizational participant would try to select his group memberships so as to keep at a low level the conflict imposed by differences in the demands made upon him.

Each of the three propositions specifies prior conditions for decision-making conflict: to the extent that withdrawal from one of the groups in the situation represents a solution to this type of conflict, we can infer the relations we have specified. Specific studies, however, have been aimed at the relations between primary factors and turnover (or absenteeism) without clearly defining the intervening factors we have identified; and it is from the propositions that follow that we infer support for the mechanisms proposed above.

Consider, first, empirical data relating to variations in the conformity of the job to the employee's self-characterization. Three types of individual evaluations of self appear to be significant: estimates of one's independence, one's worth and one's specialized competences or interests. The greater the *consistency of supervisory practices with employee independence* (4.9), the less the conflict between job characteristics and individual self-image [4.6 : 4.9]. Thus, Reynolds and Shister (1949) have found that the most frequently cited reason for job dissatisfaction is an adverse conception of the independence and control provided by the work situation. So long as an individual desires independence in decision making, the more authoritarian the supervisory practices, the greater the dissatisfaction aroused and the greater the pressure to withdraw (Morse, 1953; Morse and Reimer, 1956). Where physical egress is blocked, there is some evidence that withdrawal through rejection and in some cases psychoneurosis is stimulated (Stouffer *et al.*, 1949).

The larger the *amount of rewards* (4.10) offered by the organization (in terms of status or money), the less the conflict between the job and the individual's self-image [4.6 : 4.10]. This proposition (other things being equal) is almost universally accepted, but the mechanisms through which it operates need to be specified. It is not as obvious a proposition as marginal economic analysis suggests. Studies of the labor market have cast considerable doubt on the traditional description of that market, particularly the extent to which wage and salary information is widely shared among employees (Reynolds, 1951). We are suggesting here that an employee has a conception of what he is worth in money and status, that his conception is not totally unrelated to the labor market value of his services, but that it is far from totally dependent on the market value.

The greater the *individual's participation in job assignment* (4.11), the less the conflict between the job and the individual's self-image [4.6 : 4.11]. Studies in both army and industrial units suggest the not-surprising finding that, although the act of joining the organization commits the individual momentarily to whatever task is assigned him (since that is the nature of his employment contract) and all such tasks are perceived initially as yielding a favorable inducements-contributions balance, the employee is not indifferent to the several alternatives but prefers some to others (Bolanovich, 1948; Stouffer *et al.*, 1949). Consequently, an employee assigned according to personal preference will have a more favorable inducements-contributions balance than an employee not so assigned.

Self-conceptions change. In particular, they respond to environmental conditions as aspiration levels do. Status, wage and job activity aspirations change as a function of experience and comparison with others whom the individual considers comparable. What can we say about changes in the perceived desirability of movement from our knowledge about aspiration-level changes?

Within a given occupational level, the higher the *level of education* (4.12), the greater the conflict between the job and the individual's self-image [4.6 : 4.12]. Some evidence for this hypothesis is reported by Reynolds (1951). He found that in a group of manual workers those with a high school education were more likely to want to leave their present jobs than those without high school education. Similar findings were obtained in the army during the Second World War (Morse, 1953; Stouffer *et al.*, 1949). Whether the relation holds at a higher level in an organization is not clear.

Within a given promotional ladder, the greater the *rate of change* of status and/or income (4.13) in the past, the greater the disparity between the job and the individual's self-image [4.6 : 4.13]. Using such a precise term as the 'rate of change' may overstate what is meant. Individual participants make estimates of their worth on the basis of some projection of past achievement. For example, where promotions or salary increases occur regularly, the extrapolation is made in terms of future similar increases. Where, at some point in a promotional ladder, there is a substantial decrease in either the percentage or absolute increment, we would predict that discontent, voluntary withdrawal or both would be produced (Morse, 1953; Stockford and Kunze, 1950). Comparability of the job with the self-characterization of the individual bears a close relation to the compatibility of the job with other roles demanded by society.

Consequently, we would predict that the greater the extent to which the activities demanded by the job make it difficult or impossible to fulfil ordinary expectations in other social groups, the greater the perceived desirability of movement (Bullock, 1952). To generate specific predictions from this generalization, we need some estimate of the 'normal' from which deviations are to be measured. Most obvious among these are work schedules. The greater the *congruence of work time patterns with those of other roles* (4.14), the greater the compatibility of the job and other roles [4.8 : 4.14]. Problems arise when the requirements of the job deviate significantly from the expectation of an eight-hour day and five-day week, a holiday on Sunday and normal daylight work hours. All of these, and particularly the latter, are clearly artifacts of a particular culture. To the extent that this is a correct characterization of a cultural pattern, we can make specific predictions: the perceived desirability of movement will be greater among workers on the night shift than among workers on the day shift (Brissenden and Frankel, 1922). The perceived desirability of movement will be greater among workers who must be absent from their homes for periods of time greater than a normal working day than among others. The perceived desirability of movement will be greater among workers whose jobs involve frequent geographical moves than among others.

Propositions like those just cited are based on cultural norms and the pressures they exert through institutions like the family or the community. The norms are taken as given and the compatibility of the work with them is evaluated. However, there are many roles (e.g. friendship roles) where the compatibility of job with other activities depends as much on the characteristics of the other groups as it does on the characteristics of the job. For the individual, potential problems arise from the demands of overlapping group membership. Where the job stimulates the development of a number of single-purpose groups with overlapping membership, workers can be expected to find the work less pleasant than where a multipurpose integrated group exists. Thus, we are led to a pair of anomie-like hypotheses: the smaller the *size of the work group* (4.15), the greater the compatibility of organizational and other roles [4.8 : 4.15]; the smaller the *size of the organization* (4·16), the greater the compatibility of organizational and other roles [4.8 : 4.16]; the hypotheses may well not hold in the extreme ranges: a work group of one individual will not be a very satisfactory group for most individuals. The differences between a group of one (or two) and a group of ten have not been investigated and may reverse the relation. Similarly, differences between groups of 100 and groups of 200 have not been investigated. It is quite possible that there exist critical 'optimal' group sizes. With this proviso, there is a fair amount of empirical evidence supporting the hypothesis, particularly if we use data on absences interchangeably with turnover data (Acton Society Trust, 1953; Blackett, 1928; Reynolds and Shister, 1949).

Finally, one further hypothesis may shed light on an important difference between absences and turnover. We have argued that the larger the organization, the higher the probability that the individual will become involved in overlapping and conflicting group memberships. From this, we have argued, there stems a desire to leave the organization. In general, the proposition is supported by the available data on absences. However, the data on turnover fail to support the proposition with any consistency at all. How can we explain this difference? It is probably caused by the arbitrary nature of our turnover data. The larger the organization, the greater the *perceived possibility of intraorganizational transfer* (4.17) [4.17 : 4.16] and, therefore, the less the perceived desirability of leaving the organization [4.3 : 4.17] (Brissenden and Frankel, 1922; Rice, 1951). Typically, turnover is defined as leaving the formally defined organization (e.g. the business firm). Thus, leaving a job in manufacturing to take a job in distribution will be classified as turnover if there is a change of company, but not otherwise. A substantial amount of what would be called turnover in smaller firms is classified as 'interdepartmental transfer' in larger firms.

The structure of these propositions relating to the individual participant's perceived desirability of movement is pictured in Figure 1.

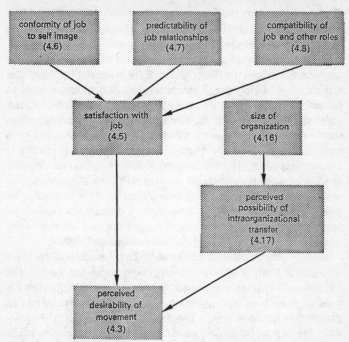

Figure 1 Major factors affecting perceived desirability of movement

Factors Affecting the Perceived Ease of Movement from the Organization

Under nearly all conditions the most accurate single predictor of labor turnover is the state of the economy. Even such a gross aggregate statistic as the national quit rate shows a strong negative relationship with the aggregate rate of discharges and lay-offs. When jobs are plentiful, voluntary movement is high; when jobs are scarce, voluntary turnover is small. It is the object of this section to suggest some possible refinements of these propositions.

We will hypothesize that perceived ease of movement for an individual depends on the availability of jobs for which he is qualified (and willing to accept) in organizations visible to him. The greater the *number of perceived extraorganizational alternatives* (4.18), the greater the perceived ease of movement [4.4 : 4.18].

We wish to explore the factors associated with both the visibility of organizations and the availability of jobs. But first, some preliminary remarks are in order.

Let us suppose that we have a population of organizations and a population of potential employees. Each potential employee has a number of attributes primarily, but not exclusively, related to his special competences as a worker. Each organization can rank combinations of such attributes so that workers can be correspondingly ranked in terms of their desirability as employees (almost independently of specific job requirements). From this it follows that when organizations expand, they do no (i.e. virtually no) firing; when they contract, they do no hiring. Even where one would not expect such a relationship to hold, in a change of political administration, it is extremely difficult to make new appointments while attempting to reduce the over-all size of the organization (e.g. the Republican administration in 1953).

Under these conditions an individual's perception of the ease of moving from a given organization will depend on (a) the number of organizations whose rankings he can scan, (b) his level in these rankings and (c) the ranking that corresponds to the current hire–fire point. The first of these factors is the visibility factor; the other two are different aspects of the job availability factor. The lower the *level of business activity* (4.19), the less the number of extraorganizational alternatives [4.18 : 4.19]. When unemployment figures are used as a criterion of the state of business, this proposition becomes almost a tautology. And since virtually all of the standard measures of business activity show a relatively high correlation with each other, it is not surprising that voluntary turnover rates should decrease when business turns downward. Shifts in business can be conceived as shifting the critical 'cut-off' points on each industry's ranking of jobs and hence changing the alternatives open to an employee. For specific predictions in specific industries, differences in the impact of the business cycle may result in differences in turnover, but the impact of a recession in one area spreads beyond that area, since the change in the cut-off point in one industry alters the alternatives open to individuals not only in that industry but also in related industries.

The evidence for the proposition is substantial. Reynolds (1951) reports that in the 1948-9 recession, the average voluntary separation in thirty-nine companies surveyed fell from 3·5 per cent per month to 1·6 per cent per month and that, in general, market demand for labor is a dominant factor in voluntary turnover. Similar results are reported by Behrend (1953), Blackett, (1928), Brissenden and Frankel (1922), Palmer (1954), and Woytinsky (1942).

Not all of the variance in behavior, however, can be explained in this fashion. Individual attributes define the individual's employability rank and, therefore, determine differential effects of changes in the state of business. Consequently, we wish to be able to specify factors that affect individual ranks.

The perceived availability of outside alternatives is a function of the *sex of the participant* (4.20) [4.18 : 4.20]. Male workers will perceive movement to be easier than will female workers. In general, studies have reported a higher turnover rate among males than among females, although a careful study should probably distinguish between marriageable and non-marriageable females. Brissenden and Frankel (1922), Myers and Mac-Laurin (1943) and Palmer (Bakke *et al.*, 1954) have reported data supporting the proposition (in Palmer's case the differences are slight). Yoder (Bakke *et al.*, 1954), however, failed to find a significant difference. Hauser (Bakke *et al.*, 1954) has some data that indicate a close relationship between female turnover rates and marriage. For the female worker the family organization is an alternative to work.

The perceived availability of outside alternatives is a function of the *age of participant* (4.21) [4.16 : 4.21]. The older the worker, the less the perceived ease of movement. A second way in which age affects the perceived ease of movement is indicated below. The mechanism just cited is clearly important. In ranking job attributes, age is a negatively valued characteristic. Consequently, turnover among younger persons will be higher than among older persons – even when skill and other attributes are held constant (Bakke *et al.*, 1954; Myers and MacLaurin, 1943; Reynolds, 1951).

The perceived availability of outside alternatives is a function of the *social status of the participant* (4.22) [4.18 : 4.22]. Members of low status groups will perceive movement to be more difficult than will members of high status groups. Thus, we would predict lower voluntary turnover among Negroes than among whites, lower among Jews than among Gentiles, lower among foreign-born than among native-born citizens.

All the propositions just cited refer to more or less static conditions in organizations operating within the contemporary American culture. However, some important features influencing the employability of an individual reflect somewhat more dynamic characteristics. The perceived availability of outside alternatives is a function of the *technology* of the economy (4.23) [4.18 : 4.23] (Jaffe and Stewart, 1951; Palmer and Ratner, 1949). For example, recent changes in technology have tended to raise the relative ranks of female workers and white-collar employees by increasing the range of jobs for which they are employable. Automation will presumably have a quite similar shuffling effect on the rankings.

The longer the *length of service* (4.24) of the employee, the greater his *specialization* (4.25) [4.25 : 4.24]; the greater his specialization, the fewer the extraorganizational alternatives perceived [4.18 : 4.25]. Where the previous proposition dealt with changes in the ratings of attributes, the present one depends on changes in the attributes of a given individual. When an individual remains in an organization for a long time, his skills become more and more specific to the organization in question. Consequently, he becomes more and more indispensible to that organization but more and more dispensible to other organizations. In specialization we approach a theoretically very interesting limiting case where the demand and supply of a particular bundle of abilities tends to decrease until we have an organization that can find a replacement only at prohibitive cost and an employee who can find another job only at prohibitive loss. At executive levels this case of bilateral monopoly is probably quite common, with salaries determined by bargaining and/or rules of thumb. Data on the compensation of business executives are consistent with this characterization of the situation (Roberts, 1956; Simon, 1957). A number of studies substantiate the negative relationship between skill level and voluntary turnover (Brissenden and Frankel, 1922; Morse, 1953; Reynolds, 1951).

All of the propositions thus far listed operate through changes (or differences) in the actual availability of jobs – either through differences in the hire–fire point, or through individual differences in employability. However, these are not the only factors involved. The perception of alternatives depends partly on the actual alternatives available and partly on evoking mechanisms. As a result, the range of organizational alternatives visible to a particular potential participant varies from individual to individual, from organization to organization, and from situation to situation (Reynolds, 1951).

The larger the *number of organizations visible* (4.26) to the participant, the greater the number of perceived extraorganizational alternatives [4.18 : 4.26]. This is one of the basic propositions stemming from our conception of the labor market. The greater the number of organizations scanned, the higher the probability that the scanning will include an alternative job that is above the cut-off point. What factors affect the visibility of organizations to participants? Certain characteristics of organizations make some more visible than others, and certain characteristics of individuals make more organizations visible to them than to other individuals. With respect to the latter, we can specify a simple mechanism that leads to a number of specific propositions. The greater the *prestige of the organization* (4.27), the greater the *visibility of the organization* (4.28) [4.28 : 4.27]. If we now apply the propositions relating to organizational prestige that were cited in chapter 3 [not included in this excerpt], we can use these to generate a series of specific predictions. The larger the organization, the more visible it will be. The more the organization produces a distinguishable product, the more visible it will be (Reynolds and Shister, 1949). The greater the number of high status occupations and/or individuals in the organization, the more visible it will be. The faster the rate of growth of the organization, the more visible it will be.

Individuals who are valued by organizations with high visibility will, in general, perceive movement to be easier than will individuals whose skills are demanded by less visible organizations.

It has been found that typical scanning procedures for potential members of business organizations are limited by geography (Reynolds, 1951). Scanning for job opportunities is typically largely by word of mouth and depends on the range of organizations included in the individual's usual contacts. Knowledge of organizations decreases rapidly with distance, except for special cases of individuals with relatively high mobility expectations or preferences.

Thus, the greater the *heterogeneity of personal contacts* (4.29) for the employee, the greater the number of organizations visible [4.26 : 4.29] (Reynolds, 1951). From this one can make a number of subsidiary predictions, for which, however, there appear to be no data. For example, the perceived ease of movement will be greater among residents of suburbs than among residents of central cities (on the assumption that bedroom communities exhibit somewhat greater organizational heterogeneity than comparable central areas). There will be an increase over time in the perceived ease of movement, because of increased commuting. The more non-work organizations in which the individual participates, the greater his perceived ease of movement. For example, it has been observed that craft union members frequently use their union to learn about available jobs (Reynolds, 1951).

Organizational recruitment, however, is not simply a matter of individual scanning of alternatives. Simultaneously, organizations are searching for personnel. The job seeks the man as well as vice versa. Consequently, factors that determine the mode of search used by organizations will affect the success of the individual's search.

The greater the *visibility of an individual* (4.30) to organizations, the greater the visibility of organizations to him [4.26 : 4.30]. With available data there is no certain way to define the important factors that affect the visibility of an individual in a job market. However, there is every reason to assume a strong feedback relationship between organizational visibility to the individual and that individual's visibility to the organization. Thus, the greater the visibility of organizations to an individual, the greater his visibility to relevant organizations [4.30 : 4.26]. The scanning process involved in the job market is necessarily, at least in part, a two-way scanning in which it is probable that if one sees, he will be seen. However, the mechanism is not a typical case of feedback, for with a change in either visibility of the individual or visibility of organizations to him, the other adjusts immediately to an equilibrium position, remaining fixed until one variable or the other is changed by some independent factor.

We have already specified at least some of the independent factors that might affect the visibility of organizations. Now we shall indicate some characteristics of individuals that would affect their visibility. The greater the range of organizations in which an individual has personal contacts, the more visible he is [4.30 : 4.29]. The higher the social status of an individual, the more visible he is [4.30 : 4.22]. The greater the *uniqueness of the individual* (4.31), the more visible he is [4.30 : 4.31]. In the absence of empirical evidence little can be said about these propositions except that they conform to our own experience and intuitions.

Finally, we need to consider an explicitly motivational factor: the individual's propensity to engage in search activities. At any point, the individual must decide not only what alternative to choose on the available evidence, but also whether he should search for additional evidence (or alternatives). The greater the *individual's propensity to search* (4.32), the greater the visibility of organizations to him [4.26 : 4.32]. In the literature, we can distinguish two major mechanisms by means of which search propensities are varied. Both of them are discussed elsewhere in more general terms, but the present case represents an important specific instance. On the one hand, search is generated by dissatisfaction. On the other hand, it is regulated by the habituation of the individual to the situation.

The greater the individual's satisfaction with his job, the less the propensity to search for alternative jobs; in general, there will be a critical level of satisfaction above which search is quite restricted and below which search is quite extensive [4.32 : 4.5] (Reynolds, 1951). We have argued previously that there is a critical level on the satisfaction–dissatisfaction scale at which the individual commences to scan alternatives not previously considered. Indeed, the whole section on the perceived desirability of movement can be viewed as a set of propositions bearing on this problem. Although the perceived desirability of movement and the perceived ease of movement are two distinct factors, the propositions relating to search show that they have considerable interdependence. Dissatisfaction makes movement more desirable and also (by stimulating search) makes it appear more feasible.

Satisfaction: Its Determinants and Effects

Habit also operates to restrict search. The greater the *habituation to a particular job or organization* (4.33), the less the propensity to search for alternative work opportunities [4.32 : 4.33] (Hill and Trist, 1955). In a sense, this is included in the prior proposition, since habitual choice of an alternative indicates that

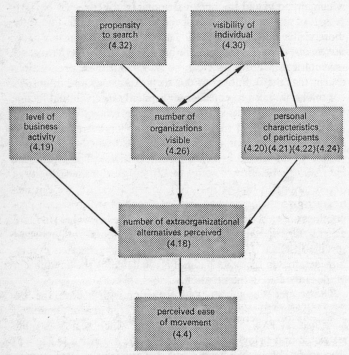

Figure 2 Major factors affecting perceived ease of movement

it is an acceptable alternative. However, it may be desirable to separate current satisfactoriness from historical satisfactoriness – particularly where we allow some adjustments in aspiration levels. Thus, if search is restricted in a mildly unsatisfactory situation, adjustment to the situation can occur before the factors restricting search are overcome (or recognized). Habituation serves to narrow severely the range of alternatives considered. It tends to

James G. March and Herbert A. Simon

remove the particular decision (in this case the choice of organization) from the realm of evaluation and choice so that the job comes to be treated less as a variable in the control of the individual than as a constant defined for him.

Unfortunately, the specific propositions relating to habituation are somewhat contaminated by other factors. For example, we would hypothesize that habituation is a function of both the length of service and the age of the participant [4.32 : 4.21, 4.24]. But results relating length of service and age to turnover are susceptible to a number of different explanations and this is only one of the mechanisms at work.

The major propositions in this section (i.e. those relating to the perceived ease of movement) are summarized in Figure 2. Along with those previously indicated in Figure 1, they constitute the major factors affecting employee participation in an organization.

References

ACTON SOCIETY TRUST (1953), *Size and Morale*.

BAKKE, E. W., HAUSER, P. M., PALMER, G. L., MYERS, C. A., YODER D., and KERR, C. (1954), *Labor Mobility, and Economic Opportunity*, MIT Press.

BARNARD, C. I. (1938), *The Functions of the Executive*, Harvard U.P.

BEHREND, J. (1953), 'Absence and labour turnover in a changing economic climate', *Occup. Psychol.*, vol. 27, pp. 69–79.

BLACKETT, D. W. (1928), 'Factory labor turnover in Michigan', *University of Michigan Business Studies*, vol. 2.

BOLANOVICH, D. J. (1948), 'Interest tests reduce factory turnover', *Personn. Psychol.*, vol. 1, pp. 81–92.

BRAYFIELD, A. H., and CROCKETT, W. H. (1955), 'Employee attitudes and employee performance', *Psychol. Bull.*, vol. 52, pp. 396–424. [Reading 5.]

BRINTON, C. C. (1952), *The Anatomy of Revolutions*, Prentice-Hall.

BRISSENDEN, P. F., and FRANKEL, E. (1922), *Labor Turnover in Industry*, Macmillan.

BULLOCK, R. P. (1952), *Social Factors Related to Job Satisfaction*, Ohio State University Bureau of Business Research.

CURLE, A. (1949), 'Incentives to work: an anthropological appraisal', *Hum. Rel.*, vol. 2, pp. 41–7.

HILL, J. M. M., and TRIST, E. L. (1955), 'Changes in accidents and other absences with length of service', *Hum. Rel.*, vol. 8, pp. 121–50.

JAFFE, A. J., and STEWART, C. D. (1951), *Manpower Resources and Utilization*, Wiley.

MORSE, N. C. (1953), *Satisfaction in the White-Collar Job*, Survey Research Center, University of Michigan.

MORSE, N. C., and REIMER, E. (1956), 'Experimental change of a major organizational variable', *J. abnorm. soc. Psychol.*, vol. 52, pp. 120–29.

MYERS, C. A., and MACLAURIN, W. R. (1943), *The Movement of Factory Workers*, Wiley and Chapman & Hall.

PALMER, G. L. (1954), *Labor Mobility in Six Cities*, Social Science Research Council.

PALMER, G. L., and RATNER, A. (1949), *Industrial and Occupational Trends in National Employment*, University of Pennsylvania Press.

REYNOLDS, L. G. (1951), *The Structure of Labor Markets*, Harper.

REYNOLDS, L. G., and SHISTER, J. (1949), *Job Horizons*, Harper.

RICE, A. K. (1951), 'An examination of the boundaries of part institutions: an illustrative study of departmental turnover in industry', *Hum. Rel.*, vol. 4, pp. 393–400.

ROBERTS, D. R. (1956), 'A general theory of executive compensation based on statistically tested propositions', *Quart. J. Econ.*, vol. 70, pp. 270–95.

SIMON, H. A. (1947), *Administrative Behavior*, Macmillan, New York. [Reading 1.]

SIMON, H. A. (1952–3), 'A comparison of organizational theories', *Rev. econ. Stud.*, vol. 20, pp. 40–8.

SIMON, H. A. (1957), 'The compensation of executives', *Sociometry*, vol. 20, pp. 32–5.

STOCKFORD, L. O., and KUNZE, K. R. (1950), 'Psychology and the pay check', *Personnel*, vol. 27, pp. 2–15.

STOUFFER, S. A. *et al.* (1949), *The American Soldier: Adjustment during Army Life*, Princeton U.P.

WOYTINSKY, W. S. (1942), *Three Aspects of Labor Dynamics*, Social Science Research Council.

Part Three Motivation and Performance: The Effects of Some Specific Job Characteristics

In the previous Part, it was apparent that a distinction must be made between a person's satisfaction with his job and his motivation to perform it effectively. The conditions in the job or work environment which make people more satisfied do not necessarily result in their expending a higher level of effort in the performance of their jobs. In this Part and the one following we are concerned with the motivational processes involved in work performance. This Part deals with evidence concerning the effects of several specific facets of the job and work situation.

Opsahl and Dunnette (Reading 10) survey and critically evaluate available theories and research related to the effects of financial compensation on employee motivation. Lawler (Reading 11) deals with the design of the job itself and asks why job design is related to performance and what specific changes in job design might be expected to lead to certain kinds of performance. Argyle, Gardner and Cioffi (Reading 12) summarize the reports of numerous investigations into the effects of supervisory behaviour on productivity and then present the results of a field study carried out in a British factory. This is followed by a report by Morse and Reimer (Reading 13) of an exceedingly ambitious field experiment which sought to apply what had been learned about the effects of supervision on productivity in a large insurance company. The excerpt by Likert (Reading 14) discusses some implications of the results of this experiment. Reading 15 by Tannenbaum presents the major conclusions that can be drawn from research on the effects of the work group on productivity.

10 Robert L. Opsahl and Marvin D. Dunnette

The Role of Financial Compensation in Industrial
Motivation

Abridged from Robert L. Opsahl and Marvin D. Dunnette, 'The role of
financial compensation in industrial motivation', *Psychological Bulletin*,
vol. 66, 1966, pp. 94–118.

In this review, we have attempted to identify and summarize
research studies designed to show how opportunities to get
money affect the way people actually do their work. It was
decided to focus attention on the role of money in motivating
behavior *on the job*. The large body of literature on manpower
economics relevant to relationships between wage and salary
practices and manpower mobility has been largely ignored. Thus,
we review here those theories and studies designed to illuminate
possible effects of financial compensation for inducing greater
effort in the job setting, and we ignore those theories and studies
related to money's effects in inducing employees to take jobs,
persist in them or to leave them. First, several theories offered to
explain how money affects behavior and research studies relevant to these theories are considered. Second, the behavioral
consequences of compensation are examined by stressing and
analysing the variables relevant to the money–motivation
relationship. Throughout, our purpose is to pinpoint the role of
financial compensation in industrial job motivation. We seek to
summarize and to evaluate critically what is already known and
to suggest directions for future research.

Theories of the Role of Money

Does money serve to stimulate job effort? If so, why does it do
so? How does it take on value in our industrial society? There are
at least five theories or interpretations of the role of money in
affecting the job behavior of employees.

Money as a generalized conditioned reinforcer

One widely held hypothesis is that money acts as a generalized
conditioned reinforcer because of its repeated pairings with

primary reinforcers (Holland and Skinner, 1961; Kelleher and Gollub, 1962; Skinner, 1953). Skinner (1953) has stated that such a generalized reinforcer should be extremely effective because some deprivation will usually exist for which the conditioned reinforcer is appropriate. Unfortunately, solid evidence of the behavioral effectiveness of such reinforcers is lacking, and what evidence there is has been based almost entirely on animal studies.

In a series of experiments conducted by Wike and Barrientos (1958), a goal box (containing wet mash) paired with both food and water deprivation proved to be a more effective reinforcer for rats than different goal boxes paired with food or water deprivation alone. The implications of these results are that money ought to be more potent when its attainment is paired with many, rather than only single, needs. Unfortunately, the magnitude of the difference in preferences in the above study, though statistically significant, was extremely small. In fifteen test trials in a T-maze, rats turned to the goal box previously paired with both deprivations an average of only 0·62 trials more often than to the goal box paired only with food deprivation.

Moreover, this and most other studies on generalized conditioned reinforcers can be criticized because of the non-independence of food and water as primary reinforcers (Grice and Davis, 1957; Verplanck and Hayes, 1953). A water-deprived rat eats less than his normal intake of food. What is needed are studies with human subjects in which a stimulus has been paired with many independent reinforcers. In one such study (Ferster and DeMyer, 1962), coins paired with games and candy were used successfully with autistic children to develop and maintain complex operant behaviors. Although the effectiveness of the coins was well-demonstrated by the increased frequencies of responding contingent on their presentation, their effectiveness under different conditions of deprivation was not studied, nor was their relative effectiveness compared with that of coins operating as simple conditioned reinforcers.

Some theorists (e.g. Brown, 1961; Dollard and Miller, 1950) have referred to the token-reward studies of Wolfe (1936) and Cowles (1937) as examples of how money acquires value. In these studies, initially neutral poker chips apparently acquired reinforcement value because they could be exchanged for various foods. The analogy between the poker chips and the industrial use of money as wages is incomplete, however, because the reinforcement value of the poker chips came about because of their association with removing deprivation in a single primary area, whereas the theory of money's generalized reinforcing role would hypothesize that it is valued quite aside from and independent of any particular state of deprivation. It should be apparent that evidence in support of money as a generalized conditioned reinforcer is, at best, limited and inconclusive.

Money as a conditioned incentive

According to this hypothesis, repeated pairings of money with primary incentives[1] establish a new learned drive for money (Dollard and Miller, 1950). For example, in Wolfe's (1936) study, the sight of a poker chip out of reach served as an incentive to motivate the chimpanzee to pull it in. The fact that chimpanzees refused to work if given a free supply of poker chips suggests that the act of obtaining the chips served a drive-reducing function (Dollard and Miller, 1950). Presumably, money could become a generalized conditioned incentive in the same manner that it is presumed by some to become a generalized conditioned reinforcer – that is, by many pairings with many different types of incentives. Perhaps the main difference between the conditioned reinforcer and conditioned incentive interpretations is the introduction of drive reduction in the incentive hypothesis. In contrast, no such drive need be hypothesized under empirical reinforcement principles.

Money as an anxiety reducer

Brown (1953, 1961) also utilized the concept of drive in an effort to explain how money affects behavior. He suggested that one learns to become anxious in the presence of a variety of cues signifying the absence of money. Presumably, anxiety related to the absence of money is acquired in childhood through a process of higher-order conditioning. The first stage consists of pairings of pain with cues of warning or alarm provided by adults. For

1. Incentive: 'an object or external condition, perceived as capable of satisfying an aroused motive, that tends to elicit action to obtain the object or condition' (English and English, 1958).

example, before a child actually touches a hot stove, a near-by adult may provide facial gestures of alarm and warnings such as 'Look out, you'll get hurt!' These cues eventually elicit anxiety without the unconditioned stimulus. In the second stage, anxiety-arousing warnings are conditioned to a wide variety of cues indicating lack of money. After such learning, the child becomes anxious upon hearing phrases such as 'That costs too much money', or 'We can't afford to buy that'. The actual presence of money produces cues for the cessation of anxiety. This concept of anxiety as a learned motivating agent for money-seeking responses in no way contradicts the possible action of money according to the two previous hypotheses; money as an anxiety-reducer could operate jointly with them as an additional explanatory device.

Harlow (1953), however, has taken issue with Brown's thesis, stating: 'It is hard to believe that parental expression at the time a child suffers injury is identical with or highly similar to a parent's expression when he says "we have no money"' (p. 22). Harlow pointed out further that an infant's ability to recognize emotional expression when suffering pain has not been reliably demonstrated. Unfortunately, Brown presented no experimental evidence bearing on his theory.

Money as a 'hygiene factor'

Herzberg, Mausner and Snyderman (1959) postulated that money is a so-called 'hygiene factor' serving as a potential dissatisfier if it is not present in appropriate amounts, but not as a potential satisfier or positive motivator. According to them, improvements in salary may only remove impediments to job satisfaction but do not actually generate job satisfaction. The main value of money, according to them, is that it leads to both the avoidance of economic deprivation and the avoidance of feelings of being treated unfairly. Thus, its hygienic role is one of avoiding pain and dissatisfaction ('disease') but not one of promoting heightened motivation ('health'). These notions were originally derived from content analyses of anecdotal accounts of unusually satisfying and unusually dissatisfying job events elicited from 200 engineers and accountants. Fifteen per cent of their descriptions of satisfying events involved the mention of salary and 17 per cent of their descriptions of dissatisfying events involved salary. Moreover, Herzberg *et al.* suggested that salary may be viewed as a 'dissatisfier' because its impact on favorable job feelings was largely short-term while its impact on unfavorable feelings was long-term – extending over periods of several months. Herzberg *et al.*'s use of this finding to argue that money acts only as a potential dissatisfier is mystifying. It becomes even more so when their data are examined more carefully. In all of the descriptions of unusually good job feelings, salary was mentioned as a major reason for the feelings 19 per cent of the time. Of the unusually good job feelings that lasted several months, salary was reported as a causal factor 22 per cent of the time; of the short-term feelings, it was a factor 5 per cent of the time. In contrast, salary was named as a major cause of unusually bad job feelings only 13 per cent of the time. Of the unusually bad job feelings lasting several months, it was mentioned only 18 per cent of the time (in contrast with the 22 per cent of long-term good feelings mentioned above).

These data seem inconsistent with the interpretations and lend no substantial support to hypotheses of a so-called differential role for money in leading to job satisfaction or job dissatisfaction.

Money as an instrument for gaining desired outcomes

Vroom's (1964) cognitive model of motivation has implications for understanding how money functions in affecting behavior. According to Vroom's interpretation, money acquires valence as a result of its perceived instrumentality for obtaining other desired outcomes. The concept of valence refers simply to affective orientations towards particular outcomes and has no direct implications for behavioral consequences. However, the 'force' impelling a person towards action was postulated to be the product of the valence of an outcome and the person's expectancy that a certain action will lead to attainment of the outcome. Thus, for example, if money is perceived by a given person as instrumental to obtaining security, and if security is desired, money itself acquires positive valence. The probability, then, of his making money-seeking responses depends on the degree of his desire for security *multiplied* by his expectancy that certain designated job behaviors lead to attaining money. Although Vroom summarized studies giving general support to his theory, the

131

specific role of money in his theory was not dealt with in any detail.

Gellerman's (1963) statement of how money functions in industry also stressed its instrumental role. According to him, money in itself has no intrinsic meaning and acquires significant motivating power only when it comes to symbolize intangible goals. Money acts as a symbol in different ways, for different persons, and for the same person at different times. Gellerman presented the interesting notion that money can be interpreted as a projective device – a man's reaction to money 'summarizes his biography to date: his early economic environment, his competence training, the various non-financial motives he has acquired, and his current financial status' (p. 166). Gellerman's evidence was largely anecdotal, but none the less rather convincing.

Behavioral Consequences of Compensation

The major research problem in industrial compensation is to determine exactly what effects monetary rewards have for motivating various behaviors. More specifically, we need to understand more precisely how money can be used to induce employees to perform at high levels. Relevant research centers around two major groupings: studies related to the job or the job content and studies related to personal characteristics – preferences, perceptions, opinions and other responses – made by the job incumbent. The first of these, the job or task variables, include primarily the policies and practices constituting the 'compensation package' for any given job or job setting. The personal or subject variables influence not only the way a job holder responds to the specific policies and practices in any given situation, but they also vary as a function of these task or job variables. Thus, it is necessary to give careful attention to the interaction between job and personal variables which is frequently overlooked in research designs and has an important bearing on the interpretations to be attached to the results of such research studies.

Job and Task Variables

Compensation policies

Our assumption is that the manner in which financial compensation is administered may account for a large amount of the variation in job behavior. The particular schedule of payment, the degree of secrecy surrounding the amount of pay one receives, how the level of salary or pay is determined and the individual's long-term or career pay history all have important potential effects on how the employee responds to any specific amount of money.

Schedules of pay. In this review we shall be concerned solely with 'incentive' payment systems[2] which are based on behavioral criteria (usually amount of output) rather than biographical factors such as education, seniority and experience. Incentive pay schemes of various sorts are believed to function primarily to 'increase or maintain some already initiated activity or ... to encourage some new form of activity ...' (Marriott, 1957, p. 12).

There is considerable evidence that installation of such plans usually results in greater output per man hour, lower unit costs and higher wages in comparison with outcomes associated with straight payments systems (e.g. Dale. 1959; Rath, 1960; Viteles, 1953). However, the installation of an incentive plan is not and can never be an isolated event. Frequently, changes in work methods, management policies and organization accompany the changeover, and it is difficult to determine the amount of behavioral variance that each of these other events may contribute. This would seem to constitute a persuasive argument for placing workers in a controlled laboratory situation and analysing the effectiveness of different methods of payment, isolated from the usual changes accompanying their installation. Unfortunately, there have been few studies of this nature.[3]

Incentive plans can be based on either the worker's own output or on the total output of his working group. The relative efficiency of the two methods are dependent upon such factors as the nature of the task performed (Babchuk and Goode, 1951; Marriott, 1957), the size of the working group (Campbell, 1952; Marriott, 1949, 1951; Marriott and Denerley, 1955; Shimmin, Williams and Buck, 1956), the social environment (Selekman, 1941) and the

2. We will not attempt to evaluate all the evidence on incentive plans. For an excellent review and evaluation of these, see Marriott (1957).

3. Marriott (1957) mentioned only three experimental studies, all in an industrial setting and all conducted at least thirty years ago: Burnett (1925), Roethlisberger and Dickson (1939) and Wyatt (1934).

particular group or individual plan employed. The chief disadvantage with group incentives is the likelihood of a low correlation between a worker's own individual performance and his pay in larger groups. There is also evidence (Campbell, 1952) that individual output decreases as the size of the work group increases and this is apparently due to workers' perceiving a decreased probability that their efforts will yield increased outcomes (i.e. the workers have less knowledge of the relationships between effort and earnings). Both of these effects run counter to the main principle of incentive plans – immediate reward for desired job behaviors.

Not only do financial incentives operate with different efficacy in different situations, but often they do not even lead to increased production. Group standards and social pressures frequently induce workers to perform considerably below their potential.

Hickson (1961) has divided the causes of rate restriction into five categories. Three of the causes are essentially negative or avoidance reasons: uncertainty about the continuance of the existing 'effort-bargain' between the workers and management, uncertainty about the continuance of employment and uncertainty about the continuance of existing social relationships. The other two causes are positive or approach-type factors: the desire to continue social satisfactions derived from the practice of restriction and a desire for at least a minimal area of external control over one's own behavior.

The most intensive analysis of rate restriction was undertaken by Whyte (1952, 1955). It was the thesis of Whyte and his co-workers that many piece-rate incentive situations actually resemble the conditions of experimentally induced neurosis. He reasoned that most incentive 'packages' do not provide the employee with sufficient cues to allow him to discriminate effectively between stimuli signaling the onset of punishing circumstances (loss of co-worker respect, etc.) and stimuli signaling the onset of rewarding circumstances (more pay, higher job success, etc.) (Whyte, 1955). Thus, money itself is only *one* of many possible rewards and punishments that invariably accompany any incentive situation.

Whyte's effort to show similarity between piece-rate incentive systems and the conditions accompanying experimental neurosis is misleading. The discriminative stimuli for the rewards and punishments administered by the work group and by management seem to be clearly differentiable. A double approach–avoidance conflict between the rewards and punishments of management and the work group is more descriptive of the situation.

Secret pay policies. In addition to the particular kind of pay plan, the secrecy surrounding the amount of money given an employee may have motivational implications. Lawler (1967) has evidence which indicates that secret pay policies may contribute to dissatisfaction with pay and to the possibility of lowered job performance. He found that managers overestimated the pay of subordinates and peers, and underestimated their superiors' pay; they saw their own pay as being too low by comparison with all three groups. Moreover, they also underestimated the financial rewards associated with promotion. Lawler argued that these two results of pay secrecy probably reduce the motivation of managers both to perform well on their present jobs and to seek higher level jobs. Another disadvantage of secrecy is that it lowers money's effectiveness as a knowledge-of-results device to let the manager know how well he is doing in comparison to others. Lawler advocated the abandonment of secrecy policies and claims there is no reason why organizations cannot make salaries public information.

Of course, there might be negative outcomes from the sudden implementation of such policies. For example, one obvious possibility is that such action might crystallize present hierarchical 'pecking orders'; group cohesiveness could be disrupted by the sudden awareness of substantial intra-work-group differences. Most such fears stem from the prevalence of actual pay inequities related to inadequate job-performance appraisal systems and current weaknesses in administering salary payments in such a way as to reflect valid relationships with job performance.

Pay curves. An employee's periodic pay increases, as he progresses in his career with a company, constitutes another job or task variable with the potential for differentially motivating effects. Wittingly or not, every company 'assigns' each employee a 'pay curve' which is the result of successive alterations in

135

compensation and compensation policies through the years. One way of doing this (the usual way) is with little or no advanced planning; increments are given haphazardly on a year to year basis and the resulting career pay curve simply 'grows' somewhat akin to Topsy. Another alternative is to plan the future compensation program shortly after the individual enters the organization and then to modify it subsequently on the basis of his job behavior as his career unfolds. No matter which pay policy is adopted, the results will most likely affect the employee's job behavior, his aspirations and anticipations of future earnings, and his feelings of fairness with respect to his career-pay 'program'.

Most companies administer pay increments on a periodic (e.g. year-to-year) basis.[4] The rationale for this is quite simple, the usual idea being that differential pay increments may be given for differential results produced by employees on their jobs. Over a span of many years, then, we might expect a consistent pattern of positive correlations for the salary increments received by the individuals comprising any particular group of employees.

In fact, however, career pay histories for employee groups do *not* usually show such patterns of consistently positive relationships between year-to-year salary gains. Haire (1965) mapped the correlations between salary levels at the end of each year and raises over five- and ten-year periods in two large national companies. In one company, the correlations decreased over the five-years span from 0·38 to −0·06 for one executive group (median salary $41,600), and from 0·36 to −0·25 for a second group (median salary $18,000). In the second firm, the correlations between salaries and raises for adjacent years over the ten-year period varied between −0·33 and 0·83 with no consistent pattern discernible. Haire believed that his results constituted damning evidence that these two companies had no consistent policies with respect to the incentive use of salary increases; he suggested that the trend in the first company reflected a shift from a policy of distributing raises under the assumption that good performance is related to past excellence to the assumption that it is either not related at all or that it is negatively related. He also asserted that

4. Since there are innumerable ways to administer pay on a periodic basis, and since these methods are largely administrative and have little interest of a psychological nature, we will not attempt to review them.

a pattern showing extremely low correlations between present salary levels and salary increments indicates that wage increases might just as well be distributed by lottery – that the incentive character of a raise is thereby nullified and that consistent striving for job excellence would seem futile under such circumstances. Haire's assertions are provocative and they may indeed follow from his results, but we believe that other explanations may be equally compatible with his findings. For example, low correlations could just as reasonably be viewed as reflecting a successfully administered wage policy allowing for greater rather than less flexibility in using money to reward top job performance. Such a policy might suggest, in effect, that an employee who has done well in the past cannot rest on his laurels in expectation of future 'rewards' and that a lower salaried employee (with presumably a history of less effective performance) still has rich opportunities to be recognized and appropriately rewarded for improved job performance in the future. It is true that a finding of consistently low correlations would tend to refute our earlier stated assumptions about the acquisition of job skills and the consistency of job performance over time.

Industrial psychologists have too often turned prematurely to the study of employee characteristics without giving sufficient attention to the job context. The significant research reviewed here and the questions suggested testify to the potential importance of task and job content variables. Certainly the complexities of the interaction between task and job variables and subject (employee) variables, discussed in the following section, demand research evidence bearing on both. The failure to place research emphasis in either area will very likely impede progress and understanding in the other.

Subject Variables

Perceived relations between performance and pay

According to Vroom's (1964) theory of work motivation, the valence of effective performance increases as the instrumentality of effective performance for the attainment of money increases, assuming that the valence of money is positive. Vroom cited supporting evidence from experiments by Atkinson (1958),

Atkinson and Reitman (1956) and Kaufman (1962) showing a higher level of performance by subjects who were told that their earnings were contingent on the effectiveness of their performance. Georgopoulos, Mahoney and Jones' (1957) path–gaol approach theory similarly states that if a worker has a desire for a given goal and perceives a given path leading to that goal, he will utilize that path if he has freedom to do so. Georgopoulos *et al.* found that workers who perceived higher personal productivity as a means to increased earnings performed more effectively than workers who did not perceive this relationship.

The effectiveness of incentive plans in general depends upon the worker's knowledge of the relation between performance and earnings. The lack of this knowledge is one cause of failure in incentive schemes. As already mentioned, Campbell's (1952) study showed that one of the major reasons for lower productivity in large groups under group incentive plans is that the workers often do not perceive the relation between pay and productivity as well as they do in smaller groups. In the Georgopoulos *et al.* (1957) study, only 38 per cent of the workers perceived increased performance as leading to increased earnings. More amazingly, 35 per cent perceived *low* productivity as an aid to higher earnings in the long run. Lawler (1964) recently found that 600 managers perceived their training and experience to be the most important factors in determining their pay – not how well or how poorly they performed their jobs. Since Lawler found that the relation between their pay and their rated job performance also was low, their perceptions were probably quite accurate. A separate analysis of the most highly motivated managers, however, indicated that they attached greater importance to pay and felt that good job performance would lead to higher pay.

These studies confirm the importance of knowing how job performance and pay are related. The relation between performing certain desired behaviors and attainment of the pay-incentive must be explicitly specified. The foregoing statement seems so obvious as hardly to warrant mentioning. Unfortunately, as we have seen, the number of times in industry that the above *rule* is ignored is surprising. Future research must determine how goals or incentives may best be presented in association with desired behaviors. Practically nothing has been done in this area – especially for managers. In fact, programs for the recognition of individual merit are notoriously poor. Methods for tying financial compensation in with management-by-results (Schleh, 1961) or with systematic efforts to set job goals and methods of unambiguously outlining what the end result of various job behaviors will be should be developed and studied.

Personality–task interactions

Under some conditions, it appears that even specifying the relation between performance and pay is not sufficient. Early studies (Wyatt and Fraser, 1929; Wyatt, Fraser and Stock, 1929; Wyatt and Langdon, 1937) conducted on British factory workers showed that feelings of boredom are associated with reduced output even under a carefully developed program of incentive pay. More recent studies have failed to reproduce the daily output curve found by the British investigators and, moreover, indicate that boredom is not *necessarily* accompanied by reduced output (Cain, 1942; Ryan and Smith, 1954; Smith, 1953). Thus, boredom *may* lead to a decrease in performance; but, as in most other areas of investigation, a *ceteris paribus* clause must be included. Little is known of the factors which may outweigh the effects of boredom in a particular situation.

It is obvious that repetitiveness and uniformity in job tasks are likely to contribute to feelings of boredom, but personality variables are also important determinants. Smith (1955) found that susceptibility to boredom is associated with such factors as youth, restlessness in daily habits and leisure-time activities and dissatisfaction with personal, home, and plant situations not directly concerned with uniformity or repetitiveness. The commonly held assumption that workers of higher intelligence are more easily bored with repetitive work, however, is based on meager and conflicting data (Ryan and Smith, 1954).

One possible method of alleviating feelings of boredom is suggested by Wyatt and Fraser's (1929) finding that piece-rate systems lead to fewer symptoms of boredom than does straight hourly pay. This is in keeping with Whyte's (1955) contention that, in addition to money, there are three other sources of reward in a piece-rate situation: escape from fatigue, because the worker

139

has a meaningful goal to shoot at; escape from management pressure and gain control over one's own time; and 'playing the game' of trying to attain quota.

Even if piece-rate systems relieve boredom, output under such plans may still suffer if the task is disliked. This was Wyatt's (1934) finding when he compared the levels of performance of ten female workers in a British sweet factory under hourly, bonus and piece-rate payment methods. He observed a strong positive relation between an incentive plan's effectiveness (defined as increased productivity) and liking for the job. The best liked job was wrapping the candy, and employees increased their output on it 200 per cent when payment was changed from straight pay to a group bonus and finally to piece-rate payment. In contrast, unwrapping damaged packages was viewed as most onerous – 'an aimless and destructive process' – and output on this task showed no change under different conditions of pay.

The net conclusion from these studies is that repetitive tasks, destructive tasks, boring tasks and disliked tasks are apparently much less susceptible to monetary incentives. Little has been done, however, to explore other possible interactions in this area. What little data we do have suggest that non-monetary incentives are more effective for subjects who have high ability on the task being measured. Thus, Fleishman (1958) found that subjects high in ability on a complex coordination task increased their performance under incentive conditions significantly more than did low ability subjects. However, we do not know if such findings would generalize to situations in which monetary incentives are used or how the effectiveness of incentives varies as a function of other important variables such as the type of task, the amount of physical effort demanded or the degree of interpersonal interaction involved, to mention but a few examples. Without knowledge of the range of behaviors susceptible to incentives or the degree to which they are susceptible, we cannot make optimal use of them in any specific situation.

Perceived importance of pay

It seems obvious that employees must regard money as a highly desirable commodity before increased amounts of it motivate increased behavior. Results of studies in this area are extremely confusing because of the almost exclusive dependence on self-reports to estimate the relative importance of pay. For example, when Wilkins (1949, 1950) asked 18- and 19-year-old males at the British Army Reception Centre to rank various job incentives on importance, 'pay' was placed second only to 'friendly workmates'. Only 8 per cent ranked pay as most important. 'Friendly workmates', 'security' and 'future prospects' all received more first-place rankings than pay. Factor analysis of the responses revealed two broad factors: one was of long-term appeal and included 'security', 'future prospects', 'variety' and 'efficient organization'. The other factor included 'pay', 'workmates', 'working hours' and 'leave'. The second factor was interpreted as consisting of items incidental to the job and mainly of short-term appeal. When Wilkins divided the group into high and low intelligence, he found that both 'pay' and 'workmates' were relatively more important for the low intelligence group – 41 per cent of the youths in this group gave 'workmates' top ranking. He concluded that 'a large proportion of such workers would be prepared to accept lower wages if they could be with workmates they liked' (1950, p. 562).

Worthy's (1950) analysis of surveys conducted by Sears, Roebuck and Company over a twelve-year period showed that pay ranked eighth among factors related to high morale, whereas rates of pay ranked fourteenth. On the other hand, when Ganuli (1954) asked employees in a Calcutta, India, engineering factory to rank eight items relating to working conditions in order of importance, he found that 'adequate earnings' was ranked first, above such factors as 'job security', 'opportunity for promotion' and 'personal benefits'. Graham and Sluckin (1954) also found pay the most important job factor in a survey of skilled and semi-skilled workers in England.

The discrepancies in the above-mentioned studies can be partially explained by the different samples of employees used. One would not expect executives to have the same values and goals as blue-collar workers (nor, for that matter, should it be assumed that executives or blue-collar workers are homogeneous groups in themselves). Another cause of the discrepant findings is the variety in the dimensions of job incentives used. Seldom are the same variables ranked in any two studies. Also, it is probable that many of the factors are not independent. Bendig and Stillman (1958) have criticized the bulk of studies for these last two reasons. They further contended that the factors used were not selected within any theoretical framework of hypothesized dimensions of job incentives. In an attempt to isolate the fundamental dimensions of job incentives, Bendig and Stillman (1958) factor-analysed eight incentive statements given to college students. They found three orthogonal bipolar factors that they tentatively named 'need achievement *v.* fear of failure', 'interest in the job *v.* the job as an opportunity of acquiring status' and 'job autonomy of supervision *v.* supervisor dependency'. Salary loaded highest on 'the job as an opportunity for acquiring status', and had small loadings on 'fear of failure' and 'job autonomy'. Still another possible reason for discrepancies in the above studies is that they have failed to assess the degree to which various respondents' job circumstances are or are not providing sufficient rewards in each job area. For example, a respondent who perceives his present pay as adequate may rate pay as relatively less important than he would if he perceived his present pay level to be low. It is probably impossible for respondents to detach themselves sufficiently from their present circumstances to be able to give completely accurate self-report estimates of the relative importance of different job aspects.

While most self-report surveys place salary in a position of only moderate importance, it is easy to find people in industry who *behave* as if they value money highly. Why is it then that money or pay seldom is ranked commensurate with these behaviors? The answer is not simple, but it may include at least the following possibilities: (a) There is probably a social desirability response set pervading the self-reports. (b) The reinforcement contingencies present in filling out a self-report questionnaire are quite different from those in the real life situation. It is apparent that an individual is reinforced generously for actually obtaining money, but it is much less evident what the reinforcement contingencies are when he simply *admits* in a self-report checklist that attaining money may be a prime goal. Certainly one is reinforced for engaging in a bit of rationalization while filling out such self-reports. (c) Finally, as implied above, people are poor judges (and therefore poor reporters) of what they really want in a job. They do not know with certainty which job factors really attract and hold them; hence they cannot validly describe or rank these job factors.

Thus, research on the valence of money must move beyond the dependency on self-report measures and strive to establish the actual linkages between money and behavior by more sophisticated observational techniques. Laboratory studies and experimental observations of the behavioral effects of money are needed here just as in the many other areas we have discussed.

These may, in part, be supplemented with more sophisticated techniques of scaling. Some modification of the paired-comparison technique used by Jones and Jeffrey (1964) in which a more inclusive domain of job incentive aspects are compared against some monetary standard would be a promising start. We should also heed Bendig and Stillman's (1958) plea for the isolation of basic independent job incentive dimensions in future research in order to unify research and allow for cross-study comparisons. In sum, the question, 'How do people value money?' will not be answered accurately simply by asking them.

Pay preferences

Although money *per se* is usually accorded a middle position in any ranking of job factors, different ways of making salary payments are differentially preferred. Mahoney (1964) found that managers prefer straight salary over various types of management incentive payments (such as stock options, deferred compensation, etc.). This is in keeping with the results of other surveys. Jaques, Rice and Hill (1951), for example, reported that the majority of both workers and management in an English factory were in favor of a change from individual piece-rates to hourly wages. Likewise, Davis (1948) found that 60 per cent of a sample of building operatives were opposed to incentive schemes, with only 21 per cent expressing definite or conditional approval. The main arguments against incentive systems, as reported by Davis, include the fear that the incentive would inhibit other strong and pleasurable motives for working, such as the pleasure of work for its own sake and the solidarity and good fellowship of the working group.

A study conducted by the Michigan Survey Research Center

(Larke, 1953) revealed that group incentive payments were favored by fewer than 50 per cent of the employees who already were under such plans. Similarly, Mahoney (1964) found that his sample of managers also preferred individual to group pay plans. On the other hand, Wyatt and Marriott (1956) found more approval than disapproval of group incentives by 62 per cent of the workers sampled in three factories. With respect to particular types of incentives Spriegal and Dale (1953) found individual piece-work much more popular than group piece-work.

Using paired-comparison techniques, Nealey (1963) found that a large sample ($N = 1133$) of electrical workers accorded direct pay increases a lower position than such fringe benefits as sick leave, extra vacation time or hospital insurance. He also discovered that such preferences do not follow a simple dollar value. For example, dental insurance cost the company less than life insurance but was preferred by more workers. Jones and Jeffrey (1964) asked employees in two electrical equipment plants to make paired comparisons among sixteen alternative compensation plans, each characterized by a combination of four features and having identical over-all costs to the company. The unique aspect of this study is the possibility of directly comparing the average value of each compensation characteristic with that of a pay raise and, thus, attaching a monetary equivalent to each preferred characteristic. Results showed that the average value of a change from hourly wage to weekly salary is judged to be equivalent to a pay increase of between one and two cents an hour. A piece-rate incentive plan was perceived as equivalent to a five- to ten-cent hourly pay increase and was preferred mainly by the skilled workers who already had experience with such a plan. At the non-union plant, a supervisory merit-rating incentive was considered equal to a four-cent pay raise. At the union plant, however, the scheme was so disliked that the absence of the plan was considered worth more than a six-cent hourly raise.

Jones and Jeffrey believed that their approach may have direct bearing upon administrative decisions concerning changes in compensation plans. If the monetary value equivalent of the change, perceived by the worker, substantially exceeds the actual cost to the company of a change in benefits, then it may be considered – if it does not hinder other compensation goals. Basing company compensation policies directly on the measured perceptions of employees regarding the policies also has the additional advantage of designing the pay schemes directly to fit the motive (or preference) systems of the employees being compensated under the plans. The Nealey study and the Jones and Jeffrey study provide rare examples of the analysis of employee's preferences by sophisticated scaling techniques. They well deserve to be emulated by other researchers in this area.

Mahoney (1964, p. 144) concluded that preferences for alternative forms of compensation are relatively uniform and that 'fine distinctions among alternative forms of compensation probably are considerably less important in managerial motivation than is often suggested'. Such preferences should not be the sole criterion for assessing the effects of compensation on motivation if we are mainly interested in actual job behavior, not satisfaction,[5] since the relation between the two is complex and, in many instances, unknown. From stated preferences one cannot easily infer that the compensation program is optimally motivating.

Although there has been a fair amount of research done in determining the pay preferences of managers and other employees, no work has been done on the relation between preference for a particular plan and the actual incentive value of that plan. The implicit, but unwarranted, assumption in all the above-mentioned studies is that if a person has a pay plan he likes, this plan will motivate behavior more than one that he does not like. Although this is an appealing assumption, future studies, in addition to determining employees' pay-plan preferences, should seek to map the relation between such preferences and the incentive value of different plans. The motivation of behavior, *not* the preference for compensation policies, is the prime goal of company pay plans, and research strategies should be directed toward this end.

5. There is correlational evidence that amount of pay is positively associated with satisfaction with pay (Andrews and Henry, 1963; Lawler and Porter, 1963), job satisfaction (Barnett *et al.*, 1952; Centers and Cantril, 1946; Marriott and Denerly, 1955; Miller and Form, 1951; Smith and Kendall, 1963; Thompson, 1939; all as reported in Vroom, 1964) and with need satisfaction (Lawler and Porter, 1963; Porter, 1962). However, it is not known to what degree the satisfaction is a result of the level of pay or the changes in job status, duties and privileges that so often accompany higher pay.

Concept of equitable payment

Several theories have been independently advanced proposing that employees seek a just or equitable return for what they have contributed to the job (Adams, 1963a, 1965; Homans, 1961; Jaques, 1961; Patchen, 1961; Sayles, 1958; Zaleznik, Christensen and Roethlisberger, 1958). A common feature of these theories is the assumption that compensation either above or below that which is perceived by the employee to be 'equitable' results in tension and dissatisfaction due to dissonant cognitions. The tension, in turn, causes the employee to attempt to restore consonance by a variety of behavioral or cognitive methods.

One of the earlier theorists in this area was Homans, who suggested the concept of distributive justice – that is, justice in the way the rewards and costs of activities are distributed among men. He postulated that:

A man in an exchange relation with another will expect that the rewards of each man be proportional to his costs – the greater the rewards, the greater the costs – and that the net rewards, or profits of each man, be proportional to his investments – the greater the investments, the greater the profits (Homans, 1961, p. 232).

Schematically, then, there is distributive justice when

$$\frac{\text{person A's rewards minus his costs}}{\text{A's investments}} = \frac{\text{person B's rewards minus his costs}}{\text{B's investments}}$$

(after Adams, 1965). If the two ratios are unequal, the members of the exchange experience feelings of injustice, one or the other perceiving that he is on the short end in terms of profits. Either member sensing injustice will attempt to bring his profits and investments into line through various behaviors or, perhaps, by changing his perception of the situation.

Another formulation of a theory of equity is found in the work of Patchen (1961). He postulated that equitable payment is achieved when the following two ratios are congruent:

$$\frac{\text{my pay}}{\text{his (their) pay}} \text{ compared to } \frac{\text{my position on dimensions related to pay}}{\text{his (their) position on dimensions related to pay}}$$

A unique aspect of this theory is the concept of potential, or future, perceived equitable payment. This results from the congruence of these ratios:

$$\frac{\text{my pay now}}{\text{his (their) pay now}} \text{ compared to}$$

$$\frac{\text{my future position on dimensions related to pay}}{\text{his (their) present position on dimensions related to pay}}.$$

Thus, although a person perceives a wage comparison as presently equitable, he may still perceive future inequity. This would occur, for example, if the comparison person(s) is someone more skilled, but the person feels he should receive gradual pay increases as his own skill improves – that is, as he becomes more like his comparison person(s) on dimensions related to pay. Such dissonant comparisons may provide a basis for mobility (promotional) aspirations for the person; he may feel that a higher status would be more appropriate for him. Under these circumstances, it is quite possible that dissatisfaction from future perceived inequity may be tolerated.

Substantiation of Patchen's theory comes from interviews with 489 employees in a Canadian oil refinery (Patchen, 1961). The employees were asked to name two persons whose yearly earnings were different from theirs. Those who chose objectively dissonant comparisons (e.g. comparison persons who were of similar status but whose earnings were greater) judged the comparison unsatisfactory. They explained their feelings in terms of dissonance between the wage difference and other related differences. For example, 75 per cent of the employees justified their feelings by pointing out their own equality or superiority with respect to the comparison person on factors directly relevant to pay – such as education, seniority and skill. Those employees who were satisfied with their comparisons based their feelings of satisfaction on a perceived consonance between the wage difference and other related differences between the workers.

Further effects of within and outside company wage comparisons are found in Andrews and Henry's (1963) study of 228 managers in five companies. They found that, at a given level of management, over-all satisfaction with pay was more highly related to the similarity between the pay of managers in one company and the average pay of managers in the other four companies than to the similarity between their pay and the average pay of other managers in their own company. Together, these two studies suggest that both mobility aspirations and wage comparisons, particularly comparisons outside of one's own company, are important determinants of wage satisfaction. Further studies along these lines should increase our meager knowledge concerning the factors influencing wage comparisons.

The most rigorous and best researched theory of equity is that of Adams (1963a, 1965). His theory is derived mostly from the postulates of Festinger's cognitive dissonance theory (1957) but was influenced also by Stouffer *et al.*'s (1949) earlier work on relative deprivation and by Homans' (1961) research on distributive justice. Adams' most recent definition of inequity stated that

inequity exists for Person[6] whenever he perceives that the ratio of his outcomes to inputs and the ratio of Other's outcomes to Other's inputs are unequal, either (a) when he and Other are in a direct exchange or (b) when both are in an exchange relationship with a third party and Person compares himself to Other (1965, p. 22).

This implies, as do all the above-mentioned theories, that an inequitable relation occurs not only when the exchange is not in Person's favor, but when it is to his advantage as well. Adams, like Homans, hypothesized that the thresholds for under-reward and over-reward differ. Thus, a certain amount of over-reward may be written off as 'good luck', whereas similar deviations in the direction of under-reward will not be so easily tolerated.

Inputs mentioned in the definition are anything a worker perceives as constituting his contribution to the job – age, skill, education, experience and amount of effort expended on the job. Outcomes, or rewards from the job, are also dependent upon the worker's perception and would normally include pay, status symbols, intrinsic job satisfaction and fringe benefits, to mention a few examples.

The existence of equity or inequity is not an all-or-none phenomenon. Many degrees of inequity can be distinguished, and the

6. Person is anyone for whom equity or inequity exists. Other is any individual or group used by Person as a referent in social comparisons of what he contributes to and what he receives from an exchange.

magnitude of the inequity is assumed to be some increasing monotonic function of the size of the difference between the ratios of outcomes to inputs. Thus, it is not the absolute magnitudes of perceived inputs and outcomes that are important, but rather the discrepancy between the two ratios. Inequity may exist for both Person and Other, so long as each perceives discrepant ratios. The greatest inequity exists when both inputs and outcomes are discrepant.

The presence of inequity creates tension within a person in an amount proportional to the magnitude of the inequity. This tension creates a drive to reduce the inequity feelings, the strength of the drive being proportional to the tension created. Adams (1963a, 1965) suggested several possible avenues of achieving an equitable state. A person may increase or decrease his inputs (e.g. by increasing or decreasing either the quality or quantity of his work); he may increase or decrease his outcomes (by asking for a raise, or by giving part of his pay to charity, for example); he may change his comparison group or cognitively alter its inputs or outcomes, or force it out of the field; he may leave the field himself (by quitting, transferring or being absent); or he may cognitively distort his own inputs and outcomes. It is not yet clear what principles govern the choice of method for inequity reduction, although Lawler and O'Gara (1967) have recently obtained evidence that the choice is related to such personality 'traits' as self-esteem and responsibility.

A series of experiments to test this theory have been undertaken (Adams, 1963a, 1963b, 1965; Adams and Jacobsen, 1964; Adams and Rosenbaum, 1962; Arrowood, 1961). These studies have all been directed towards the effects of overcompensation on behavior. In Adams and Rosenbaum (1962), the hypothesis that workers who felt they were overpaid would reduce their feelings of inequity by increasing the amount of work performed was tested. Twenty-two college students were hired to conduct interviews at $3·50 per hour; half of them were made to feel qualified and equitably paid, and the other half were made to feel unqualified and thus overpaid. As predicted, the overpaid group conducted significantly more interviews within the allotted time than did the control group.

It could reasonably be hypothesized that the group made to

149

feel overpaid for the job worked harder because they felt insecure and were afraid of being fired. Another experiment was performed by Arrowood (1961, reported in Adams, 1963a, 1965) with the same design – but with the addition of a 'private' group that was under the impression that their employer would never see their work. Within this private group, the students who felt over-compensated also conducted significantly more interviews than the students who felt equitably compensated, thus showing the predicted effect is still obtained when pains are taken to remove the insecurity motive.

Although it is predicted from the theory that workers overpaid on an hourly basis will increase the quantity of their work, workers overpaid on a piece-work basis would actually increase feelings of inequity if they produced more since they would be increasing the amount of their overpayment. Therefore, it was hypothesized that these workers would reduce inequity by redu-cing the quantity of their output – a procedure which increases inputs and decreases outcomes. Adams and Jacobsen (1964) tested this hypothesis on students hired for a proof-reading task. Persons in the overpaid, experimental group were told they were not qualified but would be paid the usual rate of 30 cents per page anyway. Persons in one equitably paid control group were made to feel qualified and were also paid 30 cents per page. Persons in a second equitably paid control group were made to feel unquali-fied but were paid the more equitable rate of only 20 cents per page. Adams also sought to assess any possible effects due to differing feelings of job security by manipulating the perceived possibility of future employment. This was done because it was reasoned that subjects made to feel overpaid and unqualified might perceive an implication that their tenure was in jeopardy unless they showed they were good workers. Thus, for half the subjects in each group, Adams created a condition in which they perceived that there was something to lose (i.e. insecurity) and for the other half a condition in which they perceived that there was nothing to lose (i.e. relative security). Adams reasoned that if job security were important, the overpaid secure subjects would work fast but carelessly whereas the overpaid insecure subjects ought to work with much greater care.

The index of quantity was the number of pages proof-read, and the index of quality was the number of implanted errors detected (each page, averaging 450 words, had an average of twelve errors implanted in the text, such as mis-spellings or grammatical, punctuational and typographical errors).

At first glance, the results substantiate the hypothesis. They show that the overpaid experimental group proofed significantly fewer pages and detected significantly more implanted errors per page than the two equitably paid groups. The job security manipulation had no significant effect, which was in keeping with the hypothesis that quality and productivity should vary with feelings of equity and not as a function of perceived job security.

It should be noted, however, that quality was not entirely adequately measured in the experiment. Detecting implanted errors is only one possible evidence of quality in proof-reading. Another aspect of quality not included in Adams's quality score is the number of words detected as errors, but which were actually correctly spelled or punctuated. If a proof-reader detected all of the real errors in a text, but also claimed several words or punctuation marks to be in error when they actually were correct, his stay on the job probably would be short-lived. Yet, in the experiment just described, he would get a perfect quality score because the specification of detecting non-errors as errors was ignored. Significantly more of these non-errors were falsely called errors by the overpaid group. If these 'errors' had been taken into account their quality scores would have been considerably lower. It can be argued, of course, that such non-error detection simply illustrates the increased effort and conscientiousness that these subjects were devoting to the task, and this would then be further evidence in favor of the theory and of the effectiveness of the experimental manipulation. Even so, the net effect of 'correcting' non-errors is to reduce the job effectiveness of a proof-reader; and it is not entirely clear whether this aspect of ineffectiveness was due to the equity manipulation, the different emphasis on detecting errors in two sets of directions, or some interaction of the two.

Recent research (e.g. Freedman, 1963; Leventhal, 1964; Weick and Penner, 1965 – all mentioned in Weick, 1965; Linder, 1965) indicates that predictions derived from equity theory in cases of under-reward may require modification. All of the above studies

151

showed that underpaid persons work harder, and also like the task more than persons who are overpaid or equitably paid.

Weick (1965) hypothesized that high effort for insufficient pay represents an attempt to raise outcomes, and suggested that proponents of equity theory give greater consideration to the proposition that persons may control their outcomes to reduce inequity. Thus, in the above-mentioned studies, increased satisfaction gained from performing the task may heighten outcomes and bring them more in line with the person's inputs. So far, with the exception of the recent paper by Lawler and O'Gara (1967), research directed towards testing equity theory has dealt only with overpayment, but the effects of insufficient reward are equally important in industry. We hope that more attention is devoted to this area in future research on equity theory.

Several additions to the theory may help to increase its efficiency of prediction. First and most important, there is need for specifying the conditions governing the choice of one mode of resolution over another. The theory itself does not specify any priority of different methods, and, since there are so many potential methods of reducing inequity, the mere prediction that some one of them will occur is not a very useful or meaningful one. Several propositions about the choice of a method have been advanced tentatively by Adams (1965). These include the following hypotheses:

1. Person will maximize positively valent outcomes and the valence of outcomes.
2. He will minimize increasing inputs that are effortful and costly to change.
3. He will resist real and cognitive changes in inputs that are central to his self-concept and to his self-esteem.
4. He will be more resistant to changing cognitions about his own outcomes and inputs than to changing his cognitions about Other's outcomes and inputs.
5. Leaving the field will be resorted to only when the magnitude of inequity is high and other means of reducing it are unavailable (p. 46).

However, the above hypotheses have not yet been tightly incorporated into equity theory. Since so many modes for resolving inequity are possible, the difficulty of specifying exactly when any specific mode may or may not be used renders the theory more 'hazy' and less directly testable than we would like to see it. For example, if an over-compensated group failed to show increased input (in the form of higher quantity or quality), might this be regarded as disconfirmation of the theory or merely an instance of the subjects' choosing another mode (e.g. altering their perceptions of their own or others' inputs or of the nature of the job being performed) for reducing feelings of inequity? Because the principles specifying the choice of mode have not yet been specified, tightly reasoned deductions cannot yet be derived from the theory.

As implied above, it is quite likely that people differ substantially from one another in the mode they might choose for resolving feelings of inequity; moreover, these differences are undoubtedly a function of individual motive configurations and ability, interest, and personality variables. Lawler and O'Gara (1967) have shown, for example, that persons scoring higher on the Responsibility scale of the California Psychological Inventory (CPI) were less likely to sacrifice quality of work for quantity, when underpaid, than were persons scoring low on the scale. In similar fashion, underpaid persons scoring high on CPI scales of Dominance and Self Assurance were less likely to react with high productivity than those scoring low. Apparently, there are distinct differences in the way different kinds of people respond to feelings of inequity. The incorporation of such variables into the theory may increase its explanatory power. As it stands, the theory ignores individual differences.

Not only may motivational variables determine methods of resolution, but it has been hypothesized that the number and kinds of similarities on which Person compares himself to Other may also affect his choice of how he resolves inequity (Weick, 1965). For example, if a person compares himself with someone who is similar only with respect to education, perhaps education inputs will be the only salient means for resolving inequity when it occurs. Similarly, as Weick pointed out, as comparability increases and Person compares himself to Other with respect to many variables, it is plausible to expect that the intensity of discomfort associated with inequity will change. These two hypotheses, unfortunately, have not yet been investigated.

As it stands, the theory fails to specify methods of resolution

153

relating to various kinds of perceptual alteration. Weick (1965) has pointed out that the theory overlooks such possibilities as denial, differentiation, toleration of the discrepancy, alteration of the object of judgement, bolstering and task enhancement. This last method seems particularly important. If a person had proportionately low outcomes, task enhancement would be a relatively easy way to increase his outcomes without alienating his co-workers in the process.

One of the major problems with which equity theory must cope, therefore, is the obvious fact of the large number of variables, the complexities of their interaction and the inadequacy of the operational definitions. Vroom (1964) pointed out that, according to the theory, a worker's satisfaction with his pay is a function of:

1. His beliefs concerning the degree to which he possesses various characteristics.

2. His convictions concerning the degree to which these characteristics should result in the attainment of rewarding outcomes from his job, i.e. their value as inputs.

3. His beliefs concerning the degree to which he receives these rewarding outcomes from his job.

4. His beliefs concerning the degree to which others possess these characteristics.

5. His beliefs concerning the degree to which others receive rewarding outcomes from their jobs.

6. The extent to which he compares himself with these others (p. 171).

We agree with Vroom's conclusion that the complexity of equity theory makes conclusive tests difficult, and that 'a great deal of theoretical and methodological refinement remains to be carried out before this approach can be properly evaluated' (1964, p. 172).

None the less, Adams is to be commended for beginning the difficult task of trying to work through some of the complexities related to an understanding of how pay and employees' perceptions of pay affect the way they work on the job. These early studies on equity, though subject to some criticism, certainly bear the stamp of careful thought and careful experimentation, and we hope that Adams and others will continue in their efforts to explicate more fully some of the questions which have been raised here.

References

ADAMS, J. S. (1963a), 'Toward an understanding of inequity', *J. abnorm. soc. Psychol.*, vol. 67, pp. 422–36.

ADAMS, J. S. (1963b), 'Wage inequities, productivity, and work quality', *Indust. Rel.*, vol. 3, pp. 9–16.

ADAMS, J. S. (1965), 'Injustice to social change', in L. Berkowitz (ed.), *Advances in Experimental Social Psychology*, vol. 2, Academic Press, pp. 267–99.

ADAMS, J. S., and JACOBSEN, P. (1964), 'Effects of wage inequities on work quality', *J. abnorm. soc. Psychol.*, vol. 69, pp. 19–25.

ADAMS, J. S., and ROSENBAUM, W. B. (1962), 'The relationship of worker productivity to cognitive dissonance about wage inequities', *J. appl. Psychol.*, vol. 46, pp. 161–4.

ANDREWS, I. R., and HENRY, M. M. (1963), 'Management attitudes toward pay', *Indust. Rel.*, vol. 3, pp. 29–39.

ARROWOOD, A. J. (1961), Some effects on productivity of justified and unjustified levels of reward under public and private conditions, *Unpublished Doctoral Dissertation, University of Minnesota.*

ATKINSON, J. W. (ed.) (1958), *Motives in Fantasy, Action, and Society*, Van Nostrand.

ATKINSON, J. W., and REITMAN, W. R. (1956), 'Performance as a function of motive strength and expectancy of goal attainment', *J. abnorm. soc. Psychol*, vol. 53, pp. 361–6.

BABCHUK, N., and GOODE, W. J. (1951), 'Work incentives in a self-determined group', *Amer. soc. Rev.*, vol. 16, pp. 679–87.

BARNETT, G. J., HANDELSMAN, I., STEWART, L. H., and SUPER, D. E. (1952), 'The occupational level scale as a measure of drive', *Psychol. Monog.*, vol. 66, no. 10 (whole no. 342).

BENDIG, A. W., and STILLMAN, E. L. (1958), 'Dimensions of job incentives among college students', *J. appl. Psychol.*, vol. 42, pp. 367–71.

BROWN, J. S. (1953), 'Problems presented by the concept of acquired drives', in *Current Theory and Research in Motivation: A Symposium*, University of Nebraska Press, pp. 1–21.

BROWN, J. S. (1961), *The Motivation of Behavior*, McGraw-Hill.

BURNETT, F. (1925), An experimental investigation into repetitive work, *Industrial Fatigue Research Report*, no. 30, H.M.S.O.

CAIN, P. A. (1942), Individual differences in susceptibility to monotony, *Unpublished Doctoral Dissertation, Cornell University.*

CAMPBELL, H. (1952), 'Group incentive payment schemes: the effects of lack of understanding and group size', *Occup. Psychol.*, vol. 26, pp. 15–21.

CENTERS, R., and CANTRIL, H. (1946), 'Income satisfaction and income aspiration', *J. abnorm. soc. Psychol.*, vol. 41, pp. 64–9.

COWLES, J. T. (1937), 'Food-tokens as incentives for learning by chimpanzees', *Comp. Psychol. Monog.*, vol. 14, pp. 1–96.

DALE, J. (1959), 'Increase productivity 50 per cent in one year with sound wage incentives', *Manag. Meth.*, vol. 16, pp. 38–42.

Motivation and Performance: Some Specific Job Characteristics

DAVIS, N. M. (1948), 'Attitudes to work among building operatives',
    Occup. Psychol., vol. 22, pp. 56–62.
DOLLARD, J., and MILLER, N. E. (1950), *Personality and Psychotherapy*,
    McGraw-Hill.
ENGLISH, H. B., and ENGLISH, C. A. (1958), *A Comprehensive Dictionary
    of Psychological and Psychoanalytical Terms*, McKay.
FERSTER, C. B., and DeMYER, M. K. (1962), 'A method for the
    experimental analysis of the behavior of autistic children', *Amer. J.
    Orthopsychiat.*, vol. 32, pp. 89–98.
FESTINGER, L. (1957), *A Theory of Cognitive Dissonance*, Row,
    Peterson.
FLEISHMAN, E. A. (1958), 'A relationship between incentive motivation
    and ability level in psychomotor performance', *J. exp. Psychol.*, vol. 56,
    pp. 78–81.
FREEDMAN, J. L. (1963), 'Attitudinal effects of inadequate justification',
    J. Personal., vol. 31, pp. 371–85.
GANULI, H. C. (1954), 'An inquiry into incentives for working in an
    engineering factory', *Ind. J. soc. Work*, vol. 15, pp. 30–40.
GELLERMAN, S. W. (1963), *Motivation and Productivity*, American
    Management Association.
GEORGOPOULOS, B. S., MAHONEY, G. M., and JONES, N. W. (1957),
    'Path–goal approach to productivity', *J. appl. Psychol.*, vol. 41,
    pp. 345–53. [Reading 17.]
GRAHAM, D., and SLUCKIN, W. (1954), 'Different kinds of reward as
    industrial incentives', *Res. Rev.*, *Durham*, vol. 5, pp. 54–6.
GRICE, G. R., and DAVIS, J. D. (1957), 'Effect of irrelevant thirst
    motivation on a response learned with food reward', *J. exp. Psychol.*,
    vol. 53, pp. 347–52.
HAIRE, M. (1965), 'The incentive character of pay', in R. Andrews (ed.),
    Managerial Compensation, Foundation for Research on Human
    Behavior, Ann Arbor, Michigan, pp. 13–17.
HARLOW, H. F. (1953), 'Comments on Professor Brown's paper', in
    Current Theory and Research in Motivation, University of Nebraska
    Press, pp. 22–3.
HERZBERG, F., MAUSNER, B., and SNYDERMAN, B. (1959), *The
    Motivation to Work*, Wiley, 2nd edn. [See Reading 7.]
HICKSON, D. J. (1961), 'Motives of work people who restrict their output',
    Occup. Psychol., vol. 35, pp. 110–21.
HOLLAND, J. G., and SKINNER, B. F. (1961), *The Analysis of Behavior*,
    McGraw-Hill.
HOMANS, G. C. (1961), *Social Behavior: Its Elementary Forms*, Harcourt,
    Brace.
JAQUES, E. (1961), *Equitable Payment*, Wiley.
JAQUES, E., RICE, A. K., and HILL, J. M. (1951), 'The social and
    psychological impact of a change in method of wage payment',
    Hum. Rel., vol. 4, pp. 315–40.

JONES, L. V., and JEFFREY, T. E. (1964), 'A quantitative analysis of expressed preferences for compensation plans', *J. appl. Psychol.*, vol. 49, pp. 201–10.

KAUFMAN, H. (1962), Task performance, expected performance, and responses to failure as functions of imbalance in the self-concept, *Unpublished Doctoral Dissertation, University of Pennsylvania.*

KELLEHER, R. T., and GOLLUB, L. R. (1962), 'A review of positive conditioned reinforcement', *J. exp. anal. Behav.*, vol. 5, pp. 543–97.

LARKE, A. G. (1953), 'Workers' attitudes on incentives', in *Dun's Review and Modern Industry*, pp. 61–3.

LAWLER, E. E. (1964), Managers' job performance and their attitudes toward their pay, *Unpublished Doctoral Dissertation, University of California.*

LAWLER, E. E. (1967), 'Secrecy about management compensation: are there hidden costs?', *Org. Behav. hum. Perf.*, vol. 2, pp. 182–9.

LAWLER, E. E., and O'GARA, P. W. (1967), 'The effects of inequity produced by underpayment on work output, work quality, and attitudes toward the work', *J. appl. Psychol.*, vol. 51, pp. 403–10.

LAWLER, E. E., and PORTER, L. W. (1963), 'Perceptions regarding management compensation', *Indust. Rel.*, vol. 3, pp. 41–9.

LEVENTHAL, G. S. (1964), Reward magnitude and liking for instrumental activity: further test of a two-process model, *Unpublished Manuscript, Yale University.*

LINDER, D. E. (1965), Some psychological processes which mediate task liking, *Unpublished Doctoral Dissertation, University of Minnesota.*

MAHONEY, T. (1964), 'Compensation preferences of managers', *Indust. Rel.*, vol. 3, pp. 135–44.

MARRIOTT, R. (1949), 'Size of working group and output', *Occup. Psychol.*, vol. 23, pp. 47–57.

MARRIOTT, R. (1951), 'Socio-psychological factors in productivity', *Occup. Psychol.*, vol. 25, pp. 15–24.

MARRIOTT, R. (1957), *Incentive Payment Systems: A Review of Research and Opinion*, Staples Press.

MARRIOTT, R., and DENERLEY, R. A. (1955), 'A method of interviewing used in studies of workers' attitudes: II. Validity of the method and discussion of the results', *Occup. Psychol.*, vol. 29, pp. 69–81.

MILLER, D. C., and FORM, W. H. (1951), *Industrial Sociology*, Harper.

NATIONAL INDUSTRIAL CONFERENCE BOARD (1947), Factors affecting employee morale, *Studies in Personal Policy*, no. 85.

NEALEY, S. (1963), 'Pay and benefit preferences', *Indust. Rel.*, vol. 1, pp. 17–28.

PATCHEN, M. (1961), *The Choice of Wage Comparisons*, Prentice-Hall.

PORTER, L. W. (1962), 'Job attitudes in management: I. Perceived deficiencies in need fulfillment as a function of job level', *J. appl. Psychol.* vol. 46, pp. 375–84.

RATH, A. A. (1960), 'The case for individual incentives', *Personn. J.*, vol. 39, pp. 172–5.

157

ROETHLISBERGER, F. J., and DICKSON, W. J. (1939), *Management and the Worker*, Harvard U.P.

RYAN, R. A., and SMITH, P. C. (1954), *Principles of Industrial Psychology*, Ronald Press.

SAYLES, L. R. (1958), *Behavior of Industrial Work Groups: Prediction and Control*, Wiley.

SCHLEH, E. C. (1961), *Management by Results: The Dynamics of Profitable Management*, McGraw-Hill.

SELEKMAN, B. M. (1941), 'Living with collective bargaining', *Harv. bus. Rev.*, vol. 22, pp. 21–3.

SHIMMIN, S., WILLIAMS, J., and BUCK, L. (1956), Studies of some factors in incentive payment systems, *Report to the Medical Research Council, Industrial Psychology Research Group* (mimeo.).

SKINNER, B. F. (1953), *Science and Human Behavior*, Macmillan, New York.

SMITH, P. C. (1955), 'The prediction of individual differences in susceptibility to industrial monotony', *J. appl. Psychol.*, vol. 39, pp. 322–9.

SMITH, P. C., and KENDALL, L. M. (1963), Cornell studies of job satisfaction: VI. Implications for the future, *Unpublished Manuscript, Cornell University*.

SPRIEGEL, W. R., and DALE, A. G. (1953), 'Trends in personnel selection and induction', *Personnel*, vol. 30, pp. 169–75.

STOUFFER, S. A., SUCHMAN, E. A., DeVINNEY, L. C., STAR, S. A., and WILLIAMS, R. M. (1949), *The American Soldier: Adjustment during Army Life*, vol. 1, Princeton U.P.

THOMPSON, W. A. (1939), 'Eleven years after graduation', *Occupations*, vol. 17, pp. 709–14.

VERPLANCK, W. S., and HAYES, J. R. (1953), 'Eating and drinking as a function of maintenance schedule', *J. comp. physiol. Psychol.*, vol. 46, pp. 327–33.

VITELES, M. S. (1953), *Motivation and Morale in Industry*, Norton.

VROOM, V. H. (1964), *Work and Motivation*, Wiley. [See Reading 16.]

WATSON, G. (1939), 'Work satisfaction', in G. W. Hartmann and T. Newcomb (eds.), *Industrial Conflict*, Cordon Co., pp. 114–24.

WEICK, K. E. (1966), 'The concept of equity in the perception of pay', *Admin. Sci. Quart.*, vol. 11, pp. 414–39.

WEICK, K. E., and PENNER, D. D. (1965), Comparison of two sources of inadequate and excessive justification, *Unpublished Manuscript, Purdue University*.

WHYTE, W. F. (1952), 'Economic incentives and human relations', *Harv. bus. Rev.*, vol. 30, pp. 73–80.

WHYTE, W. F. (1955), *Money and Motivation: An Analysis of Incentives in Industry*, Harper.

WIKE, E. L., and BARRIENTOS, G. (1958), 'Secondary reinforcement and multiple drive reduction', *J. comp. physiol. Psychol.*, vol. 51, pp. 640–3.

WILKINS, L. T. (1949), 'Incentives and the young worker', *Occup. Psychol.*, vol. 23, pp. 235–47.

WILKINS, L. T. (1950), 'Incentives and the young male worker in England', *Intern. J. opin, attit. Res.*, vol. 4, pp. 541–62.

WOLFE, J. B. (1936), 'Effectiveness of token-rewards for chimpanzees', *Comp. Psychol. Monog.*, vol. 12, pp. 1–72.

WORTHY, J. C. (1950), 'Factors influencing employee morale', *Harv. bus. Rev.*, vol. 28, pp. 61–73.

WYATT, S. (1934), Incentives in repetitive work: a practical experiment in a factory, *Industrial Health Research Board Report*, no. 69, H.M.S.O.

WYATT, S., and FRASER, J. A. (1929), The comparative effects of variety and uniformity in work, *Industrial Fatigue Research Board Report*, no. 52, H.M.S.O.

WYATT, S., FRASER, J. A., and STOCK, G. F. L. (1929). The effects of monotony in work, *Industrial Fatigue Research Board Report*, no. 56, H.M.S.O.

WYATT, S., and LANGDON, J. N. (1937), Fatigue and boredom in repetitive work, *Industrial Health Research Board Report*, no. 77, H.M.S.O.

WYATT, S., and MARRIOTT, R. (1956), *A Study of Attitudes to Factory Work*, H.M.S.O.

ZALEZNIK, A., CHRISTENSEN, C. R., and ROETHLISBERGER, F. J. (1958), *The Motivation, Productivity, and Satisfaction of Workers: A Prediction Study*, Harvard University, Graduate School of Business Administration.

11 Edward E. Lawler, III

Job Design and Employee Motivation

Edward E. Lawler, III, 'Job design and employee motivation', *Personnel Psychology*, vol. 22, 1969, pp. 426–35.

The psychological literature on employee motivation contains many claims that changes in job design can be expected to produce better employee job performance. Very few of these claims, however, are supported by an explanation of why changes in job design should be expected to affect performance except to indicate that they can affect employee motivation. Thus, I would like to begin by considering the *why* question with respect to job design and employee performance. That is, I want to focus on the reasons for expecting changes in job design to affect employee motivation and performance. Once this question is answered, predictions will be made about the effects on performance of specific changes in job design (e.g. job enlargement and job rotation).

A Theory of Motivation

Basic to any explanation of why people behave in a certain manner is a theory of motivation. As Jones (1959) has pointed out, motivation theory attempts to explain 'how behavior gets started, is energized, is sustained, is directed, is stopped and what kind of subjective reaction is present in the organism'. The theory of motivation that will be used to understand the effects of job design is 'expectancy theory'. Georgopoulos, Mahoney and Jones (1957), Vroom (1964) and others have recently stated expectancy theories of job performance. The particular expectancy theory that will be used in this paper is based upon this earlier work and has been more completely described elsewhere (e.g. Lawler and Porter, 1967; Porter and Lawler, 1968). According to this theory, an employee's motivation to perform effectively is determined by two variables. The first of these is contained in the concept of an effort-reward probability. This is the individual's subjective probability that directing a given amount of effort towards performing effectively will result in his obtaining a given reward or positively valued outcome. This effort-reward probability is determined by two subsidiary subjective probabilities: the probability that effort will result in performance and the probability that performance will result in the reward. Vroom refers to the first of these subjective probabilities as an 'expectancy' and to the second as an 'instrumentality'.

The second variable that is relevant here is the concept of reward value or valence. This refers to the individual's perception of the value of the reward or outcome that might be obtained by performing effectively. Although most expectancy theories do not specify why certain outcomes have reward value, for the purpose of this paper I would like to argue that the reward value of outcomes stems from their perceived ability to satisfy one or more needs. Specifically relevant here is the list of needs suggested by Maslow that includes security needs, social needs, esteem needs and self-actualization needs.

The evidence indicates that, for a given reward, reward value and the effort-reward probability combine multiplicatively in order to determine an individual's motivation. This means that if either is low or non-existent then no motivation will be present. As an illustration of this point, consider the case of a manager who very much values getting promoted but who sees no relationship between working hard and getting promoted. For him, promotion is not serving as a motivator just as it is not for a manager who sees a close connexion between being promoted and working hard but who doesn't want to be promoted. In order for motivation to be present, the manager must both value promotion and see the relationship between his efforts and promotion. Thus, for an individual reward or outcome the argument is that a multiplicative combination of its value and the appropriate effort-reward probability is necessary. However, an individual's motivation is influenced by more than one outcome. Thus, in order to determine an individual's motivation it is necessary to combine data concerned with a number of different outcomes. This can be done for an individual worker by considering all the outcomes he values and then by summing the products obtained from multiplying the value of these outcomes to him by their respective effort-reward probabilities.

According to this theory, if changes in job design are going to affect an individual's motivation they must either change the value of the outcomes that are seen to depend upon effort or positively affect the individual's beliefs about the probability that certain outcomes are dependent upon effort. The argument in this paper is that job design changes can have a positive effect on motivation, because they can change an individual's beliefs about the probability that certain rewards will result from putting forth high levels of effort. They can do this because they have the power to influence the probability that certain rewards will be seen to result from good performance, not because they can influence the perceived probability that effort will result in good performance. Stated in Vroom's language, the argument is that job design changes are more likely to affect the instrumentality of good performance than to affect the expectancy that effort will lead to performance.

But before elaborating on this point, it is important to distinguish between two kinds of rewards. The first type are those that are extrinsic to the individual. These rewards are part of the job situation and are given by others. Hence, they are externally mediated and are rewards that can best be thought of as satisfying lower-order needs. The second type of rewards are intrinsic to the individual and stem directly from the performance itself. These rewards are internally mediated since the individual rewards himself. These rewards can be thought of as satisfying higher-order needs such as self-esteem and self-actualization. They involve such outcomes as feelings of accomplishment, feelings of achievement and feelings of using and developing one's skills and abilities. The fact that these rewards are internally mediated sets them apart from the extrinsic rewards in an important way. It means that the connexion between their reception and performance is more direct than is the connexion between the reception of externally mediated rewards and performance. Hence potentially they can be excellent motivators because higher effort-reward probabilities can be established for them than can be established for extrinsic rewards. They also have the advantage that for many people rewards of this nature have a high positive value.

Job content is the critical determinant of whether employees believe that good performance on the job leads to feelings of accomplishment, growth and self-esteem. That is whether individuals will find jobs to be intrinsically motivating. Job content is important here because it serves a motive arousal function where higher-order needs are concerned and because it influences what rewards will be seen to stem from good performance. Certain tasks are more likely to arouse motives like achievement and self-actualization, and to generate among individuals who have these motives the belief that successful performance will result in outcomes that involve feelings of achievement and growth. It is precisely because changes in job content can affect the relationship between performance and the reception of intrinsically rewarding outcomes that it can have a strong influence on motivation and performance.

There appear to be three characteristics which jobs must possess if they are to arouse higher-order needs and to create conditions such that people who perform them will come to expect that good performance will lead to intrinsic rewards. The first is that the individual must receive meaningful feedback about his performance. This may well mean the individual must himself evaluate his own performance and define the kind of feedback that he is to receive. It may also mean that the person may have to work on a whole product or a meaningful part of it. The second is that the job must be perceived by the individual as requiring him to use abilities that he values in order for him to perform the job effectively. Only if an individual feels that his significant abilities are being tested by a job can feelings of accomplishment and growth be expected to result from good performance. Several laboratory studies have, in fact, shown that when people are given tasks that they see as testing their valued abilities, greater motivation does appear (e.g. Alper, 1964; French, 1955). Finally, the individual must feel he has a high degree of self-control over setting his own goals and over defining the paths to these goals. As Argyris (1964) points out, only if this condition exists will people experience psychological 'success' as a result of good performance.

Thus, it appears that the answer to the *why* question can be found in the ability of job design factors to influence employees' perceptions of the probability that good performance will be intrinsically rewarding. Certain job designs apparently encourage the perception that it will, while others do not, and because of this job design factors can determine how motivating a job will be.

Job Design Changes

Everyone seems to agree that the typical assembly-line job is not likely to fit any of the characteristics of intrinsically motivating jobs. That is, it is not likely to provide meaningful knowledge of results, to test valued abilities or to encourage self-control. Much attention has been focused recently on attempts to enlarge assembly-line jobs, and there is good reason to believe that this can lead to a situation where jobs are more intrinsically motivating. However, many proponents of job enlargement have failed to distinguish between two different kinds of job enlargement. Jobs can be enlarged on both the horizontal dimension and the vertical dimension. The horizontal dimension refers to the number and variety of the operations that an individual performs on the job. The vertical dimension refers to the degree to which the job holder controls the planning and execution of his job and participates in the setting of organization policies. The utility man on the assembly line has a job that is horizontally but not vertically enlarged, while the worker whom Argyris (1964) suggests can participate in decision making about his job while he continues to work on the assembly line, has a vertically but not a horizontally enlarged job.

The question that arises is, what kind of job enlargement is necessary if the job is going to provide intrinsic motivation? The answer that is suggested by the three factors that are necessary for a task to be motivating, is that jobs must be enlarged both vertically and horizontally. It is hard to see in terms of the theory why the utility man will see more connexion between performing well and intrinsic rewards than will the assembly-line worker. The utility man typically has no more self-control, only slightly more knowledge of results and only a slightly greater chance to test his valued abilities. Hence, for him, good performance should be only slightly more rewarding than it would be for the individual who works in one location on the line. In fact, it would seem that jobs can be over-enlarged on the horizontal dimension so that they will be less motivating than they were originally. Excessive

164

horizontal enlargement may well lead to a situation where meaningful feedback is impossible and where the job involves using many additional abilities that the worker does not value. The worker who is allowed to participate in some decisions about his work on the assembly line can hardly be expected to perceive that intrinsic rewards will stem from performing well on the line. His work on the line is still not under his control, he is not likely to get very meaningful feedback about it and his valued abilities still are not being tested by it. Thus, for him it is hard to see why he should feel that intrinsic rewards will result from good performance.

On the other hand, we should expect that a job which is both horizontally and vertically enlarged will be a job that motivates people to perform well. For example, the workers who, as Kuriloff (1966) has described, make a whole electronic instrument, check and ship it should be motivated by their jobs. This kind of job does provide meaningful feedback, it does allow for self-control and there is a good chance that it will be seen as testing valued abilities. It does not, however, guarantee that the person will see it as testing his valued abilities since we don't know what the person's valued abilities are. In summary, then, the argument is that if job enlargement is to be successful in increasing motivation, it must be enlargement that affects both the horizontal and the vertical dimensions of the job. In addition, individual differences must be taken into consideration in two respects. First and most obviously, it must only be tried with people who possess higher-order needs that can be aroused by the job design and who, therefore, will value intrinsic rewards. Second, individuals must be placed on jobs that test their valued abilities.

Let me address myself to the question of how the increased motivation, that can be generated by an enlarged job, will manifest itself in terms of behavior. Obviously, the primary change that can be expected is that the individual will devote more effort to performing well. But will this increased effort result in higher quality work, higher productivity, or both? I think this question can be answered by looking at the reasons that we gave for job content being able to affect motivation. The argument was that it does this by affecting whether intrinsic rewards will be seen to come from successful performance. It would seem that high quality work is indispensable if most individuals are to feel that they have performed well and are to experience feelings of accomplishment, achievement and self-actualization. The situation is much less clear with respect to productivity. It does not seem at all certain that an individual must produce great quantities of a product in order to feel that he has performed well. In fact, many individuals probably obtain more satisfaction from producing one very high quality product than they do from producing a number of lower quality products.

There is a second factor that may cause job enlargement to be more likely to lead to higher work quality than to higher productivity. This has to do with the advantages of division of labor and mechanization. Many job enlargement changes create a situation where, because of the losses in terms of machine assistance and optimal human movements, people actually have to put forth more energy in order to produce at the pre-job enlargement rate. Thus, people may be in effect working harder but producing less. It seems less likely that the same dilemma would arise in terms of work quality and job enlargement. That is, it would seem that if extra effort is devoted to quality, after job enlargement takes place the effort is likely to be translated into improved quality. This would come about because the machine assistance and other features of the assembly-line jobs are more of an aid in bringing about high productivity than they are in bringing about high quality.

The Research Evidence

There have been a number of studies that have attempted to measure the effect of job enlargement programs. Thus, it is possible to determine if the evidence supports the contention stated previously that both horizontal and vertical job enlargement are necessary if intrinsic motivation is to be increased. Also it can be determined if the effects of any increased motivation will be more likely to result in higher quality work than in high productivity.

In a literature search, reports of ten studies were found where jobs had been enlarged on both the horizontal and the vertical dimensions. Table 1 presents a brief summary of the results of these studies. As can be seen, every study shows that job enlargement did have some positive effect since every study reports that

Table 1

Research study	Higher quality	Higher productivity
Biggane and Stewart (1963)	yes	no
Conant and Kilbridge (1965) Kilbridge (1960)	yes	no
Davis and Valfer (1965)	yes	no
Davis and Werling (1960)	yes	yes
Elliott (1953)	yes	yes
Guest (1957)	yes	no
Kuriloff (1966)	yes	yes
Marks (1954)	yes	no
Rice (1953)	yes	yes
Walker (1950)	yes	no

job enlargement resulted in higher quality work. However, only four out of ten studies report that job enlargement led to higher productivity. This provides support for the view that the motivational effects produced by job enlargement are more likely to result in higher quality work than in higher productivity.

There are relatively few studies that have enlarged jobs only on either the horizontal or the vertical dimensions so it is difficult to test the predictions that both kinds of enlargement are necessary if motivation is to be increased. There are a few studies which have been concerned with the effects of horizontal job enlargement (e.g. Walker and Guest, 1952) while others have stressed its advantages. However, most of these studies have been concerned with its effects on job satisfaction rather than its effects on motivation. None of these studies appears to show that horizontal enlargement tends to increase either productivity or work quality. Walker and Guest, for example, talk about the higher satisfaction of the utility men but they do not report that they work harder. Thus, with respect to horizontal job enlargement the evidence does not lead to rejecting the view that it must be combined with vertical in order to increase production.

The evidence with respect to whether vertical job enlargement alone can increase motivation is less clear. As Argyris (1964) has pointed out, the Scanlon plan has stressed this kind of job enlargement with some success. However, it is hard to tell if this success stems from people actually becoming more motivated to perform their own jobs better. It is quite possible that improvements under the plan are due to better over-all decision making rather than to increased motivation. Vroom (1964) has analysed the evidence with respect to the degree to which participation in decision making *per se* leads to increased motivation. This evidence is suggestive of the fact that vertical job enlargement can lead to increased motivation when it leads to employees committing themselves to higher production goals.

Perhaps the crucial distinction here is whether the participation involves matters of company policy or whether it involves matters directly related to the employees' work process. Participation of the former type would seem to be much less likely to lead to increased motivation than would participation of the latter type. Thus, it seems to be crucial to distinguish between two quite different types of vertical job enlargement, only one of which leads to increased motivation. Considered together the evidence suggests that of the two types of job enlargement vertical is relatively more important that horizontal. Perhaps this is because it can lead to a situation where subjects do feel that their abilities are being tested and where they can exercise self-control even though horizontal enlargement does not take place. Still, the evidence with respect to situations where both types of enlargement have been jointly installed shows that much more consistent improvements in motivation can be produced by both than can be produced by vertical alone.

Summary

In summary, it has been argued that when jobs are structured in a way that makes intrinsic rewards appear to result from good performance then the jobs themselves can be very effective motivators. In addition, the point was made that if job content is to be a source of motivation, the job must allow for meaningful feedback, test the individual's valued abilities and allow a great amount of self-control by the job holder. In order for this to happen, jobs must be enlarged on both the vertical and horizontal dimensions. Further, it was predicted that job enlargement is more likely to lead to increased quality than to increased productivity. A review of the literature on job enlargement generally tended to confirm these predictions.

References

ALPER, T. G. (1964), 'Task-orientation *v.* ego-orientation in learning and retention', *Amer. J. Psychol.*, vol. 38, pp. 224–38.

ARGYRIS, C. (1964), *Integrating the Individual and the Organization,* Wiley.

BIGGANE, J. F., and STEWART, P. A. (1963), Job enlargement: a case study, *Research Series, Bureau of Labor and Management, State University of Iowa*, vol. 25.

CONANT, E. H., and KILBRIDGE, M. D. (1965), 'An interdisciplinary analysis of job enlargement: technology, costs, and behavioral implications', *Indust. Lab. Rel. Rev.*, vol. 18, pp. 377–95.

DAVIS, L. E., and VALFER, E. S. (1965), 'Intervening responses to changes in supervisor job designs', *Occup. Psychol.*, vol. 39, pp. 171–89.

DAVIS, L. E., and WERLING, R. (1960), 'Job design factors', *Occup. Psychol.*, vol. 34, pp. 109–32.

ELLIOT, J. D. (1953), 'Increasing office productivity through job enlargement', The human side of the office manager's job, *A.M.A. Office Management Series*, no. 134, pp. 5–15.

FRENCH, E. G. (1955), 'Some characteristics of achievement motivation', *J. Psychol.*, vol. 50, pp. 232–6.

GEORGOPOULOS, B. S., MAHONEY, G. M., and JONES, N. W. (1957), 'A path–goal approach to productivity', *J. appl. Psychol.*, vol. 41, pp. 345–53. [Reading 17.]

GUEST, R. H. (1957), 'Job enlargement: a revolution in job design', *Pers. Admin.*, vol. 20, pp. 9–16.

JONES, M. R. (ed.) (1959), *Nebraska Symposium on Motivation*, Nebraska U.P., vol. 7.

KILBRIDGE, M. D. (1960), 'Reduced costs through job enlargement: a case', *J. Bus.*, vol. 33, pp. 357–62.

KURILOFF, A. H. (1966), *Reality in Management*, McGraw-Hill.

LAWLER, E. E., and PORTER, L. W. (1967), 'Antecedent attitudes of effective managerial performance', *Org. Behav. hum. Perf.*, vol. 2, pp. 122–42. [See Reading 18.]

MARKS, A. R. N. (1954), An investigation of modifications of job design in an industrial situation and their effects on some measures of economic productivity, *Unpublished Ph.D. Dissertation, University of California.*

PORTER, L. W., and LAWLER, E. E. (1968), *Managerial Attitudes and Performance*, Irwin-Dorsey.

RICE, A. K. (1953), 'Productivity and social organization in an Indian weaving-shed', *Hum. Rel.*, vol. 6, pp. 297–329.

VROOM, V. H. (1964), *Work and Motivation*, Wiley. [See Reading 16.]

WALKER, C. R. (1950), 'The problem of the repetitive job', *Harv. bus. Rev.*, vol. 28, pp. 54–9.

WALKER, C. R., and GUEST, R. M. (1952), *The Man on the Assembly Line*, Harvard U.P.

12 Michael Argyle, Godfrey Gardner and Frank Cioffi

Supervisory Methods Related to Productivity, Absenteeism and Labour Turnover

Abridged from Michael Argyle, Godfrey Gardner and Frank Cioffi,
'Supervisory methods related to productivity, absenteeism, and labour
turnover', *Human Relations*, vol. 11, 1958, pp. 23–40.

Introduction

In a previous paper (4) the problems of measuring supervisory methods were discussed, and our measuring devices described. The present paper reports an investigation of ninety foremen in eight British factories manufacturing electric motors and switchgear. The aim was to discover the influence of five 'human relations' dimensions of foremanship, the degree of training of foremen and the size of working group. Our performance or 'organizational effectiveness' measures were output, measured in time-study units, voluntary absenteeism and labour turnover. The statistical comparison method was used, wherein matched departments were compared on all the variables listed above: how far this can lead to conclusions about causation is discussed below.

The previous research on these problems is reviewed in detail below, but the way this study developed out of the earlier work should perhaps be indicated. In the first place, it was planned as a British replication of earlier American studies, to see whether the same results would be obtained over here. Second, an attempt was made to improve upon previous ways of measuring supervisory behaviour, as described in the previous paper: many of the earlier studies were thought to be deficient in this respect. Third, the additional variables of voluntary absenteeism and labour turnover have been added: these are more objectively measurable than job satisfaction and are directly related to costs. At the same time they may be regarded, to some extent, as indices of job satisfaction, since they are correlated with it (25, 26).

Michael Argyle, Godfrey Gardner and Frank Cioffi

Review of Previous Research

The previous literature will be reviewed in three parts. The first will discuss the evidence concerning the size of differences in productivity between similar departments. There has been a tendency for some writers to cite anecdotal evidence suggesting enormous differences between departments, and it is supposed that these are due to social factors alone. The second section will review the various American studies of supervision, giving evidence for the influence of the five dimensions of supervision included in our study: first, the influence on productivity will be considered; second, the influence on the job satisfaction group of variables. The third part deals with the influence of other variables such as size of working group, training of foremen and sex of workers, all of which are tested in our study.

The extent of productivity differences produced by organizational variables

Despite a widespread belief to the contrary, 'social' factors have never been shown to be of very great significance as determinants of productivity differences between otherwise similar departments. The Hawthorne experiment is sometimes cited as a demonstration of the power of social factors, but as has been shown elsewhere (2), the 30 per cent increase in output could be accounted for entirely by such factors as the change in incentive system, the replacement of the two slowest girls by faster ones and the effects of the experimental rest periods themselves.

The results of some more systematic researches into social factors will now be reported, indicating the extent of the output differences produced. The style of supervision of foremen is discussed in detail later; here the quantitative effects only will be mentioned. Feldman (9) found changes of from 6 per cent to 18 per cent upon changing round a number of office supervisors, and in the Michigan office study an average difference of 10 per cent was found between matched departments with different supervisors. Handyside (14) found an increase of 8 per cent as the result of a training course for foremen. The way in which workers are grouped produces effects of a similar magnitude. Van Zelst (35) found a saving in labour costs of 12 per cent after

171

reorganizing groups of builders so that friends worked together. Marriott (28), in a study of two British motor-car factories, found that the smaller groups worked about 7 per cent faster than the larger ones. To summarize, the effect of supervision and group organization may be expected to lead to differences of the order of 7 per cent to 15 per cent when these factors are changed, or when otherwise similar work groups are compared.

The corresponding figures may now be cited for other sources of variation in productivity. It is not doubted that the introduction of incentive schemes normally leads to a substantial increase, though the amount depends on circumstances. One survey of 514 cases in the United States (30) showed an average increase of 39 per cent; this is probably an overestimation since other favourable changes are often made at the same time, as Viteles points out (36, pp. 29 ff.). On the other hand, *costs* may actually be increased – as a result of extra accounting staff, time-study men, etc. Again, the precise advantage to be gained by the introduction of improved methods of working varies enormously, depending on how inefficient the previous methods were. Fifteen case studies published by the British Productivity Council showed increases varying from 20 per cent to 200 per cent (6). Third, the increases of output per man hour that may result from the introduction of automatic equipment may be on an even greater scale, so that the number of men required on production jobs is cut to a fraction – though, of course, more skilled maintenance men are required. It may be concluded that differences produced by wage incentives, method study and the use of automatic equipment are far greater than those created by social factors.

Finally, the extent of differences in output between individual operatives may be considered. The differences between individuals are often greater than the differences between departments. The relative variability of workers in job proficiency can sometimes be expressed in a best-to-poorest-worker ratio and, where this is very large, productivity would obviously benefit by systematic selection and training. It has been calculated, for instance, that if the selection procedure has a validity of 0·80 and the ratio of best-to-poorest-worker is four to one, then the use of the selection procedure would improve proficiency by 22 per cent – providing that there is no need to select more than twenty out of every

172

hundred applicants. With a higher selection ratio, the resulting gain increases (11, p. 147). We have no figures of actual productivity increases obtained by personnel selection. As regards training, an investigation in 1943–5 in the United States showed that over these two years 63 per cent of the plants reported an improvement of 25 per cent *or over* in production following the introduction of T.W.I. courses (16, p. 198).

To conclude this section, it is clear that the kind of social factor under investigation plays a relatively small part in producing output differences, as compared with the other factors mentioned. However, it must be recognized that the capital outlay necessary for these other changes varies considerably and it may well be that the modest increases following the manipulation of social factors can be obtained at a relatively low cost to the organization and with less risk of disturbing labour relations, though there is no actual evidence for this. Another point in favour of understanding social factors is that an increase of 10 per cent on top of production already doubled by reorganization and new methods is certainly worth having.

The Relation between Various Dimensions of Foreman Behaviour and Organizational Effectiveness

In this section the findings of the most important previous studies will be summarized briefly. These include the Michigan studies of seventy-two foremen in charge of railroad maintenance gangs (24), of twenty-four Prudential Insurance office supervisors (23, 31) and of over 300 supervisors in a Caterpillar Tractor Factory (21, 22). Reference will also be made to a group of studies carried out in California, summarized by Comrey, Pfiffner and High (8).

General supervision was found to be associated with higher output than close supervision in some but not all of these inquiries. Probably there is an optimum degree of closeness depending on the intricacy of the work. On the other hand, several studies point to the conclusion that general supervision is preferred by the workers and is associated with higher job satisfaction.

Pressure for production seems either to be completely unrelated to productivity or to be inversely related to it – as was found in some of the California studies and in the office investigation. In the tractor study it was found that job satisfaction was less with high-pressure supervision.

Foremen who *spend more time on supervision* had more productive sections in the three Michigan studies, although, paradoxically, close supervision was related to low output in these same studies. It seems that to obtain high output a foreman has to tread a narrow path on which he spends a lot of time on supervision and yet does not supervise closely. Job satisfaction is also greater when more time is spent on supervision.

Foremen with relatively greater *power* are in charge of sections with greater productivity and satisfaction, as several of these studies show. Furthermore, this dimension interacts with others in that, for example, democratic supervision may result in *less* satisfaction if the foreman has not sufficient power to satisfy the aspirations for salary and promotion that he may inspire in his men (32).

Employee-centred, as opposed to production-centred supervision, is generally found to be related to high output. There are difficulties here over the validity of the dimension measurements – sometimes the relationship appears when the measure is based on interviews with the foremen but not for measures based on surveys of the men, and vice versa. The result is of some theoretical interest in that foremen who spend their energy on increasing output in fact produce less output than those primarily concerned with the welfare of the men. Job satisfaction is generally higher under employee-centred supervision.

Democratic, as opposed to autocratic, supervision was found to be related to high output in the Michigan studies. However, the actual data could be interpreted otherwise: in the railway study men in low-producing sections actually made more suggestions, but this is interpreted as being due to lack of competence on the part of the foremen (24, pp. 16–17); in the office study foremen gave more complete explanations of new jobs in low-producing sections, but this is interpreted as close, not democratic, supervision (23, pp. 18 f.). Job satisfaction is generally greater under democratic leadership, though authoritarian methods are more tolerated in larger groups (17).

Punitive methods of discipline are associated if anything with

174

low output, as was found in the railway study. There is no evidence that job satisfaction is affected.

The influence of foreman training, group size and sex of workers on organizational effectiveness

There is little evidence concerning the influence of *foreman training* on the output of their sections. Handyside (14) did find an 8 per cent increase in a before-and-after study of forty supervisors. However, he suggests that this increase may really have been due to increased cooperation between the foremen and the production-planning department. There is no convincing evidence that training foremen increases output, though possibly improved training methods might show better results. Other studies have been concerned with the effect of training on the style of supervision used by the foremen. Castle (7) found significant improvements in scores on his attitude scale for some courses, but not for others. Fleishman (10), in a study of 122 foremen at International Harvester, found that a training course made little difference to style of supervision, though this *was* influenced by the style of the foreman's own superior.

Productivity has not been found to vary much with group size, except in the special case of group incentive schemes. Marriott (28), in a study of 251 such groups in two motor-car factories, found that groups of less than ten in size produced about 7 per cent more than groups of over thirty. It is understandable that group bonus schemes would become ineffective for larger groups; furthermore, in the case of motor-car assembly lines the group would depend on the speed of the slowest worker – there is a statistically greater chance that he will be slower in larger groups. Despite a general belief among social psychologists in the superiority of small groups, there is no evidence that this is manifested in greater output.

As far as *sex differences* are concerned the output of men is generally assumed to be higher than that of women, though there is little conclusive published evidence on this. Probably the difference will vary widely between different kinds of work and for some kinds women will do better.

Job satisfaction has sometimes been studied in relation to these variables, though there are more studies of voluntary absenteeism and labour turnover. These last were included in our own study, and have been found in the past to be negatively related to job satisfaction (25, 26), and can be regarded as indices for it.

The training of foremen might be expected to have more influence on job satisfaction than on output, at least in so far as human relations training is concerned. Hariton (15) investigated this problem in a power station, but found no significant increase of job satisfaction; there was some evidence, however, that job satisfaction increased when the new methods of supervision received support from higher management. Handyside (14) found no change of job satisfaction, absenteeism or labour turnover in his follow-up study of forty supervisors.

Size of group has been found to be directly related to voluntary absenteeism: Hewitt and Parfitt (18) found the percentage of voluntary absenteeism in a car factory to be four times as great in groups of 128 as in groups of four, and proportionately in the intermediate sizes of group. The Acton Society (1) found that absence in coal mines decreased with diminishing size of group down to a group size of fifteen.

Sex differences have often been found in this area, but in different directions for the various criteria. Women have higher job satisfaction than men (16) as indicated by job-satisfaction questionnaires. The absenteeism of women, however, is greater; in Behrend's study (5) of fifty-one factories women's absences averaged 6·5 per cent, men's 3·9 per cent. They also have a higher index of voluntary absenteeism. Women's absences may partly be explained by the fact that women have less skilled jobs, since absenteeism is higher among unskilled workers. It may be due in part to domestic affairs, which impinge on women, especially married women, more than on men.

Labour turnover is nearly twice as great for women as for men on average (27), though this varies considerably between factories, and the difference is occasionally reversed. Scott and Clothier (34) found that although turnover was lower among men of high intelligence, it was not lower among intelligent women; this is probably because the intelligent men were being promoted, but not the women. Long (27) found that pregnancy accounted for only about 5 per cent of women's turnover, and women had much the same amount of turnover as unskilled men: again, it is probably the fact of being unskilled that accounts for the apparently greater turnover.

Hypotheses to be Tested

Various hypotheses were set up before the investigation began, and the results enable these to be tested.

1. All of the five dimensions of foremanship will be related to productivity. Specifically, the successful foremen will be General in their supervision, exert Low Pressure, and be Employee-centred, Democratic and Non-punitive.

2. There will be more influence on output in departments where the men are not paid on a wage incentive; where there is a direct wage incentive people already have an immediate incentive for working harder and less depends on persuasion by the foreman. Some of our departments were paid on a weekly bonus system so that increased effort was rewarded in the following week, whereas others were paid on a 'lieu rate' which depended on the merit rating of the individual, proportionally applied to the average bonus rate of the direct incentive departments in the same factory. Obviously in these 'lieu rate' departments, increased effort may eventually improve a man's merit rating but would not affect the average bonus rate, this being dependent upon the efforts of other workers in the factory.

3. The relation between supervision and output will be more marked in assembly departments than in machine shops, since in the latter output depends largely on the machines and not on the pace or effort of the workers.

4. Some of these foremanship dimensions – not necessarily those found to be related to productivity – will be related to satisfaction as indicated by voluntary absenteeism and labour turnover.

5. Trained foremen will score 'higher' on the five dimensions and will have more efficient departments.

6. Small groups will have lower absenteeism and turnover since satisfaction is usually greater here. However there is no reason to expect that output will be greater in smaller groups.

Method

We decided to use the statistical comparison kind of study as opposed to an experimental study or case study. In other words, we compared a number of foremen and their department at the same point in time, and looked for statistical relationships between our variables. This has the great advantage over the experimental method of not disturbing the behaviour to be investigated – a real danger in industrial research – and of making minimal demands on the managers. We did not simply carry out a single correlation using all the foremen, but eliminated other major sources of variation by comparing only those foremen whose departments were as nearly comparable as possible.

Measurement

Productivity. It is possible to give several different definitions of productivity, but to measure productivity in such a way that comparisons between departments can be made is by no means easy. Kahn and Morse (20) define productivity operationally as 'the number of units of work accomplished during a given time interval'. For our purposes we need to translate this into terms that have psychological meaning and assume, as they did, 'a correspondence between the number of units produced, the amount of work behaviour demonstrated by the individual and the amount of energy expended by the individual in work activity'. Allowances have to be made for the technical efficiency of any machinery that is used, the lay-out of equipment and tools and services performed for the worker either by mechanical devices or by 'unproductive' labour, in transporting supplies of materials and clearing finished articles. It is these inequalities of organizational factors which make inter-department comparisons difficult and inter-firm comparisons well-nigh impossible.

Fortunately some assistance is available where time-study has been applied. Time-study with its derivatives was not designed as a research tool for psychologists but as a basis for the payment of wages by results, as an aid in cost accounting and as a method of improving efficiency within a firm. As a research tool, therefore, it has to be used with considerable caution. Time rates may have been fixed many years ago in some firms and left unaltered, regardless of improvements in factory layout or organization and changes in tools and materials.

This is not the place to explain in detail how time allowances are computed; a brief explanation must suffice. The operation time is taken as the average of a number of 'representative' performances timed with a stop-watch. The speed or effort of the worker is estimated by the observer, relative to an average of sixty work-minutes per hour (or an arbitrary hundred may be taken as average), so that, if a slow or fast worker has been timed, his operation time can be suitably adjusted. This estimate is known as the 'effort rating' and it is highly subjective. Obviously the effort rating should be made *before* and never after the time-study expert[1] has used his stop-watch, but we have seen no evidence that this essential precaution is ever insisted upon. The operation time is multiplied by the effort rating (divided by 60 or 100 as the case may be), thus producing the 'standard time'. To this is added a number of fatigue allowances (in the form of percentages), and the total is the 'time allowed' for the particular operation. This procedure may be used for one 'element' at a time if the job has been broken down into elements in accordance with current practice.

The subjective aspects of this procedure have been emphasized before, the vulnerable points being the estimation of the operator's pace (effort rating) and the nature and amount of allowances to be included. Where time-study has been applied, it is usually possible to compute an average effort rating or bonus percentage for each separate department.

Voluntary absenteeism is often separated from absence due to sickness and other unavoidable causes, on the basis of reasons given for absence. This is highly unsatisfactory in view of the uncertainty as to whether people are telling the truth. Doctors' certificates are hardly more helpful and, in any case, are not required for periods of less than three days. A criterion based on attendance instead of on verbal excuses for absence has been suggested by Hilde Behrend (5). She made use of the fact that absenteeism follows a regular weekly pattern; in the factors she studied, Monday was the worst day and Friday the best. Our

1. 'Time-study engineer' is the usual term but is misleading because he is not usually an engineer nor does he possess any engineering qualifications. 'Time-study man' or 'time-study clerk' does not seem appropriate to his semi-professional status. 'Time-study practitioner' has sometimes been used.

procedure is to find the total absences for each day of the week over a period of six months or a year, and subtract the best from the worst day (dividing by the number of weeks and expressed per hundred workers). We call this the 'Worst Day Index' or WDI. It has been found that whereas total absence is largely due to sickness and varies with age, voluntary absence reflects social factors and is correlated with low job satisfaction.

Labour turnover, or the proportion of people leaving in the course of a year, can be assessed quite simply from the firm's records. We restricted our count to those who left for apparently voluntary causes, in other words we cut out those who were laid off, or who died, retired, became pregnant, etc. – for our purposes these were regarded as *involuntary* leavers. There were, of course, enormous variations between firms in labour turnover as a result of local conditions, but since we were only comparing departments within the same firm this did not affect our calculations. In each firm we eliminated the involuntary leavers as well as those moving to another department: thus essentially the same phenomenon was being measured in each firm, despite variability of practice in keeping such records. Labour turnover, apart from some uncertainty about how many leavers were voluntary, is the simplest of our variables to measure and caused us the least trouble.

The role of the investigator

There has been a great deal of discussion during recent years of the best role for the investigator, so the role adopted during this research should be described. In the first place this was a statistical field study, and the period for which the dependent variables were measured was immediately past. There was no danger therefore of any reaction to experimental variables, or of the men reacting to the presence of the investigator – for the dependent variables would not have been affected. In any case, these variables were assessed from records and our shop-floor appearances were quite brief.

These considerations do not apply however to our study of the foremen themselves, and this must be considered in more detail. Our initial approach to the firms was through the management, and we were looked after throughout by the managers, often a personnel manager. It was they who gave us access to records and helped us in their interpretation, and it was they who introduced us to the foremen. The manager in question, and we ourselves, did our best to make clear to the foremen that we were an independent university research team, and had no connexion with the firm. It was explained that anything said to us would be treated in complete confidence: this promise was kept.

As far as management was concerned we gave them full access to anything we extracted from the records, and to the general results, but told them absolutely nothing that we had obtained by contact with foremen or workers. Although we entered the firm 'on the side of management' it is thought that this did not affect the objectivity of the results.

Results

Differences between matched departments

It would be difficult to find any dimension related to Productivity unless Productivity itself varied sufficiently in our sample.

Our departments were not chosen on the basis of productivity differences – we were more concerned to match departments as far as possible. But we were reasonably lucky. For eighty-five departments we had productivity figures or effort ratings which would be contrasted on the basis of the percentage difference between highest and lowest departments within their respective sections. Where two or three departments were grouped together, the median difference between highest and lowest was 11 per cent; for the lieu rate sections the estimated productivity difference (using managerial estimates) for seven, ten and twelve departments were about 13 per cent between the best and worst departments in the three groups.

For six pairs of departments where productivity figures were available over periods of twelve and twenty-six weeks, it was possible to test the differences by means of Student's t. The result was that four t-values had p less than 0·001 and the remaining two had p at 0·01 and 0·05. We were reasonably satisfied therefore that our productivity differences were sufficiently great to make significant results possible.

Similar comparisons between highest and lowest were made for the twenty-two sets of absenteeism and labour turnover figures. Here the differences were even more striking, and on average the WDI for high-absence groups was three times as great as the WDI for low groups. For labour turnover (LT) the difference was almost as great – on average the high LT rates were 2·7 times those of low LT rates, though part of this difference is due to the fact that eight of our fifty-nine incentive departments had no LT at all. None of the twenty-nine lieu rate departments had any LT and so our comparisons were limited to the incentive departments.

Foremanship dimensions

We started out with the seven dimensions for which previous results have been summarized above. However, as indicated in the previous paper (4) we decided to drop two of these dimensions. 'Power' was dropped through its complete lack of cross-validity – there was actually a negative relation between managerial ratings and ratings based on questions to the foremen. 'Time spent on supervision' was dropped since the foremen found it difficult to give any satisfactory answers on this subject.

For each dimension the foremen were divided into high and low on the basis of a comparison with their opposite numbers, using their average rank-order on the three measures – Interview, Managerial Rating and Foreman Description Preference Test. Their departments were divided in the same way for productivity, for absenteeism and for labour turnover, using average effort rating, the worst day index and labour turnover (annual percentage). This made it possible to test for homogeneity by means of a 2 × 2 chi-square. The null hypothesis – that there is no relationship between the pair of variables being examined – is rejected at the 5 per cent level when the chi-square is 3·841 or more. Chi-squares less than 3·841 are regarded as not significant but if they exceed 2·706 (i.e. could have been obtained by chance ten times in every hundred) they are regarded in this paper as indicating a possible tendency. Yates's correction was applied in every case.

The data were tested separately for the incentive and lieu rate departments, and also for the combined results.

Productivity (*separate dimensions*). For the incentive departments no single dimension was significant; in lieu rate departments, dimensions V (Democratic) and VI (Non-punitive) discriminated significantly in the expected direction, i.e. foremen in charge of high-producing sections were found to be significantly more Democratic and less Punitive than the comparable foremen of low-producing sections. Combining results from all departments showed only the dimension VI to be significant in this way. This was due to a strong relationship in the assembly departments ($p < 0.01$); in winding and machine departments chi-square was not significant.

Productivity (*combined dimensions*). In our previous paper we showed some evidence for cross-validity in the measurement of dimensions I (General), V and VI, but none for II (Low Pressure) and IV (Employee-centred). It was, therefore, thought worthwhile combining scores on dimensions I, V and VI to produce a 'human relations' or HR score. The results were significant in the expected direction for lieu rate departments and all departments, but not for incentive departments separately. This confirmed our prediction that certain 'human relations' dimensions would be more important for departments not on a direct bonus scheme than for direct incentive departments. However, the output for the lieu rate departments (i.e. those not on a direct incentive) was not measured by time-study but by ratings by the managers – the same managers, who had contributed to the measurement of foremen dimensions. Could our result have been due to lack of independence of measures? On the whole this seems unlikely since (a) the managerial ratings constituted only one out of three measures of supervisory behaviour, (b) the other two measures correlated reasonably highly with them and (c) the managers did not know which end of our dimensions was related to high output and, if anything, supposed the 'wrong' ends to be so related.

Secondly, it was also predicted that these dimensions would be more important in assembly departments than in others. In so far as the chi-square for all assembly departments was 3·40 (*p* slightly greater than 0·05) with high foremen relatively higher on

183

HR score, but only 0·347 (non-significant) for other departments, this too was confirmed.

It is worth inquiring how much of the variance of output between our equated departments can be ascribed to the style of supervision. In the case of the three groups of lieu rate departments correlations were worked out between the output and combined scores on dimensions I, V and VI. The average correlation, by z-transformation, is 0·43, corresponding to 18·5 per cent of the variance.

Absenteeism. Only dimension V (Democratic) showed any significance; this was for lieu rate departments ($p < 0.02$), for all departments together ($p < 0.05$), and for all assembly departments ($p < 0.01$). In each of these cases, low absenteeism was related to Democratic supervision. The combination of dimensions produced no significant results.

Labour turnover. There were no significant results taking dimensions separately or in combination.

Summary on foreman dimensions

From this it would appear that foremen of high-producing sections exercised General rather than Close supervision and were relatively more Democratic and Non-punitive than foremen of low-producing sections. No combination of dimensions appeared to be related to either absenteeism or labour turnover. By itself dimension V was significant, Democratic supervision being related to low absenteeism, especially in lieu rate departments and assembly departments.

Other foreman variables

Two other 'foreman' variables on which we were able to obtain data were the extent of training and length of service as foremen. We did not ask for their age but, in general, this may be regarded as closely related to length of service. We found no evidence that training was related to organizational effectiveness, with one exception. There was a tendency for absenteeism to be lower in those lieu rate sections where the foreman had received training.

The effect of training on supervisory practices has nowhere been shown very clearly. In our study we took account only of the *extent* to which a foreman had received training, regardless of whether this was mainly technical or psychological. We had the impression that most courses, however short, included some instruction on 'human relations' and an enlightened approach to the problems of supervising workers. In our measurement of the five foreman dimensions we could find no evidence that trained foremen were any different in these respects from untrained foremen.

Similarly, length of service as a foreman did not appear to be related to anything that we could measure.

Other variables of the work-group

With one exception the size of the department or section was not related to productivity. Among lieu rate sections it was the larger groups that had the highest productivity ratings. However, the range of size was not very great, since the largest sections had only ten men each.

The same precaution must be observed in reporting the relation between size and absenteeism. Again it was the larger lieu rate section that had the best records (lowest absenteeism). This same trend in the incentive departments was not significant but owing to the lieu rate sections the result was significant at the 5 per cent level for all departments combined. No relationship between Size and labour turnover was discovered.

When sections were divided into three sizes, under 20, 20-30, over 30, regardless of the type of operation, a curvilinear relationship emerged showing that absenteeism was highest in the middle range, 20-30.

In some cases it was possible to compare departments composed mainly of men with those composed mainly of women, but no significant results emerged.

Relations between the dependent variables. The relations between each pair of dependent variables were tested by means of chi-square. There was no relation between productivity and absenteeism, or between absenteeism and labour turnover. However productivity and labour turnover were associated at the 5 per cent level of significance. The direction of this relationship was that *high* productivity went with *low* labour turnover. This result only held for the assembly departments – all other departments being equally distributed in the four cells.

Discussion

How does foreman behaviour influence output?

If it is accepted that certain kinds of supervision on the part of the foreman influence output, the problem then arises of explaining why this occurs.

It would be expected on the basis of common sense and of other psychological results that persuasion or social influence to work harder would produce more work. In fact this does not happen. Some earlier work reviewed above found a significantly negative relation between output and the dimensions Pressure and Production-centred. We found no relation at all between output and these dimensions, though we experienced difficulty in measuring the dimensions satisfactorily. Where the negative relation is obtained it looks as if persuasion to work harder has a boomerang effect, and actually produces the opposite of what was intended. However, all the research on this dimension has been carried out on workers paid on an incentive basis: it would be expected that persuasion would be more effective where there is no wage incentive.

Another explanation sometimes given for the effectiveness of different kinds of foreman, is that some foremen keep the men happy and that they work harder in consequence. The main objection to this theory is a logical one – job satisfaction cannot be regarded as a *cause* of output, but only as a parallel dependent variable: it is not possible to manipulate one independently of the other, but only to change causal variables that affect them both. Secondly, this theory implies that job satisfaction and output are positively related. Not only is this not generally the case, but in some studies they have been found to be negatively related (3, pp. 171–3). Halpin and Winer (13), for example, found that the leadership dimensions which increased efficiency in aircrews reduced satisfaction, and vice versa. Quite another type of explanation would be to account for the joint influence of foremanship on output and satisfaction. For example, punitiveness was found in this and previous studies to be related to low output. If it is supposed that punitiveness creates frustration, and that this in turn leads to some kind of aggression, then low ouput could be regarded as a form of aggression against the company and the foreman.

So far nothing has been said that would explain the finding that Democratic and General supervision lead to high output. As was stated above, other studies found General supervision to be effective, with the exception of railroad gangs. Democratic supervision has also usually been found to be related to high output. This means that men work harder when they are left to themselves and when they are allowed to have a say in what happens. Parallel evidence is provided from the various studies of the use of group decision methods in raising industrial output. The explanation may be that men work better when they can use their own method of working; this seems very doubtful when one considers the whole method-study movement. It may simply be a basic phenomenon in the psychology of work that men work harder when they are able to make some decision about how the work is done.

The direction of causation

It was found in this study that productivity is higher when the foreman has a certain style of supervision. What can be inferred about the causal process from this? There are three main possibilities, which are not mutually exclusive: (a) men work harder when supervised in certain ways; (b) foremen supervise differently when their men work hard; (c) there are some independent factors which produce both harder work and particular methods of supervision – for example, the existence of certain kinds of layout or equipment. Our results are, of course, perfectly compatible with all three interpretations. The only way of deciding definitely which process is taking place, wholly, or predominantly, is to do experiments: if the experimental variable is effective it can then be regarded as causal.

There are several previous experimental studies of leadership that are relevant here. The only one using foremen is that of Feldman (9) who studied an office where the supervisors of clerks were moved round. He found that the output of the sections

187

changed so that the rank-order of supervisors in relation to output of their sections remained the same: changes of output varied from 6 per cent to 18 per cent. There are several other investigations of groups of children and students that show that the style of supervision can influence the work done.

There is only one investigation in which the output of the groups has been treated as the experimental variable. Jackson (19) studied the behaviour of foremen who were moved to groups of different output and found no change in their style of supervision – as reported by the men. There is therefore no positive evidence that output is effective as a causal variable.

Are there any factors that are able to influence output and style of supervision simultaneously, thus creating an apparent relation between them? None has been shown to act in this way, but this still remains a real possibility.

In the present state of knowledge it seems most likely that the first process is operating – i.e. that the style of supervision is the cause of output differences. The second process seems unlikely, but the third is a possibility which could only be eliminated by experimentation.

Discussion of the negative results on absenteeism and labour turnover

Absenteeism was significantly (inversely) related to Democratic foremanship but not to the other foremanship dimensions. It is surprising that the General dimension was not related to absenteeism in view of the very large differences between equated departments. Previous work found a relation between General and high job satisfaction, but there have been no significant findings on Non-punitive. One explanation might be that the WDI is not a valid measure of voluntary absenteeism. We found that it was not higher among women than men, and that it was not higher in the larger lieu rate groups, both of these findings being contrary to previous results. A high score on the WDI may be a function of the size of the group. In a very small group one man absent on the odd day or two can substantially increase the WDI. In larger groups there is a statistically greater chance that odd days off will scatter randomly over the week; this might even result from mutual agreement among the men in order to avoid, say, two or three men out of ten being absent on the same day. Nevertheless it may be true that the optimum size of a non-incentive group is nearer to ten than to five.

Labour turnover, which varied in a ratio of 2·7 : 1 within the equated groups of departments, was not related to the foreman-ship dimensions or to size of groups. In the lieu rate departments there was no turnover at all during the six-month period studied: these men liked the method of payment and earned bonus without any sense of pressure, the work was not repetitive and the groups were small. Although there is little previous evidence that labour turnover and supervision are related, such a relationship was anticipated in view of the joint relationship of these variables to job satisfaction. Our results indicate therefore that for incentive departments, the behaviour of the foreman is not a significant factor in labour turnover. Previous results show a relation between turnover and size. We found a tendency for small groups to have a lower turnover, but this was not significant.

Summary

1. Ninety working groups with foremen were compared in matched batches of 2–15 groups for: (a) five dimensions of supervisory behaviour; (b) size of group; (c) training of foremen; (d) sex of operatives; (e) voluntary absenteeism; and (f) labour turnover.

2. The equated departments varied by 1 per cent to 27 per cent in productivity, and in a ratio of 1 : 3 on the index of voluntary absenteeism and 1 : 2·7 in labour turnover.

3. Taking all departments together, only the Non-punitive dimension was significantly related to productivity. A combination of General Democratic and Non-punitive tendencies was related to high output at the 0·01 level, accounting for 18·5 per cent of the variance.

4. The above relationship was more marked in departments not on a wage incentive and not on machine-paced work.

5. Absenteeism was less under Democratic foremen, but was not related to the other dimensions of supervision. Labour turnover was not related to supervision at all.

6. Training of foremen was not related to any of the effectiveness variables, nor did trained foremen display a different style of supervision from untrained foremen.

7. Size of group was not markedly related to the effectiveness variables, save that absenteeism was lowest over the range 20–30.

8. No difference between men and women appeared on the effectiveness variables.

9. High productivity was associated with low labour turnover in assembly departments.

References
1. ACTON SOCIETY TRUST, *Size and Morale*, London, 1953.
2. M. ARGYLE, 'The relay assembly test room in retrospect', *Occup. Psychol.*, vol. 27 (1953), pp. 98–103.
3. M. ARGYLE, *The Scientific Study of Social Behavior*, Methuen, 1957.
4. M. ARGYLE, G. GARDNER and F. CIOFFI, 'The measurement of supervisory methods', *Hum. Rel.*, vol. 10 (1957), pp. 295–313.
5. H. BEHREND, Absence under full employment, *University of Birmingham* (mimeo.), 1951.
6. BRITISH PRODUCTIVITY COUNCIL, *Case Studies: Work Study*, 1955.
7. P. F. C. CASTLE, 'The evaluation of human relations training for supervisors', *Occup. Psychol.*, vol. 26 (1952), pp. 191–205.
8. A. L. COMREY, J. M. PFIFFNER and W. S. HIGH, Factors influencing organisational effectiveness, *University of S. California* (mimeo.), 1954.
9. H. FELDMAN, *Problems in Labor Relations*, Macmillan, New York, 1937.
10. E. A. FLEISHMAN, 'Leadership climate, human relations training and supervisory behaviour', *Personn. Psychol.*, vol. 6 (1953), pp. 205–22.
11. E. E. GHISELLI and C. W. BROWN, *Personnel and Industrial Psychology*, McGraw-Hill, 1948.
12. A. P. GRAY and M. ABRAMS, *Construction of Esso Refinery, Fawley*, British Institute of Management, 1954.
13. H. W. HALPIN and B. J. WINER, *The Leadership Behavior of the Airplane Commander*, Colombus Ohio State University, Research Foundation, 1952.
14. J. D. HANDYSIDE, The effectiveness of supervisory training: a survey of recent experimental studies, *Paper read to B.P.S.*, 1955.
15. T. HARITON, Conditions affecting the effects of training foremen in human relations, *Ph.D. thesis, University of Michigan* (quoted by Viteles, 1954, p. 446), 1951.
16. T. W. HARRELL, *Industrial Psychology*, Rinehart, 1949.
17. J. K. HEMPHILL, 'Relations between size of group and the behaviour of "superior" leaders', *J. soc. Psychol.*, vol. 32 (1950), pp. 11–22.
18. D. HEWITT and J. PARFITT, 'A note on working morale and size of group', *Occup. Psychol.*, vol 27 (1953), pp. 38–42.

19. J. M. JACKSON, 'The effect of changing the leadership of small work groups', *Hum. Rel.*, vol. 6 (1953), pp. 25–44.
20. R. L. KAHN and N. C. MORSE, 'The relationship of productivity to morale', *J. soc. Iss.*, vol. 7 (1951), pp. 8–17.
21. D. KATZ and R. L. KAHN, Factors related to productivity, *The Caterpillar Tractor Co. Study*, vol. 5, University of Michigan (mimeo.), 1951.
22. D. KATZ and R. L. KAHN, Factors related to job satisfaction, *The Caterpillar Tractor Co. Study*, vol. 6, University of Michigan (mimeo.) 1951.
23. D. KATZ, N. MACCOBY and N. C. MORSE, *Productivity, Supervision and Morale in the Office Situation*, University of Michigan, Institute for Social Research, 1950.
24. D. KATZ, *et al.*, *Productivity, Supervision and Morale among Railroad Workers*, University of Michigan, Institute for Social Research, 1951.
25. W. A. KERR, 'Labour turnover and its correlates', *J. appl. Psychol.*, vol. 31 (1947), pp. 366–71.
26. W. A. KERR, G. J. KOPPEIMEIER and J. J. SULLIVAN, 'Absenteeism, turnover and morale in a metals fabrication factory', *Occup. Psychol.*, vol. 25 (1951), pp. 50–55.
27. J. R. LONG, Labour turnover under full employment, *University of Birmingham* (mimeo.), 1951.
28. R. MARRIOTT, 'Size of working group and output', *Occup. Psychol.*, vol. 23 (1949), pp. 47–57.
29. T. U. MATTHEW, 'The accuracy and use of time-study', *Oper. Res. Quart.*, vol. 6 (1955), pp. 9–15.
30. *Modern Industry* staff writer, 'Pay plans for higher production', *Modern Industry*, vol. 11 (1946), pp. 51–64 (quoted by Viteles, 1954, p. 27).
31. N. C. MORSE, *Satisfactions in the White-Collar Job*, University of Michigan, Institute for Social Research, 1953.
32. D. C. PELZ, 'Influence: a key to effective leadership in the first-line supervisor', *Personnel*, vol. 3 (1952), pp. 209–17.
33. W. RODGERS and J. M. HAMMERSLEY, 'The consistency of stop-watch time study practitioners', *Occup. Psychol.*, vol. 28 (1954), pp. 61–76.
34. W. D. SCOTT and R. C. CLOTHIER, *Personnel Management*, McGraw-Hill, 1923.
35. R. H. VAN ZELST, 'Sociometrically selected work teams increase production', *Personn. Psychol.*, vol. 5 (1952), pp. 175–85.
36. M. S. VITELES, *Motivation and Morale in Industry*, Staples, 1954.

13 Nancy C. Morse and Everett Reimer

The Experimental Change of a
Major Organizational Variable

Nancy C. Morse and Everett Reimer, 'The experimental change of a
major organization variable', *Journal of Abnormal and Social Psychology*,
vol. 52, 1956, pp. 120–29.

This experiment is one in a series of studies of social behavior in
large-scale organizations undertaken by the Human Relations
Program of the Survey Research Center. Its primary aim is to
investigate the relationship between the allocation of decision-
making processes in a large hierarchical organization and (a) the
individual satisfactions of the members of the organization, (b)
the productivity of the organization.

The results of several previous studies suggested that the individual's role in decision making might affect his satisfaction and
productivity. The effectiveness of decision making in small
groups shown by Lewin, Lippitt and others (4, 5) and the successful application of small-group decision making to method
changes in an industrial setting by Coch and French (1) both
indicated the possibilities for enlarging the role of the rank and
file in the on-going decision making of an organization. The
practical experience of Sears, Roebuck *et al.*, with a 'flat',
administratively decentralized structure, described by Worthy (8),
pointed in the same direction, as did the survey findings by Katz,
Maccoby and Morse (2), that supervisors delegating greater
authority had more productive work groups. The logical next
step seemed to be the controlled testing of hypotheses concerning
the relationship between role in organizational decision making
and two aspects of organizational effectiveness: satisfaction and
productivity. Two broad hypotheses were formulated:

Hypothesis I. An increased role in the decision making processes for rank-and-file groups increases their satisfaction (while
a decreased role in decision making reduces satisfaction).

Hypothesis II. An increased role in decision making for rank-
and-file groups increases their productivity (while a decreased
role in decision making decreases productivity).

Both these hypotheses deal with the effects on the rank and file of different hierarchical allocations of the decision-making processes of the organization. The rationale for the satisfaction hypothesis (I) predicts different and more need-satisfying decisions when the rank and file has decision-making power than when the upper echelons of the hierarchy have that power. Furthermore, the process of decision making itself is expected to be satisfying to the majority of people brought up in American traditions. Underlying the productivity hypothesis (II) was the consideration that local unit policy making would increase motivation to produce and thus productivity. Motivation should rise when productivity becomes a path for greater need satisfaction. The productivity hypothesis predicts a higher degree of need satisfaction (as does Hypothesis I) *and* an increase in the degree of dependence of satisfactions upon productivity under conditions of greater rank-and-file decision making. It is expected that when rank-and-file members work out and put into effect their own rules and regulations, their maintenance in the organization (and thus their satisfactions) will depend much more directly upon their performance.

Procedure

The experiment was conducted in one department of a non-unionized industrial organization which had four parallel divisions engaged in relatively routine clerical work. The design involved increasing rank-and-file decision making in two of the divisions and increasing upper-level decision making in the other two divisions. The time span was one and a half years: a before measurement, a half year of training supervisors to create the experimental conditions, one year under the experimental conditions, and then remeasurement. The two pairs of two divisions each were comparable on relevant variables such as initial allocation of the decision-making processes, satisfaction and productivity, as well as on such background factors as type of work, type of personnel and type of supervisory structure.

The rank-and-file employees were women, mostly young and unmarried, with high school education. The usual clerk's plans were for marriage and a family rather than a career. The population used in the analysis, except where noted, is a subgroup of the clerks, the 'matched' population. These clerks were present throughout the one and a half year period and their before and after questionnaires were individually matched. While they comprise somewhat less than half of the clerks present in these divisions at any one time, they are comparable to the total group, except on such expected variables as length of time in the division, in the work section and on the job.

One aspect of the work situation should be mentioned, as it bears on the adequacy of the setting for a test of the productivity hypothesis. The amount of work done by the divisions was completely dependent upon the flow of work to them, i.e. the total number of units to be done was not within the control of the divisions. With volume fixed, productivity depends upon the number of clerks needed to do the work, and increased productivity can be achieved only by out-placement of clerks or by foregoing replacement of clerks who leave for other reasons.

The development of the experimental conditions

Creating the experimental programs included three steps: (a) planning by research staff and company officials; (b) introducing the programs to the division supervisory personnel and training of the supervisors for their new roles; and (c) introduction to the clerks and operation under the experimental conditions.

The experiment was carried out within the larger framework of company operations. The introduction, training, and operations were in the hands of company personnel. The experimental changes were not made through personnel shifts; the changes were in what people did in their jobs with respect to the decision-making processes of the organization.

Two main change processes were used in both the autonomy program, designed to increase rank-and-file decision making, and in the hierarchically controlled program, designed to increase the upper management role in the decision-making processes. First, there were formal structural changes to create a new organizational environment for the divisions in each program. In both programs the hierarchical legitimization of new roles preceded the taking of the new roles.[1] In the autonomy program authority

1. Weber and others have used the word 'legitimization' to refer to the acceptance by subordinates of the authority of superiors. We are using the

194

was delegated by upper management to lower levels in the hierarchy with the understanding that they would redelegate it to the
clerical work groups. In the hierachically controlled program,
authority was given to the higher line officials to increase their
role in the running of the divisions and to the staff officials to
increase their power to institute changes within the two divisions
in that program. Second, there were training programs for the
supervisors of the divisions to ensure that the formal changes
would result in actual changes in relations between people. (For
a longer description of the change programs see Reimer, 6.)

Measurement

The results of the changes were gauged through before and after
measurements and through continuing measurements during the
experimental period. The major emphasis was on the attitudes
and perceptions of the clerks as reflected in extensive questionnaires. In addition, the training programs and the operations
phase of the experiment were observed. Before and after interviews were conducted with the supervisory personnel of the division. Data from company records such as productivity rates,
turnover figures, etc., were also included.

The data reported here will be confined to material most
pertinent to the testing of the two hypotheses. For other related
aspects of the experiment, see Tannenbaum's study of the relationship of personality characteristics and adjustment to the two
programs (7), Kaye's study of organizational goal achievement
under the autonomy program (3), as well as forthcoming publications.

Results[2]

Success of experimental manipulation

The first question was to discover whether or not the change

word in quite a different sense. By hierarchical legitimization we mean the
formal delegation of authority by superiors to subordinates. This delegation
legitimizes the subordinates' utilization of this authority.

2. For the statistical tests used in this section, we have assumed that
individuals were randomly chosen, while the selection of individuals by
divisions undoubtedly results in some clustering effect. The levels of
significance should, therefore, be considered as general guides rather than
in any absolute sense.

programs were successful in creating the conditions under which the hypotheses could be tested. Two types of data are pertinent. The first is descriptive data concerning the actual operations of the two programs. The second is perceptual data from the clerical employees themselves indicating the degree to which they saw changes in their role in organizational decisions.

The operations of the divisions in fact changed in the direction expected. In the autonomy program the clerical work groups came to make group decisions about many of the things which affected them and which were important to them. The range of the decisions was very great, including work methods and processes, and personnel matters, such as recess periods, the handling of tardiness, etc. Probably the most important area in which the clerks were not able to make decisions was the area of salary. Some of the work groups were more active in the decision-making process than others, but all made a very great variety of decisions in areas important to them. In the hierarchically controlled program the changes decreased the degree to which the employees could control and regulate their own activities. One of the main ways in which this greater limitation was manifested was through the individual work standards that staff officials developed for the various jobs. Also the greater role of upper line and staff officials in the operation of the divisions meant that the indirect influence which the clerks could have on decisions when they were made by managers and section supervisors was reduced.

The clerks were operating under different conditions in the two programs as the result of the experimental changes, but did they perceive these changes? The method of measuring the perception of changes in decision making was by asking clerks about their part and about the part of people above their rank in decisions with respect to a wide variety of areas of company operations, or company systems. The following questions were asked about each major area of company operations or system: 'To what degree do company officers or any employees of a higher rank than yours decide how the ____ system is set up and decide the policies, rules, procedures or methods of the ____ system?' (followed by a line with the landmark statements: not at all, to a slight degree, to some degree, to a fairly high degree and to a very high degree) and, 'To what degree do you and the girls in your section decide how the ___ system is set up and decide the policies, rules, procedures or methods of the ___ system?' (followed by a line with the same landmark statements as the first question).

The extreme degree of perceived hierarchical control of the decision-making processes would be shown by the clerks answering that employees of a higher rank than theirs made the decisions 'to a very high degree' and the clerks made them 'not at all'. Table 1 shows the number of systems where there are half or more of the clerks endorsing these two statements for the before

Table 1

Number of Company Systems in which Clerks Perceive Very High Upper-Level Control of Decision-Making Allocation

| Response | *Number of Systems in which Half or More Clerks gave Specified Response* | | |
| | | *After* | |
	Before all Divs.	*Program I Divs.*	*Program II Divs.*
Upper levels decided policies to a very high degree	20	7	24
Clerks did not decide policies at all	25	9	23
Total number of systems measured	27	24	24

situation and for the two experimental situations. (The autonomy program is designated in Table 1 and thereafter as program I and the hierachically controlled program as program II.) Questions were asked for twenty-seven company systems in the before measurement and twenty-four systems in the after measurement.

Table 1 shows that the clerks perceived the decision-making processes for most of the company operations measured as located at hierarchical levels above their own, prior to the introduction of the experimental changes. The experimental changes in the autonomy program divisions resulted in their seeing decision-making activities as much less exclusively confined to levels above theirs. The changes in the hierarchically controlled program were less striking but they resulted in the clerks judging that all of the systems about which they were asked in the after situation had their policies molded to a very high degree by people above their level.

The relative role of the hierachy compared to the rank and file as perceived by the clerks was measured by assigning scores from 1 to 9 for the landmark positions on the scales for the two questions and then dividing the score for upper-level decision making by the score for rank-and-file decision making. The theoretical range for the resulting index is from 9·0 to 0, with numbers less than 1 indicating greater local control than upper-level control. Table 2 includes the average index scores for the systems from the before and after measurements calculated by division.

Table 2 indicates the change in the divisions in the autonomy program towards greater perceived rank-and-file role in decision making, but also shows that the upper levels are seen as still having the major role in the after situation. (The downward shift in perceived decision-making control in the autonomy program is significant above the 1 per cent level by the Student's t-test for paired data. A statistically significant, but slight, change towards greater upper-level control took place in the hierarchically controlled program.)

Both Tables 1 and 2 show that the clerks in the autonomy program perceive, as predicted, a significant shift away from upper-

Table 2

Effect of Change Programs on Perception of Decision-Making Allocation

Experimental groups		Index of Perceived Decision-Making Allocation				
		Before mean	After mean	Diff.	SE Diff.	N
Program I	Div. A	5·69	4·39	−1·30*	0·24	61
	Div. B	6·49	4·08	−2·41*	0·26	57
	Average	6·08	4·24	−1·84*	0·18	118
Program II	Div. C	6·15	6·87	+0·72*	0·22	44
	Div. D	6·78	7·13	+0·35	0·26	44
	Average	6·41	7·00	+0·59*	0·17	88

Note: Higher values corresponded to perception of predominance of upper levels of organization in decision making.

* Significant at the 1 per cent level.

level control when their before–after answers are compared, and that the clerks in the hierarchically controlled program see some increase in upper-level control over policy making, even though it was already perceived as highly controlled from above before the experiment.

These measures of successful experimental manipulation suggest that the conditions in the two programs are sufficiently different to permit tests of the experimental hypotheses.

Hypothesis I

This hypothesis states that an increase in the decision-making role of individuals results in increased satisfactions, while a decrease in opportunity for decision making is followed by decreased satisfaction. The general hypothesis was tested for a variety of specific areas of satisfaction. The attitudinal areas to be reported include: (a) self-actualization and growth, (b) satisfaction with supervisors, (c) liking for working for the company, (d) job satisfaction, (e) liking for program. Student's one-tailed t-test for paired data was used for tests of significance. Results reaching the 5 per cent level or above are considered significant.

Self-actualization. One of the hypotheses of the study was that greater opportunity for regulating and controlling their own activities within the company structure would increase the degree to which individuals could express their various and diverse needs and could move in the direction of fully exploiting their potentialities. An increase in upper-management control on the other hand was predicted to decrease the opportunities for employee self-actualization and growth.

Five questions were used to measure this area:

1. Is your job a real challenge to what you think you can do?

2. How much chance does your job give you to learn things you're interested in?

3. Are the things you're learning in your job helping to train you for a better job in the company?

4. How much chance do you have to try out your ideas on the job?

5. How much does your job give you a chance to do the things you're best at?

These five items, which were answered by checking one position on a five-point scale, were intercorrelated and then combined to form an index.[3] Table 3 shows the means for the four divisions and two groups on the self-actualization and growth index.

Table 3

Effect of Change Programs on Feelings of Self-Actualization on Job

		Index of Perceived Self-Actualization				
Experimental groups		Mean before	Mean after	Diff.	SE Diff.	N
Program I	Div. A	2·67	2·74	+0·07	0·09	52
	Div. B	2·18	2·39	+0·21*	0·11	47
	Average	2·43	2·57	+0·14*	0·07	99
Program II	Div. C	2·43	2·24	−0·19	0·14	43
	Div. D	2·30	2·23	−0·07	0·10	38
	Average	2·37	2·24	−0·13*	0·07	81

Note: Scale runs from 1, low degree of self-actualization, to 5, a high degree.

* Significant at the 5 per cent level, one-tailed *t*-test for paired data.

While both groups of clerks indicated that their jobs throughout the course of the experiment did not give them a very high degree of self-actualization, the experimental programs produced significant changes. In the autonomy program, self-actualization increased significantly from before to after, and a corresponding decrease was shown in the hierarchically controlled program. At the end of the experimental period, the autonomy program is significantly higher on this variable than the hierarchically controlled program.

Satisfaction with supervision. A variety of indices were developed in order to test the hypothesis that the autonomy program would improve satisfactions with supervisors and that the hierarchically

3. The items were intercorrelated by the tetrachoric method. When these correlations were converted to z-scores the average intercorrelation was 0·62; corrected for length of test, a reliability index of 0·89 was obtained.

controlled program would reduce such satisfactions. Two general types of attitudes were separately measured: (a) satisfaction with relations with supervisors and (b) satisfaction with supervisors as a representative. These two types of attitudes were studied before and after the experimental period with respect to three levels of supervision: the first-line supervisor, the assistant manager of the division and the manager of the division. The following three questions were asked for each of these levels in order to tap the clerks' degree of satisfaction with relations with supervisors:

1. How good is your supervisor (assistant manager, manager) at handling people?

2. Can you count on having good relations with your supervisor (assistant manager, manager) under all circumstances?

3. In general, how well do you like your supervisor (assistant manager, manager) as a person to work with?

These three questions were combined to form indices of satisfaction with relations with supervisors, assistant manager and manager. (The items were intercorrelated for the satisfaction with relations with supervisor index. Through converting to z-scores, the average intercorrelation of items is found to be 0·78. Correcting for length of test, i.e. using three items to form the index rather than one, the reliability index is 0·91 with an N of 360.)

Table 4 shows that in general there was a shift towards greater satisfaction with supervisors in the autonomy program and towards less satisfaction with supervisors in the hierarchically controlled program. The divisions, however, show certain characteristic differences in satisfaction at the outset and shift in the expected direction to different degrees.

Both divisions in the hierarchically controlled program show a decrease in satisfaction with the first-line supervisor, although the changes are not statistically significant. The after differences between the autonomy and the hierarchically controlled programs are, however, significant.

Satisfaction with relations with both the assistant manager and the manager increased significantly in the autonomy program and decreased significantly in the hierarchically controlled program. Each of the divisions within the groups likewise shifted in the hypothesized directions for the two managerial indices. In the

Table 4

Effect of Change Programs on Satisfaction with Relations
with Three Levels of Supervision

Experimental groups		Index of Satisfaction				
		Mean before	Mean after	Diff.	SE Diff.	N
		Relations with supervisor				
Program I	Div. A	4·18	4·15	−0·03	0·09	62
	Div. B	3·19	3·50	+0·31*	0·14	54
	Average	3·71	3·80	+0·09	0·08	116
Program II	Div. C	3·80	3·67	−0·13	0·11	46
	Div. D	3·43	3·29	−0·14	0·16	45
	Average	3·64	3·48	−0·16	0·10	91
		Relations with assistant manager				
Program I	Div. A	3·49	3·61	+0·12	0·12	59
	Div. B	3·97	4·11	+0·14	0·11	53
	Average	3·71	3·86	+0·15*	0·08	112
Program II	Div. C	3·80	3·34	−0·46†	0·12	43
	Div. D	3·57	3·22	−0·35†	0·11	43
	Average	3·64	3·28	−0·36†	0·08	86
		Relations with manager				
Program I	Div. A	3·84	4·11	+0·27†	0·08	62
	Div. B	4·04	4·20	+0·16*	0·09	52
	Average	3·93	4·15	+0·22†	0·06	114
Program II	Div. C	3·23	2·59	−0·64†	0·15	43
	Div. D	3·87	3·37	−0·50†	0·13	40
	Average	3·50	3·01	−0·49†	0·10	83

Note: Degree of satisfaction with relations with supervision: five-point
scale ranging from 1, low degree of satisfaction, to 5, high degree of satisfaction.

* Significant at the 5 per cent level, one-tailed t-test for paired data.

† Significant at the 1 per cent level.

autonomy program the assistant manager index shifted in the
right direction for both divisions, but the changes were not statistically significant when each division was tested separately.

Thus while the employees were generally quite satisfied with their relations with their different supervisors, the experimental programs did have the expected effects of increasing the satisfaction of those in the autonomy program and decreasing the satisfaction of those in the hierarchically controlled program. The effects of the programs appear to be most evident in attitudes towards the managerial level and least marked in attitudes towards the first-line supervisors, probably because the managers, occupy the key or pivotal positions in the structure (see Kaye, 3).

The second type of attitude towards supervisors measured was satisfaction with the supervisors as representatives of the employees. Three questions were asked employees as a measure of this type of satisfaction:

1. How much does your supervisor (assistant manager, manager) go out of her (his) way to help get things for the girls in the section?

2. How effective is she (he) in helping you and the other girls get what you want in your jobs?

3. How much does your supervisor (assistant manager, manager) try to help people in your section get ahead in the company?

These three items were intercorrelated for the attitudes towards the supervisor as a representative index and the average intercorrelation was 0.83 with a corrected reliability of 0.94 (N of 340).

The findings for the three levels of supervision on the satisfaction with supervisors as representatives index are shown in Table 5.

The employees' attitudes towards their supervisors as effective representatives of their interest show significant changes in the predicted directions in the two programs. Those in the autonomy program became more satisfied than they had been previously, while those in the hierarchically controlled program became less satisfied. On satisfaction with the first-line supervisor as a representative both Division B in the autonomy program and Division D in the hierarchically controlled program shifted significantly in the hypothesized directions, although the other two divisions did not shift significantly. The two program groups were not matched on degree of satisfaction with manager and assistant manager as a representative at the beginning of the experiment,

Table 5

The Effect of Change Programs on Satisfaction with Three
Levels of Supervision as Representatives of Employees

Experimental groups		Index of Satisfaction				
		Mean before	Mean after	Diff.	SE Diff.	N
Supervisor as representative of employees						
Program I	Div. A	3·98	4·06	+0·08	0·12	59
	Div. B	2·91	3·43	+0·52†	0·14	49
	Average	3·48	3·74	+0·26†	0·09	108
Program II	Div. C	3·73	3·67	−0·06	0·13	45
	Div. D	3·52	3·15	−0·36*	0·18	41
	Average	3·59	3·43	−0·16	0·11	86
Assistant manager as representative of employees						
Program I	Div. A	3·32	3·75	+0·43†	0·14	51
	Div. B	3·54	3·76	+0·22*	0·13	53
	Average	3·43	3·75	+0·32†	0·09	104
Program II	Div. C	3·07	2·81	−0·26*	0·12	41
	Div. D	3·23	2·92	−0·31*	0·13	42
	Average	3·15	2·86	−0·29†	0·10	83
Manager as representative of employees						
Program I	Div. A	3·82	4·37	+0·55†	0·11	57
	Div. B	3·76	3·96	+0·20*	0·10	53
	Average	3·79	4·17	+0·38†	0·07	110
Program II	Div. C	2·70	2·19	−0·51†	0·13	41
	Div. D	3·14	2·92	−0·22	0·16	30
	Average	2·92	2·52	−0·40†	0·10	71

Note: Five-point scale ranging from 1, low degree of satisfaction, to 5,
high degree of satisfaction.

* Significant at the 5 per cent level, one-tailed t-test for paired data.

† Significant at the 1 per cent level.

as there was significantly more satisfaction in the autonomy
program divisions than there was in program II. However, the
changes for both groups of divisions were statistically significant
and in the predicted direction. For attitude towards manager all
of the division differences are in the predicted direction and all
except Division D are statistically significant.

Satisfaction with the company. One general question was used to measure company satisfaction: 'Taking things as a whole, how do you like working for — (the name of the company)?'

The answers for this question, presented in Table 6, indicate an

Table 6

The Effect of Change Programs on Satisfaction with the Company

		Index of Satisfaction with Company				
Experimental groups		*Before mean*	*After mean*	*Diff.*	*SE Diff.*	*N*
Program I	Div. A	4·16	4·32	+0·16*	0·09	62
	Div. B	3·83	4·02	+0·19	0·13	53
	Average	4·01	4·18	+0·17*	0·08	115
Program II	Div. C	4·04	3·80	−0·24*	0·14	46
	Div. D	4·26	3·95	−0·31†	0·12	43
	Average	4·15	3·88	−0·27†	0·09	89

Note: Five-point scale ranging from 1, low degree of satisfaction, to 5, high degree of satisfaction.
* Significant at the 5 per cent level, one-tailed *t*-test for paired data.
† Significant at the 1 per cent level.

increase in favourableness towards the company under the autonomy program and a decrease under the hierarchically controlled program.

All of the changes are significant in the predicted direction, except for the before–after difference in Division B which is only at the 10 per cent level of significance.

Job satisfaction. Three questions were used as an index of job satisfaction:

1. Does your job ever get monotonous?
2. How important do you feel your job is compared with other jobs at — (the company)?
3. In general, how well do you like the sort of work you're doing in your job?

These three questions showed an average intercorrelation of

0·47 with a corrected reliability of 0·73 (N of 369). The results on this index are reported in Table 7.

Table 7
The Effect of Change Programs on Job Satisfaction

		Index of Job Satisfaction			
Experimental groups		Before mean	After mean	Diff.	SE Diff.	N
Program I	Div. A	3·29	3·29	0	0·08	58
	Div. B	3·03	3·09	+0·06	0·09	55
	Average	3·16	3·19	+0·03	0·06	113
Program II	Div. C	3·14	2·94	−0·20*	0·10	42
	Div. D	3·12	3·07	−0·05	0·12	46
	Average	3·13	3·00	−0·13*	0·07	88

Note: A five-point scale ranging from 1, low degree of satisfaction, to 5 a high degree of satisfaction.
*Significant at the 5 per cent level, one-tailed t-test for paired data.

While the trends for the changes in job satisfaction are in the direction predicted, the differences are not sufficiently great to be statistically significant except for Division C. The lack of change in job satisfaction in the autonomy program may be due to the fact that the job content remained about the same. It is also possible that the increases in complexity and variety of their total work were offset by a rise in their level of aspiration, so that they expected more interesting and varied work.

Satisfaction with the program. In the after measurement additional questions were asked concerning attitudes towards the programs. Most of these questions were open-ended and required the employee to write her response in her own words. Although less than half of the clerks taking the after measurement filled them out, the results on questions relevant to the satisfaction hypothesis deserve brief mention. The clerks in the autonomy program typically: wanted their program to last indefinitely, did not like the other program, felt that the clerks were one of the groups gaining the most from the program and described both positive and negative changes in interpersonal relations among the girls. The clerks in the hierarchically controlled program, on the other hand, most frequently: wanted their program to end immediately, liked the other program and felt that the company gained the most from their program. Not one single person in the hierarchically controlled program mentioned an improvement in interpersonal relations as a result of this program. All of the noted changes were for the worse, with increases in friction and tension being most frequently mentioned.

Taking all of these results on the attitudinal questions together, the first hypothesis would appear to be verified. Increasing local decision making increased satisfaction, while decreasing the role of rank-and-file members of the organization in decision making decreased it.

Hypothesis II

This hypothesis predicts a direct relationship between degree of rank-and-file decision making and productivity. Thus, in order for the hypothesis to be verified, productivity should increase significantly in the autonomy program, and should decrease significantly in the hierarchically controlled program.

We have previously described the problems of assuming a direct relationship between motivation to produce and productivity in a situation in which volume is not controllable by employees and level of productivity depends upon the number of people doing a fixed amount of work. The autonomy program was handicapped by both the fact that increasing productivity required reducing the size of their own work group and the fact that the upper management staff and line costs were not included in the measure of costs per volume of work.

The measure of productivity, then, is a measure of clerical costs. These clerical costs are expressed in percentage figures, calculated by dividing the actual clerical costs by a constant standard of cost expected for that volume. Since this way of estimating productivity makes the higher figures indicate lower productivity, we have reversed the signs for purposes of presentation. The results for this measure are shown in Table 8.

The clerical costs have gone down in each division and thus productivity has increased. All these increases in productivity are statistically significant (by t-tests). In addition, the productivity increase in the hierarchically controlled program is significantly greater than that in the autonomy program. These increases in productivity do not seem to be accounted for by a general rise in productivity throughout the company, since the divisions outside the experimental groups which were most comparable to them showed no significant gain in productivity during this period. The rise in productivity appears to be the result of the experimental

Table 8

Comparison of the Four Divisions on Clerical Productivity for Year Control Period and Year Experimental Period

Experimental groups		Index of Productivity				
		Mean control period	Mean experimental period	Diff.	SE Diff.	N
Program I	Div. A	46·3	55·2	+ 8·9*	1·3	12
	Div. B	51·0	62·0	+11·0*	1·3	12
	Average	48·6	58·6	+10·0*	1·2	24
Program II	Div. C	50·2	63·2	+13·0*	1·2	12
	Div. D.	46·8	62·0	+15·2*	1·1	12
	Average	48·5	62·6	+14·1*	0·9	24

Note: Higher values correspond to great productivity.
* Significant at the 1 per cent level.

treatments. The two divisions initially low in productivity showed the greatest differential change. Division D increased its productivity the most of the four while Division A increased the least.

A second measure of the organizational costs of the two programs is the degree of turnover which could be attributed to on-the-job factors. A method of control and regulation which reduces clerical costs, but which produces the hidden costs of training new employees is of greater cost to the organization than would at first appear evident. In this company turnover, however, is not high and much of the turnover that does occur is due to personal reasons (marriage, pregnancy, etc.) rather than on-the-job reasons. Out of the fifty-four employees who left the company from the four divisions during the time of the experiment, only nine resigned for other jobs or because of dissatisfaction. Out of these nine, however, all but one were in the hierarchically controlled program. In the exit interviews conducted by the company personnel department twenty-three of the girls leaving made unfavorable comments about pressure, work standards, etc. Nineteen of these girls were from the hierarchically controlled program.

These results indicate that the productivity hypothesis is clearly not verified in terms of direct clerical costs, since the hierarchically controlled program decreased these costs more than the autonomy program, contrary to the prediction. The indirect costs for the hierarchically controlled program are probably somewhat greater. But even when this is considered the evidence does not support the hypothesis.

Discussion

The results on productivity might suggest a 'Hawthorne effect' if it were not for the satisfaction findings. The increase in satisfaction under the autonomy program and the decrease under the hierarchically controlled program make an explanation of productivity changes in terms of a common attention effect unlikely.[4]

The hierarchically controlled program reduced staff costs by ordering reductions in the number of employees assigned to the tasks. Increases in productivity for Divisions C and D were brought about as simply as that. This temporary increase in one measure of productivity is not surprising and is traditional history in industry. In the autonomy program, decrease in costs was more complex but can be simply stated as follows. The autonomy program increased the motivation of the employees to produce and thus they did not feel the need for replacing the staff-members who left the section. In addition, they were willing to make an effort to try to outplace some of their members in other

4. It is unlikely that even in the Hawthorne experiment the results were due to attention. There were a number of changes in addition to an increase in attention, including relaxation of rules, better supervisors, no change in piece-rates despite raises in productivity – to name a few.

jobs which they might like. The reductions in staff in the two programs came about in different ways. Those occurring by order in the hierarchically controlled program surpassed in number those occurring by group decision in the autonomy program, but it is not clear how long the superiority of the hierarchically controlled program would have lasted.

The results of the experiment need to be placed in a larger theoretical framework in order to contribute to the understanding of the functioning of large-scale organizations. We shall first consider briefly the role and function of the social control processes, as it is these processes which were changed by the experimental manipulations.

The high degree of rationality which is characteristic of the institutional behavior of man is achieved through a complex system for controlling and regulating human behavior. Hierarchy is a requirement because human beings must be fitted to a rational model. There are essentially two functions which the usual hierarchy serves: a *binding-in* function and a *binding-between* function. By *binding-in* we mean insuring that there will be individuals present to fill the necessary roles. The role behavior required by the organization must be a path to individual goals. Money is the most important means used for binding-in, but all ways to motivate a person to enter and remain in the system are means of binding-in. By *binding-between* we mean the insurance of the rationality of action, that is, the setting up and continuation of institutional processes which will accomplish the ends for which the organization is designed. The role behavior of individuals must be integrated into a pattern to produce interrelated action directed towards the goals of the organization. The development of assignments, work charts, job specifications, etc., are but a few examples of the many means used by organizations for binding-between.

Any means for controlling and regulating human behavior in a large organizational setting, then, needs to serve these two functions. The experiment shows that the allocation of decision-making processes to the upper hierarchy results in a greater emphasis on the binding-between function, while the function of binding-in is handled by an external reward system. Such a direct stress on the binding-between function was shown in the hierarchically controlled program and resulted in the increase in productivity (an indication of binding-between) and a decrease in employee satisfaction (an indication of degree of binding-in) and some increase in turnover (another indication of binding-in).

The greater allocation of the decision-making processes to the rank-and-file employees in the autonomy program resulted in an emphasis on both the binding-between and the binding-in functions. Thus there was both an increase in productivity and an increase in satisfaction. While the program is addressed primarily to the binding-in function, in such a context the binding-between function is also served.

The problems of the hierarchically controlled system are maintaining the employee effectively 'bound-in' to the organization and continuing favorable relations between the supervisory personnel who have involvement in the organization and the rank and file who must do the work. Indications of these problems are dissatisfaction, distortions in communications up the hierarchy, the tendency to 'goof off' and cut corners in the work, and the greater turnover.

The autonomy program is an integrated means of handling both the binding-between and the binding-in functions, but it requires in the long run that the organization be willing to grant employee decision making in the key areas of binding-in such as pay and promotions. The granting of 'safe' areas of decision making and the withholding of 'hot' ones is not likely to work for long. It is necessary for the rank and file to be sufficiently bound into the organization for them to want to make decisions which are rational for the system. But the rationality of their decisions will also depend upon the orientation of the key supervisors whose values they will interiorize. (Thus the clerks in Division B were more organizationally oriented than those in Division A – see Kaye, 3.)

Summary

A field experiment in an industrial setting was conducted in order to test hypotheses concerning the relationship between the means by which organizational decisions are made and (a) individual satisfaction and (b) productivity.

Using four parallel divisions of the clerical operations of an organization, two programs of changes were introduced. One program, the autonomy program involving two of the divisions, was designed to increase the role of the rank-and-file employees in the decision-making processes of the organization. The other two divisions received a program designed to increase the role of upper management in the decision-making processes (the hierarchically controlled program). The phases of the experiment included: (a) before measurement, (b) training programs for supervisory personnel lasting approximately six months, (c) an operations period of a year for the two experimental programs and (d) after measurement. In addition, certain measurements were taken during the training and operational phases of the experiment. Findings are reported on the question of the experimental 'take' and on the general hypotheses on individual satisfactions and productivity. Briefly, it was found that:

1. The experimental programs produced changes in decision-making allocations in the direction required for the testing of the hypotheses.

2. The individual satisfactions of the members of the work groups increased significantly in the autonomous program and decreased significantly in the hierarchically controlled program.

3. Using one measure of productivity, both decision-making systems increased productivity, with the hierarchically controlled program resulting in a greater increase.

The relationship of the findings to the so-called 'Hawthorne effect' is examined and the experimental programs and their results are considered in the light of a theoretical description of the role of the control and regulation processes of large organizations.

References
1. L. COCH and J. R. P. FRENCH, JR, 'Overcoming resistance to change', *Hum. Rel.*, vol. 1 (1948), pp. 512–32.
2. D. KATZ, N. MACCOBY and N. MORSE, *Productivity, Supervision and Morale in an Office Situation*, Survey Research Center, University of Michigan, 1950.
3. C. KAYE, *The Effect on an Organizational Goal Achievement of a Change in the Structure of Roles*, Survey Research Center, University of Michigan, 1954 (mimeo.).

4. K. LEWIN, 'Group decisions and social change', in G. E. Swanson, T. M. Newcomb and E. L. Hartley (eds.), *Readings in Social Psychology*, Holt, 2nd edn 1952, pp. 459–73.

5. R. LIPPITT and R. K. WHITE, 'An experimental study of leadership and group life', in G. E. Swanson, T. M. Newcomb and E. L. Hartley (eds.), *Readings in Social Psychology*, Holt, 2nd edn 1952, pp. 340–54.

6. E. REIMER, *Creating Experimental Social Change in an Organization*, Survey Research Center, University of Michigan, 1954 (mimeo.).

7. A. TANNENBAUM, *The Relationship between Personality Variables and Adjustment to Contrasting Types of Social Structure*, Survey Research Center, University of Michigan, 1954 (mimeo.).

8. J. C. WORTHY, 'Factors influencing employee morale', *Harv. bus. Rev.*, vol. 28 (1950), pp. 61–73.

14 Rensis Likert

The Effects of Measurements on Management Practices

Abridged from chapter 5 of Rensis Likert, *New Patterns of Management*, McGraw-Hill, 1961.

Most companies have a fair amount of information about the market and their share of it. Some companies have continuous information as to customer reactions to their products and to competing products.

Much less attention is given, however, to another class of variables which significantly influence the end results. These variables, seriously neglected in present measurements, reflect the current condition of the internal state of the organization: its loyalty, skills, motivations, and capacity for effective interaction, communication and decision making. For easy reference these variables will be called *intervening* variables. In a few companies, experimental programs are now under way to develop measurements of these intervening variables so that the quality and performance capacity of its human organization will be revealed.

The present practice of watching closely only the level of performance of the end-result variables such as production, sales, cost and earnings is leading to faulty conclusions as to what kinds of management and leadership yield the best results. What often confuses the situation is that pressure-oriented, threatening supervision can achieve impressive short-run results, particularly when coupled with high technical competence. There is clear-cut evidence that for a period of at least one year, supervision which increases the direct pressure for productivity can achieve, typically, significant increases in production if the operations are highly functionalized and if standard procedures have been established. Such increases, however, are obtained at a substantial and serious cost to the organization. (Direct pressure for increased performance does not seem to yield even short-run improvement in jobs, such as conducting research, which have not been or cannot be highly functionalized and standardized.)

The deceptive effect of increased supervisory pressure was made clear by an experimental study conducted by the Institute for Social Research in a large corporation (Morse and Reimer, 1956).

Although both programs in the Morse and Reimer study achieved increases in productivity, they yielded significantly different results in other respects. The productivity increases in the hierarchically controlled program were accompanied by shifts in an *adverse* direction in such factors as loyalty, attitudes, interest and involvement in the work. Just the opposite was true in the participative program.

The attitudes, loyalties and motivations which improved the most in the participative program and deteriorated the most in the hierarchically controlled program are those which these studies have consistently shown to be most closely related *in the long run* to employee motivation and productivity. Turnover and the adverse attitudes created by the hierarchically controlled program tend typically to affect productivity adversely over a long period of time.

Apparently, the hierarchically controlled program, at the end of one year, was in a state of unstable equilibrium. Although productivity was then high, forces were being created, as the measures of the intervening variables and turnover indicated, which subsequently would adversely affect the high level of productivity. Good people were leaving the organization because of feeling 'too much pressure on them to produce'. Hostility towards high producers and towards supervision, decreased confidence and trust in management, these and similar attitudes were being developed. Such attitudes create counterforces to management's pressure for high productivity. These developments would gradually cause the productivity level to become lower.

The results which reflect the typical, long-range situation, however, give every reason to believe that had the clerical experiment been continued for another year or two, productivity and quality of work would have continued to increase in the participative program, while in the hierarchically controlled program productivity and quality of work would have declined as a result of the hostility, resentment, and turnover evoked by the program.

In the light of these data, let us look at the situation which virtually all supervisors and managers face today. The only measurements provided them are measurements of such end-result variables as productivity and costs. With only this information available and knowing that they are being appraised in terms of it, what conclusions are managers likely to draw as to the kind of leadership they should use to achieve the level of performance expected by higher management? In considering the answer to this question, it is important to keep in mind that these managers usually experience rewards and promotions for achieving high production and low costs over the short run rather than the long run. Moreover, since many managers are transferred after about two years, their attention is focused primarily on short-run results. Given these conditions, the answer is clear. If we look *only* at the productivity and cost data in the clerical experiment, the hierarchically controlled pattern of leadership is superior, at least for a period of one year.

The great majority of managers in charge of low-producing units and a substantial proportion of managers who achieve moderately good results have reached this conclusion and have adopted an authoritarian style of leadership.

In using this method of leadership, managers may be worried from time to time by seeing the absence and turnover in their units become greater than they wish. And they may be concerned by the high scrap loss in their departments and the excessive attention to inspection and quality control required for their units. They may also be disturbed by the resentment and hostility displayed by subordinates, and they may be perplexed by the higher rates of grievances, slowdowns and similar disturbances in their units. All such developments as these may lead them to ease up from time to time on the tight controls and the threatening pressure for production. They may attribute the difficulties and hostility which they encounter to perverse human nature or the unreasonable hostility of labor leaders. But they would have little objective evidence to persuade them that their present leadership practices are inefficient and inadequate. This would be especially true in situations where their own bosses shared their views as to what leadership principles achieve the best results (Harris, 1952).

For this reason, if managers are to make the best use of their experience, they need measurements which will paint for them a full and accurate picture of their experience. This will not happen until the measurements which companies obtain routinely are far more extensive and complete than is now the case.

The clerical experiment and the subsequent discussion of the relationships between the different kinds of variables help to clarify an important research finding. The different variables such as the intervening and end result variables need not necessarily change in the same direction (e.g. favorable) at the same time. For example, in the participative program of the clerical experiment, attitudes became more favorable while productivity was increasing. In the hierarchically controlled program, however, the opposite pattern occurred: *attitudes became less favorable while productivity was increasing.*

These results help to illustrate the point that widely different trends can occur among the intervening and end-result variables, depending upon the character of the causal variables. Hierarchically controlled patterns of supervision yield different trends and relationships than do participative patterns.

A second aspect of this general finding is that, at any one point in time, each of the different variables may or may not display corresponding degrees of favorableness. Thus, production may be reasonably high for a time even though relatively unfavorable attitudes exist; or at a given point in time, high productivity can be accompanied by favorable attitudes towards job-related matters; or, at certain times, there may be no relationship at all between level of productivity and the degree of favorableness of employee attitudes. To assume, as is often done, that there is or should be a simple correspondence in the relationships between the intervening and end-result variables is unwarranted. The interrelationships are much more complex than this assumption implies.

References

HARRIS, E. F. (1952), Measuring industrial leadership and its implications for training supervisors, *Unpublished Doctoral Dissertation, Ohio State University.*

MORSE, N. C., and REIMER, E. (1956), 'The experimental change of a major organizational variable', *J. abnorm. soc. Psychol.*, vol. 52, pp. 120–29. [Reading 13.]

15 Arnold S. Tannenbaum

The Group in Organizations

Abridged from chapter 5 of Arnold S. Tannenbaum, *Social Psychology of the Work Organization*, Wadsworth, 1966.

Conformity

In the 1920s F. H. Allport reported the results of several experiments he conducted among graduate students at Harvard (1). In these experiments the students made judgements about the weights of objects and the unpleasantness of odors. The students made these judgements alone and in the presence of others, and each subject recorded his judgements on paper without revealing them to the other subjects. Allport found that subjects made less extreme evaluations in the presence of others than when alone. Although the subjects did not know the judgements of others in the group, they imagined how the others were reacting and they avoided what they thought would be extreme and deviant responses. Allport attributed this moderation of judgement to an 'attitude of social conformity' that persons adopt in social situations, even in the absence of communication among them.

Normally, members of a group communicate with one another, and Sherif demonstrated how members develop common standards as they become aware of the opinions of others in the group (11). He placed subjects in a darkened room where they could observe a pinpoint of light. Although the light does not move, most persons experience the illusion of movement, an illusion known as the *autokinetic effect*. Subjects who experience this effect while alone establish individual norms representing the average distances which they judge the light to move. However, subjects tested in groups gradually alter their individual judgements to agree more closely with the judgements reported by the others in their group. A common standard thus becomes established as the norm for the group.

Once a norm is established, members do not deviate easily from it, and some members may conform even against their 'better' judgement. Asch asked persons in groups to estimate which of three lines of varying lengths was equal to a fourth line (2). Only one person in each experimental group, however, was a real subject; the others pretended to be subjects but were really confederates of the experimenter, instructed to make erroneous judgements. The lone subject was therefore confronted with others who, in direct contradiction to the subject's own senses, unanimously and repeatedly chose the wrong line. About one-third of the real subjects who underwent this experience changed their reported judgements to conform to that of the group – even though the lengths of the lines were not the least bit ambiguous, as demonstrated by subjects who made virtually no errors in judgement when not confronted with contrary group pressures.

These studies illustrate the power of the group as an instrument of influence or control over members. However, not all groups are equally effective in establishing or maintaining conformity. Festinger, Schachter, Back, and others have investigated group conditions that are conducive to conformity (3, 5, 6, 9). These psychologists find support in their research for a number of propositions, of which we list three:

1. The more attractive a group is to members, the more likely members are to change their views to conform with those of others in the group.

2. If an individual fails to conform, the group is likely to reject him; and the more attractive the group is to its members, the more decisively they will reject this individual.

3. Members are more likely to be rejected for deviancy on an issue that is important to the group than on an issue that is unimportant.

These propositions suggest that members, implicitly or explicitly, demand conformity because it helps maintain the group that is 'attractive' to them. A general basis for the attractiveness of the group is the satisfaction that people derive from their social relations in it. In the work organization informal social behaviors – friendly remarks, jokes and conversations about matters of mutual interest – give expression to many personal needs that are frustrated by the formal limits of work roles. Groups also provide *support* to their members, and this is an especially important basis for members' attraction to the group in the context of the frustration members face on the job.

Support

Support by a group occurs in several forms. When members face a frustrating or threatening environment, the group may (a) afford some sense of comfort or consolation to members, (b) help or protect members by acting against the source of threat or frustration and (c) strengthen the individual member in his own opposition to the source of adversity.

Research by Schachter illustrates the comfort that persons undergoing threat derive through associating with others in a group (9). This pyschologist compared the behavior of two groups of college students. Subjects in the first group were told they would undergo an experiment involving severe electric shock, while those in the second group were instructed that the experiment would involve only a very slight shock, equivalent to a tickle. The experimenter then informed the subjects that they might choose to wait their turns alone or together with others. They were also told that in the 'together' situation they would not be permitted to talk to one another. Schachter thus ruled out the possibility that the subjects who waited together might plan some joint-action. None the less nearly two-thirds of the subjects in the 'severe-shock' group preferred to wait in a room with others, whereas approximately the same proportion of subjects in the second group did not care whether they waited with others or alone.

Schachter's research suggests that people are drawn to each other *psychologically* under conditions of threat or frustration. We stress the word *psychologically* because there may be no apparent benefit to members from their affiliation beyond whatever gratification or comfort is derived from the mere presence of others. The group, in other words, need not *do* anything about the source of threat in order to attract members. However, groups can sometimes act or attempt to act against the source of threat, and they may in this way afford protection or hope of protection to members. Thus a pragmatic form of support may be added to the 'psychological' support that comes from the mere presence of others.

A group may also provide support to a member by strengthening him psychologically in his opposition to a source of frustration. Stotland, for example, found that subjects' reactions to a restrictive authority figure during the course of an experiment were affected by their opportunities to talk to other subjects (12). Unlike those who had no social contact, subjects who spent some time with other subjects (a) were more aggressive and hostile towards their supervisor, (b) disagreed with the supervisor more often, (c) expressed greater dissatisfaction with the supervisor's failure to give reasons for his behavior and (d) argued strenuously for *their own* positions as opposed to that of the supervisor.

Implications of the Group for the Work Organization

Organizations are full of informal face-to-face groups that offer satisfying interpersonal relations and support to their members in the face of frustrations on the job. These groups form among workers operating around a common machine, or among workers who are near one another on the shop floor, or among workers who meet at lunch or in rest rooms or while moving around the plant. Many such groups develop norms that are relevant to the performance of the job. Members who do not conform to the group's norms face disapproval, ostracism or expulsion from the group. And if these sanctions fail, physical force may be employed. Thus relationships within these informal groups – particularly groups that are highly attractive to members – imply control and conformity as well as satisfaction and support. These characteristics help make group action the *concerted* or *mobilized* effort that it sometimes is.

Effects of the group on adjustment

Near the end of the Second World War, mass-production technology was introduced into British coal mines, in order to make mining more efficient. However, the new methods produced some unexpected results (13). For instance, psychosomatic ailments of epidemic proportions broke out among miners, and worker morale dropped to a low ebb. Absenteeism, conflicts and

221

tensions among workers rapidly increased – and productivity did not rise as it should have. At fault was the new technology, which – however sound from an engineering standpoint – did not take into account some of the social and psychological facts of life for the miner on the job; it did not consider the function of the social group.

Coal mines are dark, lonely and dangerous. The miners had coped with these adverse working conditions by forming small, tight-knit work groups. The members of these groups chose one another, knew one another and relied on one another. Thus, they gained some sense of security against the dark, the danger and other hardships of mining. Outside the mine, these supportive groups operated through the friendship and kinship relations within the community. When a miner died as a result of a mine accident, the members of his group often assumed responsibility for his family.

These group relations changed radically under the new technology. The new method of extracting coal relocated workers over a large area in the mine, so that they could no longer talk with one another easily. Their jobs, redefined by the new, large-scale machinery, isolated them further; they no longer collaborated closely and directly in getting the coal from the seam and out of the mine. Because of the new machinery, each worker specialized in a very limited part of the total process of extracting coal, which formerly was the responsibility of the group. Thus, the groups of mutually interdependent miners, which were functionally compatible with the earlier system of mining, became inappropriate. The mass-production technology disrupted these important social ties and, where adjustments were not made to substitute new social arrangements for the old, the mental health, morale, and productive efforts of the miners suffered.

Research on absenteeism and turnover in industry also suggest the importance of the group. Trist and Bamforth's study of British miners (13), illustrates some of the possible effects of groups on morale and on absenteeism. Research in other organizations generally supports the hypothesis that membership in a cohesive group helps increase job satisfaction and reduce absenteeism and turnover. Coch and French, for example, studied a group of textile workers who were required to adapt to changes in work methods. The turnover rates for these workers were quite high, but those who belonged to groups with strong 'we feeling' quit at a much lower rate – even though they had strong antagonistic feelings towards the company – than those who did not belong to 'cohesive' groups (4). Mann and Baumgartel (7) show how a sense of group belongingness, group spirit, group pride or group solidarity on the part of workers relates inversely to rates of absenteeism. In groups where workers were absent at least four times during a six-month period, only 21 per cent report that their crew is better than others in sticking together. However, 62 per cent of workers in groups with an average of only one absence during the six-month period report this kind of cohesiveness among members.

The group also appears to have important effects on the adjustment of organization members. In a number of respects, workers who belong to cohesive groups appear 'better adjusted' in the organization than those who do not have these informal attachments. Workers who belong to such groups are likely to have higher rates of job satisfaction and lower rates of tension, absenteeism and turnover than workers who do not belong to cohesive groups. The better adjustment of members of cohesive groups is due in part to the satisfactions and the psychological support that groups provide. The better adjustment may also reflect the lesser tendency for persons who are inept in social relations to join groups in the first place. But what implications does the group have for workers' productive efforts?

Effects of the group on productivity

In the Hawthorne research[1], the formation of a tight-knit group in the relay-assembly test room seemed to be responsible for the steadily increasing productivity (8). Increased productivity, however, is not the inevitable result of cohesive groups. Quite the contrary: when cohesive groups are formed in opposition to the organization, productivity drops.

The men in the test room at Hawthorne established norms to which they all conformed. One of these norms concerned the way they acted when the supervisor was present and when he was

1. See Reading 21 by J. A. C. Brown in this volume for further details on the Hawthorne studies – *Editor*.

away: all was seriousness and industry in his presence; but in his absence, levity and relaxation were the rule. Furthermore the wiremen established their own standard for production, and each employee consistently produced about what the group considered the 'proper' amount of work.

It was apparent to the observer that the men maintained a lower level of production than they could very easily have achieved. They did this despite the 'logic' of a wage-incentive system that would have rewarded them with larger pay checks, had they been less restrictive. In the *workers*' 'logic', higher production would only lead the company to raise the piece-rates, canceling out whatever additional earnings they might have made. The group, its restrictive norm and its control over members were natural consequences of this state of conflict. This control applied to members who produced at levels below the informal norm as well as to those who exceeded it. Low producers were called 'chiselers' and were admonished for not carrying their own weight. More often, however, the group imposed its sanctions on the 'rate busters' or 'slaves', who were producing at dangerously high levels.

Hawthorne drew the attention of social scientists to the group in industry, and soon a number of other researchers conducted studies on the effects of the group on worker productivity. Coch and French found that workers in informal social groups lowered their productivity in order to resist innovations in work methods introduced by the company, and that more cohesive groups – those with strong 'we feeling' – provided greater support to members who opposed the innovations (4). Seashore showed that workers in cohesive groups were neither more nor less productive on the average than workers in noncohesive groups, but in the cohesive groups workers were more *uniform* in their productivity – they all produced pretty much the same amount (10).

This uniformity is brought about through pressures against deviancy. These pressures can have an effect in changing the behavior of a newcomer to a group (4). Coch and French illustrate this with an example of a female textile worker. The newcomer unwittingly learned her job too well; and she began, after only a few days on the job, to exceed the group's production norm of about fifty units. On the thirteenth day, the group began to express its antagonism, with the desired effect: her productivity dropped. On the twentieth day, however, when all the members except the newcomer were transferred to other jobs, the group disbanded. Without the group to guide her productive efforts, her production climbed to an almost impossible level compared to what she and the group had been doing just a few days earlier.

Some Questions about the Group in Organizations

The informal group in organizations poses a paradox: groups can act with considerable effectiveness as law-enforcement agencies within the larger formal structure of the organization, but groups can direct the efforts of their members in opposition to organizational goals just as readily as they can direct members' efforts towards the support of these goals. This paradox caused students of organization to wonder how they might harness the power of the cohesive group. The answer seemed to lie in the approach taken by the Hawthorne experimenters in the relay-assembly test room, where the group worked towards the goal of efficient production. Why was the group so productive there and not in the bank-wiring room or on the shop floor?

Although part of the answer seemed to be the morale and job satisfaction – the 'fun' – that the girls felt in the relay test room, job satisfaction alone is not the answer. Neither is the mere existence of friendly social relations and a tight-knit group. The results of the Hawthorne study suggested another element in the puzzle – namely, the friendly and permissive behavior of the test-room supervisor.

References
1. F. H. ALLPORT, *Social Psychology*, Houghton Mifflin, 1924.
2. S. E. ASCH, 'The effects of group pressure upon the modification and distortion of judgments', in E. E. Maccoby, T. E. Newcomb and E. L. Hartley (eds.), *Readings in Social Psychology*, Holt, 1958, pp. 174–83.
3. K. BACK, 'The exertion of influence through social communication', *J. abnorm. soc. Psychol.*, vol. 46 (1951), pp. 9–23.
4. L. COCH and J. R. P. FRENCH, JR, 'Overcoming resistance to change', *Hum. Rel.*, vol. 1 (1948), pp. 512–33.
5. L. FESTINGER, S. SCHACHTER and K. BACK, *Social Pressures in Informal Groups: A Study of a Housing Project*, Harper, 1950.

6. L. FESTINGER and J. THIBAUT, 'Interpersonal communication in small groups', *J. abnorm. soc. Psychol.*, vol. 46 (1951), pp. 92–9.

7. F. C. MANN and H. G. BAUMGARTEL, *Absences and Employee Attitudes in an Electric Power Company*, Survey Research Center, University of Michigan, 1952.

8. F. J. ROETHLISBERGER and W. J. DICKSON, *Management and the Worker*, Harvard U.P., 1964.

9. S. SCHACHTER, 'Deviation, rejection and communication', *J. abnorm. soc. Psychol.*, vol. 46 (1951), pp. 190–207.

10. S. E. SEASHORE, *Group Cohesiveness in the Industrial Work Group*, Survey Research Center, University of Michigan, 1954.

11. M. SHERIF, *The Psychology of Social Norms*, Harper, 1936.

12. E. STOTLAND, 'Peer groups and reactions to power figures', in D. Cartwright (ed.), *Studies in Social Power*, Institute for Social Research, University of Michigan, 1959, pp. 53–68.

13. E. TRIST and K. BAMFORTH, 'Some social and psychological consequences of the Longwall method of coal-getting', *Hum. Rel.*, vol. 4 (1951), pp. 3–38.

Part Four Motivation and Performance: General Formulations

There is increasing interest among behavioural scientists in the possibility of developing models or theories which are capable of integrating the results of specific investigations of motivational influences on performance. Ultimately, it should be possible to explain the effects of such diverse job characteristics as the compensation system, job content, supervision and the work group in terms of a unified set of concepts and relationships.

In this part, we present the results of efforts directed towards this objective. Vroom (Reading 16) is concerned with the shape of the relationship between amount of motivation and the effectiveness of performance. Georgopoulos, Mahoney and Jones (Reading 17) and Lawler and Porter (Reading 18) view motivation for effective performance as a specific case of utility maximization and formulate models which include the desirability or utility of work related outcomes and the conditional probability that such outcomes will be attained. The Lawler and Porter model is the more comprehensive in the sense that it attempts to incorporate the effects of abilities and role perceptions as well as motivational variables.

Finally, Katz (Reading 19) offers a broad and integrative view of the concepts needed to understand the role of motivation in individual and organizational performance.

16 Victor H. Vroom

The Nature of the Relationship between Motivation and Performance

Excerpt from Victor H. Vroom, *Work and Motivation*, Wiley, 1964, pp. 204-9.

One could assume that, given some value of ability greater than zero, level of performance is a constantly increasing function of amount of motivation. In other words, the more motivated the worker to perform effectively, the more effective his performance. This kind of relationship is shown by the straight line in Figure 1.

There are at least two other plausible alternatives to this type of relationship. The first of these is a negatively accelerated curve approaching an upper limit. This possibility is shown in Figure 1 by a dotted line. It implies a law of diminishing returns – succeeding increments in motivation of identical amounts result in smaller and smaller increments in performance until a point is reached at which there is no further increase in performance. The second of these two alternative possibilities, an inverted U-function, is shown by a broken line. It is similar to the first except for a reduction in performance under high levels of motivation. Performance is low at low levels of motivation, reaches its maximum point under moderate levels of motivation and then drops off again under high levels of motivation.

Difficulties in measuring amount of motivation with any degree of precision make any very accurate determination of the nature of the functional relationship between amount of motivation and level of performance impossible. At best we can measure or manipulate motivation on an ordinal scale, i.e. we can specify that one level is higher than another but not how much higher it is. The admittedly imprecise nature of this measurement rules out the determination of the slope of the relationship between these two variables (e.g. positively accelerated, linear or negatively accelerated). It should still be possible, however, to determine changes in direction of the relationship (e.g. from positive to zero to negative). Thus, we can determine whether increases in motivation, when level of motivation is already at a high level, have positive effects on performance (as shown in the straight line), have no effect on performance (as shown in the dotted line), or have negative effects on performance (as shown in the broken line).

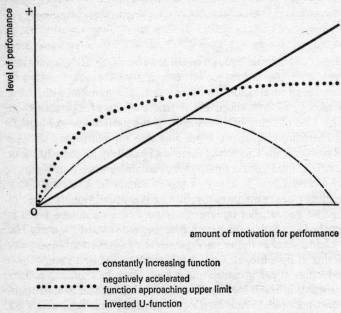

constantly increasing function

•••••••••• negatively accelerated function approaching upper limit

—— —— —— inverted U-function

Figure 1 Hypothetical relationships between amount of motivation and level of performance

There is considerable evidence that performance increases with an increase in the magnitude of the reward offered for successful performance. However, a few investigators have shown decrements in performance under very high levels of motivation. In a very early study, Yerkes and Dodson (1908) showed that maximum motivation did not lead to the most rapid learning, particularly if the tasks were difficult. They attempted to train mice to choose a white box over a black one by shocking them for entering the black box. Amount of motivation was varied by using different intensities of shock, and the difficulty of the task was varied by changing the difference in brightness between the white and black boxes. When the boxes differed only slightly in brightness, and consequently the task of discriminating among them was difficult, the relationship between amount of motivation and performance approximated the inverted U-function. The optimal level of motivation was neither the highest nor the lowest. When the task was made somewhat easier (by increasing the brightness difference between the boxes), the optimal level of motivation increased but there was still a decrement in performance under the highest motivation levels. Only when the brightness difference between the boxes was made very great was there a continuous increase in performance with increases in level of motivation.

Patrick (1934) obtained further evidence for the inverted U-function. In his experiment, he placed human subjects in a compartment which contained exit doors. Their problem was to escape from the compartment by discovering which one of the doors was unlocked. Inasmuch as the unlocked door was varied in random fashion from one trial to another and was never the same on two adjacent trials, there was no possibility for the subjects to learn a permanent solution to the problem. Under normal motivation, subjects went about trying to solve the problem in a highly rational fashion, avoiding repeated attempts to open the same door or avoiding the door that was unlocked on the previous trial. However, when the experimenter increased their motivation to escape by spraying them with a cold shower, shocking them through their bare feet or sounding a loud Klaxon horn, the subjects demonstrated more stereotyped and less efficient performance on the task.

Additional data suggesting the disruptive effects of high levels of motivation are found in an experiment carried out by Birch (1945). Six young chimpanzees were given a series of problems to solve under various lengths of food deprivation. The solution of each of the problems required the animals to use the materials provided (e.g. string, rope or sticks) to obtain food. Birch found the intermediate lengths of food deprivation, which we can assume to represent the intermediate levels of motivation to get food, to be most conducive to problem-solving efficiency. Relatively short and relatively long periods of food deprivation resulted in less efficient behavior. Birch's description of the behavior of the animals illuminates the different bases for the ineffective performance of animals under conditions of very low and very high motivation.

When motivation is very low the animals are easily diverted from the problem by extraneous factors and behavior tends to deteriorate into a series of non-goal-directed acts. Under conditions of very intense motivation, the animals concentrated upon the goal to the relative exclusion of other features of the situation which were essential to the solution of the problem. Also, the frequent occurrence of frustration responses, such as tantrums and screaming, when a given stereotyped pattern of response proved to be inadequate, hindered the animals in their problem-solving efforts (Birch, 1945, p. 316).

While the form of the relationship between amount of motivation and level of performance may vary somewhat with the nature of the task confronting the subject, most investigators have suggested that the inverted U-function most closely approximates the actual state of affairs. McClelland (1951) concludes that

... as a motive increases in intensity it first leads to an increase in the efficiency of instrumental activity and then to a decrease. Thus it would appear that as far as adjustment is concerned there is a certain optimum level of motive intensity, a level of 'creative anxiety', which leads to maximum problem-solving efficiency. Too little motivation leads to sluggishness and inertia, too much to disruption and defense against anxiety. The theoretical problems still unsolved are the discovery of what this area of optimum intensity is and why higher intensities lead to inefficiency (McClelland, 1951, p. 485).

How can the decrement in performance under very high levels of motivation be accounted for? There are at least two possible explanations. One explanation is based on the assumption, made by Tolman (1948), that a high level of motivation is accompanied by a 'narrowing of the cognitive field'. A highly motivated person may attend only to those cues which he expects to be useful in the attainment of his goals. If the task or problem is a novel or difficult one, his intense motivation may lead to his ignoring relevant information. Supporting Tolman's assumption are at least two experiments (Bruner, Matter and Papanek, 1955;

Johnson, 1952) showing substantially less incidental learning among animals trained under high levels of motivation. The possibility that a narrowing of the cognitive field represents the basis for the decrement in performance under very high motivation is further suggested by Birch's observation that the chimpanzees who had been deprived of food for forty-eight hours concentrated so intensely on the food that they ignored other objects in the cage which could be used to solve the problem.

The second explanation involves the supposition that a high level of motivation to attain a goal tends to be associated with anxiety or some other strong emotional state which in turn impairs performance. The idea that high levels of motivation tend to be accompanied by anxiety is not intuitively unreasonable. Anxiety has been defined by Mowrer (1939) as a learned anticipatory response to cues that have in the past been followed by injury or pain. It might be argued that the anticipation of failure in a situation in which failure has high negative valence could be the source of considerable anxiety. Since such a situation would also tend to be one in which the subject strongly prefers success to failure, anxiety and intense motivation may frequently accompany one another.

What about the assertion that anxiety impairs performance? There is considerable anecdotal and experimental evidence which suggests that this is in fact the case. On the anecdotal side are the frequently heard stories about the student who was so frightened by the prospects of failing an examination that his mind went 'blank' or the actor who, on 'opening night', forgot the lines that he knew so well during rehearsal. In experiments, it has been shown that when individuals are placed in a stressful situation designed to create anxiety, their performance tends to be lower than when the situation is non-stressful (Alper, 1946; Lantz, 1945; McClelland and Apicella, 1947; McKinney, 1933; Sears, 1937; Williams, 1947). It has also been found that persons obtaining high scores on the Taylor Manifest Anxiety Scale (Taylor, 1953) perform less effectively on relatively complex verbal and non-verbal training tasks than those obtaining low scores (Farber and Spence, 1953; Montague, 1953; Raymond, 1953; Taylor and Spence, 1952).

Why should anxiety impair performance? For one thing, there

233

are involuntary autonomic responses associated with anxiety which could interfere with execution of a task. The pianist may find it difficult to play when his hands are perspiring and his heart pounding and the actor may find his mouth so dry that he is incapable of delivering his lines. It is also possible that the highly anxious person's actions will become directed towards reducing his anxiety rather than performing the task. The anxious soldier may flee from the battlefield and the anxious executive may lapse into fantasy or turn to alcohol for the solution of his problems.

The disruption in performance resulting from anxiety seems to be greatest for relatively difficult tasks. Studies by Farber and Spence, (1953), Montague (1953) and Raymond (1953) show that superiority in rate of learning of non-anxious subjects (as measured by the Taylor Manifest Anxiety Scale) increases with the difficulty of the material to be learned. It has even been shown that, in the very simple eye-blink conditioning situation, anxious persons learn more quickly than non-anxious persons (Spence and Farber, 1953, 1954; Spence and Taylor, 1951; Taylor, 1951).

A recent series of field experiments by Schachter *et al.* (1961) demonstrate that situationally produced emotional disturbances result in a greater impairment in workers' performance of novel non-stereotyped tasks. These experiments were conducted on groups of assembly workers in General Electric factories. The experiments were similar in design, although details varied from factory to factory. In each experiment, matched groups performing identical operations were selected. Half of the groups, called disfavored, were subjected to a series of annoyances with the intent of making them 'disturbed and upset'. The other half of the groups, called favored, were confronted with situations designed to produce 'contentment and satisfaction'. Production data was gathered before these manipulations and during the manipulation period which lasted from two to four weeks. At the end of this time, the manipulations were halted and identical changes in work procedure were introduced into the favored and disfavored groups. The results indicate little difference in productivity between the favored and disfavored groups before the changeover. However, after the changeover, when the task required relearning on the part of the workers, the disfavored groups displayed lower productivity than the favored groups. The authors conclude that, 'emotional disturbance has little effect on stereotyped activity, but does have a disrupting effect on non-stereotyped activity'.

Both explanations of the decrement in performance under intense motivation are logically plausible and consistent with some empirical observations. Further research on the relationship between strength of motivation and performance for a wide range of different tasks and subjects should shed further light on the underlying processes.

References

ALPER, T. G. (1946), 'Memory for completed and incompleted tasks as a function of personality: an analysis of group data', *J. abnorm. soc. Psychol.*, vol. 41, pp. 403–21.

BIRCH, H. G. (1945), 'The role of motivational factors in insightful problem solving', *J. comp. Psychol.*, vol. 38, pp. 293–317.

BRUNER, J. S., MATTER, J., and PAPANEK, M. L. (1955), 'Breadth of learning as a function of drive level and mechanization', *Psychol. Rev.*, vol. 62, pp. 1–10.

FARBER, I. E., and SPENCE, K. W. (1953), 'Complex learning and conditioning as a function of anxiety', *J. exp. Psychol.*, vol. 45, pp. 120–5.

JOHNSON, E. E. (1952), 'The role of motivational strength in latent learning', *J. comp. physiol. Psychol.*, vol. 45, pp. 526–30.

LANTZ, B. (1945), 'Some dynamic aspects of success and failure', *Psychol. Monog.*, vol. 59, no. 1 (whole no. 271).

McCLELLAND, D. C. (1951), *Personality*, Sloane.

McCLELLAND, D. C., and APICELLA, F. S. (1947), 'Reminiscence following experimentally induced failure', *J. exp. Psychol.*, vol. 37, pp. 159–69.

McKINNEY, F. (1933), 'Certain emotional factors in learning and efficiency', *J. gen. Psychol.*, vol. 9, pp. 101–16.

MONTAGUE, E. K. (1953), 'The role of anxiety in serial rote learning', *J. exp. Psychol.*, vol. 45, pp. 91–6.

MOWRER, O. H. (1939), 'A stimulus–response analysis of anxiety and its role as a reinforcing agent', *Psychol. Rev.*, vol. 46, pp. 553–65.

PATRICK, J. R. (1934), 'Studies in rational behavior and emotional excitement: the effect of emotional excitement on rational behavior in human subjects', *J. comp. Psychol.*, vol. 18, pp. 153–95.

RAYMOND, C. K. (1953), 'Anxiety and task as determiners of verbal performance', *J. exp. Psychol.*, vol. 46, pp. 120–24.

SCHACHTER, S., WILLERMAN, B., FESTINGER, L., and HYMAN, R. (1961), 'Emotional disruption and industrial productivity', *J. appl. Psychol.*, vol. 45, pp. 201–13.

SEARS, R. P. (1937), 'Initiation of the repression sequence by experienced failure', *J. exp. Psychol.*, vol. 20, pp. 570–80.

SPENCE, K. W., and FARBER, L. E. (1953), 'Conditioning and extinction as a function of anxiety', *J. exp. Psychol.*, vol. 45, pp. 116–19.

SPENCE, K. W., and FARBER, I. E. (1954), 'The relation of anxiety to differentially applied conditioning', *J. exp. Psychol.*, vol. 47, pp. 127–34.

SPENCE, K. W., and TAYLOR, J. (1951), 'Anxiety and strength of the UCS as determiners of the amount of eyelid conditioning', *J. exp. Psychol.*, vol. 42, pp. 183–8.

TAYLOR, J. (1951), 'The relationship of anxiety to the conditioned eyelid response', *J. exp. Psychol.*, vol. 41, pp. 81–92.

TAYLOR, J. (1953), 'A personality scale of manifest anxiety', *J. abnorm. soc. Psychol.*, vol. 48, pp. 285–90.

TAYLOR, J., and SPENCE, K. W. (1952), 'The relationship of anxiety level to performance in serial learning', *J. exp. Psychol.*, vol. 44, pp. 61–4.

TOLMAN, E. C. (1948), 'Cognitive maps in rats and man', *Psychol. Rev.*, vol. 55, pp. 189–208.

WILLIAMS, M. (1947), 'An experimental study of intellectual control under stress and associated Rorschach factors', *J. consult. Psychol.*, vol. 11, pp. 21–9.

YERKES, R. M., and DODSON, J. D. (1908), 'The relation of strength of stimulus to rapidity of habit formation', *J. comp. Psychol.*, vol. 18, pp. 459–82.

17 Basil S. Georgopoulos, Gerald M. Mahoney and Nyle W. Jones

A Path–Goal Approach to Productivity

Basil S. Georgopoulos, Gerald M. Mahoney and Nyle W. Jones,
'A path–goal approach to productivity', *Journal of Applied Psychology*,
vol. 41, 1957, pp. 345–53.

The problem of the adequate uncovering and proper evaluation
of social-psychological factors in the area of organizational effectiveness constitutes a major aspect of current thinking and research. Since it entails considerable theoretical interest as well as
action implications, it has received constant attention in the
programmatic planning of the Organizational Behavior and
Human Relations Program, Survey Research Center. In general,
the program has focused upon the variable of productivity as one
type of organizational effectiveness. According to this position,
the performance of people in organizations may be considered as
reflecting the relative attainment of important organizational
objectives, and its prediction should contribute to our understanding of human behavior. In the present article, we shall be
concerned with the prediction of individual productivity in
industrial settings, approaching an old problem in a new way.

Problem

The question is why some workers tend to be high producers, or
why persons of largely similar background who are engaged in
the same activity under comparable conditions exhibit considerable variability in output. Specifically, what determines high
productivity? In attempting to provide an answer to this problem
previous studies in the program have explored the relationship of
several factors to productivity, employing various approaches.
These included 'morale', certain job satisfactions, supervisory
practices and group cohesiveness (1, 2, 3, 4, 7, 8). The results,
inconsistent and inconclusive in many cases, pointed to the complexity of the problem, suggesting a number of hypotheses. It

clearly emerged that productivity is the resultant of a complex of factors, both individual and situational, both phenomenal and objective. On either side, both rational and non-rational factors appeared to be involved, some being forces toward and others against high productivity.

The path–goal hypothesis

Beginning with the notions that individuals in the work situation have certain goals in common, the achievement of which would satisfy certain corresponding needs, and that behavior is in part a function of rational calculability, or decision making in terms of goal-directedness, we arrived at a path–goal approach. This approach is based on the following assumptions: individual productivity is, among other things, a function of one's motivation to produce at a given level; in turn, such motivation depends upon (a) the particular needs of the individual as reflected in the goals towards which he is moving, and (b) his perception regarding the relative usefulness of productivity behavior as an instrumentality, or as a path to the attainment of these goals.

People have certain needs in common so that, brought into a common situation, they will seek and pursue among available goals those which promise to satisfy their needs. The path to be followed in a given case will be a function of the expectations of the individual. If high productivity is perceived as the appropriate path, the individual should become a high producer. This formulation may be simply stated in the form of the following general hypothesis, labelled as the 'path-goal hypothesis': *If a worker sees high productivity as a path leading to the attainment of one or more of his personal goals, he will tend to be a high producer. Conversely, if he sees low productivity as a path to the achievement of his goals, he will tend to be a low producer.* The first aspect of this hypothesis is probably more general and relevant in our society; it is doubtful whether many people see low productivity as helping the achievement of many of their goals.

According to this hypothesis, if, for example, a worker has a need to be liked by his co-workers and he sees high (or low) productivity as a path to the attainment of his goal to get along well with the work group, we will predict that he is likely to follow this path and, in effect, become a high (or low) producer.

Such likelihood, however, depends on at least two important conditions: the path will be presumably chosen if his need(s) is sufficiently high, or if his goal(s) is relatively salient and if no other more effective and economical paths are available to him. And while the latter condition ordinarily holds in the work situation, the former must be determined.

Furthermore, even if the high productivity path is chosen, i.e. the worker is motivated to produce at a high level, we cannot be sure that he will in fact become a high producer. This would be the case if there were no restraining forces, if no barriers blocked the desired path. Such factors, acting as limiting conditions, may hinder the translation of motivation to produce into actual productive behavior of a given level. This, therefore, requires that the person be relatively free to follow the desired path. In view of these qualifications, the relationship between path–goal perception and productivity should be more pronounced among workers who have a high need for a given goal and who encounter no barriers. This suggests that the path–goal hypothesis should hold better under the condition of high need and under the condition of freedom from restraining factors, and that it should hold best under high need and freedom combined.

The major independent variable studied is the worker's perception of the usefulness or of the instrumentality of productivity as a path leading to job related goals. Such path–goal perceptions may be conceived as expectations or psychological probabilities of varying amounts of environmental return of a given kind, or as a consequence of certain behavior. A path–goal perception pattern would seem to reduce to the question, 'How much payoff is there for me towards attaining a personal goal while expending so much effort toward the achievement of an assigned organizational objective?' We, of course, recognize that several factors affect the emergence, patterning, and change of path–goal perceptions. In this study, however, these perceptions, as reported by the workers, are considered as 'given', and reference is made to only one kind of behavior – productivity. In addition to the path–goal perception variant, the role of two other pertinent conditions is taken into account. These are the level of need of the person, or the relative significance of each of his particular goals, and his level of freedom from constraining factors.

239

In summary, according to the present approach, behavior is viewed as a function of needs, expectations, and situations. Productivity level is seen as representing purposive behavior which is determined through the interaction of both facilitating and inhibiting forces, forces in the individual and in the environment. More specifically, it is seen as a function of *path–goal perception, level of need* and *level of freedom.* These three factors should in part determine one's productivity behavior. Theoretically, additional social–psychological variables, such as group norms, should account for the rest of the variance in individual performance.

This orientation is similar to the theoretical positions of Lewin and Tolman. Lewin contended that behavior (locomotion) takes place over paths, some of which are more direct than others in relation to a given goal (5). He also distinguished between driving forces towards a goal and barriers, which impede locomotion, and asserted that a behavioral possibility depends on the nature of the existing forces and the valence, positive or negative, of the particular goal (6). Similarly, according to Tolman's model, the possibility of a behavior is a function of the needs and of the 'means–end readiness' of the individual in the given stimulus situation (9).

The sample of the study

The path–goal hypothesis was submitted to a first test in connexion with a more encompassing research project in a medium-size, unionized, household appliances company. The relevant data, in the form of a questionnaire, were collected from the company's entire individual incentive worker population. However, from the 722 workers, sixty-two were excluded for low questionnaire comprehension (having also been excluded from the larger project); another thirty-nine workers of non-ascertained productivity level were also excluded, thus leaving a sample of 621 cases in the two plants operated by this organization.

Nearly all of the workers (92 per cent) were union members, and most were male (78 per cent) and married (77 per cent), having one or two dependents (72 per cent). Most grew up on farms or in small towns (76 per cent). The average age of the group was 35, with 30 per cent being in their 20s and 46 per cent

240

being between 30 and 39. In terms of education, 35 per cent had less than high school education, another 31 per cent had some high school and 32 per cent had completed high school. Nearly half of these workers (43 per cent) had less than one year of experience on the job. Finally, a fact of relevance is that the majority of these people (58 per cent) felt that on-the-job satisfactions are as important as those gained off the job.

The incentive plan under which these people operated is of the 'standard hour' type. Workers are periodically evaluated for selected time intervals, and an engineer estimates the relative effort of the person. With 1·00 assumed as normal effort, a fast worker may be rated 1·30 or 30 per cent over normal, etc. Finally, a series of allowances for such things as unavoidable delays, fatigue, personal time, etc., and 5 per cent constant allowance are added to determine the standard time for a unit of production. At the end, it may turn out that a worker producing exactly at his normal work standard is paid at the rate of 118 per cent of the hourly base rate for that job classification, his productivity being 118 per cent. A person may raise his performance, and his wages, by increasing his effort or work pace.

Method and Procedure

As the operational definition and relevant measure of the path–goal perception concept, responses to two groups of questionnaire items were utilized. One group was designed to ascertain how instrumental high productivity is seen for attaining certain job related goals, the other to ascertain how instrumental low productivity is seen for achieving these same goals. For each of a number of goal items, this was done by having the worker evaluate high productivity on a five-point scale, from 'helping' to 'hurting' the attainment of a given goal; the same evaluation was separately made for low productivity. We, therefore, have the *instrumentality of high productivity* and the *instrumentality of low productivity*, respectively representing the two evaluations.

In the case of the instrumentality of high productivity, a worker who evaluates high productivity as helping the attainment of a given goal is said to have a *positive* path–goal perception, one who sees it as hurting to have a *negative* perception, and one who perceives neither to be the case to have a *neutral* (irrelevant perception).[1] For the instrumentality of low productivity the terminology is reversed. One who sees low productivity as helping is said to have a *negative* perception from the point of view of his productivity behavior, and one who sees it as hurting to have a *positive* perception; a *neutral* alternative is also used. According to the theory, high producers would be those who have positive path–goal perceptions (high productivity helps or low productivity hurts). Those who express a neutral perception, when possible (where the analysis cells are large enough to work with), are eliminated from the analysis. Where this is not possible, the neutral perception group is combined with the negative to yield more cases for study.

Among the specific goal items studied in connexion with the two productivity instrumentalities are, 'making more money in the long run', 'getting along well with the work group' and 'promotion to a higher base rate'. The first item is unlike the other two in that it did not present the respondent with a neutral perception alternative. Of a series of ten job related items, these three were selected for full study because of their relatively higher importance to the sample as a whole, as determined by rank-ordering on the part of the respondents. With 10·00 being the lowest possible mean-rank that could result from the combined judgements of all individuals in the sample and 1·00 being the highest, the mean-rank relevance of these items was 5·1, 4·5 and 5·1, respectively.

For each goal item, the level of need of each individual was determined inferentially. Those ranking a particular goal as 1, 2 or 3 on a scale of importance from 1 to 10 (the number of items ranked) were pooled to form the *high-need* group; the remainder constitute the *low-need* group with respect to the same goal. The level of freedom for each individual was ascertained by combining three job relevant factors, each of which was expected from past experience to be related to productivity and was in fact found to

1. Thus, the term 'instrumentality' is used to refer to the level of productivity, high or low, which is the object of a path–goal perception; the terms 'positive', 'negative' and 'neutral' are used to refer to the nature of the valence (value or sign) of this perception, from the point of view of productivity behavior.

bear such a significant positive relationship at the 0·01 level. Specifically, those who stated that they were free to set their work pace, who had a minimum of six months' experience on the job, and who were aged between twenty and fifty-nine years inclusive constitute the *free* group; the remainder, lacking in one or more of these characteristics, form the *not-free* group. The rationale for this combination is that absence of any of the three characteristics may act as a barrier with respect to the freedom of a person to vary his productivity so that he can produce at a desired high level. The reader should note that while the free/not-free groups are the same for all three goal items studied, the high-/low-need groups vary from item to item.

Finally, the measure used to ascertain productivity level is based on the question: 'What productivity percentage figure do you usually hit in a day? (write in the per cent below) — per cent? It was decided that this reported, rather than a seemingly more 'objective', measure be used. This was due to the anonymity of the questionnaires, the difficulty in choosing a suitable time base-line for the computation of a person's average productivity, and imperfections in company records. Although the precise validity of this measure cannot be determined from the data themselves, past experience with similar cases gives us no reason to question its validity for the sample as a whole.

The division of the sample into high and low producers was made on the basis of the obtained productivity distribution. The median productivity for the sample was 140 per cent, the range being from 50 per cent to 200 per cent but with very few cases falling at either extreme. However, a disproportionately large number of workers, 24 per cent of the sample, reported a productivity of 140 per cent, i.e. at the median point. This argued in favor of dichotomizing the distribution at the point between 140 per cent and 141 per cent, i.e. just above the median, in order that we could be sure that 'high' producers are sufficiently differentiated from 'low' producers. Thus, the dichotomy resulted in the creation of a *high* productivity group (productivity of 141 per cent or more) and a *low* productivity group (140 per cent or less). This dichotomy gave data of relative symmetry and comparability, thus not suggesting separate treatment for the two company plants from which the sample derives. Similar percentages of

243

high as against low producers characterized each of the two plants as well as the total sample. We found that 27 per cent of the 390 workers in the one plant and 29 per cent of the 231 workers in the other were categorized as high producers, while 28 per cent of the total sample of 621 individuals were so classified as a result of the above procedure.

Results

The first operational prediction investigated constitutes a restatement of the path–goal hypothesis:

Hypothesis 1

With respect to a given goal item, the percentage of high producers will be greater among workers having a positive path–goal perception (high productivity helps or low productivity hurts) than among those having a negative perception (high productivity hurts or low productivity helps).

Table 1 shows the relationship between path–goal perception and productivity in terms of percentages of high producers with reference to each of three goal items, separately for the instrumentality of high and the instrumentality of low productivity. These data support the hypothesis that high productivity will more often occur among those who have a positive path–goal perception. For example, of those who perceive high productivity positively with respect to making more money in the long run, 38 per cent are high producers, in contrast to only 21 per cent of those who see it negatively; similarly, of those who perceive low productivity positively (as hurting), 30 per cent are high producers as against 22 per cent of those having a negative path–goal perception. Similar results obtain for the goal items of getting along well with the work group and promotion to a higher base rate. All six percentage comparisons between positive and negative perceivers are as predicted by Hypothesis 1. Three of these differences, moreover, are statistically significant, by chi-square test corrected for continuity, at the 0·05 level or better. The data also show that the hypothesis holds equally as well for the instrumentality of low productivity as for the instrumentality of high productivity, since the pattern of results is about the same in both cases.

Table 1

The Relationship between Path–Goal Perception and Productivity
(Percentage of High Producers[a])

| | Path–Goal Perception | | | |
| | Instrumentality of high productivity | | Instrumentality of low productivity | |
Goal Item Involved in Path–Goal Perception	Positive (high productivity 'helps')	Negative (high productivity 'hurts')	Positive (low productivity 'hurts')	Negative (low productivity 'helps')
More money in the long run	38%(234)>21%(376)*		30%(380)>22%(215)*	
Getting along well with work group	32% (66)>23%(195)		33%(189)>28% (36)	
Promotion to a higher base rate	26%(236)>23% (31)		32%(298)>12% (43)*	

* These percentage differences are significant, by chi-square test, at the 0·05 level or better and in the predicted direction.

[a] Percentages are based on the number in the corresponding parenthesis, the complement of each percentage, not appearing in the table, represents the percentage of low producers in each case.

The substantiation of the path–goal hypothesis also depends on the demonstration that it holds better among workers who have a high rather than a low need for a given goal item:

Hypothesis 2

With respect to a given goal item, the percentage difference of high producers between those having a positive and those having a negative (and/or neutral)[2] path–goal perception will be greater among workers who have a high than among those who have a low need for the same goal.

Table 2 presents the data which test Hypothesis 2. Comparing for each goal item the percentage difference between columns 1 and 2 (high need), with the corresponding difference between columns 3 and 4 (low need), we should expect in each case the former difference to be higher than the latter, according to the hypothesis. As an example, if we consider the goal of making more money in the long run in the case of the instrumentality of high productivity, we find that under the condition of high need the difference in high producers between positive and negative

2. For Tables 2, 3 and 4, from the data of which Hypotheses 2, 3 and 4 are tested, as was earlier mentioned, the neutral is combined with the negative perception category to yield enough cases for study. This does not apply to the goal item 'making more money in the long run', however, since the respondents had not been offered a neutral choice in this case.

Table 2

The Relationship between Path–Goal Perception and Productivity When Controlling for Level of Need (Percentage of High Producers[a])

| | Path–Goal Perception | | | |
| | High Need | | Low Need | |
Goal Item	Positive (1)	Negative and/or neutral (2)	Positive (3)	Negative and/or neutral (4)
	Instrumentality of high productivity			
More money in the long run	38% (86)*	14% (119)	36% (129)*	25% (229)
Getting along well with work group	40% (25)	28% (181)	28% (36)	27% (326)
Promotion to a higher base rate	28% (87)	23% (117)	26% (137)	32% (213)
	Instrumentality of low productivity			
More money in the long run	26% (136)	17% (66)	32% (213)	25% (128)
Getting along well with work group	33% (66)	26% (135)	33% (109)	23% (234)
Promotion to a higher base rate	28% (93)	19% (107)	33% (180)	25% (159)

* These percentage differences are significant, by chi-square test, at the 0·05 level and in the predicted direction.
[a] Percentages are based on the number in the corresponding parentheses; the complement of each percentage, not appearing in the table, represents the percentage of low producers in each case.

path–goal perceivers is 24 per cent, compared to 11 per cent under the condition of low need. In all, six such comparisons are possible, and five of these yield differences as predicted by the theory. Therefore Hypothesis 2 receives considerable support from the data. The data also show that the original path–goal hypothesis holds also when we control for level of need; regardless of level of need, high productivity occurs more often among positive rather than negative perceivers. This is shown from the fact that eleven of the twelve possible differences between positive and negative perceivers are as predicted by Hypothesis 1.

The third hypothesis is introducing the condition of freedom:

Hypothesis 3

With respect to a given goal item, the percentage difference of high producers between those having a positive and those having a negative (and/or neutral) path–goal perception will be greater among workers who are free than among workers who are not free from constraining forces. That is, the path–goal hypothesis will hold better under the condition of freedom.

Table 3 presents the data which test Hypothesis 3. A comparison identical with the one made with the data of Table 2 in connexion with Hypothesis 2 (comparing the percentage differences between columns 1 and 2 with the corresponding differences between columns 3 and 4) shows that five of the six possible percentage differences between positive and negative perceivers who are free, on the one hand, and positive and negative perceivers who are not free, on the other, are as predicted by Hypothesis 3.

Table 3

The Relationship between Path–Goal Perception and Productivity When Controlling for Level of Freedom (Percentage of High Producers[a])

| | Path–Goal Perception | | | |
| | Free | | Not Free | |
Goal Item	Positive (1)	Negative and/or neutral (2)	Positive (3)	Negative and/or neutral (4)
	Instrumentality of high productivity			
More money in the long run	52% (103)*	35% (127)	27% (131)*	14% (249)
Getting along well with work group	38% (29)	43% (201)	21% (37)	18% (344)
Promotion to a higher base rate	43% (88)	43% (140)	16% (148)	21% (228)
	Instrumentality of low productivity			
More money in the long run	44% (158)	38% (65)	20% (222)	15% (150)
Getting along well with work group	52% (81)*	37% (138)	19% (108)	17% (260)
Promotion to a higher base rate	52% (114)*	33% (108)	20% (184)	16% (184)

* These percentage differences are significant, by chi-square test, at the 0·05 level and in the predicted direction.
[a] Percentages are based on the number in the corresponding parentheses; the complement of each percentage, not appearing in the table, represents the percentage of low producers in each case.

Under the condition of freedom, the difference in high producers between those who have a positive and those who have a negative (and/or neutral) path–goal perception is greater than under the condition of no freedom. Furthermore, as in the case of level of need, the data show that the original path–goal hypothesis also holds when we control for level of freedom, since, regardless of level of freedom, high productivity more often occurs among positive rather than negative perceivers. If the twelve possible comparisons between positive and negative path–goal perception are made, it will be found that nine of these are as predicted by

Table 4 The Relationship between Path–Goal Perception and Productivity When Controlling for Level of Need and Freedom (Percentage of High Producers[a])

	Path–Goal Perception							
	High Need				Low Need			
	Free		Not free		Free		Not free	
Goal Term	Positive (1)	Negative and/or neutral (2)	Positive (3)	Negative and/or neutral (4)	Positive (5)	Negative and/or neutral (6)	Positive (7)	Negative and/or neutral (8)
Instrumentality of high productivity								
More money in the long run	66% (38)*	22% (37)	40% (57)	39% (79)	17% (48)	11% (82)	33% (72)*	17% (146)
Getting along well with work group	40% (10)	39% (66)	44% (16)	43% (126)	40% (15)	21% (115)	15% (20)	16% (200)
Promotion to a higher base rate	46% (35)	44% (39)	42% (48)	39% (87)	15% (52)	13% (78)	17% (89)	27% (126)
Instrumentality of low productivity								
More money in the long run	49% (53)	26% (19)	40% (91)	41% (41)	11% (83)	13% (47)	27% (122)	17% (87)
Getting along well with work group	50% (28)	32% (47)	52% (48)	38% (84)	21% (38)	23% (86)	18% (61)	15% (150)
Promotion to a higher base rate	56% (33)*	31% (39)	47% (70)	33% (61)	12% (60)	12% (68)	24% (110)	20% (98)

* These percentage differences are significant by chi-square test, at the 0·05 level or better and in the predicted direction.

[a] Percentages are based on the number in the corresponding parentheses; the complement of each percentage, not appearing in the table, represents the percentage of low producers in each case.

Hypothesis 1, there is no difference in one case, and only two comparisons result in differences of an opposite direction.

To substantiate the path–goal orientation, the data should finally demonstrate that the path–goal hypothesis holds best among workers who have a high need for a given goal and who, at the same time, are free from barriers:

Hypothesis 4

With respect to a given goal item, the percentage difference of high producers between those having a positive and those having a negative (and/or neutral) path–goal perception will be greater among workers who have a high need and are free than among workers characterized by any other combination of need and freedom.

Table 4 presents the data which are relevant to our last hypothesis. The pertinent comparisons which test this hypothesis are the comparisons of the percentage differences between columns 1 and 2 in relation to the corresponding differences between columns 3 and 4, 5 and 6, 7 and 8. Columns 1 and 2 represent workers who have a high need and who are also free; the other three pairs of columns respectively represent workers who have high need but are not free, who have low need but are free, and who have low need and are not free. The first column in each pair represents positive, and the second negative (and/or neutral) path–goal perceivers. Hypothesis 4 predicts that, for a given goal item, the percentage difference between columns 1 and 2 will in each case be greater than the corresponding difference from any of the other three pairs of columns.

According to the above specifications, eighteen separate comparisons, six for each goal item, are possible on the basis of the data in Table 4. Half of these comparisons pertain to the instrumentality of high productivity and the other half to the instrumentality of low productivity. The results are generally as predicted. Thus, considering the goal of making more money in the long run, instrumentality of high productivity, we find that, whereas there is a difference in high producers of 44 per cent between columns 1 and 2, the corresponding differences between columns 3 and 4, 5 and 6, and 7 and 8, are only 1 per cent, 6 per cent and 16 per cent, respectively. In short, the difference in high producers between positive and negative path–goal perceivers is greatest for the high need-free group workers. In all, fourteen of the eighteen possible comparisons yield expected differences, two show zero differences and two comparisons result in differences in the opposite direction. Considering the fact that many of the comparisons involved represent cells of relatively few cases, Hypothesis 4 receives substantial support from the findings. The data of Table 4 also support the original path–goal hypothesis: eighteen of the twenty-four possible comparisons between positive and negative perceivers are as predicted by Hypothesis 1, there is a zero difference in one case, and five differences are not as predicted. Therefore, the relationship between path–goal perception and productivity remains fairly clear when we control for level of need and level of freedom simultaneously.

Discussion

Four hypotheses deriving from the theory were supported by the data. The findings indicate that if a worker sees high (or low) productivity as a path to the attainment of his personal goals, he will tend to be a high (or low) producer. This relationship is more pronounced among workers who have a high need with respect to a given goal and who are free from constraining forces than among workers lacking in these characteristics. When compared across tables, the results also show that, functionally, high productivity viewed by the person as instrumental to the attainment of a goal does not operate differently from low productivity when the latter is viewed as impeding goal attainment, and vice versa. In both cases, the path–goal perception variables seems to be a significant determinant of individual productivity.

It cannot be expected, however, that all of the variance in individual productivity could be accounted for in path–goal terms. First, this approach deliberately emphasizes the role of rational aspects in human behavior while, as is known, non-rational aspects are also important. Second, a separate attempt at multivariate analysis, by means of a modified multiple correlation technique, indicated that only a modest portion of the variance in productivity was explained in path–goal terms. Finally, other social psychological variables, e.g. group norms, also have a determining influence on productivity, especially in situations where cooperative effort is essential. Therefore, the path–goal approach should be considered as supplementing and not as a substitute for other useful approaches.

A comparison of the findings shows that the path–goal approach holds perceptibly better for the goal item 'making more money in the long run' than for the items 'getting along well with the work group' and 'promotion to a higher base rate'. This suggests that goals may function differentially with respect to the perception–productivity relationship. In this connexion, moreover, work with some other goal items which, as was earlier indicated, were of lower relevance to the sample than the above three items yielded less clearcut results, confirming the importance of goal relevance. Still another problem may arise from the fact that several congruent goals, regardless of their particular relevance to a given population, might be simultaneously attained by the individual through production at a given level. These phenomena require further exploration so that a fuller statement of the relationship among goals attainable in the work situation can be made possible.

Future improvements might include: (a) the development of more adequate measures for the concepts of level of need and level of freedom; (b) the study of social factors in the work situation which affect or determine an individual's path–goal perceptions; (c) a study of the implications of goal relevance or salience and of goal congruence; (d) efforts towards the acquisition of an adequate sample of goal items from the variety of significant items which may be found in the work situation; and (e) the application of the path–goal approach to additional samples and settings, e.g. non-incentive work populations, under various conditions.

Summary

In this article, we have presented a path–goal approach to productivity. In an effort to understand the effects of certain social psychological factors on individual productivity in organizations, we tested four hypotheses deriving from the following formulation: if a worker sees high (or low) productivity as a path to the attainment of one or more of his personal goals in the work situation,

251

he will tend to be a high (or low) producer, assuming that his need is sufficiently high, or his goal is relatively salient, and that he is free from barriers to follow the desired path (high or low productivity). The results of this study provide support for the predictions made and, within limits, indicate the usefulness of a rational approach to the problem in question. They provide a clear confirmation of the importance of the role of rational aspects in the determination of productivity behavior and serve to re-emphasize the fact that productivity is a function of both facilitating and inhibiting forces, forces of an individual as well as of a situational character. However, a number of implications of the path–goal orientation for the understanding of what determines productivity level, our initial question, still remain to be worked out.

References
1. R. L. KAHN and D. KATZ, 'Leadership practices in relation to productivity and morale', in D. Cartwright and A. Zander (eds.), *Group Dynamics: Research and Theory*, Row, Peterson, 1953, pp. 612–28.
2. R. L. KAHN and N. C. MORSE, 'The relationship of productivity to morale', *J. soc. Issues*, vol. 7 (1951), pp. 8–17.
3. D. KATZ, N. MACCOBY and N. C. MORSE, *Productivity, Supervision and Morale in an Office Situation*, Institute for Social Research, University of Michigan, 1950.
4. D. KATZ, N. MACCOBY, G. GURIN and L. G. FLOOR, *Productivity, Supervision and Morale among Railroad Workers*, Institute for Social Research, University of Michigan, 1951.
5. K. LEWIN, *The Conceptual Representation and the Measurement of Psychological Forces*, Duke U.P., 1938.
6. K. LEWIN, *Field Theory and Social Science*, Harper, 1951.
7. N. C. MORSE, *Satisfactions in the White-Collar Job*, Institute for Social Research, University of Michigan, 1953.
8. S. E. SEASHORE, *Group Cohesiveness in the Industrial Work Group*, Institute for Social Research, University of Michigan, 1954.
9. E. C. TOLMAN, 'A psychological model', in T. Parsons and E. A. Shils (eds.), *Toward a General Theory of Action*, Harvard U.P., 1951, pp. 277–361.

18 Edward E. Lawler, III, and Lyman Porter

Antecedent Attitudes of Effective Managerial Performance

Excerpt from Edward E. Lawler, III, and Lyman Porter, 'Antecedent attitudes of effective managerial performance', *Organizational Behavior and Human Performance*, vol. 2, 1967, pp. 122–42.

The purpose of this article is to explore some of the attitudes of managers that are presumed to be related to effective job performance. This will be approached by presenting a conceptual model that attempts to tie these attitude variables to task performance.

We shall refer to the attitudes we are about to discuss as 'antecedent' attitudes because we believe they help to determine job performance rather than being the result of such performance. At the outset, however, let us note that this set of antecedent attitudes does *not* include the type of attitude most frequently studied in investigations of the attitudes–performance relationship in industrial psychology, namely, job satisfaction. For too long, in our opinion, psychologists interested in work behavior have acted as if job satisfaction were the only type of attitude that has any theoretical significance in the understanding of individual differences in job performance. Our position is that attitudes that can be classified under the satisfaction label are only one type, and perhaps not the most important type of attitudes that are in some way associated with behavior in the job situation. More importantly, we would hypothesize that job satisfaction is primarily a dependent variable in relation to job performance and that other types of attitudes may have a much more crucial role in determining task behavior. Therefore, in this article, which is addressed to the attitudinal antecedents of managerial job performance, we shall focus on other types of job attitudes than that of satisfaction with the job. In future studies we will expand the model presented in this article to include job satisfaction attitudes and other variables that are dependent variables in relation to job performance. Further elaboration of the model is also expected to include some feedback loops from the dependent variables to the antecedent attitudes. However only that part of the model which deals with antecedent variables will be considered here.

The Previous Literature

Before presenting the elements of our model we need to review briefly the relevant literature – both empirical and theoretical. By now the results of the two major surveys of the empirical investigations (carried out prior to 1955) of the relationship of job attitudes to job performance – the Brayfield and Crockett (1955) review and the Herzberg *et al.* (1957) review – have themselves become well embedded in the literature on this topic. The authors of the former survey concluded that 'there is little evidence in the available literature that employee attitudes ... bear any simple ... or appreciable relationship to performance on the job,' whereas Herzberg and his colleagues concluded that 'there is frequent evidence for the often suggested opinion that positive job attitudes are favorable to increased productivity.' However – and this is often overlooked when the findings of the two surveys are compared – Herzberg *et al.* went on to say that 'the correlations obtained in many of the positive studies were low... in addition, the large number of studies in which morale and productivity were not related must be stressed.' Hence, though Herzberg *et al.* take a somewhat more sanguine view of the evidence, both reviews are in essential agreement that the research findings prior to 1955 did not show strong positive relationships between job satisfaction and morale, on the one hand, and productivity, on the other. (Both surveys did find more consistent evidence for relationships in the expected directions between job satisfaction and turnover and absenteeism.)

An important feature to note in both of these reviews of the pre-1955 literature is that the types of attitudes dealt with were almost always concerned with 'liking or disliking' some feature or features of the job situation. The attitude-measuring instruments usually were described as measuring job satisfaction or morale, and involved the subject's like–dislike feelings towards such aspects of his work situation as his job, his work group, his pay, his supervisor, his company, etc. Seldom were other kinds of thoughts or opinions concerning the work situation investigated in relation to job performance.

Vroom (1964) has partially updated the review of the literature appearing since the Brayfield and Crockett and the Herzberg surveys by tabulating the results from correlational type job attitude/job performance studies appearing through 1963. His survey findings differ little from those previously mentioned. Though most of the studies obtained positive satisfaction–productivity correlations, the median correlation across twenty investigations amounted to only 0·14. Here, again, most of the studies included in this latest review involved like–dislike measures of job attitudes.

A further point to note concerning the studies covered in all three reviews is that practically every investigation involved *non*-management employees. This is not to say that the skill levels of the various samples of employees were always low – though quite typically they were – but it does serve to place some limitations on the generalizations to be drawn from available research findings. At the present time, empirically speaking, we do not know whether job satisfaction (let alone other types of attitudes) and job performance are related for samples of managers. Whether we should expect stronger attitude–performance relationships for managers than for non-managerial employees is an unanswered question.

Until recently, little attention was given to the possible theoretical explanations of why job attitudes should be related to job performance. Many of the individual studies providing empirical data either ignore the theoretical underpinnings of their findings or else implicitly assume that attitudes ought to be related to performance. Brayfield and Crockett pointed this out in their review and proceeded to given an excellent discussion of some of the theoretical issues involved. More currently, Vroom (1964) has dealt extensively with a theoretical approach to this topic. As he himself points out, his ideas are similar to those of Lewin, Atkinson, Peak and others. As will be seen, our own conceptual model has been strongly influenced by these various sources, especially Vroom with his emphasis on the concepts of valence, expectancy and force. In addition, the statement of a path–goal

255

approach to productivity by Georgopoulos, Mahoney and Jones (1957) has served as a specific stimulus to our own thinking.

The Theoretical Model

That part of our conceptual model that we will deal with in this article is addressed to two basic questions: What factors determine the *effort* a person puts into his job? What factors affect the relationship between effort and *performance*? To answer these two questions, we have diagrammed our view of the relationships involved among six relevant variables (see Figure 1). We will proceed to define each variable and try to indicate how they interact in determining task-relevant performance.

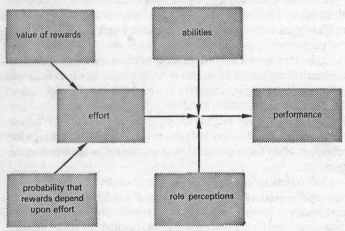

Figure 1 Diagram of the theoretical model

Factors determining effort

As can be seen from Figure 1, we posit that there are two variables that must be considered in answering the question: 'What factors determine the *effort* a person puts into his job?' These two variables are value of rewards and probability that rewards depend upon effort. We define the first of these variables as the attractiveness of possible rewards or outcomes to the individual. We are here not particularly concerned about how different rewards come to be thought of as differentially desirable by a given individual – although this is an important question in itself. All that is hypothesized is that for any given individual at any particular point in time there is a variety of possible outcomes that he differentially desires. Although, as Vroom (1964) has pointed out, some outcomes may have aversive qualities that lead them to have negative value, the focus in the present paper will be upon positively valued outcomes or rewards. Specifically the emphasis will be upon rewards that are relevant to the list of needs suggested by Maslow (1954) with the modifications of Porter (1961). The expectation is that rewards will be valued by an individual to the extent that he believes they will provide satisfaction of his security, social esteem, autonomy and self-actualization needs. Although there is a certain degree of stability to the value of rewards over time for a given person, it is also clear that the values can and do change, depending upon various circumstances in the environment. This concept is similar to the subjective utility concept that is used in behavioral decision theories (e.g. Davidson, Suppes and Siegel 1957; Edwards, 1961).

To measure the variable of value of rewards for an individual at a specific point in time, there are several possible methods that can be employed by the investigator. One method is to have the individual rank order a number of potential rewards or, alternatively, have him rank them by successive paired comparisons. In this case, we obtain a measure of the relative value of different rewards. A second method would be to obtain the absolute value for the individual of various rewards by having him rate them on, say, a seven-point scale running from zero value to maximum possible value. A third way to measure the value might be by administering some sort of projective device, such as the TAT, in which the investigator would infer the values from the responses of the subject. Still a fourth way would be to provide the individual with an actual choice of two or more rewards. Whereas the latter method is quite feasible in the laboratory, its practicality in the field setting is limited.

Our second variable is the probability that rewards depend upon effort. This variable refers to an individual's subjective expectancy about the likelihood that rewards that he desires will follow from putting forth certain levels of effort, and is similar to the concept of subjective probability. Such an expectation can be thought of as representing the combination of two separate subsidiary expectancies, namely: (a) the probability that rewards depend upon performance; and (b) the probability that performance depends upon effort.

Let us use an example to clarify these points. Suppose that a manager in charge of a manufacturing unit in a large plant desires a promotion to a higher-level job. (Such a promotion would be considered as having a high 'value of reward' in our terms, since it appears to satisfy several needs.) The manager may believe that obtaining the promotion does not depend upon his performance (i.e. the output and efficiency of his unit). He may feel that the promotion will more likely be made on the basis of straight seniority. Or, he may feel that no matter how well his unit performs he will not be promoted (in the reasonable future) because there are no openings above him to which he could be promoted even if the company desired to do so. In such instances, if the manger reports that this is how he sees the situation, we would say he has a low perceived probability that rewards depend upon performance, and therefore his perceived probability that rewards depend upon effort is also low. However, let us suppose the manager does feel that rewards do depend upon performance and that the next promotion will go to the manager whose unit is performing most effectively. Even in this case, his expectations that rewards depend upon effort may still be low. The reason for this is that although he feels that promotions are made on the basis of performance in his company, he may feel that no amount of additional effort on his part will improve the performance of his group. He may feel this, for example, simply because of his belief that the situational factors governing the performance of his unit are beyond his control, or because he does not think he has the necessary abilities to perform the job well enough to deserve a reward. He is saying, in effect, 'No matter how much effort I put into the job, I probably won't get that promotion.'

A further complication that may arise with respect to the probability dimension is that the manager may feel that effort may result in rewards even though it does not necessarily result in performance. This would be the case where an organization pays off for trying but not for performing. Where this is true, the probability that effort can be converted into performance will be irrelevant in determining how much effort an individual will put forth on the job. In this case the prediction would be that the individual would put forth effort but that it would be rather diffuse and not necessarily productive.

It is necessary to keep in mind that when we are referring to this second variable in our model – the probability that rewards depend upon effort – we are talking about the *perceived* probability or subjective expectancy, not about actual probabilities. In our example, even though the manager might think that the promotion will be based strictly on seniority, he may be incorrect in that higher officials are actually planning to decide on the basis of who has the best performing unit. In such a circumstance the manager's perceived probability is low and this will have a deleterious effect on his effort, even though his perceptions are, in fact, wrong. It is clear, then, that to measure this variable we need to obtain an estimation from the individual himself as to his beliefs concerning probabilities or expectancies – that is, perceptions of path (effort) and goal (rewards) relationships. Such perceptions can be obtained about the effort-reward probabilities directly, or by combining the two separate subsidiary probabilities, namely, performance-reward, and effort-performance. In the latter case, we would contend that such probabilities should be combined in a multiplicative way to obtain the over-all effort-reward probability that is specified in the diagram of the model.

We are now faced with the question of how the first two variables – value of rewards and probability that rewards depend upon effort – combine to determine effort. To do this, we first need to define effort. In our model, effort refers to the amount of energy an individual expends in a given situation. In non-psychological terms it refers to how hard the person is trying to perform a task. Effort, of course, is to be distinguished from performance which refers to the amount of task accomplishment. A student may put in great effort (i.e. review his notes and assigned readings for many hours) in studying for a test, but his achievement on the test may be low. Effort is the variable in our model that most closely corresponds to the motivational component in typical discussions of the motivation of performance.

Effort can be measured in several different ways. For certain

259

limited types of tasks, especially in laboratory-type settings, objective physical measurements can be obtained. In typical managerial jobs, of course, such measurements are essentially irrelevant. Here we must rely either on self-reports or the judgements of qualified observers. The problem is that in many instances the two kinds of reports may not agree, and the investigator is left with the problem of determining which is *the* measure of effort. (We do not pretend to have a solution to this problem. For the moment, we are willing to use either or both measures to indicate 'effort' in our model.)

Returning now to the question of how value of reward and probability that rewards depend upon effort determine effort, we can state the basic hypothesis: *the greater the value of a set of rewards and the higher the probability that receiving each of these rewards depends upon effort, the greater the effort that will be put forth in a given situation.* Stating the hypothesis in this form still leaves unanswered the question of the exact nature of the interaction between reward value and probability in determining effort. Although there is little previous research that is relevant to the question, we hypothesize that the interaction is essentially a multiplicative one. Thus, for each reward it is necessary to multiply its value by the perceived probability that receiving it depends on effort. In other words, either variable alone is a necessary but not sufficient condition for effort. If an individual highly values a reward that is potentially available in the situation and if he believes that its attainment in no way at all depends upon his level of effort, he will put forth minimum effort. Likewise, if a reward is provided and the person feels its attainment does depend strongly upon his level of effort, he may still put in a minimum of effort if the reward has very low value for him.

The hypothesis emphasizes the point that the amount of effort put forth is determined by a number of different rewards. Thus, it is necessary to consider the products obtained from multiplying each reward value by the probability that it depends on effort in order to determine how much effort will be put forth. Here we hypothesize that the best way to combine the products obtained from multiplying the reward values and probabilities is by addition. It is necessary to consider all rewards because in a given situation individuals may be putting forth the same amount of effort in order to obtain entirely different rewards. It may also be that an individual sees only one reward as related to effort, while another sees one reward plus several others as related to effort, and therefore works harder. In summary, then, it has been argued that the amount of effort that will be expended is a function of the sum of reward value × perceived probability that effort leads to the reward, where all rewards relevant to the list of needs suggested by Maslow (1954) are considered.

Factors affecting the relationship between effort and performance

As we pointed out above, effort is not synonymous with performance. This is another way of saying that other variables in addition to effort affect task achievement. With this in mind, let us now turn to the second of the two major questions addressed in our model: 'What factors affect the relationship between effort and performance?' As can be seen in Figure 1, our model points to two major categories of variables that combine with effort in determining performance. These two variables are abilities (including personality traits) and role perceptions.

For our purposes in the model, we have defined ability as the individual's currently developed power to perform. The set of variables encompassed under the term 'ability' refers to such characteristics of the individual as intelligence, manual skills, personality traits, etc. To a certain extent it is a sort of catch-all category of individual difference variables with the important common feature of being relatively stable and composed of long-term characteristics of the individual. They can be modified, but they typically do not change very much over the short run. In this sense, then, abilities are relatively independent of immediate environmental circumstances. Measurement of abilities depends upon the specific ability being considered, but typically such measurements involve tests of some sort – intelligence tests, aptitude tests, personality inventories, and the like. Also, of course, it is possible for other individuals to estimate a given person's abilities in a particular area, although it is obvious that frequently such estimates might be quite at variance with supposedly more valid test data.

In contrast to abilities and their long-term nature, the variable of role perceptions in our model refers to a more situationally modified variable, namely, the kinds of activities and behavior the individual feels he should engage in to perform his job successfully. In other words, role perceptions determine the *direction* in which the individual applies his effort. Since they can be affected by immediate cues coming from the environment, they are much more dynamic in their character than are relatively static abilities. There are many important situational factors other than role perceptions which can and do influence performance. For example, the production-line worker is frequently limited in terms of the variability of his performance regardless of how much effort he puts forth (Walker and Guest, 1952). Thus, there are many situational factors which influence performance that could potentially be included along with role perceptions as moderators of the relationship between effort and performance. Argyris (1964) has discussed many of the relevant situational factors such as job design and managerial controls. However, for the purposes of the present study we have decided to focus on only one kind of situational factor – role perceptions – because they are a psychological or human variable rather than an environmental one, and because they can relatively easily be subjected to empirical study.

An individual's role perceptions can be termed accurate ('good') if his views about where he should apply his effort correspond closely with the views of those who will be evaluating his performance. If the individual's role perceptions are inaccurate he may expend a great deal of effort without performing at a high level, even though his abilities are more than adequate for superior performance. Measuring role perceptions involves, by definition, acquiring information as to how the individual himself views the requirements of a particular job. Thus, some sort of report must be obtained from the individual. This can be in several forms: narrative descriptions of the job, answers to open-ended questions concerning the job or answers to directive-type, closed-end questions.

As we have previously noted, the sixth and final term in the theoretical model presented here is performance, defined as the amount of successful role achievement. Broadly considered, the model does appear to be potentially applicable with respect to explaining the amount of successful role achievement an individual will obtain in any number of behavioral situations. Thus, the model presumably can explain an individual's performance on the golf course as well as his job performance. In the present study, however, the focus is upon job performance which traditionally has been measured in three ways: (a) objective indices (rate of output of a manufacturing unit, amount of sales, amount of profits, etc.); (b) appraisals and ratings by individuals other than the person whose performance is being evaluated; and (c) self-appraisals and self-ratings. Although objective measures of performance are usually considered to be the most advantageous for the researcher, we can note that in many instances (e.g. management jobs) ratings – especially ratings of the person by other individuals – often have greater over-all relevance for the goals of the organization than certain objective measures that may cover only minor or peripheral aspects of the job.

Now, how do traits and role perceptions modify the relationship between effort and performance? We hypothesize that higher effort will lead to higher performance, the greater the extent to which the individual possesses task relevant abilities and the greater the extent to which his role perceptions are congruent with those who will be evaluating his performance.

More specifically, we hypothesize that both abilities and role perceptions interact multiplicatively with effort to produce performance. The evidence for the multiplicative interaction of effort and abilities has been reviewed in detail by Vroom (1964) and by Lawler (1966) and though it is not extensive we find it convincing. Evidence for the interactive nature of effort and role perceptions is essentially non-existent, but it is our thesis that the degree of accuracy of role perceptions determines the proportion of effort that is relevant for task achievement.

If we were going to put the above ideas into a purely hypothetical example, we could consider the following: assume that the amount of possible effort that can be expended runs from nil (no effort) to ten (maximum effort) units, the amount of a particular ability in a given situation runs from nil (no ability) to ten (maximum ability) units and that accuracy of role perceptions runs from 0 per cent (completely inaccurate) to 100 per cent (completely accurate). Then, hypothetically, these values could be combined multiplicatively in an equation to derive the task achievement that would be expected from a given individual in a given situation: e.g. eight units of effort × six units of ability × 80 per cent role perception accuracy = 38·4 units of task performance (out of a theoretical maximum of a hundred units).

The important point to keep in mind in the above hypothetical equation is that attitudes are involved in affecting performance primarily through only two of the three antecedent variables, namely, effort and role perceptions. Two types of attitudes – value of rewards and probability that rewards depend on effort – are involved in determining effort, and role perceptions are themselves a particular type of attitude. Thus, according to our model, if it is desired to modify performance through changing attitudes, the three specific types of attitude just mentioned are the ones we consider to be the most crucial antecedent attitudes of effective managerial performance.

References
ARGYRIS, C. (1964), *Integrating the Individual and the Organization*, Wiley.
BRAYFIELD, A. H., and CROCKETT, W. H. (1955), 'Employee attitudes and employee performance', *Psychol. Bull.*, vol. 52, pp. 396–424. [See Reading 5.]
DAVIDSON, D., SUPPES, P., and SIEGEL, S. (1957), *Decision Making: An Experimental Approach*, Stanford U.P.
EDWARDS, W. (1961), 'Behavioral decision theory', in P. R. Farnsworth (ed.), *Annual Review of Psychology*, vol. 12, pp. 473–98, Annual Reviews.
GEORGOPOULOS, B. S., MAHONEY, G., and JONES, N. (1957), 'A path–goal approach to productivity', *J. appl. Psychol.*, vol. 41, pp. 345–53. [Reading 17.]
HERZBERG, F., MAUSNER, B., PETERSON, R. O., and CAPWELL, D. F. (1957), *Job Attitudes: Review of Research and Opinion*, Psychological Services of Pittsburgh.
LAWLER, E. E. (1966), 'Ability as a moderator of the relationship between job attitudes and job performance', *Personn. Psychol.*, vol. 19, pp. 153–64.
MASLOW, A. H. (1954), *Motivation and Personality*, Harper.
PORTER, L. W. (1961), 'A study of perceived need satisfactions in bottom and middle management jobs', *J. appl. Psychol.*, vol. 45, pp. 1–10.
VROOM, V. H. (1964), *Work and Motivation*, Wiley. [See Reading 16.]
WALKER, C. R., and GUEST, R. H. (1952), *The Man on the Assembly Line*, Harvard U.P.

19 Daniel Katz

The Motivational Basis of Organizational Behaviour

Daniel Katz, 'The motivational basis of organizational behavior', *Behavioral Science*, vol. 9, 1964, pp. 131–46.

The basic problem to which I shall address myself is how people are tied into social and organizational structures so that they become effective functioning units of social systems. What is the nature of their involvement in a system or their commitment to it?

The major input into social organizations consists of people. The economist or the culturologist may concentrate on inputs of resources, raw materials, technology. To the extent that human factors are recognized, they are assumed to be constants in the total equation and are neglected. At the practical level, however, as well as for a more precise theoretical accounting, we need to cope with such organizational realities as the attracting of people into organizations, holding them within the system, insuring reliable performance and, in addition, stimulating actions which are generally facilitative of organizational accomplishment. The material and psychic returns to organizational members thus constitute major determinants, not only of the level of effectiveness of organizational functioning, but of the very existence of the organization.

The complexities of motivational problems in organizations can be understood if we develop an analytic framework which will be comprehensive enough to identify the major sources of variance and detailed enough to contain sufficient specification for predictive purposes. The framework we propose calls for three steps in an analysis process, namely, the formulation of answers to these types of questions:

1. What are the types of behavior required for effective organizational functioning? Any organization will require not one, but several patterns of behavior from most of its members. And

the motivational bases of these various behavioral requirements may differ.

2. What are the motivational patterns which are used and which can be used in organizational settings? How do they differ in their logic and psycho-logic? What are the differential consequences of the various types of motivational patterns for the behavioral requirements essential for organizational functioning? One motivational pattern may be very effective in bringing about one type of necessary behavior and completely ineffective in leading to another.

3. What are the conditions for eliciting a given motivational pattern in an organizational setting? We may be able to identify the type of motivation we think most appropriate for producing a given behavioral outcome but we still need to know how this motive can be aroused or produced in the organization (Katz, 1962).

Behavioral Requirements

Our major dependent variables are the behavioral requirements of the organization. Three basic types of behavior are essential for a functioning organization:

1. People must be induced to enter and remain within the system.

2. They must carry out their role assignments in a dependable fashion.

3. There must be innovative and spontaneous activity in achieving organizational objectives which go beyond the role specifications.

Attracting and holding people in a system

First of all, sufficient personnel must be kept within the system to man its essential functions. Thus people must be induced to enter the system at a sufficiently rapid rate to counteract the amount of defection. High turnover is costly. Moreover, there is some optimum period for their staying within the system. And while they are members of the system they must validate their membership by constant attendance. Turnover and absenteeism are both measures of organizational effectiveness and productivity, though they are partial measures. People may, of course, be within the system physically but may be psychological absentees. The child may be regular and punctual in his school attendance and yet day-dream in his classes. It is not enough, then, to hold people within a system.

Dependable role performance

The great range of variable human behavior must be reduced to a limited number of predictable patterns. In other words, the assigned roles must be carried out and must meet some minimal level of quantity and quality of performance. A common measure of productivity is the amount of work turned out by the individual or by the group carrying out their assigned tasks. Quality of performance is not as easily measured and the problem is met by quality controls which set minimal standards for the pieces of work sampled. In general, the major role of the member is clearly set forth by organizational protocol and leadership. The man on the assembly line, the nurse in the hospital, the teacher in the elementary school all know what their major job is. To do a lot of it and to do it well are, then, the most conspicuous behavioral requirements of the organization. It may be, of course, that given role requirements are not functionally related to organizational accomplishment. This is a different type of problem and we are recognizing here only the fact that some major role requirements are necessary.

Innovative and spontaneous behavior

A neglected set of requirements consists of those actions not specified by role prescriptions which nevertheless facilitate the accomplishment of organizational goals. The great paradox of a social organization is that it must not only reduce human variability to insure reliable role performance but that it must also allow room for some variability and in fact encourage it.

There must always be a supportive number of actions of an innovative or relatively spontaneous sort. No organizational planning can foresee all contingencies within its operations, or can anticipate with perfect accuracy all environmental changes, or can control perfectly all human variability. The resources of people in innovation, in spontaneous cooperation, in protective and creative behavior are thus vital to organizational survival and effectiveness. An organization which depends solely upon its blueprints of prescribed behavior is a very fragile social system.

Cooperation

The patterned activity which makes up an organization is so intrinsically a cooperative set of interrelationships, that we are not aware of the cooperative nexus any more than we are of any habitual behavior like walking. Within every work group in a factory, within any division in a government bureau or within any department of a university are countless acts of cooperation without which the system would break down. We take these everyday acts for granted, and few, if any, of them form the role prescriptions for any job. One man will call the attention of his companion on the next machine to some indication that his machine is getting jammed, or will pass along some tool that his companion needs or will borrow some bit of material he is short of. Or men will come to the aid of a fellow who is behind on his quota. In a study of clerical workers in an insurance company one of the two factors differentiating high-producing from low-producing sections was the greater cooperative activity of the girls in the high-producing sections coming to one another's help in meeting production quotas (Katz, Maccoby and Morse, 1950). In most factories specialization develops around informal types of help. One man will be expert in first aid, another will be expert in machine diagnosis, etc. We recognize the need for cooperative relationships by raising this specific question when a man is considered for a job. How well does he relate to his fellows, is he a good team man, will he fit in?

Protection

Another subcategory of behavior facilitative of organizational functioning is the action which protects the organization against disaster. There is nothing in the role prescriptions of the worker which specifies that he be on the alert to save life and property in the organization. Yet the worker who goes out of his way to remove the boulder accidentally lodged in the path of a freight car on the railway spur, or to secure a rampant piece of machinery or even to disobey orders when they obviously are wrong and dangerous, is an invaluable man for the organization.

Constructive ideas

Another subcategory of acts beyond the line of duty consists of creative suggestions for the improvement of methods of production or of maintenance. Some organizations encourage their members to feed constructive suggestions into the system, but coming up with good ideas for the organization and formulating them to management is not the typical role of the worker. An organization that can stimulate its members to contribute ideas for organizational improvement is a more effective organization in that people who are close to operating problems can often furnish informative suggestions about such operations. The system which does not have this stream of contributions from its members is not utilizing its potential resources effectively.

Self-training

Still another subcategory under the heading of behavior beyond the call of duty concerns the self-training of members for doing their own jobs better and self-education for assuming more responsible positions in the organization. There may be no requirement that men prepare themselves for better positions. But the organization which has men spending their own time to master knowledge and skills for more responsible jobs in the system has an additional resource for effective functioning.

Favorable attitude

Finally, members of a group can contribute to its operations by helping to create a favorable climate for it in the community, or communities, which surround the organization. Employees may talk to friends, relatives and acquaintances about the excellent or the poor qualities of the company for which they work. A favorable climate may help in problems of recruitment and, sometimes, product disposal.

In short, for effective organizational functioning many members must be willing on occasion to do more than their job prescriptions specify. If the system were to follow the letter of the law according to job descriptions and protocol, it would soon grind to a halt. There have to be many actions of mutual cooperation and many anticipations of organizational objectives to make the system viable.

Now these three major types of behavior, and even the sub-categories, though related, are not necessarily motivated by the same drives and needs. The motivational pattern that will attract and hold people to an organization is not necessarily the same as that which will lead to higher productivity. Nor are the motives which make for higher productivity invariably the same as those which sustain cooperative interrelationships in the interests of organizational accomplishment. Hence, when we speak about organizational practices and procedures which will further the attainment of its mission, we need to specify the type of behavioral requirement involved.

Types of Motivational Patterns

It is profitable to consider the possible motivational patterns in organizations under six major headings. Before considering their specific modes of operation and their effects, let me briefly describe the six motivational patterns which seem most relevant. These patterns are: (a) conformity to legal norms or rule compliance; (b) instrumental system rewards; (c) instrumental individual rewards; (d) intrinsic satisfaction from role performance; (e) internalization of organizational goals and values; and (f) involvement in primary-group relationships.

Rule compliance or conformity to system norms

Conformity constitutes a significant motivational basis for certain types of organizational behavior. Though people may conform for different reasons I am concerned here with one common type of reason, namely, a generalized acceptance of the rules of the game. Once people enter a system they accept the fact that membership in the system means complying with its legitimate rules. In our culture we build up, during the course of the socialization process, a generalized expectation of conforming to the recognized rules of the game if we want to remain in the game. We develop a role readiness, i.e. a readiness to play almost any given role according to the established norms in those systems in which we become involved.

Instrumental system rewards

These are the benefits which accrue to individuals by virtue of their membership in the system. They are the across-the-board rewards which apply to all people in a given classification in an organization. Examples would be the fringe benefits, the recreational facilities and the working conditions which are available to all members of the system or subsystem. These rewards are instrumental in that they provide incentives for entering and remaining in the system and thus are instrumental for the need satisfaction of people.

Instrumental reward geared to individual effort or performance

System rewards apply in blanket fashion to all members of a subsystem. Individual rewards of an instrumental character are attained by differential performance. For example, the piece-rate in industry or the singling out of individuals for honors for their specific contributions would fall into this category of instrumental individual rewards.

Intrinsic satisfactions accruing from specific role performance

Here the gratification comes not because the activity leads to or is instrumental to other satisfactions such as earning more money but because the activity is gratifying in itself. The individual may find his work so interesting or so much the type of thing he really wants to do that it would take a heavy financial inducement to shift to a job less congenial to his interests. It is difficult to get professors in many universities to take administrative posts such as departmental chairmanships or deanships because so many of them prefer teaching and research. This motivational pattern has to do with the opportunities which the organizational role provides for the expressions of the skills and talents of the individual.

Internalized values of the individual which embrace the goals of the organization

Here the individual again finds his organizational behavior rewarding in itself, not so much because his job gives him a chance to express his skill, but because he has taken over the goals of the organization as his own. The person who derives his gratifications from being a good teacher could be equally happy in teaching in many institutions but unhappy as an administrator in any one. The person who has identified himself with the goals of his own particular university and its specific problems, potentialities and progress wants to stay on at his university and, moreover, is willing to accept other assignments than a teaching assignment.

Social satisfactions derived from primary-group relationships

This is an important source of gratification for organizational members. One of the things people miss most when they have to withdraw from organizations is the sharing of experiences with like-minded colleagues, the belonging to a group with which they have become identified. Whether or not these social satisfactions become channeled for organizational objectives leads us to a consideration of the two basic questions with which we started:

1. What are the consequences of these motivational patterns for the various organizational requirements of holding people in the system, maximizing their role performance, and stimulating innovative behavior?

2. What are the conditions under which these patterns will lead to a given organizational outcome?

Motivational Patterns: Consequences and Conditions

Compliance with legitimized rules

In discussing bureaucratic functioning Max Weber pointed out that the acceptance of legal rules was the basis for much of organizational behavior (Weber, 1947). Compliance is to some extent a function of sanctions but to a greater extent a function of generalized habits and attitudes towards symbols of authority. In other words, for the citizen of modern society the observance of legitimized rules has become a generalized value. A great deal of behavior can be predicted once we know what the rules of the game are. It is not necessary to take representative samplings of the behavior of many people to know how people will conduct themselves in structured situations. All we need is a single informant who can tell us the legitimate norms and appropriate symbols of authority for given types of behavioral settings. Individuals often assume that they can control their participation with respect to organizational requirements when they enter an organization. Before they are aware of it, however, they are acting like other organizational members and complying with the rules and the authorized decisions.

The major impact of compliance with the legitimate rules of the organization primarily concerns only one type of organizational requirement, namely, reliable role performance. The way in which any given role occupant is to perform in carrying out his job can be determined by the rules of the organization. But individuals cannot be held in the system by rule enforcement save for exceptions like the armed services. Nor can innovative behavior and actions beyond the call of duty be prescribed.

Though compliance with legitimate rules is effective for insuring reliable role performance it operates to insure minimal observance of role requirements. In other words, the minimal standards for quantity and quality of work soon become the maximum standards. The logic of meeting legal norms is to avoid infractions of the rules and not to go beyond their requirements, for as Allport has pointed out (1934), it is difficult, if not impossible, to be more proper than proper. Why, however, cannot the legal norms be set to require high standards with respect to both quantity and quality of production? Why cannot higher production be legislated? It can, but there is an important force working against such raising of standards by changing rules. The rule which sets a performance standard in a large organization is also setting a uniform standard for large numbers of people. Hence it must be geared to what the great majority are prepared to do. If not, there will be so many defections that the rule itself will break down. Timing of jobs in industry illustrates this principle. Management does not want a loose standard, but if the standards are set so that many workers can meet them only with difficulty, management is in for trouble.

In the third area of behavior necessary for effective organizational functioning, namely, innovative and spontaneous acts which go beyond the call of duty, rule compliance is useless by definition. There can be exceptions, in that rules can be devised to reward unusual behavior under specified conditions. The army, for example, will move the man who has pulled off a brilliant military exploit from a court martial to a court of honors. Though such exceptions may occur, organizations cannot stimulate innovative actions by decreeing them. In general the greater the emphasis upon compliance with rules the less the motivation will be for individuals to do more than is specified by their role prescriptions. The great weakness of a system run according to rules is the lack of the corrective factor of human enterprise and spontaneity when something goes wrong. In 1962 in a hospital in New York State several infants died because salt rather than sugar was put into the formula. The large container for sugar had been erroneously filled with salt. The tragic fact was that day after day for about a week the nurses fed the babies milk saturated with salt in spite of the fact that the infants reacted violently to the food, crying and vomiting after each feeding session. But the hospital continued poisoning the children until many of them died. Not a single nurse, attendant, supervisor or person connected with the nursery tasted the milk to see what was wrong. The error was discovered only when a hospital employee broke a rule and used some of the substance in the sugar container in her own coffee.

Conditions conducive to the activation of rule acceptance

Though compliance with rules can bring about reliable role performance, the use of rules must take account of the following three conditions for maximum effectiveness: (a) the appropriateness of the symbols of authority and the relevance of rules to the social system involved; (b) the clarity of the legal norms and rule structure; and (c) the reinforcing character of sanctions.

Appropriateness and relevance. The acceptance of communications and directives on the basis of legitimacy requires the use of symbols and procedures recognized as the proper and appropriate sources of authority in the system under consideration. The worker may grumble at the foreman's order but he recognizes the right of the foreman to give such an order. The particular directives which are accepted as legitimate will depend upon their matching the types of authority structure of the system. The civilian in the army with officer status, uniform and unassimilated rank is not accepted by the enlisted man as the proper giver of orders. In a representative democracy a policy decision of an administrator may be rejected since it lacks the legal stamp of the accepted procedures of the system. An industrial company may have a contract with a union that changes in the speed of the assembly line have to be agreed to by both organizations. The workers accordingly will accept a speedup in the line if it is sanctioned by the union–management agreement, but not if it is the work of a foreman attempting to impress his superiors.

The acceptance of legal rules is also restricted to the relevant sphere of activity. Union policy as formulated in its authority structure is binding upon its members only as it relates to relations with the company. The edicts of union officials on matters of desegregation or of support of political parties are not necessarily seen as legal compulsions by union members. In similar fashion, employees do not regard the jurisdiction of the company as applying to their private lives outside the plant. And areas of private behavior and personal taste are regarded in our democratic society as outside the realm of coercive laws. The most spectacular instance of the violation of a national law occurred in the case of the Volstead Act. While people were willing to accept laws about the social consequences resulting from drinking, such as reckless driving, many of them were not willing to accept the notion that their private lives were subject to federal regulation.

Another prerequisite to the use of rules as the appropriate norms of the system is their impersonal character. They are the rules of the system and are not the arbitrary, capricious decisions of a superior aimed at particular individuals. The equivalents of bills of attainder in an organization undermine rule compliance. We speak of the officiousness of given individuals in positions of authority when they use their rank in an arbitrary and personal fashion.

Clarity. A related condition for the acceptance of legal norms is the clarity of authority symbols, of proper procedures and the content of the legitimized decisions. Lack of clarity can be due to the vagueness of the stimulus situation or to the conflict between opposed stimulus cues. In some organizations, symbols of authority are sharply enough defined, but the relationship between competing symbols may lack such clarity of definition. One difficulty of using group decision in limited areas in an otherwise authoritarian structure is that group members may not perceive the democratic procedure as legitimized by the structure. They will question the compelling effect of any decisions they reach. And often they may be right. Moreover, the procedure for the exercise of power may not be consistent with the type of authority structure. The classic case is that *of ordering* a people to be democratic.

Specific laws can be ambiguous in their substance. They can be so complex, so technical or so obscure that people will not know what the law is. The multiplication of technical rulings and the patchwork of legislation with respect to tax structure means that while people may feel some internal compulsion to pay taxes, they also feel they should pay as little as they can without risking legal prosecution. A counter dynamic will arise to the tendency to comply with legal requirements, namely, the use of legal loopholes to defy the spirit of the law. Any complex maze of rules in an organization will be utilized by the guardhouse lawyers in the system to their own advantage.

Though our argument has been that legal compliance makes for role performance rather than for holding people in a system, the clarity of a situation with well-defined rules is often urged as a condition making for system attractiveness. People know what is expected of them and what they should expect in turn from others, and they much prefer this clarity to a state of uncertainty and ambiguity. There is merit in this contention, but it does not take into account all the relevant variables. The armed services were not able to hold personnel after the Second World War, and recruitment into systems characterized by rules and regulations is traditionally difficult in the United States. The mere multiplication of rules does not produce clarity. Even when certainty and clarity prevail they are not relished if it means that individuals are certain only of non-advancement and restrictions on their behavior.

In brief, the essence of legal compliance rests upon the psychological belief that there are specific imperatives or laws which all good citizens obey. If there is doubt about what the imperative is, if there are many varying interpretations, then the law is not seen as having a character of its own but as the means for obtaining individual advantage. To this extent, the legitimacy basis of compliance is undermined.

Reinforcement. To maintain the internalized acceptance of legitimate authority there has to be some reinforcement in the form of penalties for violation of the rules. If there is no policing of laws governing speeding, speed limits will lose their force over time for many people. Sometimes the penalties can come from the social disapproval of the group as well as from legal penalties. But the very concept of law as an imperative binding upon everyone in the system requires penalties for violation either from above or below. Where there is no enforcement by authorities and no sanctions for infractions from the group itself, the rule in question becomes a dead letter.

Instrumental system rewards

It is important to distinguish between rewards which are administered in relation to individual effort and performance and the system rewards which accrue to people by virtue of their membership in the system. In the former category would belong piece-rate incentives, promotion for outstanding performance, or any special recognition bestowed in acknowledgement of differential contributions to organizational functioning. In the category of system rewards would go fringe benefits, recreational facilities, cost of living raises, across-the-board upgrading, job security save for those guilty of moral turpitude, pleasant working conditions. System rewards differ, then, from individual rewards in that they are not allocated on the basis of differential effort and performance but on the basis of membership in the system. The major differentiation for system rewards is seniority in the system – a higher pension for thirty years of service than for twenty years of service. Management will often overlook the distinction between individual and system rewards and will operate as if rewards administered across the board were the same in their effects as individual rewards.

System rewards are more effective for holding members within the organization than for maximizing other organizational behaviors. Since the rewards are distributed on the basis of length of tenure in the system, people will want to stay with an attractive set-up which becomes increasingly attractive over time. Again the limiting factor is the competition with the relative attraction of other systems. As the system increases its attractions, other things being equal, it should reduce its problems of turnover. In fact, it may sometimes have the problem of too low turnover with too many poorly motivated people staying on until retirement.

System rewards will not, however, lead to higher quality of work or greater quantity than the minimum required to stay in the organization. Since rewards are given across-the-board to all members or differentially to them in terms of their seniority, they are not motivated to do more than meet the standards for remaining in the system. It is sometimes assumed that the liking for the organization created by system rewards will generalize to greater productive effort within the system. Such generalization of motivation may occur to a very limited extent, but it is not a reliable basis for the expectation of higher productivity. Management may expect gratitude from workers because it has added some special fringe benefit or some new recreational facility. The more likely outcome is that employees will feel more desirous of staying in an enterprise with such advantages than of working harder for the company for the next twelve months.

System rewards will do little, moreover, to motivate performance beyond the line of duty, with two possible exceptions. Since people may develop a liking for the attractions of the organization they may be in a more favorable mood to reciprocate in cooperative relations with their fellows towards organizational goals, provided that the initiation of task-oriented cooperation comes from some other source. Otherwise, they may just be cooperative with respect to taking advantage of the system's attractions, such as the new bowling alley. Another possible consequence of system rewards for activity supportive of organizational goals is the favorable climate of opinion for the system in the external environment to which the members contribute. It may be easier for a company to recruit personnel in a community in which its employees have talked about what a good place it is to work.

Though the effects of system rewards are to maintain the level of productivity not much above the minimum required to stay in the system, there still may be large differences between systems with respect to the quantity and quality of production as a function of system rewards. An organization with substantially better wage rates and fringe benefits than its competitors may be able to set a higher level of performance as a minimal requirement for its workers than the other firms and still hold its employees. In other words, system rewards can be related to the differential productivity of organizations as a whole, though they are not effective in maximizing the potential contributions of the majority of individuals within the organization. They may account for differences in motivation between systems rather than for differences in motivation between individuals in the same system. They operate through their effects upon the minimal standards for all people in the system. They act indirectly in that their effect is to make people want to stay in the organization; to do so people must be willing to accept the legitimately derived standards of role performance in that system. Hence, the direct mechanism for insuring performance is compliance with legitimacy, but the legal requirements of the organization will not hold members if their demands are too great with respect to the demands of other organizations. The mediating variable in accounting for organizational differences based upon system rewards is the relative attractiveness of the system for the individual compared to other available systems in relation to the effort requirements of the system. If the individual has the choice of a job with another company in the same community which requires a little more effort but offers much greater system rewards in the way of wages and other benefits, he will in all probability take it. If, however, the higher requirements of the competing system are accompanied by very modest increases in system rewards, he will probably stay where he is.

Conditions conducive to effective system rewards

We have just described one of the essential conditions for making system rewards effective in calling attention to the need to make the system as attractive as competing systems which are realistic alternatives for the individual. In this context seniority becomes an important organizational principle in that the member can acquire more of the rewards of the system the longer he stays in it. The present trends to permit the transfer of fringe benefits of all types across systems undercuts the advantages to any one system of length of membership in it, though of course there are other advantages to permitting people to retain their investment in seniority when they move across systems.

Another condition which is important for the effective use of system rewards is their uniform application for all members of the system or for major groupings within the system. People will perceive as inequitable distinctions in amounts of rewards which go to members by virtue of their membership in the system where such differences favor some groups over other groups. Management is frequently surprised by resentment of differential system rewards when there has been no corresponding resentment of differential individual rewards. One public utility, for example, inaugurated an attractive retirement system for its employees before fringe benefits were the acceptable pattern. Its employees were objectively much better off because of the new benefits and yet the most hated feature about the whole company was the retirement system. Employees' complaints centered on two issues: years of employment in the company before the age of thirty did not count towards retirement pensions, and company officials could retire on livable incomes because of their higher salaries. The employees felt intensely that if they were being rewarded for service to the company it was unfair to rule out years of service before age thirty. This provision gave no recognition for the man who started for the company at age twenty compared to the one who started at age thirty. Moreover, the workers felt a lifetime of service to the company should enable them to retire on a livable income just as it made this possible for company officials. The company house organ directed considerable space over a few years to showing how much the worker actually benefited from the plan, as in fact was the case. On the occasion of a company-wide survey, this campaign was found to have had little effect. The most common complaint still focused about the patent unfairness of the retirement system.

The critical point, then, is that system rewards have a logic of their own. Since they accrue to people by virtue of their membership or length of service in an organization, they will be perceived as inequitable if they are not uniformly administered. The perception of the organization member is that all members are equal in their access to organizational benefits. Office employees will not be upset by differences in individual reward for differences in responsibility. If, however, their organization gives them free meals in a cafeteria and sets aside a special dining room for their bosses, many of them will be upset. In our culture we accept individual differences in income but we do not accept differences in classes of citizenship. To be a member of an organization is to be a citizen in that community, and all citizens are equal in their membership rights. A university which does not extend the same tenure rights and the same fringe benefits accorded its teaching staff to its research workers may have a morale problem on its hands.

Instrumental individual rewards

The traditional philosophy of the free-enterprise system gives priority to an individual reward system based upon the quality and quantity of the individual effort and contribution. This type of motivation may operate effectively for the entrepreneur or even for the small organization with considerable independence of its supporting environment. It encounters great difficulties, however, in its application to large organizations which are in nature highly interdependent cooperative structures. We shall examine these difficulties in analysing the conditions under which individual rewards of an instrumental character are effective.

Basically the monetary and recognition rewards to the individual for his organizational performance are directed at a high level of quality and quantity of work. In other words, they can be applied most readily to obtain optimal role performance rather than to innovative and non-specific organizational needs. They may also help to hold the individual in the organization, if he feels that his differential efforts are properly recognized. None the less there is less generalization, or rubbing off, of an instrumental individual reward to love for the organization than might be anticipated. If another organization offers higher individual rewards to a person, his own institution may have to match the offer to hold him.

Individual rewards are difficult to apply to contributions to organizational functioning which are not part of the role

281

requirements. Spectacular instances of innovative behavior can be singled out for recognition and awards. In the armed services, heroism beyond the call of duty is the basis for medals and decorations, but the everyday cooperative activities which keep an organization from falling apart are more difficult to recognize and reward. Creative suggestions for organizational improvement are sometimes encouraged through substantial financial rewards for employees' suggestions. The experience with suggestion systems of this sort has not been uniformly positive though under special conditions they have proved of value.

Conditions conducive to effective individual instrumental rewards

If rewards such as pay incentives are to work as they are intended they must meet three primary conditions.

1. They must be clearly perceived as large enough in amount to justify the additional effort required to obtain them.

2. They must be perceived as directly related to the required performance and follow directly on its accomplishment.

3. They must be perceived as equitable by the majority of system members, many of whom will not receive them.

These conditions suggest some of the reasons why individual rewards can work so well in some situations and yet be so difficult of application in large organizations. The facts are that most enterprises have not been able to use incentive pay, or piece-rates, as reliable methods for raising the quality and quantity of production (McGregor, 1960).

In terms of the first criterion many companies have attempted incentive pay without making the differential between increased effort and increased reward proportional from the point of view of the worker. If he can double his pay by working at a considerably increased tempo, that is one thing. But if such increased expenditure means a possible 10 per cent increase, that is another. Moreover, there is the tradition among workers, and it is not without some factual basis, that management cannot be relied upon to maintain a high rate of pay for those making considerably more than the standard and that their increased efforts will only result in their 'being sweated'. There is, then, the temporal dimension of whether the piece-rates which seem attractive today will be maintained tomorrow.

More significant, however, is the fact that a large-scale organization consists of many people engaging in similar and interdependent tasks. The work of any one man is highly dependent upon what his colleagues are doing. Hence individual piece-rates are difficult to apply on any equitable basis. Group incentives are more logical but, as the size of the interdependent group grows, we move towards system, rather than towards individual, rewards. Moreover, in large-scale production enterprises the role performance is controlled by the tempo of the machines and their co-ordination. The speed of the worker on the assembly line is not determined by his decision but by the speed of the assembly line. An individual piece-rate just does not accord with the systemic nature of the coordinated collectivity. Motivational factors about the amount of effort to be expended on the job enter the picture not on the floor of the factory but during the negotiations of the union and management about the manning of a particular assembly line. Heads of corporations may believe in the philosophy of individual enterprise, but when they deal with reward systems in their own organizations they become realists and accept the pragmatic notion of collective rewards.

Since there is such a high degree of collective interdependence among rank-and-file workers the attempts to use individual rewards are often perceived as inequitable. Informal norms develop to protect the group against efforts which are seen as divisive or exploitative. Differential rates for subsystems within the organization will be accepted much more than invidious distinctions within the same subgrouping. Hence promotion or upgrading may be the most potent type of individual reward. The employee is rewarded by being moved to a different category of workers on a better pay schedule. Some of the same problems apply, of course, to this type of reward. Since differential performance is difficult to assess in assembly-type operations, promotion is often based upon such criteria as conformity to company requirements with respect to attendance and absenteeism, observance of rules and seniority. None of these criteria are related to individual performance on the job. Moreover, promotion is greatly limited by the technical and professional education of the worker.

It is true, of course, that many organizations are not assembly-line operations and, even for those which are, the conditions described here do not apply to the upper echelons. Thus General Motors can follow a policy of high individual rewards to division managers based upon the profits achieved by a given division. A university can increase the amount of research productivity of its staff by making publication the essential criterion for promotion. In general, where assessment of individual performance is feasible and where the basis of the reward system is clear, instrumental individual rewards can play an important part in raising productivity.

Intrinsic job satisfaction

The motivational pathway to high productivity and to high-quality production can be reached through the development of intrinsic job satisfaction. The man who finds the type of work he delights in doing is the man who will not worry about the fact that the role requires a given amount of production of a certain quality. His gratifications accrue from accomplishment, from the expression of his own abilities, from the exercise of his own decisions. Craftsmanship was the old term to refer to the skilled performer who was high in intrinsic job satisfaction. This type of performer is not the clock watcher, nor the shoddy performer. On the other hand, such a person is not necessarily tied to a given organization. As a good carpenter or a good mechanic, it may matter little to him where he does work, provided that he is given ample opportunity to do the kind of job he is interested in doing. He may, moreover, contribute little to organizational goals beyond his specific role.

Conditions conducive to arousal of intrinsic job satisfaction

If intrinsic job satisfaction or identification with the work is to be aroused and maximized, then the job itself must provide sufficient variety, sufficient complexity, sufficient challenge and sufficient skill to engage the abilities of the worker. If there is one confirmed finding in all the studies of worker morale and satisfaction, it is the correlation between the variety and challenge of the job and the gratifications which accure to workers (Morse, 1953). There are, of course, people who do not want more responsibility and people who become demoralized by being placed in jobs which are

284

too difficult for them. These are, however, the exceptions. By and large people seek more responsibility, more skill-demanding jobs than they hold, and as they are able to attain these more demanding jobs, they become happier and better adjusted. Obviously, the condition for securing higher motivation to produce, and to produce quality work, necessitates changes in organizational structure – specifically job enlargement rather than job fractionization. And yet the tendency in large-scale organizations is towards increasing specialization and routinization of jobs. Workers would be better motivated towards higher individual production and towards better quality work if we discarded the assembly line and moved towards the craftsmanlike operations of the old Rolls-Royce type of production. Industry has demonstrated, however, that it is more efficient to produce via assembly-line methods with lowered motivation and job satisfaction than with highly motivated craftsmen with a large area of responsibility in turning out their part of the total product. The preferred path to the attainment of production goals in turning out cars or other mass physical products is, then, the path of organizational controls and not the path of internalized motivation. The quality of production may suffer somewhat, but it is still cheaper to buy several mass-produced cars, allowing for programming for obsolescence, than it is to buy a single quality product like the Rolls-Royce.

In the production of physical objects intended for mass consumption, the assembly line may furnish the best model. This may also apply to service operations in which the process can be sufficiently simplified to provide service to masses of consumers. When, however, we move to organizations which have the modifications of human beings as their product, as in educational institutions, or when we deal with treating basic problems of human beings, as in hospitals, clinics and remedial institutions, we do not want to rely solely upon an organizational control to guarantee minimum effort of employees. We want employees with high motivation and high identification with their jobs. Jobs cannot profitably be fractionated very far, and standardized and coordinated to a rigorous time schedule in a research laboratory, in a medical clinic, in an educational institution or in a hospital.

In addition to the recognition of the inapplicability of organizational devices of the factory and the army to all organizations, it is also true that not all factory operations can be left to institutional controls without regard to the motivations of employees. It frequently happens that job fractionization can be pushed to the point of diminishing returns even in industry. The success of the Tavistock workers in raising productivity in the British coal mines through job enlargement was due to the fact that the specialization of American Longwall methods of coal mining did not yield adequate returns when applied to the difficult and variable conditions under which British miners had to operate (Trist and Bamforth, 1951). The question of whether to move towards greater specialization and standardization in an industrial operation or whether to move in the opposite direction is generally an empirical one to be answered by research. One rule of thumb can be applied, however. If the job can be so simplified and standardized that it is readily convertible to automated machines, then the direction to take is that of further institutionalization until automation is possible. If, however, the overall performance requires complex judgement, the differential weighing of factors which are not markedly identifiable, or creativity, then the human mind is a far superior instrument to the computer.

The paradox is that where automation is feasible, it can actually increase the motivational potential among the employees who are left on the job after the changeover. Mann and Hoffman (1960) conclude from their study of automation in an electric power plant that the remaining jobs for workers can be more interesting, that there can be freer association among colleagues, and that the elimination of supervisory levels brings the top and bottom of the organization closer together.

Internalization of organizational goals and values

The pattern of motivation associated with value expression and self-identification has great potentialities for the internalization of the goals of subsystems and of the total system, and thus for the activation of behavior not prescribed by specific roles. Where this pattern prevails individuals take over organizational objectives as part of their own personal goals. They identify not with the organization as a safe and secure haven but with its major purposes. The internalization of organizational objectives is

generally confined to the upper echelons or to the officer personnel. In voluntary organizations it extends into some of the rank
and file, and in fact most voluntary organizations need a core of
dedicated people – who are generally referred to as the dedicated
damn fools.

Now the internalization of organizational goals is not as common as two types of more partial internalization. The first has to
do with some general organizational purposes which are not
unique to the organization. A scientist may have internalized
some of the research values of his profession but not necessarily
of the specific institution to which he is attached. As long as he
stays in that institution, he may be a well-motivated worker. But
he may find it just as easy to work for the things in which he
believes in another institution. There is not the same set of
alternative organizations open to liberals who are political acti-
vists and who are part of the core of dedicated damn fools in the
Democratic party. They have no other place to go, so they find
some way of rationalizing the party's deviation from their liberal
ideals.

A second type of partial internalization concerns the values and
goals of a subsystem of the organization. It is often easier for the
person to take over the values of his own unit. We may be
attached to our own department in a university more than to the
goals of the university as a whole.

Conditions conducive to internalization of system goals

Internalization of organization objectives can come about through
the utilization of the socialization process in childhood or
through the adult socialization which takes place in the organization itself. In the first instance, the selective process, either by
the person or the organization, matches the personality with the
system. A youngster growing up in the tradition of one of the
military services may have always thought of himself as an Air
Force officer. Similarly, the crusader for civil liberties and the
American Civil Liberties Union find one another.

The adult socialization process in the organization can build
upon the personal values of its members and integrate them about
an attractive model of its ideals. People can thus identify with
the organizational mission. If the task of an organization has

287

emotional significance, the organization enjoys an advantage in the creation of an attractive image. If the task is attended by hazard as in the tracking down of criminals by the FBI, or of high adventure as in the early days of flying, or of high service to humanity as in a cancer research unit, it is not difficult to develop a convincing model of the organization's mission.

The imaginative leader can also help in the development of an attractive picture of the organization by some new conceptualization of its mission. The police force, entrusted with the routine and dirty business of law enforcement carried out by dumb cops and 'flatfeet', can be energized by seeing themselves as a corps of professional officers devoted to the highest form of public service. Reality factors limit the innovative use of symbols for the glorification of organizations. Occupational groups, however, constantly strive to achieve a more attractive picture of themselves, as in the instances of press agents who have become public relations specialists or undertakers who have become morticians.

Internalization of subgroup norms can come about through identification with fellow group members who share the same common fate. People take over the values of their group because they identify with their own kind and see themselves as good group members, and as good group members they model their actions and aspirations in terms of group norms. This subgroup identification can work for organizational objectives only if there is agreement between the group norms and the organizational objectives. Often in industry the norms of the work group are much closer to union objectives than to company objectives.

This suggests three additional factors which contribute to internalization of group objectives: (a) participating in important decisions about group objectives; (b) contributing to group performance in a significant way: and (c) sharing in the rewards of group accomplishment. When these three conditions are met, the individual can regard the group as his, for he in fact has helped to make it.

Social satisfactions from primary-group relationships

Human beings are social animals and cannot exist in physical or psychological isolation. The stimulation, the approval and the support they derive from interacting with one another comprise one of the most potent forms of motivation. Strictly speaking, such affiliative motivation is another form of instrumental reward seeking, but some of its qualitative aspects are sufficiently different from the instrumental system and individual rewards previously described to warrant separate discussion.

The desire to be part of a group in itself will do no more than hold people in the system. The studies of Elton Mayo and his colleagues during the Second World War showed that work groups which provided their members' social satisfactions had less absenteeism than less cohesive work groups (Mayo and Lombard, 1944). Mann and Baumgartel (1953) corroborated these findings in a study of the Detroit Edison Company. With respect to role performance, moreover, Seashore (1954) has demonstrated that identification with one's work group can make for either above-average or below-average productivity depending upon the norms of the particular group. In the Seashore study the highly-cohesive groups, compared to the low-cohesive groups, moved to either extreme in being above or below the production standards for the company.

Other studies have demonstrated that though the group can provide important socioemotional satisfactions for the members it can also detract from task orientation (Bass, 1960). Members can have such a pleasant time interacting with one another that they neglect their work. Again the critical mediating variable is the character of the values and norms of the group. The affiliative motive can lead to innovative and cooperative behavior, but often this assumes the form of protecting the group rather than maximizing organizational objectives. So the major question in dealing with the affiliative motive is how this motive can be harnessed to organizational goals.

The Likert theory

What are the conditions under which the cohesive group with all the motivational force of primary-group relationships can gear its members to organizational goals? There is the possibility that our fifth factor of internalization of organizational objectives can be mediated through identification with subgroups whose informal norms reflect these purposes. Likert (1961) has devoted his book, *New Patterns of Management*, to this problem. The Likert thesis is that the factors making for internalization of organizational objectives can be realized by involving all the subgroups of the organization in group decision making of a task-oriented character. The task orientation is provided by an overlapping set of organizational families and by giving each such family some responsibility in decision making.

Specifically the Likert theory is based upon four essential concepts: (a) the efficacy of group process in maximizing motivation of organizational members; (b) the channeling of this motivation towards group goals by the use of overlapping organizational families; (c) the key role of a member of two families in his linking-pin function; and (d) the development of short feedback cycles through the use of research on the functioning of both the social and the technical system. This theory thus takes account of the hierarchical authority structure of organizations, but also ties in every individual in the organization through his attachment to his own group, and presumably integrates the needs of all subgroups. For example, the president of an organization can meet with his vice-presidents as the top organizational family, and as a group they can work through problems ordinarily handled by the president alone or by the president meeting individually with his vice-presidents. In turn each vice-president meets with his department heads and again the problems at this level are met through group process, with the vice-president forming the link to top management and interpreting company policy. Department heads meet with their division heads, and so on down the line. When a department head meets with his fellow department heads and their superior, the vice-president, he functions not only as a member of that group but as a representative of his own group of division heads. These meetings take on a task-oriented character, in good part through the continuing use of research and measurement on the group's own activities.

Decisions are made at the level of the structure which is the relevant locus for the amount of organizational space involved. If a decision affects only the people within a sub-unit, then it should be made in that sub-unit. Thus top management is relieved of many small decisions which can well be made down the line. Every member of the organization, save at the very top and bottom levels, thus serves as a linking-pin in functioning as a member of two organizational families. The bond between organizational levels is always personally mediated. Every group in the organizational structure has a voice in decision making. It decides how its task should be implemented. Though its task is set primarily by the level above it, it has some participation at this higher level through its representative.

Problems

There are, however, difficulties with the Likert theory, not because of the nature of the approach but because the approach is not pushed far enough in dealing with the walls of the maze. Specifically, the following problems still remain.

1. The voice of the rank-and-file member of the organization is greatly attenuated in its representation up the line. By the time the ordinary member's voice is reinterpreted through several levels of the organizational structure it may be so faint as to be ghostlike.

2. A related weakness is that the Likert model is primarily directed at the technical and task problems of the organization. The interest-group conflicts in organizations over the distribution of rewards, privileges, and prerequisites between hierarchical levels are difficult to meet in this system of organizational families. In contrast, the worker's union which cuts across all organizational families at the rank-and-file level, is still the worker's best chance of gaining representation of his interests. Legitimate differences in interests between groups may in fact be obscured by an application of the Likert model.

3. Not all motivational problems of the large-scale organization are solved by decisions made in overlapping family groups. The loss of a feeling of worth in an organization when an individual performs a routinized role which can be performed by ten million others or by a machine is still a basic issue. The internalization of organizational goals is not insured by involvement in very limited decisions. In other words, the specialization of labor, the job fractionization and the alienation of the worker from any meaningful work process are matters of organizational structure which may still prove to be overriding factors in sociotechnical systems.

4. Finally, there is the limitation upon group process when it

has to be carefully kept to a limited set of decisions, especially when these limits are imposed upon the group as fixed policies and boundaries. Workers may prefer their own unions, where their elected officers make some of their decisions for them, to their work group where they do not elect their leader and have no voice in larger issues. Group process generates its own dynamic and people involved in it want to go beyond their limited directives. Students who are given disciplinary policies by the university administration and given the task of their implementation soon raise questions about the policies themselves. Representative democracy may be a more powerful organizational form than group process hamstrung by being restricted to means rather than to goals.

References

ALLPORT, F. H. (1934), 'The J-curve hypothesis of conforming behavior', *J. soc. Psychol.*, vol. 5, pp. 141–83.

BASS, B. M. (1960), *Leadership, Psychology, and Organizational Behavior*, Harper.

KATZ, D. (1962), 'Human interrelationships and organizational behavior', in S. Mallick and E. H. Van Ness (eds.), *Concepts and Issues in Administrative Behavior*, Prentice-Hall, pp. 166–86.

KATZ, D., MACCOBY, N., and MORSE, N. (1950), *Productivity, Supervision and Morale in an Office Situation*, Institute for Social Research, University of Michigan.

LIKERT, R. (1961), *New Patterns of Management*, McGraw-Hill. [See Readings 14 and 23.]

MANN, F. C., and BAUMGARTEL, H. J. (1953), *Absences and Employee Attitudes in an Electric Power Company*, Institute for Social Research, University of Michigan.

MANN, F. C., and HOFFMAN, L. R. (1960), *Automation and the Worker*, Holt, Rinehart & Winston.

MAYO, E., and LOMBARD, G. (1944), Teamwork and labor turnover in the aircraft industry of Southern California, *Business Research Studies, Harvard University*, no. 32.

MCGREGOR, D. (1960), *The Human Side of Enterprise*, McGraw-Hill.

MORSE, N. (1953), *Satisfactions in the White-Collar Job*, Institute for Social Research, University of Michigan.

SEASHORE, S. (1954), *Group Cohesiveness in the Industrial Work Group*, Institute for Social Research, University of Michigan.

TRIST, E., and BAMFORTH, K. W. (1951), 'Some social and psychological consequences of the Longwall method of coal-getting', *Hum. Rel.*, vol. 4, pp. 3–38.

WEBER, M. (1947), *The Theory of Social and Economic Organization*, Free Press.

Part Five
Theories of Motivation and Management

To a large extent, the job of management involves the efficien: utilization of the organization's human resources. Accordingly. an important component of the manager's task is to maintain a high level of motivation in his subordinates to insure that they will carry out their jobs effectively.

In this Part we present attempts at the construction of theories of management based on assumptions about human motivation. The Readings have been selected to give the reader a sense of both the historical evolution and some of the current diversity in thinking on this problem.

Historically, the first major management theorist to concern himself with motivation was 'the father of scientific management', Frederick Winslow Taylor. Taylor's views, summarized in Reading 20, have had their largest impact on the management of rank-and-file workers. The worker is seen as an economic man to be induced to work effectively through wage incentives established by time and motion study. Taylor stresses the necessity of establishing the best method of doing each job through application of his principles and also of insuring that each worker utilizes that method.

Brown (Reading 21) criticizes the assumption that man is driven primarily by economic motives, and places emphasis on the affiliative or social motives. He supports these views by citing work of Elton Mayo, who is often considered to be the founder of the human relations movement which followed, and stands in sharp contrast to scientific management.

In Reading 22, McGregor discusses the various human needs (based heavily on Maslow, Reading 2) and considers them significant for the managerial process. He, along with Likert (Reading

23) and Maier and Hayes (Reading 24), views man as intrinsically motivated, willing to accept responsibility and striving towards actualization. In his selection, Likert discusses the idea of supportiveness of workers; Maier and Hayes focus on participative decision making.

Finally, Leavitt (Reading 25) warns that attempts to construct normative theories of management based on the assumption that the principle task is the co-ordination of human effort, are too limited in scope. He seeks to put the assumptions underlying participative management into perspective along with recent developments in the communication and systems sciences.

20 Frederick W. Taylor

The Principles of Scientific Management

Excerpts from Frederick W. Taylor, 'The principles of scientific management', in *Scientific Management*, Harper, 1947, pp. 36–9, 100–101, 117–22.

Under the old type of management, success depends almost entirely upon getting the 'initiative' of the workmen, and it is indeed a rare case in which this initiative is really attained. Under scientific management the 'initiative' of the workmen (that is, their hard work, their goodwill and their ingenuity) is obtained with absolute uniformity and to a greater extent than is possible under the old system; and in addition to this improvement on the part of the men, the managers assume new burdens, new duties and responsibilities never dreamed of in the past. The managers assume, for instance, the burden of gathering together all of the traditional knowledge which in the past has been possessed by the workmen and then of classifying, tabulating and reducing this knowledge to rules, laws and formulae which are immensely helpful to the workmen in doing their daily work. In addition to developing a *science* in this way, the management take on three other types of duties which involve new and heavy burdens for themselves.

These new duties are grouped under four heads:

1. They develop a science for each element of a man's work, which replaces the old rule-of-thumb method.

2. They scientifically select and then train, teach and develop the workman, whereas in the past he chose his own work and trained himself as best he could.

3. They heartily cooperate with the men so as to insure all of the work being done in accordance with the principles of the science which has been developed.

4. There is an almost equal division of the work and the responsibility between the management and the workmen. The management take over all work for which they are better fitted than the

workmen, while in the past almost all of the work and the greater part of the responsibility were thrown upon the men.

It is this combination of the initiative of the workmen, coupled with the new types of work done by the management, that makes scientific management so much more efficient than the old plan.

Three of these elements exist in many cases in a small and rudimentary way, under the management of 'initiative and incentive', but they are then of minor importance, whereas under scientific management they form the very essence of the whole system.

The fourth of these elements, 'an almost equal division of the responsibility between the management and the workmen', requires further explanation. The philosophy of the management of 'initiative and incentive' makes it necessary for each workman to bear almost the entire responsibility for the general plan as well as for each detail of his work, and in many cases for his implements as well. In addition to this he must do all of the actual physical labor. The development of a science, on the other hand, involves the establishment of many rules, laws and formulae which replace the judgement of the individual workman and which can be effectively used only after having been systematically recorded, indexed, etc. The practical use of scientific data also calls for a room in which to keep the books, records,[1] etc., and a desk for the planner to work at. Thus all of the planning which under the old system was done by the workman, as a result of his personal experience, must of necessity under the new system be done by the management in accordance with the laws of the science; because even if the workman was well suited to the development and use of scientific data, it would be physically impossible for him to work at his machine and at a desk at the same time. It is also clear that in most cases one type of man is needed to plan ahead and an entirely different type to execute the work.

The man in the planning room, whose speciality under scientific management is planning ahead, invariably finds that the work can be done better and more economically by a subdivision of the labor; each act of each mechanic, for example, should be preceded

1. For example, the records containing the data used under scientific management in an ordinary machine-shop fill thousands of pages.

by various preparatory acts done by other men. And all of this involves, as we have said, 'an almost equal division of the responsibility and the work between the management and the workman'.

To summarize: under the management of 'initiative and incentive' practically the whole problem is 'up to the workman', while under scientific management fully one-half of the problem is 'up to the management'.

Perhaps the most prominent single element in modern scientific management is the task idea. The work of every workman is fully planned out by the management at least one day in advance, and each man receives in most cases complete written instructions, describing in detail the task which he is to accomplish, as well as the means to be used in doing the work. And the work planned in advance in this way constitutes a task which is to be solved, as explained above, not by the workman alone, but in almost all cases by the joint effort of the workman and the management. This task specifies not only what is to be done but how it is to be done and the exact time allowed for doing it. And whenever the workman succeeds in doing his task right, and within the time limit specified, he receives an addition of from 30 per cent to 100 per cent to his ordinary wages. These tasks are carefully planned, so that both good and careful work are called for in their performance, but it should be distinctly understood that in no case is the workman called upon to work at a pace which would be injurious to his health. The task is always so regulated that the man who is well suited to his job will thrive while working at this rate during a long term of years and grow happier and more prosperous, instead of being overworked. Scientific management consists very largely in preparing for and carrying out these tasks. [. . .]

The change from rule-of-thumb management to scientific management involves not only a study of what is the proper speed for doing the work and a remodeling of the tools and the implements in the shop, but also a complete change in the mental attitude of all the men in the shop towards their work and towards their employers. The physical improvements in the machines necessary to insure large gains, and the motion study followed by minute study with a stop-watch of the time in which each workman should do his work, can be made comparatively quickly. But the change in the mental attitude and in the habits of the 300 or more workmen can be brought about only slowly and through a long series of object-lessons, which finally demonstrates to each man the great advantage which he will gain by heartily cooperating in his everyday work with the men in the management. [. . .]

In most trades, the science is developed through a comparatively simple analysis and time study of the movements required by the workmen to do some small part of his work, and this study is usually made by a man equipped merely with a stop-watch and a properly ruled notebook. Hundreds of these 'time-study men' are now engaged in developing elementary scientific knowledge where before existed only rule of thumb. Even the motion study of Mr Gilbreth in bricklaying involves a much more elaborate investigation than that which occurs in most cases. The general steps to be taken in developing a simple law of this class are as follows:

1. Find, say, ten to fifteen different men (preferably in as many separate establishments and different parts of the country) who are especially skilful in doing the particular work to be analysed.

2. Study the exact series of elementary operations or motions which each of these men uses in doing the work which is being investigated, as well as the implements each man uses.

3. Study with a stop-watch the time required to make each of these elementary movements and then select the quickest way of doing each element of the work.

4. Eliminate all false movements, slow movements and useless movements.

5. After doing away with all unnecessary movements, collect into one series the quickest and best movements as well as the best implements.

This one new method, involving that series of motions which can be made quickest and best, is then substituted in place of the ten or fifteen inferior series which were formerly in use. This best method becomes standard, and remains standard, to be taught first to the teachers (or functional foremen) and by them to every workman in the establishment until it is superseded by a quicker and better series of movements. In this simple way one element after another of the science is developed.

In the same way each type of implement used in a trade is

studied. Under the philosophy of the management of 'initiative and incentive' each workman is called upon to use his own best judgement, so as to do the work in the quickest time, and from this results in all cases a large variety in the shapes and types of implements which are used for any specific purpose. Scientific management requires, first, a careful investigation of each of the many modifications of the same implement, developed under rule of thumb; and second, after a time study has been made of the speed attainable with each of these implements, that the good points of several of them shall be united in a single standard implement, which will enable the workman to work faster and with greater ease than he could before. This one implement, then, is adopted as standard in place of the many different kinds before in use, and it remains standard for all workmen to use until superseded by an implement which has been shown, through motion and time study, to be still better.

With this explanation it will be seen that the development of a science to replace rule of thumb is in most cases by no means a formidable undertaking, and that it can be accomplished by ordinary, everyday men without any elaborate scientific training; but that, on the other hand, the successful use of even the simplest improvement of this kind calls for records, system and cooperation where in the past existed only individual effort.

There is another type of scientific investigation which should receive special attention, namely, the accurate study of the motives which influence men. At first it may appear that this is a matter for individual observation and judgement and is not a proper subject for exact scientific experiments. It is true that the laws which result from experiments of this class, owing to the fact that the very complex organism – the human being – is being experimented with, are subject to a larger number of exceptions than is the case with laws relating to material things. And yet laws of this kind, which apply to a large majority of men, unquestionably exist, and when clearly defined are of great value as a guide in dealing with men. In developing these laws, accurate, carefully planned and executed experiments, extending through a term of years, have been made, similar in a general way to the experiments upon various other elements which have been referred to in this paper.

Perhaps the most important law belonging to this class, in its relation to scientific management, is the effect which the task idea has upon the efficiency of the workman. This, in fact, has become such an important element of the mechanism of scientific management that, by a great number of people, scientific management has come to be known as 'task management'.

There is absolutely nothing new in the task idea. Each one of us will remember that in his own case this idea was applied with good results in his schoolboy days. No efficient teacher would think of giving a class of students an indefinite lesson to learn. Each day a definite, clear-cut task is set by the teacher before each scholar, stating that he must learn just so much of the subject; and it is only by this means that proper, systematic progress can be made by the students. The average boy would go very slowly if, instead of being given a task, he were told to do as much as he could. All of us are grown-up children, and it is equally true that the average workman will work with the greatest satisfaction, both to himself and to his employer, when he is given each day a definite task which he is to perform in a given time, and which constitutes a proper day's work for a good workman. This furnishes the workman with a clear-cut standard, by which he can throughout the day measure his own progress, and the accomplishment of which affords him the greatest satisfaction.

The writer has described in other papers a series of experiments made upon workmen, which have resulted in demonstrating the fact that it is impossible, through any long period of time, to get workmen to work much harder than the average men around them, unless they are assured a large and a permanent increase in their pay. This series of experiments, however, also proved that plenty of workmen can be found who are willing to work at their best speed, provided they are given this liberal increase in wages. The workman must, however, be fully assured that this increase beyond the average is to be permanent. Our experiments have shown that the exact percentage of increase required to make a workman work at his highest speed depends upon the kind of work which the man is doing.

It is absolutely necessary, then, when workmen are daily given a task which calls for a high rate of speed on their part, that they should also be insured the necessary high rate of pay whenever they are successful. This involves not only fixing for each man his daily task, but also paying him a large bonus, or premium, each time that he succeeds in doing his task in the given time. It is difficult to appreciate in full measure the help which the proper use of these two elements is to the workman in elevating him to the highest standard of efficiency and speed in his trade, and then keeping him there, unless one has seen first the old plan and afterwards the new tried upon the same man. And, in fact, until one has seen similar accurate experiments made upon various grades of workmen engaged in doing widely different types of work. The remarkable and almost uniformly good results from the *correct* application of the task and the bonus must be seen to be appreciated.

21 J. A. C. Brown

The Social Psychology of Industry

Abridged from J. A. C. Brown, *The Social Psychology of Industry*,
Penguin Books, 1954.

But there was another side to the F. W. Taylor success story.
Taylor, who stood with his stop-watch over the workers, timing
their rest-pauses and their every movement, altering the layout of
the plant and changing the traditional ways of doing things, was
not very popular. Years later he wrote of this period of his life:
'I was a young man in years but I give you my word I was a great
deal older than I am now, what with the worry, meanness and
contemptibleness of the whole damn thing. It's a horrid life for
any man to live not being able to look any workman in the face
without seeing hostility there, and a feeling that every man around
you is your virtual enemy.' The movement which, as it now
appears, Taylor had hoped would increase not only industrial
efficiency but also the standard of living and the health of the
worker was to appear to many workers as a form of exploitation,
a means of increasing output for the benefit of the owners. Since
the success of his work was measured in part by the number of
workers who could be discarded when the new methods were
applied, and Taylor himself took the view that 'all employees
should bear in mind that each shop exists first, last and all the
time, for the purpose of paying dividends to its owners', the attitude of the workers is hardly surprising. The researches of Taylor
and his successor Frank B. Gilbreth came to form the basis of
what is now known as time and motion study, while the professional psychologists studied for the most part such problems as
fatigue and conditions of work or the devising of selection tests for
vocational guidance.

What, to the modern student, is most striking about this early
work is not so much its specific content as the assumptions upon
which it is based. It is clear that the psychologists and efficiency

experts of this period had accepted the attitudes of management which arose during the early stages of the Industrial Revolution and these tended to form the background to all their investigations. Behind each experiment there lies the tacit implication that human nature is possessed of certain fixed properties which decree that most men find work distasteful, are naturally lazy, solely motivated by fear or greed (a motive now described as 'the carrot and the stick'), and always do as little work as possible for the largest possible wage.

In this view of mankind, every detail is completely fallacious. There is no such thing as a fixed human nature, either good or bad, which determines minutely how people shall behave. There is no evidence that men are naturally competitive or self-interested and there are many things which are more important to the worker than his wages. Human beings are not machines in any significant sense of the word, nor does a good physical environment, in itself, make them happy.

The Work of Elton Mayo

The inadequacy of the assumptions on which most of the early work in industrial psychology had been based was first shown by the failure of certain experiments carried out at the Hawthorne Works of the Western Electric Company in Chicago between 1924 and 1927.

Mayo began this early piece of research with the introduction of rest periods which amounted to two ten-minute breaks in the morning and two in the afternoon. The workers were encouraged to sleep for these periods, which initially were made available to only one-third of the men in the department. The results were impressive, since labour turnover decreased and output went up. It was further noted that morale had improved and the men were more friendly in their attitude. But what was at that time quite inexplicable to Mayo, was that there was an almost equivalent rise in production and decrease in labour turnover among the two-thirds of the men who had been excluded from the experiment although they worked in the same department. By the end of the first month, production efficiency had reached nearly 80 per cent and the workers received their first bonus. Within four months the level of production was 82 per cent.

At this point, certain difficulties began to arise. The supervisors of the department had never liked the new system and, it seems probable, shared with many other supervisors a dislike of what they considered to be pampering the workers in the name of science. They believed that the rest pauses should be earned (that is to say that the men should be expected to complete certain jobs before being authorized to rest), and, when a special rush order was received, they abandoned the rest pauses completely. (The assumption that, the longer the hours of work, the more goods should be produced, dies hard.) Within five days, conditions were back to what they had been when the experiment started, production was the lowest for months, absenteeism went up and morale went down. The supervisors were, not unnaturally, upset, and brought back the rest periods once more, but, this time strictly on an earned basis. Again the workers failed to respond, and production was back at 70 per cent. The position was a desperate one for the firm, since it looked as if the rush order would never be completed. But, at this moment, the President of the company, in consultation with Mayo, took charge. He ordered that during the rest pauses the machines should be shut down so that everyone in the department would be compelled to rest whether he was worker or supervisor. The supervisors were still more alarmed, for it seemed impossible that the time lost on the job could ever be recovered. But once more absenteeism diminished, morale went up, and production increased to $77\frac{1}{2}$ per cent. Subsequent changes permitted the men to select their own rest pauses which alternated with each other, so that the machines could be kept running continuously. This was the final phase of the experiment. Production reached $86\frac{1}{2}$ per cent, and several years later the President of the company was able to report that labour turnover had never since exceeded 5 to 6 per cent – that is, it was the same in the spinning department as in the rest of the factory. The problem had been solved.

Mayo gives an explanation of the results, in view of his later work. [. . .]

He pointed out that, firstly, the mere fact of the research being carried out demonstrated to the workers that their problems were not being ignored. That, secondly, the President of the company had always been popular with his employees, and was never more so than when he took the side of the workers against the supervisors who had put a stop to the rest pauses. But, finally, and most important of all, a crowd of solitary workers had been transformed into a group with a sense of social responsibility when they had themselves been given control over their rest periods.

Miller and Form in their *Industrial Sociology* (Harper, 1951) summarize in detail some conclusions to be drawn from this and other of Mayo's research.

1. Work is a group activity.

2. The social world of the adult is primarily patterned about work activity.

3. The need for recognition, security and sense of belonging is more important in determining workers' morale and productivity than the physical conditions under which he works.

4. A complaint is not necessarily an objective recital of facts; it is commonly a *symptom* manifesting disturbance of an individual's status position.

5. The worker is a person whose attitudes and effectiveness are conditioned by social demands from both inside and outside the work plant.

6. Informal groups within the work plant exercise strong social controls over the work habits and attitudes of the individual worker.

7. The change from an established to an adaptive society (i.e. from the older type of community life to the atomistic society of isolated individuals, from eotechnic to paleotechnic society) tends continually to disrupt the social organization of a work plant and industry generally.

8. Group collaboration does not occur by accident; it must be planned for and developed. If group collaboration is achieved, the work relations within a work plant may reach a cohesion which resists the disrupting effects of adaptive society.

22 Douglas M. McGregor

The Human Side of Enterprise

Douglas M. McGregor, 'The human side of enterprise', in *Adventures in Thought and Action*, Proceedings of the Fifth Anniversary Convocation of the School of Industrial Management, Massachusetts Institute of Technology, 1957, pp. 23–30.

It has become trite to say that the most significant developments of the next quarter century will take place not in the physical but in the social sciences, that industry – the economic organ of society – has the fundamental know-how to utilize physical science and technology for the material benefit of mankind, and that we must now learn how to utilize the social sciences to make our human organizations truly effective.

Many people agree in principle with such statements; but so far they represent a pious hope – and little else. Consider with me, if you will, something of what may be involved when we attempt to transform the hope into reality.

I

Let me begin with an analogy. A quarter century ago basic conceptions of the nature of matter and energy had changed profoundly from what they had been since Newton's time. The physical scientists were persuaded that under proper conditions new and hitherto unimagined sources of energy could be made available to mankind.

We know what has happened since then. First came the bomb. Then, during the past decade, have come many other attempts to exploit these scientific discoveries – some successful, some not.

The point of my analogy, however, is that the application of theory in this field is a slow and costly matter. We expect it always to be thus. No one is impatient with the scientist because he cannot tell industry how to build a simple, cheap, all-purpose source of atomic energy today. That it will take at least another decade and the investment of billions of dollars to achieve results which are economically competitive with present sources of power is understood and accepted.

It is transparently pretentious to suggest any *direct similarity* between the developments in the physical sciences leading to the harnessing of atomic energy and potential developments in the social sciences. Nevertheless, the analogy is not as absurd as it might appear to be at first glance.

To a lesser degree, and in a much more tentative fashion, we are in a position in the social sciences today like that of the physical sciences with respect to atomic energy in the thirties. We know that past conceptions of the nature of man are inadequate and in many ways incorrect. We are becoming quite certain that, under proper conditions, unimagined resources of creative human energy could become available within the organizational setting.

We cannot tell industrial management how to apply this new knowledge in simple, economic ways. We know it will require years of exploration, much costly development research and a substantial amount of creative imagination on the part of management to discover how to apply this growing knowledge to the organization of human effort in industry.

May I ask that you keep this analogy in mind – overdrawn and pretentious though it may be – as a framework for what I have to say.

Management's task: conventional view

The conventional conception of management's task in harnessing human energy to organizational requirements can be stated broadly in terms of three propositions. In order to avoid the complications introduced by a label, I shall call this set of propositions 'Theory X':

1. Management is responsible for organizing the elements of productive enterprise – money, materials, equipment, people – in the interest of economic ends.

2. With respect to people, this is a process of directing their efforts, motivating them, controlling their actions, modifying their behavior to fit the needs of the organization.

3. Without this active intervention by management, people would be passive – even resistant – to organizational needs. They must therefore be persuaded, rewarded, punished, controlled

– their activities must be directed. This is management's task – in managing subordinate managers or workers. We often sum it up by saying that management consists of getting things done through other people.

Behind this conventional theory there are several additional beliefs – less explicit, but widespread:

4. The average man is by nature indolent – he works as little as possible.

5. He lacks ambition, dislikes responsibility, prefers to be led.

6. He is inherently self-centred, indifferent to organizational needs.

7. He is by nature resistant to change.

8. He is gullible, not very bright, the ready dupe of the charlatan and the demagogue.

The human side of economic enterprise today is fashioned from propositions and beliefs such as these. Conventional organization structures, managerial policies, practices and programs reflect these assumptions.

In accomplishing its task – with these assumptions as guides – management has conceived of a range of possibilities between two extremes.

The hard or the soft approach?

At one extreme, management can be 'hard' or 'strong'. The methods for directing behavior involve coercion and threat (usually disguised), close supervision, tight controls over behavior. At the other extreme management can be 'soft' or 'weak'. The methods for directing behavior involve being permissive, satisfying people's demands, achieving harmony. Then they will be tractable and accept direction.

This range has been fairly completely explored during the past half century, and management has learned some things from the exploration. There are difficulties in the 'hard' approach. Force breeds counter-forces: restriction of output, antagonism, miiitant unionism, subtle but effective sabotage of management objectives. This approach is especially difficult during times of full employment.

There are also difficulties in the 'soft' approach. It leads frequently to the abdication of management – to harmony, perhaps, but to indifferent performance. People take advantage of the soft approach. They continually expect more, but they give less and less.

Currently, the popular theme is 'firm but fair'. This is an attempt to gain the advantages of both the hard and the soft approaches. It is reminiscent of Teddy Roosevelt's 'speak softly and carry a big stick'.

Is the conventional view correct?

The findings which are beginning to emerge from the social sciences challenge this whole set of beliefs about man and human nature and about the task of management. The evidence is far from conclusive, certainly, but it is suggestive. It comes from the laboratory, the clinic, the schoolroom, the home and even to a limited extent from industry itself.

The social scientist does not deny that human behavior in industrial organization today is approximately what management perceives it to be. He has, in fact, observed it and studied it fairly extensively. But he is pretty sure that this behavior is *not* a consequence of man's inherent nature. It is a consequence rather of the nature of industrial organizations, of management philosophy, policy and practice. The conventional approach of Theory X is based on mistaken notions of what is cause and what is effect.

'Well,' you ask, 'what then is the *true* nature of man? What evidence leads the social scientist to deny what is obvious?' And, if I am not mistaken, you are also thinking, 'Tell me – simply, and without a lot of scientific verbiage – what you think you know that is so unusual. Give me – without a lot of intellectual claptrap and theoretical nonsense – some practical ideas which will enable me to improve the situation in my organization. And remember, I'm faced with increasing costs and narrowing profit margins. I want proof that such ideas won't result simply in new and costly human relations frills. I want practical results, and I want them now.'

If these are your wishes, you are going to be disappointed. Such requests can no more be met by the social scientist today than could comparable ones with respect to atomic energy be met by the physicist fifteen years ago. I can, however, indicate a few of the reasons for asserting that conventional assumptions about the human side of enterprise are inadequate. And I can suggest – tentatively – some of the propositions that will comprise a more adequate theory of the management of people. The magnitude of the task that confronts us will then, I think, be apparent.

II

Perhaps the best way to indicate why the conventional approach of management is inadequate is to consider the subject of motivation. In discussing this subject I will draw heavily on the work of my colleague, Abraham Maslow of Brandeis University. His is the most fruitful approach I know. Naturally, what I have to say will be over-generalized and will ignore important qualifications. In the time at our disposal, this is inevitable.

Physiological and safety needs

Man is a wanting animal – as soon as one of his needs is satisfied, another appears in its place. This process is unending. It continues from birth to death.

Man's needs are organized in a series of levels – a hierarchy of importance. At the lowest level, but pre-eminent in importance when they are thwarted, are his physiological needs. Man lives by bread alone, when there is no bread. Unless the circumstances are unusual, his needs for love, for status, for recognition are inoperative when his stomach has been empty for a while. But when he eats regularly and adequately, hunger ceases to be an important need. The sated man has hunger only in the sense that a full bottle has emptiness. The same is true of the other physiological needs of man – for rest, exercise, shelter, protection from the elements.

A satisfied need is not a motivator of behavior! This is a fact of profound significance. It is a fact which is regularly ignored in the conventional approach to the management of people. I shall return to it later. For the moment, one example will make my point. Consider your own need for air. Except as you are deprived of it, it has no appreciable motivating effect upon your behavior.

When the physiological needs are reasonably satisfied, needs at the next higher level begin to dominate man's behavior – to motivate him. These are called safety needs. They are needs for protection against danger, threat, deprivation. Some people mistakenly refer to these as needs for security. However, unless man is in a dependent relationship where he fears arbitrary deprivation, he does not demand security. The need is for the 'fairest possible break'. When he is confident of this, he is more than willing to take risks. But when he feels threatened or dependent, his greatest need is for guarantees, for protection, for security.

The fact needs little emphasis that since every industrial employee is in a dependent relationship, safety needs may assume considerable importance. Arbitrary management actions, behavior which arouses uncertainty with respect to continued employment or which reflects favoritism or discrimination, unpredictable administration of policy – these can be powerful motivators of the safety needs in the employment relationship *at every level* from worker to vice-president.

Social needs

When man's physiological needs are satisfied and he is no longer fearful about his physical welfare, his social needs become important motivators of his behavior – for belonging, for association, for acceptance by his fellows, for giving and receiving friendship and love.

Management knows today of the existence of these needs, but it often assumes quite wrongly that they represent a threat to the organization. Many studies have demonstrated that the tightly knit, cohesive work group may, under proper conditions, be far more effective than an equal number of separate individuals in achieving organizational goals.

Yet management, fearing group hostility to its own objectives, often goes to considerable lengths to control and direct human efforts in ways that are inimical to the natural 'groupiness' of human beings. When man's social needs – and perhaps his safety needs, too – are thus thwarted, he behaves in ways which tend to defeat organizational objectives. He becomes resistant, antagonistic, uncooperative. But this behavior is a consequence, not a cause.

Ego needs

Above the social needs – in the sense that they do not become motivators until lower needs are reasonably satisfied – are the needs of greatest significance to management and to man himself. They are the egoistic needs, and they are of two kinds:

1. Those needs that relate to one's self-esteem – needs for self-confidence, for independence, for achievement, for competence, for knowledge.

2. Those needs that relate to one's reputation – needs for status, for recognition, for appreciation, for the deserved respect of one's fellows.

Unlike the lower needs, these are rarely satisfied; man seeks indefinitely for more satisfaction of these needs once they have become important to him. But they do not appear in any significant way until physiological, safety and social needs are all reasonably satisfied.

The typical industrial organization offers few opportunities for the satisfaction of these egoistic needs to people at lower levels in the hierarchy. The conventional methods of organizing work, particularly in mass-production industries, give little heed to these aspects of human motivation. If the practices of scientific management were deliberately calculated to thwart these needs – which, of course, they are not – they could hardly accomplish this purpose better than they do.

Self-fulfilment needs

Finally – a capstone, as it were, on the hierarchy of man's needs – there are what we may call the needs for self-fulfilment. These are the needs for realizing one's own potentialities, for continued self-development, for being creative in the broadest sense of that term.

It is clear that the conditions of modern life give only limited opportunity for these relatively weak needs to obtain expression. The deprivation most people experience with respect to other lower-level needs diverts their energies into the struggle to satisfy *those* needs, and the needs for self-fulfilment remain dormant.

III

Now, briefly, a few general comments about motivation. We recognize readily enough that a man suffering from a severe dietary deficiency is sick. The deprivation of physiological needs has behavioral consequences. The same is true – although less well recognized – of deprivation of higher-level needs. The man whose needs for safety, association, independence, or status are thwarted is sick just as surely as is he who has rickets. And his sickness will have behavioral consequences. We will be mistaken if we attribute his resultant passivity, his hostility, his refusal to accept responsibility to his inherent 'human nature'. These forms of behavior are *symptoms* of illness – of deprivation of his social and egoistic needs.

The man whose lower-level needs are satisfied is not motivated to satisfy those needs any longer. For practical purposes they exist no longer. (Remember my point about your need for air.) Management often asks, 'Why aren't people more productive? We pay good wages, provide good working conditions, have excellent fringe benefits and steady employment. Yet people do not seem to be willing to put forth more than minimum effort.'

The fact that management has provided for these physiological and safety needs has shifted the motivational emphasis to the egoistic needs. Unless there are opportunities *at work* to satisfy these higher-level needs, people will be deprived; and their behavior will reflect this deprivation. Under such conditions, if management continues to focus its attention on physiological needs, its efforts are bound to be ineffective.

People *will* make insistent demands for more money under these conditions. It becomes more important than ever to buy the material goods and services which can provide limited satisfaction of the thwarted needs. Although money has only limited value in satisfying many higher-level needs, it can become the focus of interest if it is the *only* means available.

The carrot and stick approach

The carrot and stick theory of motivation (like Newtonian physical theory) works reasonably well under certain circumstances. The *means* for satisfying man's physiological and (within limits) his safety needs can be provided or withheld by management. Employment itself is such a means, and so are wages, working conditions and benefits. By these means the individual can be controlled so long as he is struggling for subsistence. Man lives for bread alone when there is no bread.

But the carrot and stick theory does not work at all once man has reached an adequate subsistence level and is motivated primarily by higher needs. Management cannot provide a man with self-respect, or with the respect of his fellows, or with the satisfaction of needs for self-fulfilment. It can create conditions such that he is encouraged and enabled to seek such satisfactions *for himself*, or it can thwart him by failing to create those conditions.

But this creation of conditions is not 'control'. It is not a good device for directing behavior. And so management finds itself in an odd position. The high standard of living created by our modern technological know-how provides quite adequately for the satisfaction of physiological and safety needs. The only significant exception is where management practices have not created confidence in a 'fair break' – and thus where safety needs are thwarted. But by making possible the satisfaction of low-level needs, management has deprived itself of the ability to use as motivators the devices on which conventional theory has taught it to rely – rewards, promises, incentives, or threats and other coercive devices.

Neither hard nor soft

The philosophy of management by direction and control – *regardless of whether it is hard or soft* – is inadequate to motivate because the human needs on which this approach relies are today unimportant motivators of behavior. Direction and control are essentially useless in motivating people whose important needs are social and egoistic. Both the hard and the soft approach fail today because they are simply irrelevant to the situation.

People, deprived of opportunities to satisfy at work the needs which are now important to them, behave exactly as we might predict – with indolence, passivity, resistance to change, lack of responsibility, willingness to follow the demagogue, unreasonable demands for economic benefits. It would seem that we are caught in a web of our own weaving.

In summary, then, of these comments about motivation: management by direction and control – whether implemented with the hard, the soft, or the firm but fair approach – fails under today's conditions to provide effective motivation of human effort towards organizational objectives. It fails because direction and control are useless methods of motivating people whose physiological and safety needs are reasonably satisfied and whose social, egoistic and self-fulfilment needs are predominant.

IV

For these and many other reasons, we require a different theory of the task of managing people based on more adequate assumptions about human nature and human motivation. I am going to be so bold as to suggest the broad dimensions of such a theory. Call it 'Theory Y', if you will.

1. Management is responsible for organizing the elements of productive enterprise – money, materials, equipment, people – in the interest of economic ends.

2. People are *not* by nature passive or resistant to organizational needs. They have become so as a result of experience in organizations.

3. The motivation, the potential for development, the capacity for assuming responsibility, the readiness to direct behavior towards organizational goals are all present in people. Management does not put them there. It is a responsibility of management to make it possible for people to recognize and develop these human characteristics for themselves.

4. The essential task of management is to arrange organizational conditions and methods of operation so that people can achieve their own goals *best* by directing *their own* efforts toward organizational objectives.

This is a process primarily of creating opportunities, releasing potential, removing obstacles, encouraging growth, providing guidance. It is what Peter Drucker has called 'management by objectives' in contrast to 'management by control'.

And I hasten to add that it does *not* involve the abdication of management, the absence of leadership, the lowering of standards or the other characteristics usually associated with the 'soft' approach under Theory X. Much on the contrary: it is no more possible to create an organization today which will be a fully effective application of this theory than it was to build an atomic power plant in 1945. There are many formidable obstacles to overcome.

315

Some difficulties

The conditions imposed by conventional organization theory and by the approach of scientific management for the past half century have tied men to limited jobs which do not utilize their capabilities, have discouraged the acceptance of responsibility, have encouraged passivity, have eliminated meaning from work. Man's habits, attitudes, expectations – his whole conception of membership in an industrial organization – have been conditioned by his experience under these circumstances. Change in the direction of Theory Y will be slow, and it will require extensive modification of the attitudes of management and workers alike.

People today are accustomed to being directed, manipulated, controlled in industrial organizations and to finding satisfaction for their social, egoistic and self-fulfilment needs away from the job. This is true of much of management as well as of workers. Genuine 'industrial citizenship' – to borrow again a term from Drucker – is a remote and unrealistic idea, the meaning of which has not even been considered by most members of industrial organizations.

Another way of saying this is that Theory X places exclusive reliance upon external control of human behavior, while Theory Y relies heavily on self-control and self-direction. It is worth noting that this difference is the difference between treating people as children and treating them as mature adults. After generations of the former, we cannot expect to shift to the latter overnight.

V

Before we are overwhelmed by the obstacles, let us remember that the application of theory is always slow. Progress is usually achieved in small steps.

Consider with me a few innovative ideas which are entirely consistent with Theory Y and which are today being applied with some success.

Decentralization and delegation

These are ways of freeing people from the too-close control of conventional organization, giving them a degree of freedom to direct their own activities, to assume responsibility and, importantly, to satisfy their egoistic needs. In this connexion, the flat organization of Sears, Roebuck and Company provides an interesting example. It forces 'management by objectives' since it enlarges the number of people reporting to a manager until he cannot direct and control them in the conventional manner.

Job enlargement

This concept, pioneered by I.B.M. and Detroit Edison, is quite consistent with Theory Y. It encourages the acceptance of responsibility at the bottom of the organization; it provides opportunities for satisfying social and egoistic needs. In fact, the reorganization of work at the factory level offers one of the more challenging opportunities for innovation consistent with Theory Y. The studies by A. T. M. Wilson and his associates of British coal mining and Indian textile manufacture have added appreciably to our understanding of work organization. Moreover, the economic and psychological results achieved by this work have been substantial.

Participation and consultative management

Under proper conditions these results provide encouragement to people to direct their creative energies towards organizational objectives, give them some voice in decisions that affect them, provide significant opportunities for the satisfaction of social and egoistic needs. I need only mention the Scanlon Plan as the outstanding embodiment of these ideas in practice.

The not infrequent failure of such ideas as these to work as well as expected is often attributable to the fact that a management has 'bought the idea' but applies it within the framework of Theory X and its assumptions.

Delegation is not an effective way of exercising management by control. Participation becomes a farce when it is applied as a sales gimmick or a device for kidding people into thinking they are important. Only the management that has confidence in human capacities and is itself directed towards organizational objectives rather than towards the preservation of personal power can grasp the implications of this emerging theory. Such management will find and apply successfully other innovative ideas as we move slowly towards the full implementation of a theory like Y.

Performance appraisal

Before I stop, let me mention one other practical application of Theory Y which – while still highly tentative – may well have important consequences. This has to do with performance appraisal within the ranks of management. Even a cursory examination of conventional programs of performance appraisal will reveal how completely consistent they are with Theory X. In fact, most such programs tend to treat the individual as though he were a product under inspection on the assembly line.

Take the typical plan: substitute 'product' for 'subordinate being appraised', substitute 'inspector' for 'superior making the appraisal', substitute 'rework' for 'training or development', and, except for the attributes being judged, the human appraisal process will be virtually indistinguishable from the product inspection process.

A few companies – among them General Mills, Ansul Chemical and General Electric – have been experimenting with approaches which involve the individual in setting 'targets' or objectives *for himself* and in a *self*-evaluation of performance semi-annually or annually. Of course, the superior plays an important leadership role in this process – one, in fact, which demands substantially more competence than the conventional approach. The role is, however, considerably more congenial to many managers than the role of 'judge' or 'inspector' which is forced upon them by conventional performance. Above, all, the individual is encouraged to take a greater responsibility for planning and appraising his own contribution to organizational objectives; and the accompanying effects on egoistic and self-fulfilment needs are substantial. This approach to performance appraisal represents one more innovative idea being explored by a few managements who are moving towards the implementation of Theory Y.

VI

And now I am back where I began. I share the belief that we could realize substantial improvements in the effectiveness of industrial organizations during the next decade or two. Moreover, I believe the social sciences can contribute much to such developments. We are only beginning to grasp the implications of the growing body of knowledge in these fields. But if this conviction is to become a reality instead of a pious hope, we will need to view the process much as we view the process of releasing the energy of the atom for constructive human ends – as a slow, costly, sometimes discouraging approach toward a goal which would seem to many to be quite unrealistic.

The ingenuity and the perseverance of industrial management in the pursuit of economic ends have changed many scientific and technological dreams into commonplace realities. It is now becoming clear that the application of these same talents to the human side of enterprise will not only enhance substantially these materialistic achievements but will bring us one step closer to 'the good society'. Shall we get on with the job?

23 Rensis Likert

New Patterns of Management

Excerpt from chapter 8 of Rensis Likert, *New Patterns of Management*, McGraw-Hill, 1961, pp. 97–104.

The managers whose performance is impressive appear to be fashioning a better system of management. Two generalizations stated below are based on the available research findings:

The supervisors and managers in American industry and government who are achieving the highest productivity, lowest costs, least turnover and absence, and the highest levels of employee motivation and satisfaction display, on the average, a different pattern of leadership from those managers who are achieving less impressive results. The principles and practices of these high-producing managers are deviating in important ways from those called for by present-day management theories.

The high-producing managers whose deviations from existing theory and practice are creating improved procedures have not yet integrated their deviant principles into a theory of management. Individually, they are often clearly aware of how a particular practice of theirs differs from generally accepted methods, but the magnitude, importance and systematic nature of the differences when the total pattern is examined do not appear to be recognized.

Based upon the principles and practices of the managers who are achieving the best results, a newer theory of organization and management can be stated. An attempt will be made in this chapter to present briefly some of the over-all characteristics of such a theory and to formulate a general integrating principle which can be useful in attempts to apply it.

There is no doubt that further research and experimental testing of the theory in pilot operations will yield evidence pointing to modifications of many aspects of the newer theory suggested in this volume. Consequently, in reading this it will be well not to quarrel with the specific aspects of the newer theory as presented.

These specifics are intended as stimulants for discussion and as encouragement for experimental field tests of the theory. It will be more profitable to seek to understand the newer theory's general basic character, and whenever a specific aspect or derivation appears to be in error, to formulate more valid derivations and propositions.

Research findings indicate that the general pattern of operations of the highest-producing managers tends to differ from that of the managers of mediocre and low-producing units by more often showing the following characteristics:

A preponderance of favorable attitudes on the part of each member of the organization towards all the other members, towards superiors, towards the work, towards the organization – towards all aspects of the job. These favorable attitudes towards others reflect a high level of mutual confidence and trust throughout the organization. The favorable attitudes towards the organization and the work are not those of easy complacency, but are the attitudes of identification with the organization and its objectives and a high sense of involvement in achieving them. As a consequence, the performance goals are high and dissatisfaction may occur whenever achievement falls short of the goals set.

This highly motivated, cooperative orientation towards the organization and its objectives is achieved by harnessing effectively all the major motivational forces which can exercise significant influence in an organizational setting and which, potentially, can be accompanied by cooperative and favorable attitudes. Reliance is not placed solely or fundamentally on the economic motive of buying a man's time and using control and authority as the organizing and coordinating principle of the organization. On the contrary, the following motives are all used fully and in such a way that they function in a cumulative and reinforcing manner and yield favorable attitudes:

The ego motives. These are referred to throughout this volume as the desire to achieve and maintain a sense of personal worth and importance. This desire manifests itself in many forms, depending upon the norms and values of the persons and groups involved. Thus, it is responsible for such motivational forces as the desire for growth and significant achievement in terms of one's own values and goals, i.e. self-fulfilment, as well as the desire for status, recognition, approval, acceptance and power and the desire to undertake significant and important tasks.
The security motives.
Curiosity, creativity and the desire for new experiences.

The economic motives.

By tapping all the motives which yield favorable and cooperative attitudes, maximum motivation oriented towards realizing the organization's goals as well as the needs of each member of the organization is achieved. The substantial decrements in motivational forces which occur when powerful motives are pulling in opposite directions are thereby avoided. These conflicting forces exist, of course, when hostile and resentful attitudes are present.

The organization consists of a tightly knit, effectively functioning social system. This social system is made up of interlocking work groups with a high degree of group loyalty among the members and favorable attitudes and trust between superiors and subordinates. Sensitivity to others and relatively high levels of skill in personal interaction and the functioning of groups are also present. These skills permit effective participation in decisions on common problems. Participation is used, for example, to establish organizational objectives which are a satisfactory integration of the needs and desires of all members of the organization and of persons functionally related to it. High levels of reciprocal influence occur, and high levels of total coordinated influence are achieved in the organization. Communication is efficient and effective. There is a flow from one part of the organization to another of all the relevant information important for each decision and action. The leadership in the organization has developed what might well be called a highly effective social system for interaction and mutual influence.

Measurements of organizational performance are used primarily for self-guidance rather than for superimposed control. To tap the motives which bring cooperative and favorable rather than hostile attitudes, participation and involvement in decisions is a habitual part of the leadership process. This kind of decision making, of course, calls for the full sharing of available measurements and information. Moreover as it becomes evident in the decision-making process that additional information or measurements are needed, steps are taken to obtain them.

In achieving operations which are more often characterized by the above pattern of highly cooperative, well-coordinated activity, the highest producing managers use all the technical resources of the classical theories of management, such as time-and-motion study, budgeting and financial controls. They use these resources at least as completely as do the low-producing managers, but in quite different ways. This difference in use arises from the differences in the motives which the high-producing, in contrast to the low-producing, managers believe are important in influencing human behavior.

The low-producing managers, in keeping with traditional practice, feel that the way to motivate and direct behavior is to exercise control through authority. Jobs are organized, methods are prescribed, standards are set, performance goals and budgets are established. Compliance with them is sought through the use of hierarchical and economic pressures.

The highest-producing managers feel, generally, that this manner of functioning does not produce the best results, that the resentment created by direct exercise of authority tends to limit its effectiveness. They have learned that better results can be achieved when a different motivational process is employed. As suggested above, they strive to use all those major motives which have the potentiality of yielding favorable and cooperative attitudes in such a way that favorable attitudes are, in fact, elicited and the motivational forces are mutually reinforcing. Motivational forces stemming from the economic motive are not then blunted by such other motivations as group goals which restrict the quantity or quality of output. The full strength of all economic ego and other motives is generated and put to use.

Widespread use of participation is one of the more important approaches employed by the high-producing managers in their efforts to get full benefit from the technical resources of the classical theories of management coupled with high levels of reinforcing motivation. This use of participation applies to all aspects of the job and work, as, for example, in setting work goals and budgets, controlling costs, organizing the work, etc.

In these and comparable ways, the high-producing managers make full use of the technical resources of the classical theories of management. They use these resources in such a manner, however, that favorable and cooperative attitudes are created and all members of the organization endeavor to pull concertedly towards commonly accepted goals which they have helped to establish.

This brief description of the pattern of management which is more often characteristic of the high-producing than of the low-producing managers points to what appears to be a critical difference. The high-producing managers have developed their

323

organizations into highly coordinated, highly motivated, co-operative social systems. Under their leadership, the different motivational forces in each member of the organization have coalesced into a strong force aimed at accomplishing the mutually established objectives of the organization. This general pattern of highly motivated, cooperative members seems to be a central characteristic of the newer management system being developed by the highest-producing managers.

How do these high-producing managers build organizations which display this central characteristic? Is there any general approach or underlying principle which they rely upon in building highly motivated organizations? There seems to be; the research findings show, for example, that those supervisors and managers whose pattern of leadership yields consistently favorable attitudes more often think of employees as 'human beings rather than just as persons to get the work done'. Consistently, in study after study, the data show that treating people as 'human beings' rather than as 'cogs in a machine' is a variable highly related to the attitudes and motivation of the subordinate at every level in the organization.

The superiors who have the most favorable and cooperative attitudes in their work groups display the following characteristics:

The attitude and behavior of the superior towards the subordinate as a person, *as perceived by the subordinate*, is as follows:

He is supportive, friendly, and helpful rather than hostile. He is kind but firm, never threatening, genuinely interested in the well-being of subordinates and endeavors to treat people in a sensitive, considerate way. He is just, if not generous. He endeavors to serve the best interests of his employees as well as of the company.

He shows confidence in the integrity, ability and motivations of subordinates rather than suspicion and distrust.

His confidence in subordinates leads him to have high expectations as to their level of performance. With confidence that he will not be disappointed, he expects much, not little. (This, again, is fundamentally a supportive rather than a critical or hostile relationship.) He sees that each subordinate is well trained for his particular job. He endeavors also to help subordinates be promoted by training them for jobs at the next level. This involves giving them relevant experience and coaching whenever the opportunity offers.

He coaches and assists employees whose performance is below standard. In the case of a subordinate who is clearly misplaced and unable to do his job satisfactorily, he endeavors to find a position well suited to that employee's abilities and arranges to have the employee transferred to it.

The behavior of the superior in directing the work is characterized by such activity as:

Planning and scheduling the work to be done, training subordinates, supplying them with material and tools, initiating work activity, etc. Providing adequate technical competence, particularly in those situations where the work has not been highly standardized.

The leader develops his subordinates into a working team with high group loyalty by using participation and the other kinds of group-leadership practices.

The Integrating Principle

These results and similar data from other studies (Argyris, 1957; March and Simon, 1958; Viteles, 1953) show that subordinates react favorably to experiences which they feel are supportive and contribute to their sense of importance and personal worth. Similarly, persons react unfavorably to experiences which are threatening and decrease or minimize their sense of dignity and personal worth. These findings are supported also by substantial research on personality development (Argyris, 1957; Rogers, 1942, 1951) and group behavior (Cartwright and Zander, 1960). Each of us wants appreciation, recognition, influence, a feeling of accomplishment and a feeling that people who are important to us believe in us and respect us. We want to feel that we have a place in the world.

This pattern of reaction appears to be universal and seems to be the basis for the general principle used by the high-producing managers in developing their highly motivated, cooperative organizations. These managers have discovered that the motivational forces acting in each member of an organization are most likely to be cumulative and reinforcing when the interactions between each individual and the others in the organization are of such a character that they convey to the individual a feeling of support

325

and recognition for his importance and worth as a person. These managers, therefore, strive to have the interactions between the members of their organization of such a character that each member of the organization feels confident in his potentialities and believes that his abilities are being well used.

An individual's reaction to any situation is always a function not of the absolute character of the interaction, but of his perception of it. It is how he sees things that counts, not objective reality. Consequently, an individual member of an organization will always interpret an interaction between himself and the organization in terms of his background and culture, his experience and expectations. The pattern of supervision and the language used that might be effective with a railroad's maintenance-of-way crew, for example, would not be suitable in an office full of young women. A subordinate tends also to expect his superior to behave in ways consistent with the personality of the superior. All this means that each of us, as a subordinate or as a peer or as a superior, reacts in terms of his own particular background, experience and expectations. In order, therefore, to have an interaction viewed as supportive, it is essential that it be of such a character that the individual himself, in the light of his experience and expectations, sees it as supportive. This provides the basis for stating the general principle which the high-producing managers seem to be using and which will be referred to as the *principle of supportive relationships*. This principle, which provides an invaluable guide in any attempt to apply the newer theory of management in a specific plant or organization, can be briefly stated: *the leadership and other processes of the organization must be such as to ensure a maximum probability that in all interactions and all relationships with the organization each member will, in the light of his background, values and expectations, view the experience as supportive and one which builds and maintains his sense of personal worth and importance.*

The Principle of Supportive Relationships as an
Organizing Concept

This general principle provides a fundamental formula for obtaining the full potential of every major motive which can be constructively harnessed in a working situation. There is impressive evidence, for example, that economic motivations will be tapped more effectively when the conditions specified by the principle of supportive relationships are met (Katz and Kahn, 1951; Krulee, 1955). In addition, as motives are used in the ways called for by this general principle, the attitudes accompanying the motives will be favorable and the different motivational forces will be cumulative and reinforcing. Under these circumstances, the full power from each of the available motives will be added to that from the others to yield a maximum of coordinated, enthusiastic effort.

The principle of supportive relationships points to a dimension essential for the success of every organization, namely, that the mission of the organization be seen by its members as genuinely important. To be highly motivated, each member of the organization must feel that the organization's objectives are of significance and that his own particular task contributes in an indispensable manner to the organization's achievement of its objectives. He should see his role as difficult, important and meaningful. This is necessary if the individual is to achieve and maintain a sense of personal worth and importance. When jobs do not meet this specification they should be reorganized so that they do. This is likely to require the participation of those involved in the work.

The term 'supportive' is a key word in the principle of supportive relationships. Experiences, relationships, etc., are considered to be supportive when the individual involved sees the experience (in terms of his values, goals, expectations and aspirations) as contributing to or maintaining his sense of personal worth and importance.

The principle of supportive relationships contains within it an important clue to its effective use. To apply this general principle, a superior must take into consideration the experience and expectations of each of his subordinates. In determining what these expectations are, he cannot rely solely on his observations and impressions. It helps the superior to try to put himself in his subordinate's shoes and endeavor to see things as the subordinate sees them, but this is not enough. Too often, the superior's estimates are wrong. He needs direct evidence, if he is to know how

327

the subordinate views things and to estimate the kinds of behavior and interaction which will be seen by the subordinate as supportive. The superior needs accurate information as to how his behavior is actually seen by the subordinate. Does the subordinate, in fact, perceive the superior's behavior as supportive?

There are two major ways to obtain this evidence. In a complex organization it can be found by the use of measurements of the intervening variables. It can also be obtained by the development of work-group relationships, which not only facilitate but actually require, as part of the group building and maintenance functions, candid expressions by group members of their perceptions and reactions to the behavior of others.

References

ARGYRIS, C. (1957), *Personality and Organization*, Harper.

CARTWRIGHT, D., and ZANDER, A. (eds.) (1960), *Group Dynamics: Research and Theory*, Row, Peterson, 2nd edn.

KATZ, D., and KAHN, R. L. (1951), 'Human organization and worker motivation', in L. Reed Tripp (ed.), *Industrial Productivity*, Industrial Relations Research Association; Madison, Wisconsin.

KRULEE, G. K. (1955), 'The Scanlon plan: co-operation through participation', *J. Bus.*, vol. 28, pp. 100–13.

MARCH, J. G., and SIMON, H. A. (1958), *Organizations*, Wiley. [See Reading 9.]

ROGERS, C. R. (1942), *Counseling and Psychotherapy*, Houghton Mifflin.

ROGERS, C. R. (1951), *Client-Centered Therapy*, Houghton Mifflin.

VITELES, M. S. (1953), *Motivation and Morale in Industry*, Norton.

24 Norman R. F. Maier and John J. Hayes

Introducing Creative Management

Abridged from chapter 11 of Norman R. F. Maier and John J. Hayes, *Creative Management*, Wiley, 1962.

Effects of Organization on Behavior

Most of what businessmen know about industrial organizations has been learned from their own observation and experience. For the most part, this experience has led them to believe that employee behavior leaves much to be desired.

Rank-and-file employees, heirs to a work situation bereft of opportunities that challenge their intelligence and creative capacities, adapt to their role in selfish, defensive and sometimes hostile ways. Management employees, caught in the ideological no man's land between Man and the Organization, are frustrated by the social and economic consequences of conflict between two opposing need systems. Managers find themselves resorting to the endless search for influence and authority to control subordinate behavior and reduce the costs of negative attitudes and restrictive work practices.

Classical management theory, based on the economic nature of the industrial organization and not on its social nature, is inadequate to improve the situation, because it focuses all attention on the effects of employee apathy and irresponsibility, and ignores the basic causes of employee behavior.

When we fail to achieve the results we desire, we tend to seek the cause everywhere but where it usually lies: in our choice of inappropriate methods of control. The engineer does not blame water for flowing downhill rather than up. . . . However, when people respond to managerial decisions in undesired ways, the normal response is to blame them. It is *their* stupidity, or *their* uncooperativeness, or *their* laziness which is seized on as the explanation of what happened, not management's failure to select appropriate methods of control (McGregor, 1960, p. 10).

Overt behavior is not self-explanatory. This is a hopeless confusion of the principle of cause and effect. Unless the manager is willing to look at the underlying causes of apathy, uncooperativeness and laziness in the workplace, he will never discover approaches to management that get to the causes of the difficulty. He will back into the future by facing the past, quixotically insisting on the right to make decisions that can never be carried out.

The authoritarian theory proceeds from assumptions that human relations' concerns are irrelevant in business, and that most people are naturally dependent, indolent, self-centered and uncooperative. They are assumed to require strong direction and control by external forces if discipline is to be maintained. If most people employed in industry were in fact immature and dependent, the authoritarian theory would be appropriate; but there is no basic evidence that such behavior is inherent in human nature.

The democratic theory of organization proceeds from assumptions that mature, intelligent, educated adults in American society are capable of managing their own affairs in creative and responsible ways. People react positively to opportunities for expressing their natural human attributes and they react negatively to deprivation of such opportunities.

Since the authoritarian point of view is the more pervasive in our industrial culture, most business experience has been acquired under the circumstances where human relations and participative practices have been essentially manipulative and the employee's reaction has frequently been apathy, resistance, and irresponsibility. In this background it is hardly surprising that many people, managers as well as rank-and-file employees, remain dubious about democratic principles and methods. Even those philosophically inclined towards democratic ethics may be haunted by lingering fears of what might happen if people were left more generally to their own devices. People in business organizations have to work towards specific goals and organizational objectives, not do things just as they please. Power and authority are exercised to restrain employees from hedonistic and narrowly selfish behavior. The error in this concept is not that control and integration are necessary in organizations, but in the false assumption that without the strong guiding hand of management authority, there would be no restraints, no order, no unified purpose.

Limits on Individual Autonomy in Democratic Organizations

If we observe the functioning of small groups in reaching a decision, we can see that any primary group places numerous limits on the individualistic behavior of its members. Deviant behavior is policed by the group itself, no less than by external authority of a superior.

Democratic decision making does not provide the right or a mechanism for each individual to have his own way. This is impossible in any system of organized human activity. Differences of opinion are inescapable because people have different needs and motives, and these differences lead to diversity and conflict. In democratic organizations, the group must resolve some of its conflicting ideas and suggestions before it can proceed in any unified way towards a common goal.

If the group is small, cohesive and skilled in group problem solving, differences are usually resolved through consensus. If the group is large and loosely structured, differences may be resolved by majority rule.

In any democratic process the majority, in one way or another, imposes its collective judgements and restraints on the minority. The distinctive feature of democratic decision making is in having one's *say*, not in having one's *way*. In face-to-face meetings this *say* has its full meaning. Satisfaction is greatest when the participants feel they have had as much influence as they wish (Hoffman, Harburg and Maier, 1962)

Limits on Group Autonomy in Democratic Organizations

As individuals in a group-decision conference cannot and do not expect to have their own way all the time, subordinate subgroups in the larger organization do not expect and cannot be expected to have their way on every decision which large organizations have to reach.

Both personal freedom and subgroup autonomy are therefore limited by the extent to which they conflict with the broader needs and interests of the whole organization. Such restraints are not arbitrary, however, but are jointly needed and jointly derived by the parties concerned. Mutually agreed-on restraints do not infringe on the legitimate human freedoms which are prerequisite to responsible behavior and creative achievement.

Influence of Organizational Climate on Management Practices

Ironically, the social phenomena that restrain innovative or deviant behavior operate without discrimination as to the nature of the deviation. Centers of influence and social power within an organization tend to protect prevailing norms and standards from any innovation, good or bad, and this becomes a problem for the progressive manager.

The group problem-solving and decision-making processes, in which the idea of participation is brought to meaningful reality, are basically a democratic method of management. The group-decision leadership method creates as well as thrives in a democratic atmosphere. Industrial organizations generally do not provide this kind of atmosphere and it must be introduced by the individual leaders themselves.

Creative leadership entails fundamental theories and assumptions about people and organizations which are in striking contrast with the theories and assumptions that govern most business organizations. The convictions and procedures involved in the leadership of problem-solving conferences conflict with judgements about management practices and prerogatives which are ordinarily defined, explicitly and implicitly, by the organization's top policy makers.

The individual manager cannot ignore these contrasts. The conditions under which he operates are predetermined, in large measure, by the total organizational context. He is a superior in his relationships with his own work group; he is a subordinate in his relationships with his own boss; and an equal with other members of the group reporting to his boss. However, the initiative for change must come from someone. In any organization the supervisory practices vary considerably and there are many opportunities to move toward the leadership goals we have described. A supervisor who produces results can justify his methods.

If an individual manager's responsibilities were only to himself and his own subordinates, he would be able to approach the management role according to his best judgement of the organization's needs and interests. He would be justified in making extensive use of participation or any other management method that best fitted his problems and situations. However, such is not usually the case. Parochial interests and individual judgements are not the sole determinant of leadership practices and management methods unless they are clearly delegated to him.

Production employees require a climate of some freedom and participation in order to function creatively and responsibly as employees, just as management employees require some freedom and participation in policy making at their level in order to function effectively and creatively as managers. Organizations need professionally competent managers and, to foster their development, favorable conditions in industrial organizations need to be created.

Since these democratic principles are often in theoretical conflict with the organizational climate in which they have to operate, the nature of the total organization becomes an important consideration and deterrent to the individual manager interested in innovation and progress. Some changes in the total climate, or at least in the expression given to it by his immediate superior, may be prerequisite to any substantial improvements in leadership practices.

The situation may seem to indicate that the average manager is powerless to introduce participative forms of management, even in his own work group. Without prior initiative by top policy makers, the subordinate manager's hands may appear to be tied. In some particular situations this may be true; but before this is assumed there are important alternatives to explore.

The Individual Manager's Opportunities

The individual manager, if he is interested in holding group meetings and has the freedom as well as the facilities to operate democratically, can usually achieve positive results in upgrading business decisions within the sphere of his own primary group. This alone is worthwhile, for it can lead to needed improvements in group morale and productivity. Most important is the new satisfaction he derives from working with a group that accepts him as a helper rather than as a judge.

First of all, he must recognize the limitations on his freedom that are imposed on him from higher management. An initial reaction of many a supervisor is to think of all of the things he cannot decide. However, if he wishes to use group participation he must think of the kinds of things he can decide. In the most restricted positions, a supervisor may find that he can make job assignments, set up work schedules, plan certain aspects of a job, assign equipment, and even set or interpret standards of efficiency and quality. These are important decisions and often are the center of controversy. A supervisor who can make decisions in these areas is free to ask his group to participate in making them.

Restrictions imposed by law, union contracts, company policy and even the personal preferences of an immediate superior must be considered realistically as limiting facts. Whether we like them or not, the problem-solving approach requires that limits of freedom be accepted as part of the situation. The most that an individual supervisor can do to increase his own area of freedom is to suggest an increase to his superior. In some instances the need for more freedom may be temporary.

Let us return to problem solving in the given area of freedom. Each supervisor has an area of decision making that depends on his job and his level in the company. He can share the problem-solving and decision-making opportunities that fall within this area. In the event he does not know the limitations, which is not uncommon, he can discuss the matter with his superior.

The important rule for every supervisor, regardless of his level in the organization, is to see to it that he handles only that part of the problem that concerns his level. Like his superior, each supervisor is inclined to restrict the problem-solving function of his subordinates by going beyond the aspects of the problem that concern his function. He must resist the tendency of solving the problem in all its details and thereby denying subordinates some problem-solving opportunities.

Perhaps the most highly developed approaches and examples of participative management on a company-wide scale are in the many organizations which have adopted the so-called 'Scanlon plan' (Lesieur, 1958) or its variants.

The Scanlon plan embraces two major features. First, it is a plant-wide system of participation in decision making in which productivity improvements can be made and carried out. Second, it is a plant-wide incentive system for sharing the economic results of productivity improvements. Unfortunately, the second feature sometimes tends to obscure the significance of the first. Since incentive pay is involved, the results are often imputed to economic incentives despite the fact that other attempts at motivating employees with incentive pay achieve nowhere near such spectacular results in upgrading productivity and morale. In orthodox organizations, the highest paid employee groups may indeed often be the lowest ranking in general morale and productive effort.

The Scanlon plan complements the regular organizational hierarchy with a second network of joint labor–management committees, production committees and screening committees. These are set up to process employee suggestions and ideas, solve production problems and carry out plans of action for methods of improvement. The committee network directly involves rank-and-file employees in key policy and operating decisions that go right to the heart of the business. Productivity, costs, prices and profits become the goals around which employee participation is organized.

Here is a bold and imaginative plan for making social goals and economic goals fully compatible in the enterprise. Participation is not used as a gimmick, but as a unique concept of organization where every employee has a meaningful responsibility and personal investment in the success of the company.

Success of an activity such as is involved in the Scanlon plan requires a veritable revolution in management's conception of its functions and its behavior in relation to workers and union representatives. The management preoccupied with protecting its prerogatives had best not consider the Scanlon plan at all (Whyte, 1955, pp. 185–6).

These participative attempts capture some of the democratic values but they fall short of what is possible. Smaller group meetings with skilled leaders can accomplish much more in the utilization of human resources.

An Organizational Concept for Creative Management

It would seem that the best way to introduce democratic processes into the larger organization is to regard the problem-solving conference as the functional unit and, through interlocking membership, have these conferences multiplied until all levels and job classifications are included. This method gives all members an opportunity to participate in solving some problems, actually those that concern them the most and those that they know the most about.

The face-to-face influence on decisions permits far more participation and influence than does the democratic procedure which limits participation to voting where the choice of the majority rules, and the minority must abide by this choice. Group discussion for resolving differences permits greater opportunities for satisfaction than does casting ballots.

Voting is a form of democracy but when practiced on a large scale it tends to deny participants the opportunities to solve problems. Rather the alternatives are supplied and the participants can merely express a preference for one of them. In face-to-face discussions, the participants can create new alternatives and they can find ways to integrate or to compromise differences. The mere fact that there is more involvement in discussion than in voting is enough to favor the smaller face-to-face meeting. The question is whether or not a pattern of small group conferences is a practical approach to operate a large organization. Although this may not be practical for society in general it seems that a business organization has the framework and sufficient unity of purpose to locate problems of mutual interest.

References

HOFFMAN, L. R., HARBURG, E., and MAIER, N. R. F. (1962), 'Differences and disagreements as factors in creative group problem solving', *J. abnorm. soc. Psychol.*, vol. 64, pp. 206–14.

LESIEUR, F. G. (1958), *The Scanlon Plan*, Wiley.

MCGREGOR, D. M. (1960), *The Human Side of Enterprise*, McGraw-Hill.

WHYTE, W. F. (1955), *Money and Motivation*, Harper.

25 Harold J. Leavitt

Unhuman Organizations

Abridged from Harold J. Leavitt, 'Unhuman organizations',
Harvard Business Review, vol. 40, 1962, pp. 90–98.

The purpose of this article is to urge that we take another look at our beliefs about the place of people in organizations. They are beliefs that have matured, even oversolidified, in the 1940s and 1950s. And they are beliefs which, until the last couple of years, have seemed safe and inviolate.

Let me emphasize from the start that although this article is a critique of our 'human relations' emphasis on people, I am not worried about 'manipulation', group-think', 'softness', 'conformity' or any of the other recent criticisms. In fact, most theories and techniques of human relations are, to my mind, both sound and progressive. *The theme here is not that human relations theory is either incorrect or immoral. My argument is that it is simply insufficient. It is too narrow a perspective from which to analyse the management of organizations.* But I am not suggesting that we turn back to the earlier and even narrower beliefs of 'tough' management. What we have to do is to push beyond the plateau of present beliefs, which are becoming too deeply ingrained among managers and social scientists. Such beliefs now hold:

1. That organizations are and ought to be in their essence *human* systems.

2. Therefore, that the management of organizations is and ought to be in its essence a process of coordinating human effort.

3. Implicitly, that the best organization is the one in which each member contributes up to his 'full potential', and that the best individual manager is he who has set up conditions which maximize the creativity and commitment of his people.

4. And that management is a *unified* rather than a *differentiated*

337

process; i.e. that good management at one level or in one locale of an organization ought to be essentially the same as good management at any other level or locale in that or any other organization. This idea is so implicit, so seldom said aloud, that I cannot be perfectly sure it is really there.

Incidentally, this fourth belief in some unifying essence was, I think, held by earlier theorists about management, too. To early Taylorists, for example, 'rationalization' of work was the pure essence of good management and was, in theory, applicable anywhere and everywhere from president to sweeper.

Participative Beliefs

For simplicity, let me refer to the first three of the above as 'participative beliefs'. They have one common integrating element – the idea that organizations are essentially human. It follows that we should begin our descriptions and analyses of organizations in human terms. They have a value element in common, too – a very strong one; i.e. not only are organizations best described in human units; they *ought* to be human. It is right, many of us believe, to think about organizations from a human point of view, because people *are* more important than anything. Moreover, we are blessed (according to these beliefs) by the happy coincidence that managerial practices which place human fulfilment first also happen to be the most efficient and productive practices.

I can offer no definitive evidence to prove that these beliefs are not straw men. It may be they are not really widely shared by social scientists, managers, consultants and personnel people. If that should be the case, and they are only fat red herrings, then our re-examination may help to destroy them.

Reasons for re-examination

I urge that these beliefs be re-examined not so much because they are wrong, in any absolute sense, and certainly not because the beliefs that preceded them, especially the Tayloristic beliefs, were right. Essentially, the participative beliefs ought to be re-examined for two reasons.

1. *In so eagerly demolishing Taylorism we may have thrown out*

338

some useful parts of the baby with the bath water. We may even be repeating some of the mistakes of Taylorism that we have taken such pains to point out.

Though it is clear that Taylorism has had some large and unforeseen costs, it also seems clear that present-day Taylorism, i.e. the ideas and techniques of industrial engineering, continue to be viable and almost invariably present in American firms. Human resistance to the techniques has been a real problem, but not always an insurmountable or economically intolerable one. And partially with the naïve help of social scientists, the costs of Taylorism (the slowdown, for instance) have often been eased enough by psychological palliatives (like suggestion systems) to warrant their continued use.

2. *We have new knowledge both from the information and communication sciences and the social sciences that may be applicable to organizational problems; and if we freeze on our present beliefs, we may not be able to incorporate that knowledge.*

Two relevant sets of ideas have been emerging over the last few years. One is the development of information technology, a science in which human beings need *not* be the fundamental unit of analysis. We cannot examine that in detail here (see Leavitt and Whisler, 1958; Simon, 1960). The other set is the emerging findings from recent research on individual and group problem solving. This research in which human beings have indeed been the fundamental unit will be the subject of the rest of this discussion.

Self-programming people

Some remarkably similar findings keep turning up in a number of different places. They look irrelevant at first, but I think they are really quite to the point. For instance, given a problem to solve, people try to develop a program that will solve not only the specific problem at hand but other problems of the same 'class'. If we give a true–false test, the subject not only tries to answer each question properly; he almost invariably sets up and checks out hypotheses about the order of true and false answers.

The point, which I believe is as fundamental as many other points psychologists have made about the nature of man, is that humans have strong and apparently natural tendencies to

339

program themselves. In many cases a 'solution' to a problem is really a program for solving all problems of that class.

The second finding is that the challenge, the puzzle, the motivational impetus for the problem solver also stems in part from this same need – the need to develop a general program. Moreover, when such a general program is discovered, then any particular task within the program is likely to become trivial and uninteresting. When we 'understand' tick-tack-toe, the game stops being much fun.

These dual findings – programming oneself out of a challenging and novel situation, and then losing interest – keep showing up. And they keep reiterating the probably obvious point, so clearly observable in children, that people tend to reduce complexity to simplicity, and having done so find that the game isn't so much fun any more.

These findings lead me, very tentatively, to the generalization that high interest and high challenge may be caused as much by the job at hand (is it already programmed or not?) as by 'participation'. The players in our game participated fully – but they got bored when required routinely to operate their program, despite the fact that it was their own baby. The fun was in the making.

If we make a big jump, we can then ask: is it reasonable to think that we can, in the real world, maintain a continuously challenging 'unprogrammed' state for all members of an organization? ... especially when members themselves are always searching for more complete programs? ... and while the demands made upon the organization call for routine tasks like making the same part tomorrow, tomorrow and tomorrow that was made today?

The answer to this question is not obvious. In fact we have all witnessed the frequent demand of groups of workers for more and more highly detailed job definitions, on the one hand, accompanied by more and more complaints about 'deskilling', on the other. For instance, the airline pilot wants more and better ground-control programs to deal with increasing traffic; but once he gets them, he finds that the new programs also reduce the autonomy, the freedom and the exercise of human judgement that make flying interesting.

Which kind of structure?

Some years ago another area of reasearch got under way at the Massachusetts Institute of Technology which dealt with communication nets and their effects on problem solving by groups. As this body of experimentation has built up, it too has added reason for uneasiness about the unshakability of the participative beliefs.

Let me review the experiments very quickly. They are quite simple in their conception and purpose. They ask how the structure of communication among members of a group affects the way that group solves a given problem.

Suppose, for example, we connect up groups of five men so that they may communicate *only* through the two-way channels represented by the lines shown below. We can then ask whether comparable groups, working on the same problem, will solve it 'better' in network (a) than in network (b) or network (c).

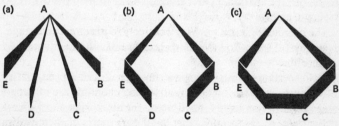

Figure 1

The men are put in booths so that they cannot see one another, and then given a simple problem to solve.

We can then measure the 'efficiency' of each net by such factors as speed of problem solving, number of messages sent, number of errors made, clarity of organizational form, specificity of each job in the organization and clarity of leadership. It turns out that on these simple tasks network (a) is far more efficient than (b) ,which in turn is more efficient than (c). In other words, groups of individuals placed in network (a) within a very few trials solve these problems in an orderly, neat, quick, clear, well-structured way – with minimum messages. In network (c), comparable groups

341

solve the same problems less quickly, less neatly, with less order and with less clarity about individual jobs and the organizational structure – and they take more paper, too.

However, if we now ask members of these three networks to indicate how *happy* they are in their jobs, we get the reverse effect. network (c) people are happier, on the average, than (b) or (a) people (though the *center* man in network (a) is apt to be quite happy). But since we are concerned with effectiveness, we may argue that happiness is not very important anyway. So let us go on to some other possible criteria of organizational effectiveness: creativity and flexibility.

We find two interesting things. First, when a bright new idea for improvement of operations is introduced into each of these nets, the rapid acceptance of the new idea is more likely in (c) than in (a). If a member of (a) comes up with the idea and passes it along, it is likely to be discarded (by the man in the middle) on the ground that he is too busy, or the idea is too hard to implement, or 'We are doing O.K. already; don't foul up the works by trying to change everything!'

Correspondingly, network (c) is better able to adapt to a change. Network (a) seems to have much greater difficulty in adapting to a more abstract and novel job.

So by certain industrial engineering-type criteria (speed, clarity of organization and job descriptions, parsimonious use of paper, and so on), the highly routinized, non-involving, centralized network (a) seems to work best. *But* if our criteria of effectiveness are more ephemeral, more general (like acceptance of creativity, flexibility in dealing with novel problems, generally high morale and loyalty), then the more egalitarian or decentralized network (c) seems to work better.

What shall we conclude? Using the common 'efficiency' criteria, the Taylorists are right. But these are narrow and inhuman, and if we use creativity and morale as criteria, modern participative beliefs are right. But are we also to conclude that the criteria of creativity and flexibility and morale are somehow *fundamentally* more important than speed and clarity and orderliness?

Or shall we (and I favor this conclusion) pragmatically conclude that if we want to achieve one kind of goal, then one kind of structure seems feasible? If we want other criteria to govern, then another structure may make sense. Certainly it is reasonable to guess that in the real (as distinct from the laboratory) world there will be locations and times which might make one set of criteria more important than the other even within the same large organization.

But participative managers, myself once included, will immediately go back to the happiness issue that I treated so cavalierly a few paragraphs ago. They will counter by arguing that network (a) cannot work long – for the growing resistance and low morale it generates in its members will eventually cause it to burst.

The evidence is negative. The *relative* importance of this resistance is apparently small. There seem to be fairly cheap ways of compensating for the low morale, yet still keeping the organization going efficiently. To the best of my capacity to speculate, and also the best of my knowledge from extended runs (sixty trials) of network (a), it can keep going indefinitely, highly programmed and unchallenging as it is to most of its members. Moreover, we could probably automate network (a) rather easily if we wanted to, and get rid of the human factor altogether.

Planned decisions

Additional research has pointed to the following as tentative findings:

1. Differentiated groups (ones in which some members are rewarded differently from others) can perform better than undifferentiated groups – whether they be rewarded cooperatively only, or both cooperatively and competitively.

2. Competitively motivated groups learn faster than cooperative ones; but their corresponding performance is dampened by their competition.

3. Groups that 'evolve' by working together directly on the problem come up with different, less clean and less simple solutions than groups in which the planning and the performing phases of their activity are separated.

These results do not directly contradict any present ideas; but they suggest that manipulation of variables like competition or differentiation of roles may yield results we cannot easily fit into our well-organized and perhaps overly rigidified beliefs about the universal effectiveness of self-determination, wholehearted co-operation and bottom-up planning.

What kinds of teams win?

Finally, in some research we have been doing recently with the complex year-long business game that has been developed at Carnegie Institute of Technology, another similar finding has turned up (Dill *et al.*, 1961). We found that those teams had the highest morale and also performed best in which there was the greatest *differentiation* of influence among team members. That is, teams whose players saw themselves as all about equally influential were less satisfied and made smaller profits than teams whose players agreed that some particular individuals were a good deal more influential than others.

Now bringing the influence problem in at this point may be another red herring. But the optimal distribution of influence, and of power that produces influence, has been one of the problems that has plagued us industrial social scientists for a long time. Does participative management mean, in its extreme form, equal distribution of power throughout the organization? If not, then how should power be distributed? What is a 'democratic' distribution? What is an autocratic one? I fear that none of us has satisfactorily resolved these questions. We have made some soft statements, pointing out that participation does not mean that everyone does the same job, and that the president ought still to be the president. But our specifications have not been clear and consistent, and we have never made a very good theoretical case for any optimal differentiation of power within an organization.

Again the finding is anti-egalitarian, and in favor of differentiation. Yet eglaitarianism of both communication and of power is often assumed to produce, through the participative beliefs, involvement, commitment and morale.

Idea of Differentiation

So it is developments in these two areas – the information sciences and bits and pieces of organizational research – that should, I submit, stimulate us to start re-examining our beliefs about the role of people in organizations. Together these developments suggest that we need to become more analytical about organizations, to separate our values from our analyses more than we have up until now; that we need also to take a more microscopic look at large organizations and to allow for the possibility of *differentiating* several kinds of structures and managerial practices within them.

Changes in this direction are, of course, already taking place but mostly at the research level (as distinct from the level of applied practice). In practice, participative management and the beliefs that accompany it are clearly very much on the rise.

But it is worth pointing out that, even at the level of current practice, participative ideas do not seem to be sweeping into the organization uniformly. In general, we have been concentrating more effort on developing participation at middle-management than at hourly levels – the Scanlon plan notwithstanding.

This differential emphasis on middle management as opposed to hourly workers is probably not a temporary accident. It represents, I believe, a general trend towards differentiating management methods at different organizational levels, roughly in accordance with the 'programmedness' of the tasks that those levels perform. It represents a new third approach to the problem of the routinization and programming of work.

The first approach was Taylor's: to routinize all work and, by routinizing, to control it. The second, the participative approach, was to strive to eliminate routine – to make all jobs challenging and novel. I suggest that the third approach – the one we are drifting into – is to do both: to routinize and control what we can; to loosen up and make challenging what we cannot. In so doing we may end up being efficient, and at once human and inhuman, depending on where, within the large organization, we choose to focus.

Conclusion

The main purposes of this article, then, have been to ask for a re-examination of the 'participative beliefs' about management, and to urge a consideration of the idea of differentiation.

In asking for a second look at the participative beliefs, I have tried not to associate myself with some others who are asking for the same thing but for quite different reasons. I do not want a return to tough management. Nor am I worried about groups replacing individuals. In my opinion the participative beliefs represent a great advance in management, one that needs now only to be placed in perspective.

In our eagerness over the last couple of decades to expand and test our new and exciting findings about participation, we may have made two serious but understandable and correctable mistakes: we have on occasion confused our observations with our values; and we have assumed that our participative beliefs represented the absolute zero of management – that there was no more basic level.

But though I believe in the values associated with the participative beliefs and in their great practical utility for solving huge present and future problems of human relationships, I ask that we try to fit them into the still broader perspective on organizations that is being generated out of the communication and systems sciences, and out of our rapidly growing understanding of the processes of thinking, organizing and problem solving.

One way of setting these beliefs into a different perspective may be, I submit, by viewing large organizations as differentiated sets of subsystems rather than as unified wholes. Such a view leads us towards a management-by-task kind of outlook – with the recognition that many subparts of the organization may perform many different kinds of tasks, and therefore may call for many different kinds of managerial practices.

References

COHEN, A. M., BENNIS, W. G., and WOLKON, G. H. (1961), 'The effects of continued practice on the behavior of problem-solving groups', *Sociometry*, December, pp. 416–31.

DILL, W. R., HOFFMAN, W., LEAVITT, H. J. and O'MARA, T. (1961), 'Experiences with a complex management', *Calif. manag. Rev.*, Spring, pp. 38–51.

LEAVITT, H. J., and WHISLER, T. L., (1958), 'Management in the 1980s', *Harv. bus. Rev.*, vol. 36, pp. 41–8.

SIMON, H. A., (1960), 'The corporation: will it be managed by machines?', in M. L. Anschen and G. L. Bach (eds.), *Management and Corporation*, McGraw-Hill.

Part Six Organizational Change

Behavioural scientists have sought not only to develop newer theories of management based on research results but also to develop methods of implementing these theories in organizations. The technology of planned change in organizations typically involves a collaborative relationship between one or more external change agents, usually behavioural scientists and the client organization. In the first Reading of this Part, Trist (Reading 26) discusses the evolution and present status of this technology, giving a comprehensive international flavour to this review. The second and final Reading by Leavitt (Reading 27) contains a widely accepted system for characterizing methods of organizational change. He distinguishes between structure, technology and people as entry points for changing organizations and notes that changes in any one are likely to create pressures for change in each of the others. Leavitt argues persuasively that the relative emphasis on each approach should depend on the nature of the task being performed by the organization.

26 Eric Trist

The Professional Facilitation of Planned Change in Organizations

Eric Trist, 'The professional facilitation of planned change in organizations', in *Reviews, Abstracts, Working Groups: XVI International Congress of Applied Psychology*, Swets & Zeitlinger, Amsterdam, 1968, pp. 111–20.

The facilitation of planned organizational change as a process involving collaborative relationships between client systems and social science professionals may now be said to have emerged as a recognized though still precarious activity in human affairs. The action research studies which provide its first models were undertaken during the Second World War independently and against the background of distinct traditions in the U.S. and Britain when conditions of crisis compelled rapid change. Subsequently, work of this kind has made its appearance in most western and in one or two eastern European countries, and in developing countries as different as India and Mexico. After the immediate post-war years came a lull during which the different norms of the academic and practical worlds were separately reasserted; but in manifold ways pressures towards change continued to mount and from the late fifties onwards collaborative activities have grown in frequency while increasing their variety, their depth, their scope and their duration. Their persistence and elaboration over the past quarter of this century suggests that they represent a response, however groping, to a widespread 'felt need' in the contemporary world. This need arises from the continuous presence in the social environment of a more rapid change-rate (stemming from an acceleration of technological innovation and scientific advance) which has created higher orders of complexity and interdependence and a higher level of uncertainty than have previously characterized the human condition. These pose new problems of adaptation for individuals and the organizations through which their relations are regulated and on which they are dependent. New attitudes and values must be found; old organizations require to renew themselves; new organizational

349

forms and behaviours have to be brought into being and tested.

One way of attempting to increase adaptive capability under these conditions is to couple the resources of the social sciences with the competences already available in organizations. One way of effecting this coupling is through establishing a collaborative, action-research type relationship between social scientists outside and independent of the organization and those inside it who represent its various systems and are directly concerned with its affairs. In such a relationship joint responsibility is accepted for bringing about organizational change towards agreed ends identified through a search process to which each party makes his own contribution, though all decisions regarding the actual introduction of any change of whatever character remain strictly with members of the client system. Frequent evaluations must be made both of what is experienced and done so that, on the one hand, a process of social learning can be released in the organization and, on the other, an increase in knowledge be returned to the scientific community.

These last two aspects are of central importance, for even if the available social science resources were the only constraint, the number of organizations able and willing to enter into thorough-going engagements of this type must be limited. Even if not formally researched, every such engagement should be regarded as a research undertaking in the formal sense, from which an attempt should be made to secure a 'multiplier effect'. This effect is beginning to be brought about in a number of ways. For example, both the organizations and the social scientists concerned in such programmes are getting to know each other within and across national boundaries. The overlapping informal sets so composed have the properties of a low register but higher order system capable of influencing neighbouring sets to which their members also belong. There are now also many more people inside organizations with varying degrees of social science competence so that there often exists a third force, an internal as well as an external, resource group, whose presence can accelerate the rate at which change can take place. The character of the organization-changing system is itself changing; it is already far more complex than the model of the single change-agent working with the single organization.

In the United States the main stream of work concerned with changing organizations derives from the field experiments on various aspects of social change carried out by Kurt Lewin (1951) and his associates during the last years of his life. These led to a field theory formulation of how to bring about social change which has affected areas of work far wider than that with which we are here concerned. It also led through the unexpected effect on the members of an experimental workshop on community relations to the discovery of the T-Group, the innovation of the laboratory method of training, the concept of the cultural island and the establishment of a new type of social science institution – the National Training Laboratories (N.T.L.). (Bradford, Gibb and Benne, 1964.) This development was premised on the need to abstract the individual from his usual organizational setting in order to learn experientially about small group processes and himself in relation to them – in the 'here and now'. In these respects the method proved to have great power, but the effects on their organizations of the abstracted members when they returned were negligible; while the effects of returning on them were often to undo what had been gained. The original model of the strangers' human relations training laboratory was not in itself a method of effecting organizational change. Its transformation into such a method took another ten years to discover.

In Britain the counterpart of the Lewin change experiments was the development in the war-time Army by a group, most of whom had been at the pre-war Tavistock Clinic, of a form of operational field psychiatry – a sort of psychological equivalent of operational research (Rees, 1945). As the tasks undertaken became more complex psychologists, sociologists and anthropologists were added to the team. Interdisciplinary collaboration was achieved in an action frame of reference, and a common set of understandings developed, based on a shared core value – commitment to the social engagement of social science both as a strategy for advancing the base of fundamental knowledge and as a way of enabling the social sciences to contribute to 'the important practical affairs of men'. The value position was the same as Lewin's – though the conceptual background was different – that of a psychoanalytically oriented, interdisciplinary, social psychiatry rather than of a social psychology based on field theory. As, however, the British group became better acquainted with Lewin's work its influence on them was far-reaching. Indeed, some mixture of these two heritages may be detected in most of the work on changing organizations that developed in the early post-war years.

The method developed by the British group depended in the first place on a free search of the military environment to discover points of relevant engagement. The right had then to be earned to have a problem which could not be met by customary military methods referred to the technical team for investigation and diagnosis. The diagnosis would next be discussed with appropriate regimental personnel and a likely remedy jointly worked out. The feasibility and acceptability of this remedy as well as its technical efficacy would be tested in a pilot scheme under protected conditions and technical control. As the pilot proved itself the scheme would become operational, control being handed back to regimental personnel, the technical team 'recreating' to advisory roles or removing their presence entirely except for purposes of monitoring and follow-up. What was learned was how to take the collaborative role in innovating special purpose service organizations with built-in social capability in a large multi-organization of which the social science professionals were themselves members – the army – under conditions of crisis.

The second phase in the theme that now unfolds covers the decade which elapsed between Lewin's death in 1947 and the fusion which took place between the training centred laboratory of N.T.L. and the consulting studies of organizational change demanded in increasing volume towards the end of the fifties by large-scale science-based industries in the United States. To illustrate the distinctive contributions of this period we shall select two well-known studies from the Institute of Social Research at the University of Michigan and two from the Tavistock Institute in London. The first two combine field studies with experimental design, the intention being to test specific hypotheses. The second two combine field studies with clinical exploration, the intention being to follow the course of a social process. All four depend on a collaborative relationship being maintained between a research team and a client system consisting of a single organization considered as a whole. All four attempt to deal with organizational as distinct from simply group or attitudinal variables, which had been the centre of concern in the previous period. All continued over long periods of time, the premature curtailment of one of the Michigan studies serving to underline the need for a long time basis.

The first Michigan study is the Morse–Reimer Experiment (Morse and Reimer, 1955, 1956) – a systematic attempt under conditions of full organizational reality to test a critical hypothesis: that degree of hierarchical control is inversely related both to worker morale and to productivity. After one year, during which contrasting programmes were in official operation following a lengthy preparatory period, results in terms of morale were in the expected direction. Productivity, however, was higher in the more hierarchically controlled group. Analysis of this unpredicted result revealed its conditionality: the character of the tasks produced a constant work flow so that only by having less workers could productivity be increased – a result easier to achieve in the more hierarchically controlled group; the character of the workers, girls, for many of whom employment was transitional to marriage made this also more easily acceptable; the character of the measure of productivity neglected labour turnover which rose in the hierarchically controlled group; its cost in the longer run could have reversed the trend. The scientific lesson of the experiment was theoretical: the need to advance in studies of organizational change from traditional concepts of discrete functional relationships to a systems approach, i.e. taking into account the characteristics of environments of groups in a wide context – sociopsychological characteristics as well as others like economic and technical ones.

The second Michigan study concerns the method of the systematic feedback of survey data for group discussion in 'organizational families', developed by Floyd Mann (1957). Data of this kind were fed back to each organizational family beginning with the top in a large company; each level had discretion to consider the implications for itself of the findings; but each level reported the outcome of its meetings up the line. Repeats were made in some parts of the company, with others omitted as control groups, at intervals which allowed for consequent actions and changes in climate to be realized. Results consistently favoured the experimental groups. This research, which lasted some four years, demonstrated the effectiveness of a method which can become self-administering and provide a basis for continuous organizational learning.

The next study, formally associated with the Tavistock in its first three years, is the Glacier Project, a continuous collaborative research into the organization and management of a total industrial concern which had been proceeding for fourteen years when Jaques last reported it (Jaques, 1964). This project established a scientific rationale and ethical rules for the 'independent role' and developed the method of 'social analysis'. Discussion with informal groups was abandoned in favour of working with individuals in their executive or representative roles or with formal groups such as managerial commands and committees. The first phase of the project was dominated by the need to undo the widespread organizational confusion which existed in the Company; the next with facilitating the extensive reorganization rendered possible by the insights gained; the third with enabling a consistent set of policies to be formulated which expressed the principles on which reorganization was based and provided a guide for the future. All managers needed to know these so that a training school was set up, later opened to members of other companies. The course of the Glacier Project therefore illustrates the opposite trend to that of N.T.L. which began in the training frame of reference and only later moved into the organizational.

A second trend in work at the Tavistock entailed a shift in the unit of analysis from the social system to the socio-technical system, which in turn required the replacement of a closed by an open system approach (Emery, 1959; Trist and Bamforth, 1951; Trist *et al.*, 1963). The studies in the British coal industry, which provided the first detailed empirical evidence of the superiority of certain forms of work organization over others for the same technological tasks, led to the concept of the joint optimization of the technical and social systems as a goal of organizational change and raised the question of the participation of the social scientists in the design process. An opportunity for such participation arose in collaborative work with the Sarabhai group of companies in India (Rice, 1958, 1963). The opening phase of this project was concerned with the sociotechnical reorganization of an automatic weaving shed where Rice became a member of a spontaneously formed design team which included the workers as well as the management and himself.

The third phase of collaborative organization research began with the wave of developments released in the United States in 1958 when Esso, through Shepard and Blake, inaugurated a series of laboratory training programmes throughout their refineries (Shepard, 1960). Other large companies followed suit so that a new pattern was established. This gave the T-Group a central position in collaborative projects on organizational change and produced such variations of the original model as 'cousin' labs, 'diagonal slice' labs and 'family' labs. These innovations turned a number of earlier assumptions inside out and forced a theoretical reappraisal that had to take account of a much wider range of processes and phenomena (Schein and Bennis, 1965). Little concensus has yet been reached.

In the writer's hypothesis (cf. Emery, 1967; Emery and Trist, 1965), these developments were occasioned by the mounting need of the science-based industries in the world's most advanced economy – in face of higher orders of complexity and environmental uncertainty – to evolve organizational forms, climates and values beyond and different from those of the more customary bureaucratic patterns which were no longer adaptive. These needs account also for the impact of Theory Y as formulated by McGregor (1960) which, by stating the direction of emergent relevant values, indicated the new type of organizational relationships likely to be required. Theory Y constituted a new 'appreciation' in Sir Geoffrey Vickers' sense (1965). Likert (1961, 1967) has brought together research evidence to show that the performance of enterprises managed in terms of 'System 4' (direction of Theory Y) is superior to that of those managed in terms of 'System 1' (direction of Theory X). The findings of the Glacier Project on the other hand favour what might be described as an enlightened form of Theory X. These differences may be accounted for by the different requirements of large-scale enterprises in advanced science-based industries in a society already in transition to post-industrialism (Bell, 1967) as compared with those of medium-sized enterprises in less advanced technologies in a society still centred in the later phase of industrialism.

In addition, current research suggests that the various subsystems of complex organizations have their own dynamics, organization characters and psychosocial climates (Katz and Kahn,1966) and that the capacity to tolerate different sub-identities within a given organization contributes significantly to the level of performance (Lawrence and Lorsch, 1967). Such studies suggest that sociological and environmental context requires to be taken into account to a greater extent than was evident in earlier versions of the still rudimentary theory and practice of changing organizations.

At the present time the practice of the leading professionals in the field is guided by an extending repertoire of concepts and techniques which they combine in 'personal styles' difficult to decode. No one knows what a Tannenbaum (Tannenbaum, Wechsler and Massarik, 1961) or an Argyris (1964) in the U.S., or a Bridger (1946), or a Hutte (1966), or a Pagès (1964), or Faucheux in Europe, in fact does, unless he works with him. Though joint work is increasing it is not in itself enough to ensure systematic advance. Much interest therefore has attached to the formulation by Blake (Blake and Mouton, 1964) of a de-personalized model capable of independent assessment. This is based on a concept of managerial styles as mixes of concern with 'production' and 'people' (the managerial grid). A high concern with both, called the '9,9' style, is regarded as optimum, and the objective of an organizational change programme is defined as a systematic attempt to induce an over-all change in management behaviour in this direction throughout the enterprise. There are six phases: (a) off-site training in 'diagonal slice' groups with an emphasis on structured exercises rather than unstructured settings to avoid too high a level of initial anxiety; (b) off-site team training based on 'family' groups; (c) on-site intergroup training to achieve better integration between functional groups; (d) discussions with various managerial groups to set goals for the total organization; (e) consultant help in implementing the consequential changes; (f) their consolidation and withdrawal of the consulting team. The over-all programme takes a minimum of four years. First attempts have been made to evaluate its application (Blake *et al.*, 1964) and some positive evidence has been adduced for its effectiveness both in terms of 'intervening' and 'outcome' variables (cf. Likert, 1961, 1967). Evaluation studies in this whole field have been remarkable by their absence. (One exception may be mentioned: Greiner, 1967.) However difficult, as Bennis (1966) says, 'the (evaluation) research effort has somehow to equal all the energy that goes into developing planned change programmes themselves. Until this effort is made the wider body of social scientists is likely to preserve its scepticism as to their worth.'

Apart from the Tavistock studies and certain projects at the Institute of Preventive Medicine in Leiden (see Hutte, 1949, 1966; van Beinum, 1963) little work on the introduction of planned change on a collaborative basis had been published in Europe up to the mid fifties. Moreover, though Wildred Bion from a psychoanalytic background had proposed some entirely novel ideas on the nature of group process in relation to task performance (Bion, 1946, 1948, 1955, 1961; Bion and Rickman, 1943) which created wide theoretical interest, their effect on the practice of those concerned with organizational change in the U.S. had been negligible. It is doubtful if even today the differences between the analogues of the T-Group which grew out of his work (Rice, 1965; Trist and Sofer, 1959) and any of the variants of the N.T.L. tradition are widely realized. But visits to Europe during 1955 and 1956 by a team of American consultants sponsored by the European Productivity Agency triggered-off widespread developments in a number of countries where a fusion took place between the N.T.L. T-Group tradition and collaborative studies of organizational change, much as it had in the United States. By this time the dynamic recovery of the European economies had become evident and these developments may be regarded as a manifestation of the renewed societal vitality of a number of these countries. Pointedly, there was little effect on Britain, despite the originality and importance of earlier British contributions. Volume of work relative to size of country has been greatest in Holland. So far, however, this has replicated American models rather than created a new tradition (by contrast with much of the Dutch work in social psychiatry). In France, however, process-centred longrange studies have been proceeding where basic anxieties of 'the human condition' are confronted in organizational contexts (Pagès, 1964) in a way which reflects the influence of Sartre, even if it is not avowedly existentialist as is the current work of Laing

357

at the Tavistock (Laing and Cooper, 1964). By contrast the work in the Scandinavian countries is task- rather than process-centred. Hjelholt (1963) has initiated a series of studies of the restructuring of roles and relationships in automated tankers. Patterns agreed in group discussion in Copenhagen were immediately tried out at sea. This work reflects a fusion of a task-centred approach to the T-Group with sociotechnical concepts. Recently, a European organization in some ways similar to the N.T.L. network and its Institute of Applied Behavioral Science (there are arrangements for overlapping membership) has emerged – the European Institute for Transnational Studies in Group and Organizational Development (E.I.T.).

The latest development has been the appearance of collaborative studies concerned with sets of organizations related to the wider societal environment as contrasted with the single organization related to its immediate environment. This has come about because the critical problems facing contemporary societies under conditions of complex turbulent environments (Emery and Trist, 1965) have taken on the character of what Chevalier (1967) has called meta-problems. These are diffuse social problems affecting major sectors of a society. Moreover, this quality of social extension is becoming perceived so that an existential dimension is added. Such problems are beyond the scope of single organizations to solve. Their solution requires the collaboration of a number of organizations.

Such problems appear first to have become accessible to collaborative social research in one or two of the smaller societies of western Europe. An example is the Industrial Democracy project in Norway (Thorsrud and Emery, 1966) which has now been proceeding for some five years as a collaborative enterprise between the Norwegian Confederations of Employers and Trade Unions and the Trondheim Institute of Industrial and Social Research and the Human Resources of the Tavistock Institute. At a later stage the Norwegian Government joined the consortium of sponsors while the Trondheim Institute had to set up a new centre in Oslo. The problem arose because of a sudden increase in the Norwegian trade unions of a demand for workers' representation on boards of management. What is remarkable is that the two confederations should have requested the assistance of social scientists in order to gain a better understanding of such a problem. The first phase of the project involved a field study of the main enterprises in Norway which included workers' representatives on their boards. The findings, having been reported back to the joint steering committee set up by the sponsors, were widely discussed not only throughout the two confederations but in the press. The redefinition of the problem obtained in the first phase set the stage for the second which has been concerned with securing, through sociotechnical experiments, improved conditions for personal participation as 'a different and perhaps more important basis for democratization of the work place than the formal systems of representation'. The third phase, recently begun, is concerned with the diffusion of organizational learning from these experiments.

Projects of this kind involved bringing into existence suitable 'institutions' under whose auspices they may be carried out. Such bodies, working intimately with the research team and sanctioned from the highest levels of the sectors of the society concerned, are essential if a shared and responsible understanding of what is required is to be created. On the research side the task is to assemble the relevant resources, which will rarely exist in one centre, so that consortia are likely to be brought into existence. Working models of improved systems must not only be established under operational conditions but must possess a cultural congruence which will permit their diffusion throughout the entire societal domain concerned.

Work of this kind will extend the interdisciplinary mix of social science professionals to include political scientists and economists and operational research workers and engineers. This extension is already happening in a number of instances. The widened nature of the societal engagement recalls something in the spirit of the pioneering efforts of Lewin and the Tavistock group during the Second World War, which was later absent. Everything that has since been learnt will be needed plus more that awaits discovery. The whole field of collaborative studies in organizational change is undergoing redefinition through the different quality in the pressure on the social scientist to take an active (but professional) role in 'the starting conditions' of social innovation (Emery, 1959, 1967). Perlmutter (1965) has suggested a concept of social architecture to express this redefinition. By social architecture he means the process of building, changing and renewing 'indispensable institutions' as distinct from 'expendable organizations'. By social architects he means the interdisciplinary set of scientific professionals who are beginning to find out how to assist the institution builders – the executive and elected leaders of all kinds – in their task of 'building better'.

References

ARGYRIS, C. (1964), *Integrating the Individual and the Organization*, Wiley.

BEINUM, H. J. J. VAN (1963), *Een Organisatie in Beweging*, Leiden Stenfert Kroese.

BELL, D. (1967), 'The year 2000. The trajectory of an idea', *Daedalus*, vol. 96, pp. 639–51.

BENNIS, W. G. (1966), 'Theory and method in applying behavioural science to planned organizational change', in J. R. Lawrence (ed.), *Operational Research and the Social Sciences*, Tavistock Publications.

BION, W. R. (1946), 'The leaderless group project', *Bull. Menninger Clin.*, vol. 10, pp. 77–81.

BION, W. R. (1948), 'Advances in group and individual therapy', in J. C. Flugel (ed.), *International Congress on Mental Health*, vol. 3, H. K. Lewis.

BION, W. R. (1952), 'Group dynamics – a review', *Intern. J. Psychoanal.*, vol. 33, pp. 335–49.

BION, W. R. (1961), *Experiences in Groups, and Other Papers*, Tavistock Publications.

BION, W. R., and RICKMAN, J. (1943), 'Intra-group tensions in therapy', *Lancet II*, November, p. 678.

BLAKE, R. R., and MOUTON, J. S. (1964), *The Managerial Grid*, Gulf.

BLAKE, R. R., MOUTON, J. S., BARNES, L. B., and GREINER, L. E. (1964), 'A breakthrough in organizational development', *Harv. bus. Rev.*, vol. 42, pp. 133–55.

BRADFORD, L. P., GIBB, J. R., and BENNE, K. D. (1964), *T-Group Theory and Laboratory Method*, Wiley.

BRIDGER, H. (1946), 'The Northfield experiment', *Bull. Menninger Clin.*, vol. 10, pp. 71–6.

CHEVALIER, M. (1967), *Stimulation of Needed Social Research for Canadian Water Resource Problems*, Privy Council Science Secretariat, Ottawa.

EMERY, F. E. (1959), *Characteristics of Socio-Technical Systems*, Tavistock Publications, no. 527.

EMERY, F. E. (1967), 'The next thirty years: concepts, methods and anticipation', *Hum. Rel.*, vol. 20, pp. 199–237.

EMERY, F. E., and TRIST, E. L. (1965), 'The causal texture of organizational environments', *Hum. Rel.*, vol. 18, pp. 21–32.

GREINER, L. E. (1967) 'Patterns of organizational change', *Harv. bus. Rev.*, vol. 45, pp. 119–30.

HIGGIN, G. W., and BRIDGER, H. (1964), 'The psychodynamics of an intergroup experience', *Hum. Rel.*, vol. 17, pp. 391–446.

HJELHOLT, G. (1963), Training for reality, *Paper of Department of Industrial Management, Leeds University.*

HUTTE, H. A. (1949), 'Experiences in studying social psychological structures in industry', *Hum. Rel.*, vol. 2, pp. 185–92.

HUTTE, H. A. (1966), *Sociatry of Work*, Royal van Gorcum Cy., Assen, Netherlands.

JAQUES, E. (1964), 'Social-analysis and the Glacier project', *Hum. Rel.*, vol. 17, pp. 361–75.

KATZ, D., and KAHN, R. L. (1966), *The Social Psychology of Organizations*, Wiley.

LAING, R. D., and COOPER, D. G. (1964), *Reason and Violence. A Decade of Sartre's Philosophy, 1950–60*, Tavistock Publications.

LAWRENCE, P. R., and LORSCH, J. W. (1967), *Organization and Environment*, Graduate School of Business Administration, Harvard University.

LEWIN, K. (1951), *Field Theory in Social Science*, with editing by D. Cartwright, Harper.

LIKERT, R. (1961), *New Patterns of Management*, McGraw-Hill. [See Readings 14 and 23.]

LIKERT, R. (1967), *The Human Organization*, McGraw-Hill.

MANN, F. (1957), Studying and creating change: a means to understanding social organization, *Industrial Relations Research Association Publication*, no. 17.

MCGREGOR, D. (1960), *The Human Side of Enterprise*, McGraw-Hill.

MORSE, N., and REIMER, E. (1955), *Report on Organizational Change*, Survey Research Center, University of Michigan.

MORSE, N., and REIMER, E. (1956), 'The experimental change of a major organizational variable', *J. abnorm. soc. Psychol.*, vol. 52, pp. 120–9. [See Reading 13.]

PAGÈS, M. (1964), in *ARIP Pédagogie et Psychologie des Groupes*, Editions de l'Epi, Paris.

PERLMUTTER, H. V. (1965), *Towards a Theory and Practice of Social Architecture*, Tavistock Publications.

REES, J. R. (1945), *The Shaping of Psychiatry by War*, Norton.

RICE, A. K. (1958), *Productivity and Social Organization, The Ahmedabad Experiment*, Tavistock Publications.

RICE, A. K. (1963), *The Enterprise and its Environment*, Tavistock Publications.

RICE, A. K. (1965), *Learning for Leadership*, Tavistock Publications.

SCHEIN, E. H., and BENNIS, W. G. (1965), *Personal and Organizational Change through Group Methods*, Wiley.

Organizational Change

SHEPARD, H. A. (1960), 'Three management programs and the theories behind them', in *An Action Research Program for Organization Improvement*, Foundation for Research on Human Behavior, Ann Arbor, Michigan.

TANNENBAUM, R., WECHSLER, I. R., and MASSARIK, F. (1961), *Leadership and Organization*, McGraw-Hill.

THORSRUD, E., and EMERY, F. E. (1966), 'Industrial conflict and industrial democracy', in J. R. Lawrence (ed.), *Operational Research and the Social Sciences*, Tavistock Publications.

TRIST, E. L., and BAMFORTH, K. W. (1951), 'Some social and psychological consequences of the Longwall method of coal-getting', *Hum. Rel.*, vol. 4, pp. 3–38.

TRIST, E. L., and SOFER, C. (1959), *Exploration in Group Relations*, Leicester U.P.

TRIST, E. L., HIGGIN, G. W., MURRAY, H., and POLLOCK, A. B. (1963), *Organizational Choice: Capabilities of Groups at the Coal Face under Changing Technologies*, Tavistock Publications.

VICKERS, G. (1965), *The Art of Judgment*, Chapman & Hall.

27 Harold J. Leavitt

Applied Organization Change in Industry: Structural, Technical and Human Approaches

Abridged from Harold J. Leavitt, 'Applied organization change in industry: structural, technical and human approaches', in W. W. Cooper, H. J. Leavitt and M. W. Shelly, II (eds.), *New Perspectives in Organizational Research*, Wiley, 1964, pp. 55–71.

This is a mapping chapter. It is part of a search for perspective on complex organizations, in this instance, through consideration of several classes of efforts to change ongoing organizations. Approaches to change provide a kind of sharp caricature of underlying beliefs and prejudices about the important dimensions of organizations. Thereby, perhaps, they provide some insights into areas of real or apparent difference among perspectives on organization theory.

To classify several major approaches to change, I have found it useful, first, to view organizations as multivariate systems, in which at least four interacting variables loom especially large: the variables of task, structure, technology and actors (usually people) (Figure 1).

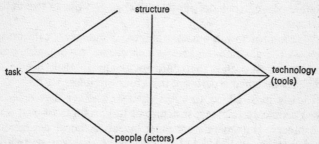

Figure 1

Roughly speaking, task refers to organizational *raisons d'être* – manufacturing, servicing, etc., including the large numbers of different, but operationally meaningful, subtasks which may exist in complex organizations.

By actors I mean mostly people, but with the qualification that

363

acts usually executed by people need not remain exclusively in the human domain.

By technology I mean technical tools – problem-solving inventions like work measurement, computers or drill presses. Note that I include both machines and programs in this category, but with some uncertainty about the line between structure and technology.

Finally, by structure I mean systems of communication, systems of authority (or other roles) and systems of work flow.

These four are highly interdependent, so that change in any one will most probably result in compensatory (or retaliatory) change in others. In discussing organizational change, therefore, I shall assume that it is one or more of these variables that we seek to change. Sometimes we may aim to change one of these as an end in itself, sometimes as a mechanism for effecting some changes in one or more of the others.

Thus, for example, structural change towards, say, decentralization should change the performance of certain organizational tasks (indeed, even the selection of tasks), the technology that is brought to bear (e.g. changes in accounting procedures), and the nature, numbers, and/or motivation and attitudes of people in the organization. Any of these changes could presumably be consciously intended; or they could occur as unforeseen and often troublesome outcomes of efforts to change only one or two of the variables.

We can turn now to our central focus of, namely, a categorization and evaluation of several approaches to organizational change – approaches that differ markedly in their degree of emphasis and their ordering of these four variables.

Clearly most efforts to effect change, whether they take off from people, technology, structure or task, soon must deal with the others. Human relators must invent technical devices for implementing their ideas, and they must evaluate alternative structures, classing some as consonant and some as dissonant with their views of the world. Structuralists must take stands on the kinds of human interaction that are supportive of their position, and the kinds that threaten to undermine it, etc.

Although I differentiate structural from technical from human approaches to organizational tasks, the differentiation is in points of origin, relative weightings and underlying conceptions and values, not in the exclusion of all other variables.

This categorization must be further complicated by the fact that the objectives of the several approaches to organizational change are not uniform. All of them do share a considerable interest in improved solutions to tasks. But while some of the technical approaches focus almost exclusively on task solutions, that is, on the *quality* of decisions, some of the people approaches are at least as interested in performance of task subsequent to decisions. Although improved task solution serves as a common goal for all of these approaches, several carry other associated objectives that weigh almost as heavily in the eyes of their proponents. Thus some of the early structural approaches were almost as concerned with maintaining a power *status quo* as with improving task performance, and some of the current people approaches are at least as interested in providing organizations that fulfil human needs as they are in efficacious performance of tasks.

The several approaches are still further complicated by variations in the causal chains by which they are supposed to bring about their intended changes. Some of the structural approaches, for example, are not aimed directly at task but at people as mediating intervening variables. In these approaches, one changes structure to change people to improve task performance. Similarly, some of the people approaches seek to change people in order to change structure and tools, to change task performance, and also to make life more fulfilling for people. We can turn now to the several varieties of efforts themselves.

The Structural Approaches

Applied efforts to change organizations by changing structure seem to fall into four classes. First, structural change has been the major mechanism of the 'classical' organization theorist. Out of the deductive, logical, largely military-based thinking of early non-empirical organization theory, there evolved the whole set of now familiar 'principles' for optimizing organizational performance by optimizing structure. These are deductive approaches carrying out their analyses from task backwards to appropriate divisions of labor and appropriate systems of authority. These early structural approaches almost always mediated their activities through people to task. One improves task performance by clarifying and defining the jobs of people and setting up appropriate relationships among these jobs.

In retrospect, most of us think of these early approaches as abstractions, formal and legalistic, and poorly anchored in empirical data. They were also almost incredibly naïve in their assumptions about human behavior. In fact, almost the only assumptions that were made were legalistic and moralistic ones: that people, having contracted to work, would then carry out the terms of their contract; that people assigned responsibility would necessarily accept that responsibility; that people when informed of the organization's goals would strive wholeheartedly to achieve those goals.

In one variation or another, such structural approaches are still widely applied. It is still commonplace for consultants or organization planning departments to try to solve organizational problems by redefining areas of responsibility and authority, enforcing the chain of command, and so on.

A second widespread approach to structural change, allied to the first, somewhat more modern and sophisticated and somewhat narrower, too, is the idea of decentralization. The idea of changing organizations by decentralizing their structure was probably more an invention of the accounting profession than anyone else, though it has been widely endorsed by structuralists and by human relators too. Almost nobody is against it.

Decentralization affects the performance of tasks partially through its intervening effects on people. By creating profit centers one presumably increases the motivation and goal-oriented behavior of local managers. One also adds flexibility so that variations in technology appropriate to the different tasks of different decentralized units now become more possible; so do subvariations in structure and local variations in the use of people. Decentralization can be thought of as a mechanism for changing organizations at a meta level, providing local autonomy for further change. Thus, within limits, decentralized units may further change themselves through the use of any one of the many alternatives available, and perhaps for this reason no group has questioned it, at least until the last couple of years.

Recently, two other structural approaches have shown up, but they have not yet reached a widespread level of application. One of them is best represented by Chappel and Sayles (7). Theirs is a form of social engineering aimed at task, but via people. They seek to modify the behavior of people in order to improve task performance, but they do it by modifying structure, in this case, the flow of work. Out of the tradition of applied anthropology, they argue that planning of work flows and groupings of specialities will directly affect the morale, behavior and output of employees. One of the failings of earlier structural models, in their view, is that the design of work was almost entirely determined by task and technical variables, and failed to take account of human social variables. They provide illustrative cases to show that appropriate redesigning of work, in a social engineering sense, affects both human attitudes and output.

I cannot overlook in this discussion of structure the implications of a second approach – the research on communication networks (10). I know of no *direct* applications of this laboratory research to the real world, though it has had some indirect influence on structural planning. In that research, variations in communication nets affect both routine and novel task performance rather significantly. The results suggest that appropriate communication structures might vary considerably within a complex organization, depending upon the type of task that any sub-unit of the organization undertakes. Thus for highly programmed repetitive tasks, highly centralized communication structures seem to operate most efficiently, but with some human costs. For more novel, ill-structured tasks, more wide-open communication nets with larger numbers of channels and less differentiation among members seem to work more effectively.

Technological Approaches to Organizational Change

My first entry in this technological category is Taylor's *Scientific Management* (24). Its birth date was around 1910, its father, Frederick W. Taylor [see Reading 20 – *Editor*].

Like the early structural approaches, scientific management was to a great extent ahuman, perhaps even inhuman. For in creating the separate planning specialist, it removed planning from its old

367

location – the head of the doer of work. Many observers, both contemporary and subsequent, saw this phase of scientific management as downright demeaning of mankind.

But despite the flurry of congressional investigations and active counterattack by Taylor's contemporaries, scientific management grew and prospered, and radically changed structure, people and the ways jobs got done.

Scientific management receded into a relatively stable and undramatic background in the late 1930s and 1940s and has never made a real comeback in its original form. But the technological approaches were by no means dead. The development of operations research and the more or less contemporaneous invention and exploitation of computers have more than revived them.

I submit that operational operations-research methods for organizational problem solving can be reasonably placed in the same category with scientific management. They have both developed a body of technical methods for solving work problems. They both are usually *external* in their approach, essentially separating the planning of problem-solving programs from the routine acting out of solutions. Operaticns research, too, is quickly developing in its operational form, a new class of hot-shot staff specialists, in many ways analogous to the earlier staff efficiency man. What is *clearly* different, of course, is the nature of the techniques, although there may be larger differences that are not yet so clear.

The operations-research and information-processing techniques are turning out to be, if not more general, at least applicable to large classes of tasks that scientific management could not touch (Schultz and Whisler, 22). Now armed with linear programming methods, one can approach a task like media selection in an advertising agency, though it would have been nonsense to time-study it.

But note the over-all similarity: change the setting of the movie from Bethlehem, Pa., to Madison Avenue, the time from 1910 to 1962; the costuming from overalls to gray flannel suits; and the tasks from simple muscular labor to complex judgemental decisions. Turn worried laborer Schmidt into worried media executive Jones. Then replace Taylor with Charnes and Cooper and supplant the stopwatch with the computer. It is the same old theme either way – the conflict between technology and humanity.

A distinction needs to be drawn, of course, between operational operations-research and other computer-based, information-processing approaches, although they are often closely allied. 'Management Science' hopefully will mean more than highly operational applications of specific techniques, and organizations are also being changed by simulation techniques and by heuristic, problem-solving methods. Their impact has not yet been felt in anything like full force; but tasks, people and structures are already being rather radically modified by them.

Without delving further into the substance of these more recent technological approaches, it may be worth pointing up one other characteristic that they share with many of their predecessors – a kind of faith in the ultimate victory of *better* problem solutions over less good ones. This faith is often perceived by people-oriented practitioners of change as sheer naïveté about the nature of man. They ascribe it to a pre-Freudian fixation on rationality; to a failure to realize that human acceptance of ideas is the real carrier of change; and that emotional human resistance is the real road block. They can point, in evidence, to a monotonously long list of cases in which technological innovations, methods changes or operations-research techniques have fallen short because they ignored the human side of the enterprise. It is not the logically better solutions that get adopted, this argument runs, but the more humanly acceptable, more feasible ones. Unless the new technologist wises up, he may end up a miserable social isolate, like his predecessor, the unhappy industrial engineer.

Often this argument fits the facts. Operations research people can be incredibly naïve in their insensitivity to human feelings. But in another, more gracious sense, one can say that the technological approaches have simply taken a more macroscopic, longer view of the world than the people approaches.

The technological approaches seem not only to predict the victory of cleaner, more logical, and more parsimonious solutions but also to *value* them. Failure of human beings to search for or use more efficient solutions is a sign, from this perspective, of human weakness and inadequacy. People must be teased or educated into greater logic, greater rationality. Resistance to better

369

solutions is proof only of the poverty of our educational system; certainly it is not in any way an indication that 'optimal' solutions are less than optimal.

The People Approaches

The people approaches try to change the organizational world by changing the behavior of actors in the organization. By changing people, it is argued, one can cause the creative invention of new tools, or one can cause modifications in structure (especially power structure). By one or another of these means, changing people will cause changes in solutions to tasks and performance of tasks as well as changes in human growth and fulfilment.

In surveying the people approaches, one is immediately struck by the fact that the literature dealing directly with organizational change is almost all people-oriented. Just in the last four or five years, for example, several volumes specifically concerned with organizational change have been published. All of them are people-type books (see 3, 9, 11, 13, 15).

This tendency to focus on the process of change itself constitutes one of the major distinguishing features of the people approaches. The technological and structural approaches tend to focus on problem-solving, sliding past the microprocesses by which new problem-solving techniques are generated and adopted.

Historically, the people approaches have moved through at least two phases: the first was essentially manipulative, responsive to the primitive and seductive question, 'How can we get people to do what we want them to do?'

Carnegie's *How to Win Friends and Influence People* (6) was first published in 1936, a few years ahead of most of what we now regard as psychological work in the same area. Like the social scientists that followed, Carnegie's model for change focused on the relationship between changer and changee, pointing out that changes in feelings and attitudes were prerequisites to voluntary changes in overt behavior.

Though social scientists have tended to reject it out of hand, current research on influence processes suggests that the Carnegie model is not technically foolish at all, although we have disavowed it as manipulative, slick and of questionable honesty.

However, Carnegie-like interest in face-to-face influence has finally become a respectable area of social scientific research. Several works of Hovland *et al.* (12) on influence and persuasion provide experimental support for the efficacy of certain behavioral techniques of influence over others.

But if we move over into the traditionally more 'legitimate' spheres of social science, we find that much of the work after the Second World War on 'overcoming resistance to change' was still responsive to the same manipulative question. Consider, for example, the now classic work by Kurt Lewin (23) and his associates on changing food habits, or the later industrial work by Coch and French (8). In both cases, A sets out to bring about a predetermined change in the behavior of B. Lewin sets out to cause housewives to purchase and consume more variety meats – a selling problem. Coch and French set out to gain acceptance of a preplanned methods change by hourly workers in a factory. In both cases the methodology included large elements of indirection with less than full information available to the changees.

But whereas Dale Carnegie built warm personal relationships and then bargained with them, neither Lewin nor Coch and French are centrally concerned about intimate relationships between changer and changee. Their concern is much more with warming up the interrelationships among changees.

Thus 32 per cent of Lewin's test housewives exposed to a group-decision method served new variety meats, as against only 3 per cent of the women exposed to lectures. Lewin accounts for these results by calling upon two concepts: 'involvement' and 'group pressure'. Lectures leave their audiences passive and unpressed by the group, whereas discussions are both active and pressing. Similarly, Coch and French, causing the girls in a pajama factory to accept a methods change, emphasize *group* methods, seeing resistance to change as partially a function of individual frustration, and partially of strong group-generated forces. Their methodology, therefore, is to provide opportunities for need satisfaction and quietly to corner the group forces and redirect them towards the desired change.

One might say that these early studies wrestled rather effectively with questions of affect and involvement, but ducked a key variable – power.

It was to be expected, then, that the next moves in the development of people approaches would be towards working out the power variable. It was obvious, too, that the direction would be towards power equalization rather than towards power differentiation. The theoretical underpinnings, the prevalent values and the initial research results all pointed that way.

But though this is what happened, it happened in a complicated and mostly implicit way. Most of the push has come from work on individuals and small groups, and has then been largely extrapolated to organizations. Client-centered therapy (Rogers, 21) and applied group dynamics (Miles, 19) have been prime movers. In both of those cases, theory and technique explicitly aimed at allocating at least equal power to the changee(s), a fact of considerable importance in later development of dicta for organizational change.

At the group level, a comparable development was occurring, namely, the development of the T- (for training) group (or sensitivity training or development group). The T-group is the core tool of programs aimed at teaching people how to lead and change groups. It has also become a core tool for effecting organizational change. T-group leaders try to bring about changes in their groups by taking extremely permissive, extremely non-authoritarian, sometimes utterly non-participative roles, thus encouraging group members not only to solve their own problems but also to define them. The T-group leader becomes, in the language of the profession, a 'resource person', not consciously trying to cause a substantive set of changes but only changes in group processes, which would then, in turn, generate substantive changes.

Though the T-group is a tool, a piece of technology, an invention, I include it in the people rather than the tool approaches, for it evolved out of those approaches as a mechanism specifically designed for effecting change in people.

In contrast to earlier group discussion tools the T-group deals with the power variable directly. Its objective is to transfer more power to the client or the group.

But these are both non-organizational situations. For the therapist, the relationship with the individual client bounds the world. For the T-group trainer, the group is the world. They can both deal more easily with the power variable than change agents working in a time-constrained and work-flow-constrained organizational setting.

At the organizational level, things therefore are a little more vague. The direction is there, in the form of movement towards power equalization, but roadblocks are many and maps are somewhat sketchy and undetailed. McGregor's (18) development of participative Theory Y to replace authoritarian Theory X is a case in point. McGregor's whole conception of Theory Y very clearly implies a shift frcm an all powerful superior dealing with impotent subordinates to something much more like a balance of power.

Bennis, Benne and Chin (3) specifically set out power equalization (PE) as one of the distinguishing features of the deliberate collaborative process they define as planned change: 'A power distribution in which the client and change agent have equal, or almost equal, opportunities to influence' is part of their definition.

In any case, power equalization has become a key idea in the prevalent people approaches, a first step in the theoretical causal chain leading towards organizational change. It has served as an initial subgoal, a necessary predecessor to creative change in structure, technology, task solving and task implementation. Although the distances are not marked, there is no unclarity about direction – a more egalitarian power distribution is better.

It is worth pointing out that the techniques for causing re-distribution of power in these models are themselves power-equalization techniques – techniques like counseling and T-group training. Thus both Lippitt, Watson and Westley (15) and Bennis, Benne and Chin (3) lay great emphasis on the need for collaboration between changer and changee in order for change to take place. But it is understandable that neither those writers nor most other workers in power equalization seriously investigate the possibility that power may be redistributed unilaterally or authoritatively (e.g. by the creation of profit centers in a large business firm or by coercion).

If we examine some of the major variables of organizational behavior, we will see rather quickly that the power-equalization approaches yield outcomes that are very different from those produced by the structural or technological approaches.

Thus in the PE models, *communication* is something to be maximized. The more channels the better, the less filtering the better, the more feedback the better. All these because power will be more equally distributed, validity of information greater, and commitment to organizational goals more intense.

Contrast these views with the earlier structural models which argued for clear but limited communication lines, never to be circumvented, and which disallowed the transmission of affective and therefore task-irrelevant information. They stand in sharp contrast, too, to some current technical views which search for optimal information flows that may be far less than maximum flows.

The PE models also focus much of their attention on issues of *group pressure*, *cohesiveness* and *conformity*. The more cohesiveness the better, for cohesiveness causes commitment. The broader the group standards, the better. The more supportive the group, the freer the individual to express his individuality.

Consider next the *decision-making* variable. Decision making, from the perspective of power equalization, is viewed not from a cognitive perspective, nor substantively, but as a problem in achieving committed agreement. The much discussed issues are commitment and consensual validation, and means for lowering and spreading decision-making opportunities.

Contrast this with the technical emphasis on working out optimal decision rules, and with the structuralist's emphasis on locating precise decision points and assigning decision-making responsibility always to individuals.

References
1. S. E. ASCH, *Social Psychology*, Prentice-Hall, 1952.
2. R. BENDIX, *Work and Authority in Industry*, Wiley, 1956.
3. W. G. BENNIS, K. D. BENNE and R. CHIN (eds.), *The Planning of Change*, Holt, Rinehart & Winston, 1961.
4. W. G. BENNIS and H. A. SHEPARD, 'A theory of group development', in W. G. Bennis, K. D. Benne and R. Chin (eds.), *The Planning of Change*, Holt, Rinehart & Winston, 1961.
5. S. E. ASCH, 'Issues in the study of social influences on judgment', in I. A. Berg and B. Bass (eds.), *Conformity and Deviation*, Harper, 1961.
6. D. CARNEGIE, *How to Win Friends and Influence People*, Simon & Schuster, 1936.

7. E. D. CHAPPLE and L. R. SAYLES, *The Measure of Management*, Macmillan, 1961.

8. L. COCH and J. R. P. FRENCH, 'Overcoming resistance to change', *Hum. Rel.*, vol. 1 (1948), pp. 512–32.

9. E. GINSBERG and E. REILLY, *Effecting Change in Large Organizations*, Columbia U.P., 1957.

10. M. GLANZER and R. GLASER, 'Techniques for the study of group structure and behavior', *Psychol. Bull.*, vol. 58 (1961), pp. 1–27.

11. R. H. GUEST, *Organizational Change: The Effect of Successful Leadership*, Dorsey, 1962.

12. C. HOVLAND, I. JANIS and H. KELLY, *Communication and Persuasion*, Yale U.P., 1953.

13. P. R. LAWRENCE, *The Changing of Organizational Behavior Patterns*, Harvard University Business School, Division of Research, 1958.

14. R. LIKERT, *New Patterns of Management*, McGraw-Hill, 1961. [See Readings 14 and 23.]

15. R. LIPPITT, J. WATSON and B. WESTLEY, *The Dynamics of Planned Change*, Harcourt, Brace, 1958.

16. J. G. MARCH (ed.), *Handbook of Organizations*, Rand McNally, 1964.

17. N. H. MARTIN and J. R. SIMMS, 'The problem of power', in W. L. Warner and N. H. Martin (eds.), *Industrial Man*, Harper, 1959.

18. D. McGREGOR, *The Human Side of Enterprise*, McGraw-Hill, 1960.

19. M. B. MILES, *Learning to Work in Groups*, Bureau of Publications, Teachers College, Columbia University, 1959.

20. F. J. ROETHLISBERGER and W. J. DICKSON, *Management and the Worker*, Harvard U.P., 1939.

21. C. R. ROGERS, *Counseling and Psychotherapy*, Houghton Mifflin, 1942,

22. G. P. SHULTZ and T. L. WHISLER (eds.), *Management Organization and the Computer*, Free Press, 1960.

23. K. LEWIN, 'Group decision and social change', in G. E. Swanson, T. Newcomb and E. Hartley (eds.), *Readings in Social Psychology*, Holt, 2nd edn. 1952.

24. F. W. TAYLOR, *Scientific Management*, Harper, 1947.

Further Reading

Why Men Work

E. Friedmann and R. Havighurst, *The Meaning of Work and Retirement*, University of Chicago Press, 1954.

D. Hall and K. Nougaim, 'An examination of Maslow's need hierarchy in an organizational setting', *Org. Behav. hum. Perf.*, vol. 3, 1968, pp. 12–35.

A. R. Heron, *Why Men Work*, Stanford U.P., 1948.

M. S. Viteles, *Motivation and Morale in Industry*, Norton, 1953.

V. H. Vroom, *Work and Motivation*, Wiley, 1964 (esp. ch. 3).

R. White, 'Motivation reconsidered: a concept of competence', *Psychol. Rev.*, vol. 66, 1959, pp. 297–333.

Satisfaction: Its Determinants and Effects

J. S. Adams, 'Toward an understanding of inequity', *J. abnorm. soc. Psychol.*, vol. 67, 1963, pp. 422–36.

E. A. Fleishman and E. F. Harris, 'Patterns of leadership behavior related to employee grievances and turnover', *Personn. Psychol.*, vol. 15, 1962, pp. 43–56.

E. Hardin, 'Job satisfaction and the desire for change', *J. appl. Psychol.*, vol. 51, 1967, pp. 20–7.

F. Herzberg, B. Mausner and B. Snyderman, *The Motivation to Work*, Wiley, 2nd edn 1959.

R. L. Kahn, 'Productivity and job satisfaction', *Personn. Psychol.*, vol. 13, 1960, pp. 275–87.

E. Lawler and P. O'Gara, 'Effects of inequity produced by underpayment on work output, work quality, and attitudes toward the work', *J. appl. Psychol.*, vol. 51, 1967, pp. 403–11.

N. C. Morse, *Satisfactions in the White-Collar Job*, Survey Research Center, University of Michigan, 1953.

L. W. Porter and E. E. Lawler, *Managerial Attitudes and Performance*, Dorsey, 1968.

A. Tannenbaum, *The Social Psychology of the Work Organization*, Wadsworth, 1966.

M. S. Viteles, *Motivation and Morale in Industry*, Norton, 1953.

V. H. Vroom, *Work and Motivation*, Wiley, 1964 (esp. chs. 5 and 6).

S. Zedeck and P. C. Smith, 'A psychophysical determination of equitable payment: a methodological study', *J. appl. Psychol.*, vol. 52, 1968, pp. 343–7.

Further Reading

Motivation and Performance:
The Effects of Some Specific Job Characteristics

L. Coch and J. R. P. French, Jr, 'Overcoming resistance to change', *Hum. Rel.*, vol. 1, 1948, pp. 512–32.

F. Fielder, *A Theory of Leadership Effectiveness*, McGraw-Hill, 1967.

J. R. P. French, J. Israel and D. As, 'An experiment on participation in a Norwegian factory', *Hum. Rel.*, vol. 13, 1960, pp. 3–19.

S. Gellerman, *Motivation and Productivity*, American Management Association, 1963.

R. L. Kahn and D. Katz, 'Leadership practices in relation to productivity and morale', in D. Cartwright and A. Zander (eds.), *Group Dynamics: Research and Theory*, Harper, 2nd edn 1960, pp. 554–70.

D. Katz, N. Maccoby, G. Gurin and L. G. Floor, *Productivity, Supervision and Morale Among Railroad Workers*, Survey Research Center, University of Michigan, 1951.

D. Katz, N. Maccoby and N. C. Morse, *Productivity, Supervision and Morale in An Office Situation*, Institute for Social Research, University of Michigan, 1950.

E. E. Lawler and L. W. Porter, 'Perceptions regarding management compensation', *Industr. Rel.*, vol. 3, 1963, pp. 41–9.

H. J. Leavitt, *Managerial Psychology*, University of Chicago Press, rev. edn 1964 (esp. ch. 15).

N. R. F. Maier, *Problem Solving Discussions and Conferences: Leadership Methods and Skills*, McGraw-Hill, 1963.

L. W. Porter and E. E. Lawler, *Managerial Attitudes and Performance*, Dorsey, 1968.

A. Tannenbaum, *The Social Psychology of the Work Organization*, Wadsworth, 1966.

E. Trist and K. Bamforth, 'Some social and psychological consequences of the Longwall method of coal-getting', *Hum. Rel.*, vol. 4, 1951, pp. 3–38.

M. S. Viteles, *Motivation and Morale in Industry*, Norton, 1953.

V. H. Vroom,' Some personality determinants of the effects of participation', *J. abnorm. soc. Psychol.*, vol. 59, 1959, pp. 322–7.

V. H. Vroom, *Work and Motivation*, Wiley, 1964. (esp. ch. 8).

K. Weick, 'Dissonance and task enhancement: a problem for compensation theory?', *Organiz. Behav. hum. Perf.*, vol. 2, 1967, pp. 190–208.

W. F. Whyte, *Money and Motivation: an Analysis of Incentives in Industry*, Harper, 1955.

Motivation and Performance: General Formulations

J. K. Galbraith and L. Cummings, 'An empirical investigation of the motivational determinants to task performance: interactive effects between instrumentality-valence and motivation-ability', *Org. Behav. hum. Perf.*, vol. 2, 1967, pp. 237–57.

D. Hall and K. Nougaim, 'An examination of Maslow's need hierarchy in an organizational setting', *Org. Behav. hum. Perf.*, vol. 3, 1968, pp. 12–35.

L. W. Porter and E. E. Lawler, *Managerial Attitudes and Performance*, Dorsey, 1968.

H. A. Simon and J. G. March, *Organizations*, Wiley, 1958 (esp. ch. 3).

M. S. Viteles, *Motivation and Morale in Industry*, Norton, 1953.

V. H. Vroom, *Work and Motivation*, Wiley, 1964 (esp. chs. 2 and 9).

Theories of Motivation and Management

S. Gellerman. *Motivation and Productivity*, American Management Association, 1963.

M. Haire, E. Ghiselli and L. Porter, *Managerial Thinking: An International Study*, Wiley, 1966.

F. Herzberg, B. Mausner and B. Snyderman, *The Motivation to Work*, Wiley, 2nd edn 1959.

D. Katz and R. Kahn. *The Social Psychology of Organizations*, Wiley, 1966 (esp. chs. 1, 2, 6, 11, 12).

R. Likert, 'Motivational approach to management development', *Harv. bus. Rev.*, vol. 37, 1959, pp. 75–82.

R. Likert, *The Human Organization*, McGraw-Hill, 1967.

N. R. F. Maier, *Problem Solving Discussions and Conferences: Leadership Methods and Skills*, McGraw-Hill, 1963.

D. McGregor, *The Human Side of Enterprise*, McGraw-Hill, 1960.

D. McGregor, *The Professional Manager*, with editing by C. McGregor and W. G. Bennis, McGraw-Hill, 1967.

H. A. Simon and J. G. March, *Organizations*, Wiley, 1958 (esp. ch. 3).

A. Tannenbaum, *The Social Psychology of the Work Organization*, Wadsworth, 1966.

M. S. Viteles, *Motivation and Morale in Industry*, Norton, 1953.

V. H. Vroom, *Work and Motivation*, Wiley, 1964.

Organizational Change

C. Argyris, *Interpersonal Competence and Organizational Effectiveness*, Irwin, 1962.

W. G. Bennis, *Changing Organizations*, McGraw-Hill, 1966.

R. Blake and J. Mouton, *The Managerial Grid: Key Orientations for Achieving Production Through People*, Gulf Publishing Company, 1964.

R. Blake, J. Mouton, L. Barnes and L. Greiner, 'Breakthrough in organizational development', *Harv. bus. Rev.*, vol. 46, 1964, pp. 133–55.

L. Coch and J. R. P. French, Jr, 'Overcoming resistance to change', *Hum. Rel.*, vol. 1, 1948, pp. 512–32.

D. Katz and R. Kahn, *The Social Psychology of Organizations*, Wiley, 1965 (esp. ch. 13).

H. J. Leavitt, *Managerial Psychology*, University of Chicago Press, rev. edn 1964 (esp. chs. 21 and 22).

Further Reading

R. Likert, 'Motivational approach to management developments', *Harv. bus. Rev.*, vol. 37 (1959), pp. 75–82.

F. S. Mann and F. W. Neff, *Managing Major Change in Organizations*, Foundation for Research on Human Behavior, Ann Arbor, Michigan, 1961.

A. J. Marrow, 'Risk and uncertainties in action research', *J. soc. Iss.*, vol. 20 (1964), pp. 5–20.

Acknowledgements

Permission to reproduce the Readings in this volume is acknowledged from the following sources:

Reading 1 The Macmillan Company, New York
Reading 2 American Psychological Association Inc. and A. H. Maslow
Reading 3 American Sociological Association, Nancy C. Morse and Robert S. Weiss
Reading 4 *Personnel Psychology*, Ian C. Ross and Alvin Zander
Reading 5 American Psychological Association Inc., Arthur H. Brayfield and Walter H. Crockett
Reading 6 John Wiley & Sons Inc.
Reading 7 World Publishing Company and Staples Press
Reading 8 Addison-Wesley Publishing Company
Reading 9 John Wiley & Sons Inc.
Reading 10 American Psychological Association Inc., Robert L. Opsahl and Marvin D. Dunnette
Reading 11 Personnel Psychology and Edward E. Lawler
Reading 12 Plenum Publishing Company Ltd
Reading 13 American Psychological Association Inc., Nancy C. Morse and Everett Reimer
Reading 14 McGraw-Hill Book Company
Reading 15 Wadsworth Publishing Company Inc.
Reading 16 John Wiley & Sons Inc.
Reading 17 American Psychological Association Inc., Basil S. Georgopoulos, Gerald M. Mahoney and Nyle W. Jones
Reading 18 Academic Press Inc., E. E. Lawler, III, and L. Porter
Reading 19 *Behavioral Science* and D. Katz
Reading 20 Harper & Row, Publishers Inc.
Reading 21 Penguin Books Ltd
Reading 22 M.I.T. Press
Reading 23 McGraw-Hill Book Company
Reading 24 John Wiley & Sons Inc.
Reading 25 *Harvard Business Review*
Reading 26 Swets & Zeitlinger N.V.
Reading 27 John Wiley & Sons Inc.

Author Index

Author Index

Index

Index

Subject Index

Subject Index

Index